That
GALLANT SHIP
U.S.S. YORKTOWN [CV-5]

That GALLANT SHIP
U.S.S. YORKTOWN (CV-5)

BY ROBERT CRESSMAN

Library of Congress
Catalog Card Number 84-62874

ISBN 0-933126-57-3

First Printing October 1985
Second Printing January 1989
Third Printing July 1993
Fourth Printing February 2000

Cover Painting: *Yorktown* (CV-5) by Paul Bender

Cover Design by Kirk Johnson

Pictorial Histories Publishing Company, Inc.
713 South Third West
Missoula, Montana 59801
(406) 549-8488   FAX (406) 728-9280
E-MAIL: phpc@montana.com

Contents

Maps

"*Yorktown* was a proud ship, with a seasoned air group that had covered both Atlantic and Pacific operations and which was supported by a veteran air department with a depth of true professionalism in warrant officers, chiefs, and leading petty officers. In gunnery we thought we had a pretty fine outfit and the same was true throughout the ship, engineers, supply, medical, etc. Add to the professionals the large number of eager and buoyant youngsters who joined the Navy to be 'Navymen' and you have Yorktown's ship's company."

—RADM John R. Wadleigh, USN (Ret.)
"Memories of Midway, Thirty Years Ago"
Shipmate, June 1972

"Carriers are the largest warships afloat, cities of 2,000-odd men. They are so incredibly vast and complicated that men who have been aboard for a year sometimes get lost when they venture out of their own bailiwick . . . If you want shoes fixed, clothes laundered, typewriter repaired, haircut, tooth paste or hundreds of other services or articles, they're here. There seems to be nothing lacking. Everything is on a big scale."

—William Hipple
Honolulu *Star-Bulletin* Correspondent
and a passenger on board *Yorktown*
from 15 February to 25 April 1942.

Preface

That Gallant Ship: USS Yorktown (CV-5) was my first book. I little realized then that it, and a subsequent work I co-authored with Mark Horan, Clark Reynolds, Steve Ewing, Barrett Tillman and Stan Cohen, *"A Glorious Page in Our History:" The Battle of Midway, 4–6 June 1942,* would serve as oft-consulted and well-thumbed reference tools on the expedition that ultimately found the subject of that first book, *Yorktown* herself. The excitement that accompanied my learning that the expedition, under noted deep-sea explorer Dr. Robert D. Ballard, had located *Yorktown* was indescribable; to see the ship I had written about!

The opportunity to revise *That Gallant Ship,* to incorporate the discovery of *Yorktown* in 1998, led to a reorganization of photographs and text to form a more coherent picture of the life of this great ship. Many photograph captions have been rewritten and expanded; individuals hitherto unknown have been identified. Photo-graphs of actions and of people have been added. Further study in Japanese materials has led to revisions in the descriptions of a portion of the Marshalls-Gilberts Raid, a total revision of the account of the Lae and Salamaua Raid, and detail changes to certain parts of the Coral Sea and Midway narratives. Hitherto unused eyewitness testimony concerning the controversial incident of two sailors left behind when *Yorktown* was abandoned on 4 June compelled a major revision of that section; there is also a reappraisal of the tragedy that occurred when a damaged VF-3 "Wildcat" made a hard landing on board *Hornet* (CV-8) during the Battle of Midway.

As I wrote in 1985, *Yorktown*'s brief but distinguished career is the stuff of a fine biography, for a ship, like a person, possesses personality and character. It is my sincere hope that the story that follows captures some of that proud ship's spirit, illustrated by some splendid photography, some of which is published here for the first time.

Acknowledgments

A HOST OF INDIVIDUALS proved of signal assistance in the research and writing of the first edition of *That Gallant Ship* as well as in the production of the new edition; as is often the case in government service, individuals move to other agencies, or retire; some have passed away in the intervening years between publication of the first edition (1985) and now. In the Naval Historical Center's Operation Archives, those who helped facilitate research include Bernard Cavalcante and his superb staff, notably Kathy Lloyd, Mike Walker, John Hodges, Regina Akers and Ariana Jacob; those who are no longer at the Operational Archives include its former head, Dr. Dean C. Allard (now retired), Martha Crawley, and the late Judy Koontz. In the Navy Department Library, the present staff under Jean Hort has been most helpful: including Glenn Helm, Barbara Auman, and Davis Elliott; those who have moved or retired include Barbara Lynch, Katherine Bowman, and John Vajda. Agnes F. Hoover of the Curator Branch Photographic Section provided her own special brand of encouragement; she is now retired. In the Ship's History Branch, John C. Reilly, Jr. has always been superbly helpful; colleagues who have left "SH" include James L. Mooney and Mary P. Walker. Roy A. Grossnick provided material from the Naval Aviation History Office and Archives; at the U.S. Naval Institute Paul Stillwell and Mary Sprawls assisted me with oral histories and photographic assistance. Last but by no means least, I especially thank Charles R. ("Chuck") Haberlein, Jr., a long-time colleague and friend at the Historical Center, whose incisive inquiries have often provided me the needed impetus to look carefully at photographic evidence. Other friends who have been particularly encouraging during the revision phase are Jeffrey G. Barlow, John D. Sherwood, Richard A. Russell and John Sillin. Long-time American Aviation Historical Society members William T. Larkins, David W. Lucabaugh, and Thomas E. Doll generously loaned me photographs from their files, as did Harry Gann of McDonnell-Douglas. Others who helped with photographs or information include John B. Lundstrom, James C. Sawruk, J. Michael Wenger, James T. Rindt, Kent Walters, and Samuel L. Morison.

During the initial work on this book I also benefitted from the spiritual support and encouragement of several special couples: Fred & Carol Burrows, Tom & Susan Hirsch, Kip & Geri Busick, John & Jean Erskine, Bill & Michele Briggs, and Bob & Patti Windsor.

Last but not least my parents, LCDR and Mrs. Wilmer H. Cressman, USN (Ret.) provided me with a loving and nurturing home as I grew to love naval history; while my wife Linda and our children Christine and Bobby showed love and much patience as I worked on this manuscript.

(See also list of participants in Bibliography.)

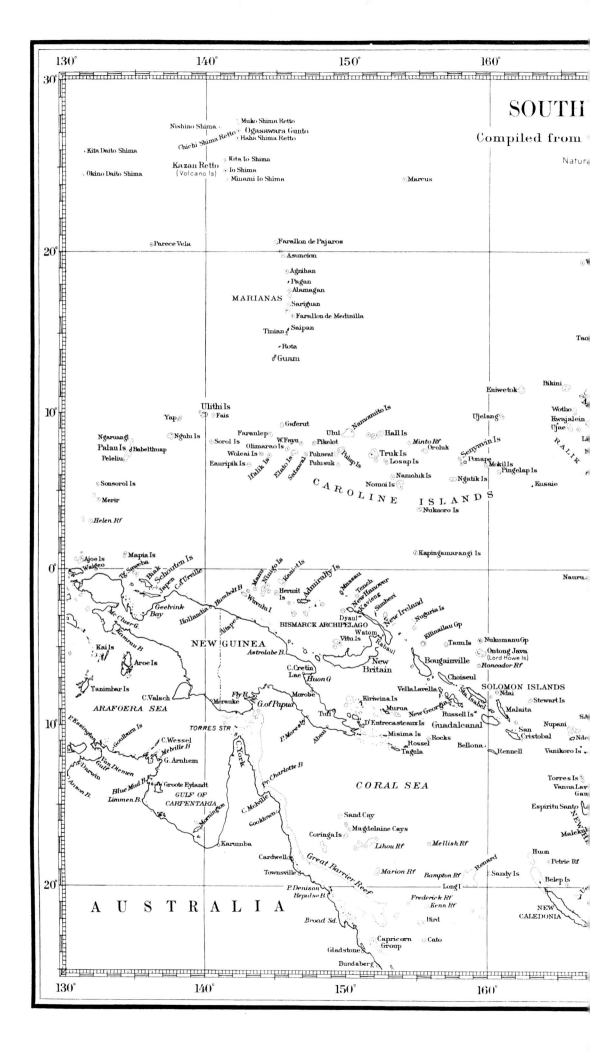

SOUTH

Compiled from

Natura

130° 140° 150° 160°

30°

Kita Daito Shima   Nishino Shima   Muko Shima Retto
                      Chichi Shima Retto   Ogasawara Gunto
                                            Haha Shima Retto
                              Kita Io Shima
Okino Daito Shima   Kazan Retto   Io Shima
                     (Volcano Is)   Minami Io Shima   Marcus

20°   Parece Vela   Farallon de Pajaros
                                                  Asuncion
                                                  Agrihan
                                                  Pagan
                                                  Alamagan
                          MARIANAS   Sariguan
                                                  Farallon de Medinilla
                                         Tinian   Saipan
                                                  Rota
                                            Guam   Tao

                                                                    Eniwetok   Bikini
10°   Ulithi Is   Ujelang   Wotho
              Yap   Fais   Namonuito Is   Kwajalein
                              Gaferut   Ujae
   Ngaruangl   Ngulu Is   Faraulep   Uhul   Hall Is   RALIK   Li
   Palau Is   W.Fayu   Pikelot   Minto Rf   Senyavin Is
   Peleliu   Babelthuap Sorol Is   Olimarao Is   Oroluk
                           Woleai Is Puluwat Truk Is   Pulap Is   Ponape
              Eauripik Is Ifalik Is Elato Is Puluwat Losap Is   Mokil Is
                           Satawal   Pulusuk   Namohuk Is   Ngatik Is Pingelap Is
   Sonsorol Is   Nomoi Is   Kusaie
                                       C A R O L I N E   I S L A N D S
     Merir   Nukuoro Is

       Helen Rf   Kapingamarangi Is

                     Ajoe Is   Mapia Is   Nauru
0°   Waigeo   Schouten Is
              Ts.Sooeba Biak   Manus Is Kaniet Is
                        Jepen   C.d'Urville   Ninigo Is Admiralty Is   Nassau   Tench
                                          Wuvulu I Hermit   New Hanover
                     Geelvink   Hollandia Humbolt B   Is   Kavieng   Sumberi
                     Bay   Aitape   Dyaul   New Ireland Nuguria Is
              Mc.Cluer G.   BISMARCK ARCHIPELAGO   Kilinailau Gp
              Kamrau B.   Watom   Nukumanu Gp
   Kai Is   NEW GUINEA   Vitu Is Rabaul   Tami Is   Ontong Java
                             Astrolabe B.   New   (Lord Howe Is)
        Aroe Is   C.Cretin   Britain   Bougainville   Roncador Rf
                                            Lae Huon G.   Choiseul
   Tanimbar Is   Morobe   Vella Lavella   SOLOMON ISLANDS
          C.Valsch   Fly R.   Kiriwina Is   Sta.Isabel Ndai
                         Merauke   G.of Papua Tufi   Murua New Georgia   Malaita Stewart Is
   ARAFOERA SEA   D'Entrecasteaux Is Russell Is   Nupani
10°   TORRES STR.   P.Moresby Abau Misima   Guadalcanal San   SA
   P.Essington   Rocks   San Cristobal Ndo
           Goulburn Is   Abau   Rossel   Bellona   Vanikoro Is
   C.Wessel   Tagula   Rennell
   Melville B.   G.Arnhem   C.York   Torres Is
   Von Diemen   Vanua Lav
   Darwin Gulf   CORAL SEA   Gau
   Anson B. Blue Mud B. Groote Eylandt   Espiritu Santo
        Limmen B.   GULF OF   NEW H Malekn
                   CARPENTARIA   C.Melville   Sand Cay
                        Mornington   Coringa Is Magdelaine Cays   Huon
                            Cooktown   Lihou Rf   Mellish Rf
                     Karumba   Petrie Rf
                        Cardwell   Renard
                        Townsville   Great Barrier Reef   Marion Rf Bampton Rf   Sandy Is Belep Is
20°   P.Denison   Long I
                                      Repulse B.   Frederick Rf   NEW
   A U S T R A L I A   Broad Sd.   Kenn Rf   Bird   CALEDONIA
                                                         Capricorn   Cato
                                          Gladstone   Group
                                          Bundaberg

130° 140° 150° 160°

PACIFIC

formation to 1938

at Lat. 0°

HAWAIIAN ISLANDS

Kure ○
Midway Is ○
○ Pearl and Hermes Rf

Lisianski ○
Laysan ○
○ *Maro Rf*
Gardner Pinnacles ○
rep. awash

French Frigate Shl ○
Necker ○
Nihoa ○

Niihau ○
Kaula ○
Kauai ○
Oahu ○
Honolulu ○
Lanai ○
Molokai ○
Maui ○
Hilo B
Kealakekua ○
Kalae ○
Hawaii

Johnston ○

dries ○ *Kingman Rf*
○ *Palmyra*

○ Washington

○ Fanning

♋ Christmas
(low)

SAK CHAIN

li ○

○ Makin
(Taritari)
○ Maraki
○ Tarawa
○ Maiana
○ Apamama
Aranuka ○
○ Nonuti
Beru ○
peteuea ○ Nukunau
○ Onotoa
Tamana ○
Arorai ○
IS

Howland ○
Baker ○

○ Jarvis

PHOENIX
○ Canton
○ Enderbury
M'Kean ○
Birnie ○
○ Phoenix
ISLANDS
Gardner ○
Hull ○
○ Sydney

○ Malden

○ Starbuck

○ Nanomea
○ Niutao
○ Nanomana
○ Nui
Vaitupu ○
ELLICE IS
○ Nuku Fetau
○ Funafuti
Nuku Lailai ○
○ Atafu
UNION
○ Nuku Nono
GROUP
○ Fakaofu

○ Penrhyn (Tongareva)

Nurakita ○

Rakahanga ○
○ Manahiki
Vostok ○

○ Rotuma
Uea ○
○ Swains
Danger Is ○
○ Nassau
Suvarov Is ○
Flint ○

SAMOA ISLANDS
Hoorn Is ○
Savaii ○
Upolu ○
Tutuila ○
Manua Is ○
○ Rose

FIJI ISLANDS
Vanua Levu
Vatoma ○
Niuafou ○
○ Tafahi
SOCIETY IS
Motu One ○
Fenua Ura ○
Mopihaa ○
Maupiti ○
Raiatea ○

Viti Levu
Eastern
Group
Fanua Lai ○
○ Vavau Gp
Late ○
Suva ○
○ Niue (Savage)
Palmerston Is ○
Aitutaki ○
Hervey Is ○
Mitiaro ○
Mauke ○
Abu ○
Tutuai Manu ○

Kanduvu ○
Matuku ○
Vatoa ○
TONGA
Haapai Gp ○
ISLANDS
○ *Beveridge Rf*
COOK ISLANDS

Tuvana Itholo ○
Ono Ilau Is ○
Tongatabu Gp ○
Rarotonga ○

Conway Rf ○
nter
Ata ○
Mangaia ○
Maria Is ○
Ruruhi ○
Rimatara ○

Minerva Rfs
(dries 3 ft)

Photo Credits

AT THE END of each extended caption will be a parenthetical credit. Numbers prefixed by 80-G, 80-PR, 80-CF, or 19-N refer to photographs held by the Still Pictures Branch of the National Archives, College Park, Maryland; those prefixed by NH are obtainable through the Naval Historical Foundation, Washington, D.C. Individuals who provided photographs either directly or through others will be credited by last name only (all USN ranks are retired): John N. Blakely, CDR James H. Cales, CAPT Tom F. Cheek, Thomas E. Doll, CDR Wilhelm G. Esders, Harry Gann, Roy M. Grossnick, RADM Paul A. Holmberg, William T. Larkins, Robert L. Lawson, LCDR Albert E. Lindsay, Richard A. Long, David W. Lucabaugh, RADM William N. Leonard, Donald S. Montgomery, CAPT John N. Myers, John C. Reilly, Jr., James C. Sawruk, CAPT William E. Scarborough, CAPT Lawrence G. Traynor, CDR John W. Trott, Mrs. Marie Urban, CAPT Stanley W. Vejtasa, Kent Walters, and J. Michael Wenger.

Photographs in author's collection are so indicated.

A Note on USN Ship Names

UNLESS OTHERWISE SPECIFIED, all USN ship names will be understood to be preceded by "USS" (United States Ship); ship's hull number will only be used once, the first time it is mentioned—such as *Yorktown* (CV-5) on page 1 will be only *Yorktown* thereafter.

All times and dates are those observed locally by the ship, with the exception of the Jaluit/Makin/Mille strikes in early 1942, which are placed on 1 February 1942 vice 31 January, the ship not having advanced the date to the proper one west of the International Date Line. The times used in the Midway chapters differ by two hours from the time zone in which Midway itself lay.

The insignia of *Yorktown* (CV-5). Painting by Thomas E. Doll

Introduction

YORKTOWNERS ARE FIERCELY PROUD of their ship—and justifiably so. In retrospect, among all of the Pacific Fleet's carriers operating between Pearl Harbor and Midway *Yorktown* seemed to be the best handled and best run; her captain—an unquestionably excellent shiphandler—among the most competent. She had operated in the Atlantic during the undeclared war with the German navy, steaming more miles on patrol than her cousins *Ranger* (CV-4) and *Wasp* (CV-7) and escorting two convoys, one east-bound, one west-, at a time of heavy U-boat activity in the North Atlantic. She had been at war a long time before her sistership *Enterprise* (CV-6) sailed for Wake Island in late November 1941 to deliver VMF-211's dozen F4F-3s.

Inclement weather limited the success of *Yorktown's* planes in her earliest raid, but she teamed with *Lexington* (CV-2) to give the Japanese cause to pause in their southward advance, at Lae and Salamaua—an attack whose true significance is only beginning to emerge after decades of being downplayed or ignored. While *Lexington, Enterprise* and *Saratoga* (CV-3) underwent refits, repairs or alterations, *Yorktown* held the line, alone, in the South Pacific, her crew enduring all of the hardships engendered by operating in the tropics. Her 101 days deployed included almost ceaseless steaming in the Coral Sea; she tarried once at Tongatabu in late April, fought the Battle of the Coral Sea along with *Lexington* (again stopping the Japanese cold); lingered at Tongatabu a second time in mid-May before sailing for Pearl Harbor and repairs. She had not had a major overhaul for a long time.

When RADM Frank Jack Fletcher brought his task force (TF-17) back to Pearl Harbor, an uncertain feeling gnawed at him about what lay ahead. Then, in a meeting with ADM Chester Nimitz, he found that he was to take TF-17 right back to sea as soon as *Yorktown* could be repaired. In the meantime, an air group was cobbled up, the result of intensive preparations after Coral Sea, and the ship sailed to take part in a pivotal battle—Midway—never returning to Pearl Harbor.

In summing up the Battle of Midway, an encounter between U.S. and Japanese fleets that unquestionably influenced the course of the war that followed, RADM Raymond A. Spruance praised the *Yorktown* air group's important part in the first attack (her planes crippled one carrier, *Sōryū*), and the search that gave the Americans the location of the one carrier—*Hiryū*—that had escaped the morning's devastation. "This enabled us to launch the late afternoon attack," Spruance wrote, "which crippled the fourth carrier and gave us incontestible mastery of the air." It was *Yorktown's* planes, operating from *Enterprise*, that sank *Hiryū*. Spruance also could not close his informal report to ADM Nimitz without expressing his admiration for the part Frank Jack Fletcher had played, for it was under Fletcher's direction that the initial part of the battle was fought. Spruance praised the "fine and smoothly working co-ordination between the two task forces [16 and 17] before the fighting commenced." Once the battle was underway, Spruance continued, "*Yorktown's* attack and the information her planes furnished were of vital importance to our success, which for some time had been hanging in the balance."

Yorktown's last battle evoked the admiration of those who witnessed it. Stopped once, she got underway again and launched planes in time to meet the second attack that stopped her again. Had not a Japanese submarine intervened, she might have survived.

"A staunch little craft and a good sea-boat," the first *Yorktown*—a 16-gun sloop-of-war—is not well represented by a good contemporary picture. However, this reproduction of a sepia wash drawing of a sistership, *Dale*, done by R.G. Skerritt (*circa* 1903) shows what *Yorktown* essentially looked like. (NH 57817)

The second *Yorktown* (Gunboat No. 1) was, despite her classification, a small cruiser, mounting a main battery of six 6-inch guns. Her paint scheme at this time was white hull and "spar"-color upperworks and masts. Note ornamental giltwork at her bow, the large number of ventilator cowls (necessary in those days before forced-air ventilation), and her open bridge, just forward of her stack. Her masts were equipped to carry sails. (NH 44265)

I Christen Thee *Yorktown*

A T THE END OF WORLD WAR I, the United States found itself thrust into a position of reluctant leadership in a world recently beset by global conflict. The country wanted to get on with its business after having—at least in its own estimation—put affairs in Europe back in order. Isolationism, while more prevalent toward things European than things Far Eastern, reasserted itself, aided by a revulsion against the destructiveness of modern warfare. Many hoped that World War I was, as President Woodrow Wilson had said, "the war to end all wars."

As the country it had served had done, the United States Navy emerged from the conflict as perhaps the most powerful in the world, the beneficiary of the first systematic building program ever enacted by the Congress. American shipyards had produced a vast fleet of naval and mercantile shipping; both the Navy and the Merchant Marine boasted of hosts of ships.

However, in the desire of the country to return to what President Warren G. Harding termed "normalcy" the number of ships in the naval and merchant service shrank as the 1920s wore on. And, between the Washington Treaty of 1922 and the London Treaty of 1930, expenditures for new naval construction never exceeded $40,000,000 and, in 1926, even fell to its lowest point in some years—$7,000,000. Corresponding decline occurred in the American shipbuilding industry, as with their services less in demand, shipyards folded; only a handful of hardy yards survived in the 1920s.

In efforts to provide less of a climate in which wars could start, the nations met after World War I to discuss arms limitations, and to sign treaties. Among the ship types discussed in these post-war talks was the "aircraft carrier." Taking airplanes to sea extended the reach of seapower, and the U.S. Navy, although behind the British and Japanese in this respect, evinced great interest in the subject.

The U.S. Navy's first aircraft carrier was converted from the fast collier, *Jupiter* (AC-13). Renamed *Langley*, for the first American who seriously attempted to fly (but failed) and designated CV-1, this experimental ship was soon followed by two massive vessels spared by the arms limitations agreements reached at Washington in 1922—*Lexington* (CV-2) and *Saratoga* (CV-3)—which had originally been laid down as battle cruisers.

Operations with *Langley* showed her to be, at least in BuAer's estimation, too small; *Lexington* and *Saratoga*, in their design stage at the time, were feared to be, potentially, too large. The next carrier therefore began life as a compromise: CV-4, named *Ranger*, was designed to be a cross between the only type of carrier with which the Navy had *had* experience (*Langley*) and one which it had *not* (the *Lexington*-class). Since operating experience with the latter had been *nil*—*Ranger* being designed before "Lex" and "Sara" joined the fleet—by the time it came around to actually laying the keel for CV-4 (1931), experience with the two giant flat-tops proved that *Ranger* would simply not be adequate. Designed to please everybody, *Ranger* emerged as a compromise that satisfied nobody.

On 10 June 1931, less than a year after the contract had been awarded to build *Ranger*, and three months before her keel was to be laid at one of the six major American shipyards that had managed to weather the depression—the Newport News Shipbuilding and Dry Dock Co., of Newport News, Va.—the General Board met to discuss modification of the accepted aircraft carrier design. Unhappy with *Ranger* even before she was laid down, BuAer proposed that the Navy needed larger carriers. The revision of the *Ranger* design prompted a series of intense discussions before the General Board—the Navy's highest policy advisory body—to determine just what the characteristics of future flat-tops should be. A big question was whether or not the Navy, which could, under the allowances of the Washington Treaty, increase its aircraft carrier tonnage by 69,000 tons, wanted three 18,000-ton ships or four 13,800-tonners. Another question brought up was how to get Congress to adopt a change in plans for the aircraft carrier design after steadfastly maintaining that *Ranger* met their needs perfectly!

Ranger lacked protection and was comparatively slow, a combination of factors that led some to contemplate her only suitable employment as that of a "battle line" carrier—operating with the battleships and seldom venturing out on her own. BuAer clearly wanted something larger, with protection falling on a scale between a battleship and a cruiser, and with speed equal to the latter type of ship. How the Navy could get what it wanted, though, would prove a tough proposition since the Great Depression had begun in 1929 and deepened as the months passed. One naval officer who attended an early General Board hearing on the matter of future aircraft construction summed it all up when he lamented: "Conditions are very much against us—national conditions, treasury conditions, and the general national situation . . ."

The discussion of design proposals went on through the summer, in three hearings before the General Board, supplemented by the necessary work in the bureaus responsible for their areas in the ship's design. What emerged from the summer's labors was a ship type substantially bigger than *Ranger*, more well-protected, faster, and better able to act as an aircraft carrier apart from the Battle Fleet. The factor of survivability weighed heavily on the conferees' minds, since the aircraft carrier had become an accepted element of the fleet in time of war, its protection a vital necessity. Keeping one's carrier in action and being able to immobilize your enemy's concerned the bureaus very much.

Ten days before Christmas of 1931, Secretary of the Navy Charles Francis Adams approved the characteristics of the new aircraft carrier design. Before the year was out, and less than two weeks after SECNAV's approval of the Board's work, BuC&R submitted a design sketch for the proposed ships. Subsequently, the initial general arrangement plan was ready by 1 February 1932, followed by contract plans one month later. Work on cruisers, however, took priority, and no monies were forthcoming for carrier construction. There the matter rested, a state of affairs changed by the 1932 presidential election.

Franklin D. Roosevelt, an avowed navalist and former Assistant Secretary of the Navy in the Wilson administration, had promised to give the American people a "New Deal" to lift them out of the depression gripping and numbing the land. Among the items of legislation enacted toward this end was the National Industrial Recovery Act (NIRA) of 16 June 1933, which provided for "the construction of naval vessels within the terms and/or limits established by the London Navy Treaty of 1930." President Roosevelt declared proudly that history would probably record the NIRA as "the most important and far-reaching legislation ever enacted by the American congress. . . "Its importance lay not only in its job provisions but in the building program that was to provide 32 new ships—including two aircraft carriers—for the U.S. Navy.

The same day that the NIRA was signed, the Navy sought a yard to undertake construction of the two carriers which, soon thereafter, received their official designations, CV-5 and CV-6, on 5 July. One month later, on 5 August, the Navy awarded the contract to the Newport News Shipbuilding and Dry Dock Co., to build the ships. On 6 September, the two vessels received their names: CV-5 was named *Yorktown*; CV-6 became *Enterprise*.

At this point a digression would be in order to reflect on the names chosen for these two ships. These were good ones, rich in American history. *Enterprise* recognized a lineage of historic ships which dated back to the early days of the Republic. *Yorktown*, however, went back even further.

Established in 1691, "Yorktown," (variously known, in its early years, as the "port of York," "Borough of York," "York," or, simply, "Town of York") was a colonial village whose roots reached back to some of the first generation of English settlers to populate the Tidewater region of Virginia. The battle fought in these environs almost a century later, in the autumn of 1781, while making the name famous, ironically brought about Yorktown's decline. Its population dwindled from around 3,000 (a populous village by 1781 standards) to about 300 by 1941.

The *name*, however, was not forgotten. The Act of Congress of 7 March 1819 established the policy that directed the naval vessels of the "third rate" (i.e., those mounting less than 20 guns) be named for cities and towns of the States of the Union. The first *Yorktown* was a 16-gun sloop of war built at the Gosport (now Norfolk) Navy Yard, in 1838. Launched in 1839 and fitted out at her builders' yard, she sailed for the Pacific on 13 December 1840.

On her maiden voyage, *Yorktown* visited the Marquesas, Society and New Zealand and Hawaiian Islands, looking after the interests of the American whaling industry and of this nation's burgeoning ocean commerce. She then "showed the flag" on the west coast of South America, still with the Pacific Squadron, until she returned to the east coast of the United States in 1843. *Yorktown* then served twice on the African Station, as part of the squadron entrusted with breaking up the odious slave trade off that continent's west coast, until she struck a reef off the island of Mayo, in the Cape Verdes, on 6 September 1850. Although the ship sank quickly, a total loss, her entire complement of officers and men gained shore safely. The sloop *John Adams* then rescued *Yorktown*'s men and brought them back to the United States.

The second *Yorktown* was a twin-screw steel-hulled gunboat built by the William Cramp and Sons Ship and Engine Building Co., of Philadelphia, Pa. Launched on 28 April 1888, amidst much pomp, and christened by the daughter of the Honorable Don Cameron, United States Senator from Pennsylvania and a member of the Senate Naval Committee, *Yorktown* (Gunboat No. 1) was schooner-rigged, provided with auxiliary sails, and carried a main battery of six 6-inch breech-loading rifles, supplemented by a secondary battery of eight rapid-fire guns of various calibers.

Yorktown began her career with the Squadron of Evolution, formed of the new steel warships of the U.S. Navy, which developed tactics for these revolutionary new vessels. Over the decades which followed, she then "showed the flag" as her predecessor had done; she operated from the Gulf of Mexico to the waters of the Far East; sought gunrunners in the Philippine Archipelago and seal poachers in the Bering Strait, interspersing these activities with the usual inactive periods of upkeep and voyage repairs. Her duties were not always as festive as showing up at the Rose Festival in Portland, Ore.—she was sometimes required to stand by to protect American lives and property on strife-torn coasts of Mexico and Nicaragua. Modern American naval gunnery was born on board *Yorktown* in September 1892, while she was operating in Alaskan waters, with the successful test of a telescopic gunsight invented and perfected by CDR Bradley Fiske, the ship's executive officer at that time. Among her commanding officers in the early 1890s was CDR Robley D. Evans, the same "Fighting Bob" who would initially command the "Great White Fleet" as it began its globe-girdling cruise in 1907.

When World War I engulfed Europe in the summer of 1914, *Yorktown* lay at the Mare Island Navy Yard, Vallejo, Calif. Upon completion of repairs and alterations, the gunboat resumed her watchful waiting off the coasts of Mexico, Nicaragua, and Honduras, maintaining this regimen for over three years,

varying this "extension of diplomacy" with investigations of local conditions as they affected Americans living or working in those areas, and periodic upkeep at Mare Island. She then sailed for the east coast of the United States on 28 April 1918, and ultimately reached New York on 20 August, to commence escort duty for coastal convoys running between New York and Halifax, Nova Scotia, a routine which she maintained through the armistice and until two days into the year of 1919, at which time she sailed for the west coast, arriving at San Diego on 15 February. Decommissioned at Mare Island on 12 June 1919, she was ultimately sold to the Union Hide Co., Oakland, Calif., on 30 September 1921.

The availability of funds to build the two new carriers, one of which was designated to bear the name *Yorktown*—this time specifically honoring the battle of 1781—prompted BuC&R to contact the General Board to see if there were to be any alterations to the original 1932 plans. There were: BuC&R itself desired a rearrangement of the 5-inch battery to allow for an increased flight deck length (729 feet, as opposed to the original 708 feet as designed); three guns forward, five aft. The former were to be mounted as follows: one on the centerline, in a shallow "well" at the bow, the other two forward disposed on the foc'sle deck, port and starboard; the after guns were to be situated with one on the main deck level, on the centerline, the other four mounted just below the gallery deck, on sponsons, two on the port side, two on the starboard. In addition, BuOrd put forth a proposal that would give the ship four quadruple-mount 1.1-inch automatic guns, weapons designed specifically to counter the threat posed by dive bombers. The General Board found both gunnery proposals acceptable, but disapproved of the subtraction of torpedo stowage—as had been done in *Ranger* as an economy measure. One further change was made to the design in November 1933, when BuAer pushed for a still-longer flight deck (794 feet), by having all the 5-inch battery placed in sponsons, forward and aft, eliminating the centerline mounts (the most forward of which would have been unusable in any but a fair sea). Weighing the pros and cons carefully, the General Board approved. The Board turned down, however, a further attempt by BuAer—shortly before keel-laying—to get still more flight deck length, deeming it too costly and too likely to cause an unacceptable delay in the construction of the ship.

Workmen laid the third *Yorktown*'s keel on 21 May 1934, and for almost two years, she—and her sistership *Enterprise*, laid down on 16 July 1934—lay a-building within the shadows cast by the towering trellises

Considering the sponsorship of a warship "by no means incompatible" with her anti-war views, Mrs. Franklin D. Roosevelt smashes the traditional bottle of champagne on *Yorktown*'s bow during christening ceremonies at Newport News on 4 April 1936. "One country," she stated after the launch, "by itself cannot limit armaments." After evincing the hope that "some day all nations will agree to arms limitations," the outspoken first lady added, "but until then we must build our Navy to treaty strength in order not to be defenseless against attack." (80-CF-80301-1)

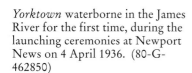

Yorktown waterborne in the James River for the first time, during the launching ceremonies at Newport News on 4 April 1936. (80-G-462850)

which comprised Newport News' two shipbuilding cradles, the gigantic steel structures which dominated the orderly aggregation of red-brick buildings that made up the yard. Newport News had a proud tradition to uphold, one enunciated by the yard's founder, Collis P. Huntington, who had once declared: "We shall build good ships here at a profit if we can, at a loss if we must, but always good ships." These words had been inscribed in bronze on a giant rock inside the entrance to the shipyard, and the company had had to live up to Huntington's words in order to survive the lean years of the 1920s and 1930s.

As *Yorktown* was to be the first of the President's NIRA-produced vessels to be launched, her sponsor was, appropriately, the first lady, Mrs. Eleanor Roosevelt. "Obviously enjoying the privilege," Mrs. Roosevelt "lustily swung the bottle, dangling on a beribboned cord, against the towering hull" that glistened bright in the spring sunshine, at 1000 on 4 April 1936, declaring "I christen thee *Yorktown* . . ." The bunting-bedecked ship then gathered momentum, gracefully proceeding down the ways; whistles shrieked, thousands of spectators cheered, and the Army's 2d Coast Artillery band played stirring music for the occasion. She rode out into the stream of the James River, high in the water, before she gradually lost way, and, soon, tugs, waiting there, nudged the ship to her outfitting pier. Mrs. Roosevelt had done more than merely break a bottle of champagne on the bulbous bow of a ship; done more than bestowed upon that ship a proud

Yorktown (foreground) lies alongside pier No. 1, Newport News Shipbuilding and Dry Dock Co., in June 1937, fitting out, her flight deck markings—chrome yellow striping and identification letters Y K T N—contrasting sharply with the maroon-stained Douglas fir flight deck planking. The light cruiser *Boise* (CL-47) is being fitted out at the second pier over, while *Yorktown*'s sistership *Enterprise* (CV-6) is in the drydock at the top center of this view. (80-G-462977)

Among the requirements for CV-5 class carriers was the ability to land planes over the bow and launch them over the stern; *Yorktown* (seen here making 17.5 knots astern during preliminary standardization trials off Rockland, Maine, on 21 July 1937) was thus equipped with two sets of arresting gear and two LSO platforms. (19-N-17422)

name. As the writer of *Yorktown*'s commissioning booklet declared: "She gave a soul to an inanimate hull which we who are to serve aboard her will come to love, cherish, and honor during the years she passes in the service of the nation that created her . . ."

Newport News put *Yorktown* through her paces the following summer, but the results of the trial did not satisfy the Navy. Reduction gear noise—"120 decibels on the engine room floor plates"—resulted in a return trip to the yard. The second trial, also run off the Virginia capes, went better, on 6 July 1937; but while the ship exceeded all machinery requirements and developed more power and speed than had been specified in the contract, the annoying, and hazardous, din in the engine room remained.

However, although the Navy considered *Yorktown*'s reduction gears as unsatisfactory after the ship's builders' trials, it decided to accept the vessel anyway—on the condition that Newport News would replace the defective machinery components. Pending the replacement, *Yorktown* would have to be operated "at reduced speeds," 25 knots being the maximum practicable. The Navy deemed this conditional acceptance to be in the best interests of the government, since it prevented deterioration of the ship "which would surely result if she were not operated"; would "permit active training of her crew" and ensure a "more rapid final completion of the vessel and her readiness to join the fleet." And, even in her "present condition" she could be employed with the Fleet in case of a "national emergency." Also, too, this would relieve Newport News of an excessive burden of costs and damages incurred, and, more importantly, protect the government's $25,000,000 investment in the ship.

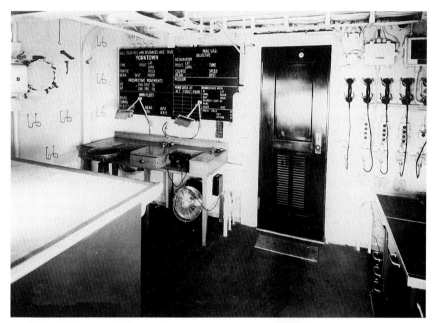

"Air plot" on 26 August 1937; note plotting board in left foreground, board on bulkhead in left background, with spaces for meteorological and flight data entries used in planning air missions, and bank of telephones to the right of the door. Object on deck beneath the desk in the left background is an electric space heater. When the ship received her CXAM radar equipment three years later, "radar plot" was constructed in this space. (19-N-17542)

View of the forward end of the island and bridge decks, 7 September 1937, showing to advantage the air officer's spacious enclosure from which he could direct flight deck operations, from the navigation bridge level. One deck up (from forward moving aft) is the closed surface rangefinder (atop the pilot house) and the forward Mk.XXXIII gun director. .50 cal. MG were mounted on this level as well, to port and starboard of the tripod foremast base. Also note flag bags and the magnetic compass platform. Fence-like object on the deck, visible on the flight deck just forward of the bridge, is the forward palisade which, when erected, served as a windbreak for planes spotted on deck. (19-N-17408)

"Sky control" on 7 September 1937, showing data transmitters on port and starboard sides, and the radio direction finder loop in its cage-like enclosure in the center. In the background is the base of the forward Mk.XXXIII gun director, with the enclosed surface rangefinder beyond. The latter was removed during the December 1941 refit at Norfolk. (19-N-17404)

One of *Yorktown*'s eight 5"/38 cal. guns, this particular mount located on the after gun platform on the starboard side. An experienced crew could load 15 rounds a minute over a sustained period of time, and could attain a short-period rate of 22 rounds per minute. Maximum horizontal range was 18,000 yards, vertical was 37,300 feet. Semifixed ammunition was used, consisting of a 54-pound projectile and a 28-pound case assembly. Note non-skid rubber matting on deck, and complete lack of any protection for the crew from either enemy fire or the elements. View taken on 27 September 1937. (19-N-17439)

All these details ironed out, *Yorktown* departed her builders' yard at 0500 on 30 September 1937, and after an hour and forty-five minutes passage, moored to the north side of Pier 7, NOB Norfolk. At 1009, *Yorktown* was placed in commission and her first watch set in a "brief but colorful" ceremony. Her first commanding officer was CAPT Ernest D. McWhorter, a portly, genial Mississippian; her first executive officer was CDR Charles P. Mason. At 1039 RADM Charles A. Blakely, COMCARDIV 2 and the man entrusted with directing the training of the *Yorktown* and *Enterprise* squadrons, read his orders "placing Carrier Division Two in commission and him in com-

CAPT Ernest D. McWhorter, USNA 1907, reads the orders giving him command of the new carrier *Yorktown*, during the commissioning ceremonies on her flight deck on 30 September 1937 at NOB Norfolk. After serving in submarines for much of his early career, during which time he received a Navy Cross for commanding the submarine *K-6* and Submarine Division 6 in European waters during World War I, McWhorter was designated a naval aviator in 1927, and over the next ten years served in various billets ashore and afloat, highlighted by command of the seaplane tenders *Jason* (AV 2) and *Wright* (AV-1). (Author)

mand of it." His blue and white flag soon flew from the main truck.

Yorktown remained at NOB Norfolk for most of the following month, proving quite an attraction for local sightseers, who flocked to get a glimpse of her on 17 October 1937, 1,338 visitors coming on board that day. Underway shortly after noon on the 28th,

Looking forward from the main deck, inside *Yorktown*'s hangar space. No. 1 elevator pit is in the center of this view; hatches on the main deck level lead to squadron offices and officers' staterooms; those on the foc'sle deck lead to "officers' country" as well. View taken on 29 September 1937.

Boat stowage on board *Yorktown* on 29 September 1937, the day before the ship was turned over to the Navy. At right is a black-hulled, white-canopied admiral's "barge," 40 feet in length; just forward is a 35-foot gig. Above, on the gallery deck level (left) is the .50 cal. machine gun platform; at right, on the same level, is a stowed outrigger.

Yorktown shares Pier 7, NOB Norfolk with the battleship *Texas* (BB-35), the destroyer *Decatur* (DD-341) and *Jacob Jones* (DD-130) and the fleet tug *Kewaydin* (AT-24) on 19 October 1937. *Yorktown* flies the flag of RADM Charles A. Blakely, COMCARDIV 2. (80-CF-2115-11)

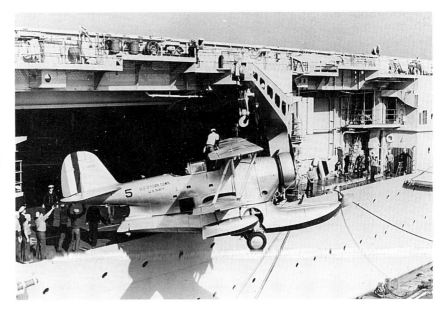

A factory-fresh Grumman J2F-1 (BuNo 0170), Plane No. 5 in *Yorktown*'s utility unit, is brought on board from pier 7, NOB Norfolk, on 26 October 1937. Each carrier was assigned such a unit which performed, as the name suggests, a variety of duties, ranging from transporting passengers and hauling light freight and mail to towing targets. Note vertical rudder stripes, peculiar to ship unit aircraft. (80-CF-5449-14)

Yorktown at anchor in Hampton Roads, on 30 October 1937, as seen from close aboard. Note details of the massive island structure, showing the bridges as originally built. The ship's prospective commanding officer took an immediate dislike to the arrangement of the navigation and flag bridges when he saw them for the first time, complaining of the fact that they severely restricted visibility—the flag bridge is that which is visible one deck below the prominent conning tower which extends around the forward end of the pilot house. Ultimately, this was changed during the ship's December 1939 overhaul at Puget Sound Navy Yard, and remained a distinctive feature of this ship for the rest of her days. Other details of interest are the boat booms, side ladders, early-pattern foremast tripod, and the projecting sponson for the hangar deck catapult which had not yet been fitted. (NH 51823)

she anchored in Hampton Roads to prepare for her scheduled training, and soon embarked the first group of naval aviation cadets for familiarization.

Soon thereafter, another significant milestone occurred in the ship's career, when *Yorktown*'s first take-off and landing took place on 10 November, carried out by the air officer, LCDR Clifton A.F. Sprague, in one of the ship utility unit Vought O3U-3s. A flurry of such evolutions followed shortly, take-offs and landings of the utility unit's Grumman J2F-1s and O3U-3s, witnessed by all of the men from the off-duty sections who, seized with the inevitable curiosity, eagerly "crowded every vantage point for a glimpse" of the operations taking place on the flight deck.

Yorktown then entered the Norfolk Navy Yard, Portsmouth, Va., on 18 November for the installation of her secondary AA battery—four 1.1-inch quadruple-mount automatic guns. She remained yard-bound until 9 December, at which time she returned to Pier 7, NOB Norfolk. The next day, *Yorktown* brought on board her assigned fighting and scouting squadrons, VF-5 and VS-5, respectively equipped with

Plane No. 4 of *Yorktown*'s utility unit, Grumman J2F-1 (BuNo 0169), spotted on no. 2 elevator, is being struck below on 2 November 1937. (80-CF-54867-2)

Plane no. 1 of *Yorktown*'s utility unit, resplendent in the blue and silver color scheme peculiar to "command" aircraft, was a Vought O3U-3 (BuNo 9329). Seen here on *Yorktown*'s flight deck on 2 November 1937, this plane, allocated to the ship's commanding officer, later became the first aircraft to be launched by a hangar deck catapult, on 9 November 1938. Grumman J2F-1s, BuNo 0169 and 0170 are visible in the right background. (80-CF-54862-2)

Grumman F2F-1s and Curtiss SBC-3s, as well as the similarly equipped VF-6 and VS-6, squadrons allocated to the still-building *Enterprise*. The ship then moved out to anchor in Hampton Roads on the 11th, and, the next morning, got underway for the Southern Drill Grounds, to qualify pilots and conduct refresher landings, *Jacob Jones* (DD-130) and *Leary* (DD-158) accompanying her as plane guards. The first day's evolutions proceeded smoothly; tragedy, however, marred the next day's.

At 1010 on 14 December, AVCDT Michael T. Leonard, USNR, was bringing in his Grumman F2F-1 (BuNo 9672) for his third landing in the series of seven he needed to qualify for routine carrier operations. Although Leonard promptly answered the LSO's "cut," he landed so close to the port side of the deck that the F2F's tail hook caught the wire near the port

yielding element. The Grumman went into the catwalk, its prop knocking AMM3c Donald A. Robinson, who was standing fire watch, overboard.

Yorktown immediately stopped all engines, fired a signal gun, dropped two Franklin life buoys and sounded her whistle to alert the plane guard destroyers. While *Jacob Jones* began searching for Robinson, *Yorktown* got underway and landed the rest of her planes, *Leary* standing by. Despite a search by all three ships, Robinson was never found. An investigation later asserted that the sailor had been killed by the propeller blade.

After resuming flight operations the following day, the carrier flew off her aircraft to land at NAS Norfolk, the pilots having completed their scheduled training, and arrived back at NOB Norfolk on the 18th. She remained there through the end of the year 1937.

While *Yorktown* was on her shakedown cruise, RADM Charles A. Blakely, COMCARDIV TWO (who would be the first flag officer to use the new carrier as his flagship), attended to administrative business at NAS Norfolk. This view, taken on 14 January 1938, shows Blakely (center, seated) with members of his staff. In front are (L-R) LCDR Leslie E. Gehres, CAPT Newton H. White (chief of staff), RADM Blakely, CDR Vernon E. Wheeler (SC), LCDR Harold F. Fick. Standing: LTs Albert Handley, Bromfield B. Nichol, Frederick Berry, Jr., Robert C. Sutcliff, Bennett W. Wright (flag lieutenant), and Warren W. Whitside (SC). Less than six months later, CAPT White would be the commissioning CO of *Yorktown*'s sistership *Enterprise* (CV-6); he would be remembered as the man who stamped *Enterprise* with the "personality" that animated her throughout her career. (80-CF-8008-4)

Yorktown anchored at Limon Bay, Cristobal, Canal Zone, on 21 February 1938, during her shakedown cruise. Parked aft of the erected palisade on her flight deck can be seen two Vought O3U-3s and two Grumman J2F-1s of the ship's utility unit. (80-G-60688-A via Reilly)

Shifting from thence to Hampton Roads on 7 January 1938, *Yorktown* got underway the following morning for Culebra, Puerto Rico, and the first leg of her "shakedown," that period in the life of every ship that serves as a "honeymoon" of sorts, where ship and crew get to know each other's idiosyncrasies.

Traveling singly, *Yorktown* reached her destination six days later, before she shifted to Charlotte Amalie, Virgin Islands, on the 14th, literally bringing home the bacon for the Marines of VMS-3. A longshoremen's strike at San Juan had prevented a shipment of fresh meat to the Marine squadron based at St. Thomas, but *Yorktown* provided 1,500 pounds of it by the simple expedient of rearranging her own consumption of meat for a day or so. The cavernous hangar "and the millions of things that make this, the newest carrier, what it is . . ." awed the Marines who visited the ship.

She steamed thence to Gonaives, Haiti, and Guantanamo Bay, Cuba, arriving at the latter place on the 21st to commence a 10-day stay. *Yorktown* then paid a return call on Gonaives and exercised at Guantanamo before she proceeded to Cristobal, Colon Bay, Canal Zone, which she reached on 21 February, greeted on her way in by three patrol planes from PATRON 2 and three from PATRON 5, whose crews thought the new ship looked like "a cross between the *Saratoga* and *Ranger*" and who had used her as the object of a search problem. On the first day of March, she sailed for Norfolk. Arriving off the Chesapeake lightship at noon on the 6th, *Yorktown* launched the five planes of her utility unit for NAS Hampton Roads and stood in, dropping anchor just after sundown.

The following day, *Yorktown* entered the Norfolk Navy Yard and commenced post-shakedown availability. Among the items of work performed was the installation of the three Type H, Mark II catapults—one on the hangar deck, running athwartships at frame 47, and the other two, port and starboard, at the forward end of the flight deck; replacement of the defective reduction gears that had plagued the ship since the previous summer; and the enclosing of her foremast fire control platform. In addition, during this period in 1938, *Yorktown* received a prominent marking—a large black Y painted on both sides of the stack—to distinguish her from her twin-sister *Enterprise*. While she lay at Norfolk, her sistership was commissioned on 12 May, and *Yorktown* hosted her first flag change-of-command, when RADM William F. Halsey, Jr. relieved RADM Blakely as COMCARDIV 2 in ceremonies on board on 28 June.

Ultimately emerging from the yard on 17 October 1938, *Yorktown* returned briefly to NOB Nor-

folk before getting underway on the 19th for the Southern Drill Grounds to carry out carrier qualifications. The only mishap to occur happened on 27 October, when a TBD-1 hit the ramp and crashed in the ship's wake; fortunately the pilot, CDR J.E. Craig, survived unhurt. Shortly before the ship returned to Pier 7, NOB Norfolk on 2 November, RADM Halsey and BGEN Humphreys, USA, were flown back to Norfolk ahead of the ship, in a TBD.

A week after the ship tied up at Pier 7, another milestone occurred when, on 9 November 1938, *Yorktown* catapulted off a Vought O3U-3 (BuNo 9329) at 1501—the first launch from a hangar deck catapult.

The next day, *Yorktown* got underway for Rockland, Maine, reaching that port on the 12th. With RADM H.L. Brinser, Chief of the Board of Inspection and Survey, embarked between 15 and 18 November, the carrier ran a series of post-overhaul trials to verify that the ship's noisy reduction gears had indeed been replaced properly. *Yorktown* ultimately returned to Norfolk on the 25th, mooring in the Navy Yard that day.

In the meantime, plans had been finalized for the fleet's next series of big exercises, Fleet Problem XX. *Yorktown* departed NOB Norfolk on 4 January 1939, in company with *Enterprise* and the destroyers *Warrington* (DD-383), *Helm* (DD-388) and *Ralph Talbot* (DD-390), *Yorktown* flying RADM Halsey's flag as COMCARDIV 2. They stood out of Hampton Roads and headed south, to join the fleet in the Guantanamo Bay-Culebra area, the carriers to take part in their first war games—the annual Fleet Problem that had become a fixture of the Navy's training cycle since the mid-1920s and the culminating event of the training year.

For these scenarios, an elaborate international situations was mapped out, slated to end in a major fleet action. Each of the major "nationalities" in the problems was given a color code. For Fleet Problem XX, the principal players were WHITE, BLACK and GREEN. Briefly, to set the stage, one powerful nation (WHITE), desired to assert political control over another—revolution-wracked GREEN. WHITE, acting before GREEN could secure help from anywhere else, sought to aid the GREEN revolutionaries. Observers cynically speculated that WHITE would later seek to exact "important advantages" for the assistance thus rendered. BLACK, although opposed to the designs of WHITE, found herself unable to employ her full naval strength because of the ominous Pacific designs of an unnamed fourth power. BLACK, learning

Douglas TBD-1s of VT-5 spotted, carrier-fashion, on the concrete ramp at NAS Hampton Roads, Va., on 24 March 1938. The third squadron to be equipped with the monoplane torpedo bomber later christened "Devastator," Torpedo 5 took delivery of its first TBD-1 (BuNo 0314) in February 1938. 5-T-4, in left foreground (BuNo 0319) was later assigned the code 5-T-1, and flew in action ranging from the strike on Jaluit in February 1942 to the attack on the Japanese carrier *Shōkaku* in the Battle of the Coral Sea. Other identifiable BuNos are 0316 (behind 0319), 0315 and 0313. (80-CF-54852-1 via Lucabaugh)

of WHITE's intent to declare early recognition of the GREEN revolutionaries, took steps to oppose WHITE and ordered a part of its fleet into the Caribbean. Strikingly, the scenario for Fleet Problem XX mirrored a situation in which the United States would have to deal with an attempt to overturn the Monroe Doctrine in the western hemisphere while having to keep a weather eye on the Japanese in the Pacific.

Yorktown, along with *Enterprise* and *Lexington*—the latter the flagship for VADM Ernest J. King, COMAIRBATFOR—was assigned to the WHITE fleet. *Ranger*

was assigned to the BLACK fleet. The Navy's fifth carrier, *Saratoga*, played no role in the problem. Shortly before the "war" started, a ship's newspaper appeared on board *Yorktown*, dubbed "The Oracle." A clever spoof, "The Oracle" even contained one story that identified the ruler of one of the mythical warring powers as "King Earnest I."

Above: Grumman F2F-1 (BuNo 9672) assigned to VF-5's CO, seen here over the Tidewater area on 17 July 1938. Plane bears the "Diving Eagle" insignia of VF-5. Cowl, fuselage band, tail surfaces and wing chevron are red. (80-G-414445)

Left: Yorktown's VB-5 was the first USN squadron to be equipped with the Northrop BT-1 monoplane dive bomber, taking deliveries of its first aircraft in April 1938. A BT-1 (BuNo 0614) flown by AVCDT Arthur B. Sweet, USNR, with ENS Robert B. Byrnes in the rear cockpit, pushes over into a dive. Note VB-5's prominent "Winged Satan" insignia. (NH 91165 via Lucabaugh)

15

Fleet Problem XX began at 0600 on 20 February, with the auxiliary *Utah* (AG-16)—representing a convoy of three merchantmen—sailing for Port William. At 0604, *Yorktown* and *Enterprise*, together with *San Francisco* (CA-38), *Quincy* (CA-39) and *Tuscaloosa* (CA-37) left the main body of the WHITE fleet to form an escort for the "convoy." Sighting *Utah* at 0850, *Yorktown* turned into the wind at 1038 and soon began launching the Curtiss SBC-3s of VS-5 for a scouting flight, together with a division of VF-5's Grumman F2F-1s to patrol above the force. For the remainder of the day, *Yorktown*'s planes carried out searches and patrols, and served as "aerial pickets" over *Utah*, in what passed for "early warning" aircraft in those pre-war days. None of *Yorktown*'s planes made any contacts during the day, and after recovering the last of her aircraft, the carrier dropped astern of the cruisers for the night.

The tempo of operations quickened, however, the following day, and continued almost relentlessly through that day and the next, as BLACK attempted—unsuccessfully—to intercept the WHITE convoy. Several surface engagements took place, resulting in each side inflicting considerable damage upon the other.

The pace at which the carriers were operating showed no signs of let-up. At 0400 on the 21st, *Yorktown* went to general quarters and, between 0600 and 0700, "intercepted numerous contact reports" telling of the presence of enemy heavy and light cruisers, and an aircraft carrier, nearing the convoy she was assigned to protect. Acting on a report of an *Enterprise* scout, *Yorktown* accordingly commenced launching her air group at 0725, consisting of 18 F2F-1s (each armed with two 100-pound bombs); 18 SBC-3s (VS-5) and 18 Northrop BT-1s (VB-5), each scout and dive bomber armed with a 1,000-pounder, and 18 Douglas TBD-1s, each carrying three 500-pound bombs, completing the evolution within 25 minutes. The group then took departure and, soon thereafter, received orders to attack the "enemy" carrier.

Yorktown's planes, though, found no such ship. They reached the position of the reported carrier but discovered that an error had been made in the contact report. Instead of a carrier they found two BLACK cruisers—*Northampton* (CA-26) and *Pensacola* (CA-24)—who soon paid the price for being bereft of air cover. For ten minutes, the *Yorktown* subjected the two ships to a punishing attack. VS-5 and VT-5 singled out *Northampton* for destruction while VF-5 and VB-5 similarly drubbed *Pensacola*, the four squadrons leaving both cruisers *hors de combat*. Later, however, an umpire for that phase of the

exercise ruled that *Northampton*'s guns had shot down two SBCs and two TBDs.

Yorktown subsequently landed her attack group between 0938 and 1032 and serviced and re-armed it for a second strike. Later that afternoon, the carrier altered course to rejoin the fleet's main body, launching her SBCs to conduct a sector search to a distance of 80 miles from the ship. Still later, *Yorktown* rejoined *Lexington*.

The following morning, *Yorktown* went to general quarters at 0400, and throughout the day served as the "duty" carrier, establishing her first outer air patrol of sixteen SBCs (the first line of aerial defense) and a combat air patrol of nine F2F-1s over the main body of the WHITE fleet. She relieved these patrols as necessary throughout the day, the inner patrol remaining comprised of Grumman fighters but the outer one varying from BT-1s to TBD-1s. On the 23d and 24th, *Yorktown* carried the responsibility of screening the WHITE fleet, as early on the former day *Lexington* and *Enterprise*, with their accompanying ships, proceeded out on a raiding mission.

The 25th of February began routinely enough, with *Yorktown* again the duty carrier, steaming with the WHITE fleet; turning into the wind at 0546, she launched her first patrol of the day, as well as established her pickets (ten SBC-3s) within a half hour. *Lexington* rejoined, along with her escorts, at 1140, but within an hour came word of enemy patrol planes lurking about—25 miles away and closing. *Yorktown* went to general quarters at 1215.

One minute later, her inner air patrol reported engaging a BLACK patrol plane at 2,500 feet; nine F2F-1s ganged up on the hapless flying boat, the umpire assessing it "completely disabled" at the cost of one fighter. Less than two hours later the same scenario occurred—with the same result—one flying boat in exchange for one fighter lost in the attack to the defending gunners. At 1607, three BLACK patrol planes managed to penetrate the air cover, emerging over the WHITE fleet and within range of *Yorktown*'s .50-caliber machine guns. Eight fighters from VF-5 pounced on the intruders, downing three at the cost of one F2F-1. Elsewhere, however, BLACK planes, from *Ranger*, had put *Enterprise* out of action.

The brush with the BLACK patrol planes punctuated the routine of search and patrol, but only proved a preliminary to the Jutlandesque last act of Fleet Problem XX. The fleets closed one another on the 26th, each side preparing its disposition for the battle the following day. To give all ships the benefit of being able to participate in the action, the umpires removed all previous damage restrictions.

As dawn broke over the Antilles on 27 February, *Yorktown* teemed with life as colorfully jerseyed plane handlers spotted the red-tailed air group on the maroon-stained flight deck. At 0605, *Yorktown* left the formation and turned into the wind to launch planes. Scouting Five soon headed out on its search, scouring the seas to a distance of 120 miles away from the ship, while the attack group then set out to take up its position, following the median line of the sector being searched by the SBCs. Nineteen fighters comprised the combat air patrol over the WHITE fleet.

Less than an hour later, at 0702, came exciting news, when Commander, VS-5, reported the enemy carrier (*Ranger*) and "many" additional ships. Ten minutes later, 5-S-10 confirmed the proximity of "many BBs, CAs, CLs and DDs"—the BLACK fleet! Between 0728 and 0735, *Yorktown*'s air group snarled down upon *Ranger*, dropping 57 500-pound bombs and 18 1,000-pounders on the BLACK carrier, inflicting heavy damage upon their adversary at no cost to themselves. One section of SBC-3s then tracked the enemy's main body while six of the returning TBD-1s, on their way back to the ship, attacked an enemy patrol plane in the vicinity of the WHITE task force, in an inconclusive skirmish that resulted in no damage to either side.

By 0932, *Yorktown* had completed the recovery of the strike group, and was already commencing the re-armament and refueling of her planes, beginning launch again at 1043. This time, VT-5s TBD-1s were armed with torpedoes, for attacks on the enemy's battle line; VS-5 and VB-5 again carried 1,000-pound bombs.

WHITE opened the battle line action, meanwhile,

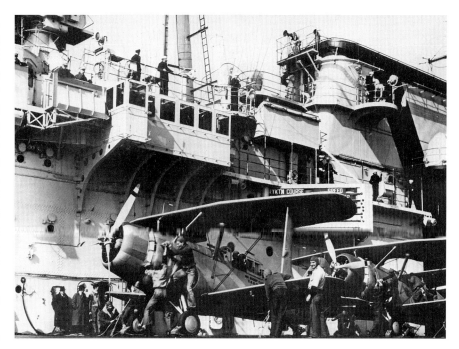

Cranking up the Air Group Commander's Curtiss SBC-3 (BuNo 0527) during carrier qualifications on the Southern Drill Grounds on 25 October 1938. Note the "billboard" (visible behind the upper wing of the YAGC's aircraft) giving information as to the ship's course and speed—an item of shipboard equipment unique to *Yorktown* and *Enterprise*. Visible just above the YAGC's plane is the air officer's enclosure, with the hinged docking bridge just forward. (80-G-5037 via Reilly)

On the eve of Fleet Problem XX, "The Oracle" appeared on board *Yorktown*. The first issue came out on 18 February 1939, and the cover page is illustrated here. The "Harrigan" of "Harrigan's Hoptoads" was LCDR Daniel W. Harrigan, CO of VB-5. The "war" referred to was Fleet Problem XX's scenario of hostilities between the BLACK and WHITE forces. It was probably the first paper to be published on board, preceding the "*Yorktown* Crier" by two months. (Naval Aviation History Office & Archives)

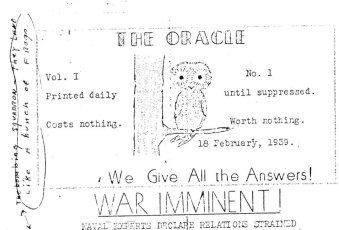

THE ORACLE

The bombing SQUADRON they call like a bunch of Frogs

Vol. I   No. 1

Printed daily   until suppressed.

Costs nothing.   Worth nothing.

18 February, 1939.

We Give All the Answers!

WAR IMMINENT!

NAVAL EXPERTS DECLARE RELATIONS STRAINED

WAR SURE, SAY HOPTOADS!
At Sea., 17 Feb. When interviewed last night by our War Correspondant, Harrigan's Hoptoads declared that from present indications war is not
(Continued on page four)

WAR POSITIVE, SAY
            MAN-O'-WAR BIRDS
At Sea, 17 Jan. (Special) - The Man-o'-War bird spokesman for Scoron FIVE last night was positive that war was merely a matter of hours and stated - "While not desiring to be quoted, 1 will say, however, that 'when war is near who better should know than the
(Continued on page four)

BERTHA SCOFFS AT
            STRAINED RELATIONS
At Sea, 18 Feb. (Special) - Torpron FIVE's Bertha told our correspondent last night that she could be quoted as sayin "As far as I know, none of m relations are or ever have b strained, and that any impli cation that they have is a
(Continued on page four)

WAR FLARES IN
            WESTERN HEMISPHERE
Port William, Bananuela, 17 Feb. It was announced to day in Blackton that the Bla Consul in Port William had i
(Continued on page four)

17

Grumman F2F-1s (one of which is 5-F-2, BuNo 9664) spotted near the island during a lull in operations during Fleet Problem XX in February 1939. Camera guns are mounted on the planes' upper wings, to record aerial gunnery practice. (80-CF-5485-2)

at 1121, with the advantage of air spot, while BLACK followed suit five minutes later. Soon after the battle had been joined, each side hurled its respective air power against the other, launching heavy and well-coordinated attacks. Four VT-5 TBDs carried out an unopposed attack on a BLACK battleship, dropping their torpedoes at 1,500 yards, at 1126. Seventeen SBCs then pushed over and dove on the lead BLACK battleship, losing four of their number to the heavy anti-aircraft fire from their quarry, and an additional SBC-3 moments later as Scouting Five attempted to disengage and clear the area. The remainder of Torpedo Five selected two other battleships as their target and attacked, suffering one plane damaged, while Bombing Five pounced on their targets, losing three Northrops in the process.

Shortly after noon, *Yorktown* changed course and began to bring her air group on board, and at 1236 received the signal to "cease present exercises"—the "war" was over. Completing the recovery of her planes by 1302, *Yorktown* secured from general and flight quarters and steamed to form up with *Lexington*. VADM King had no question as to which side emerged the victor, writing to a friend soon thereafter, ". . . I think there can be no doubt that WHITE 'won' the 'war.'" To another acquaintance he declared: "The Fleet is in the best shape in which any of us have ever seen it . . . "

This was *not* to say, of course, that there was no room for improvement: more work *was* definitely needed in

the area of "developing powers of observation," so that aircrew could communicate key data on the enemy's dispositions and character, and thus cut down on the number of erroneous contact reports and misidentified ships. Needed, too, were fast battleships to operate with raiding forces, to enhance the fleet's striking power and its mobility.

Educating the surface ship sailors in the Navy's hierarchy was also necessary, in VADM King's eyes, for carriers were often called upon, and expected, to perform too many air tasks at one time. During one phase of the action, for example, CARDIV 2 was given the jobs of locating and destroying "enemy aircraft in the air prior to their reaching the convoy," scouting with aircraft "plus sweeps in rear semi-circle" and "combat air patrol." In addition to which they were to "locate and destroy the enemy carrier . . . and destroy enemy cruisers . . . [and] provide air spot for CRUDIV 7 if cruiser-based aircraft cannot fly . . ."

When the hypothetical smoke of battle had cleared, however, few would quarrel with the fact that carrier operations, as part of the training cycle of the Fleet Problems, had come a long way since *Langley* had pioneered them in 1925. The performance of his carriers particularly pleased VADM King: "*Lexington, Yorktown* and *Enterprise* successfully completed Fleet Problem XX with no casualties to personnel and with but few material casualties of any moment. In consideration of the amount of flying and relative inexperience of Carrier Division Two this is indeed an enviable record . . . The general performance of the *Lexington* and *Yorktown* and their squadrons, and of the *Enterprise* and squadrons . . . throughout the problem are considered to have been excellent . . ."

Clearly, the two new carriers had done well in their first outing. In fact, when he compared the performance of the ships in his division to the veteran *Lexington* and *Ranger*, RADM Halsey declared confidently: ". . . the greenhorn *Yorktown* and *Enterprise* had a rugged time trying to match them, but we had no reason to be ashamed when the maneuvers were over . . ."

Fleet Problem XX—the last part of which had been witnessed by President Roosevelt from the deck of *Houston* (CA-30)—was now over, but there was still work to be done before the fleet could sail north. *Yorktown* and *Enterprise* visited Gonaives, "showed the flag" at Martinique (a "holiday port") before they carried out type training and exercises in Guantanamo Bay. From thence they steamed to Hampton Roads. Ultimately, the schedule predicted, the fleet would visit New York City to attend the opening of the World's Fair.

As the fleet shaped its course for Hampton Roads, however, a crisis was meanwhile brewing in Europe that would impact dramatically on *Yorktown*'s—and the fleet's—immediate plans. During the second week of April, 1939, Britain, in response to Italy's sending troops into Albania on 7 April, gathered her fleet in the Mediterranean and extended her defensive alliances; the Polish government summoned its army reservists to active duty. President Roosevelt, away from Washington at the onset, hurried back to the White House, returning to an "anxious" capitol on 11 April from Warm Springs, Ga., and in a press conference that day, talked of possible American involvement in a European war. He warned the country that the New World could not close its eyes to what was going on in the Old.

Although local newspaper headlines told of these disquieting tidings, Norfolk eagerly and optimistically awaited the fleet's arrival, the ships standing in past the Virginia capes shortly after daybreak on 12 April in gray grandeur, led by the Battle Force flagship *California* (BB-44). Soon, bluejackets, *Yorktowners* among them, were swarming ashore on leave and liberty by the thousands. Owners of hotels and boarding houses in the city, of hotels and cottages at Ocean View, as well as of tourist homes throughout the area all reported capacity or near-capacity bookings, while sailors bound for the immediate vicinity crowded the train and bus stations. Great plans had also been made for a naval review—the largest since President Theodore Roosevelt had sent off the "Great White Fleet" in 1907—for 27 April, the day upon which the fleet was to sail for New York.

On the morning of 15 April, however, President Roosevelt spoke out on the ominous turn of events in Europe. He entreated Hitler and Mussolini to pledge a decade of peace, and assure their neighbors that they would respect their independence. Three European countries—Austria, Czechoslovakia and Albania—had been swallowed up by Germany and Italy, as well as one African nation—Ethiopia—by Italy. Berlin and Rome, however, scornfully rejected Roosevelt's appeal. The shadow of impending war lengthened across the Old World.

Shortly after noon that day, word reached Norfolk over the Associated Press wire that the Navy Department had announced that the Fleet would return to its west coast bases two weeks early. No reason was given for the sudden move, which hit Norfolk "with a shattering impact comparable to that of the first shell from 'Big Bertha' which bombarded Paris in World War days." The Navy, declared the *Virginian-Pilot*, was "under wartime pressure for speed."

"An avalanche of telephone calls" jammed the switchboards of the *Virginian-Pilot* and *Ledger-Star* after radio station WTAR had broadcast the orders, as sailors sought confirmation of the story. A yeoman from RADM Halsey's staff tracked down the admiral in downtown Norfolk and told him of the startling order. The shore patrol visited train and bus stations, cautioning all bluejackets "not to get out of reach of possible emergency orders."

Qualification of the directive—that the fleet would leave as son as it had been fueled and provisioned—served as a calming influence, to some extent, but the questions as to "why" persisted. Locally, the *Virginian-Pilot* speculated that the Fleet's return to the Pacific "reinforced President Roosevelt's appeal for peace in Europe" as well as returned to that ocean "the only sea force able . . . to checkmate Japanese aggression in the event of a world conflagration."

Other prognosticators seized upon the Far Eastern connection: in the event of outbreak of war in Europe, one stated, a strong force would be needed to keep an eye on American interests in the Pacific. "In some important naval circles," a *New York Times* commentator posited, "the fleet order was interpreted as another effort to offset the Rome-Berlin-Tokyo Axis" in the event that Roosevelt's peace overture failed. Perceptive observers noted the congregation of the British and French fleets in the Mediterranean, leaving those nations little to send to the Far East to watch their respective interests. As the *Virginian-Pilot* editorialized, "Japan had reserved its most active depredations for the period when the European powers are too busy clawing one another to police their Far East interests."

The secrecy underlying the move to the west coast

rankled members of the 4th Estate, who said so to aides of ADM William D. Leahy, the CNO. As the *New York Times* reported it, though, Leahy's aides had told inquiring reporters "flatly and bluntly that orders of secrecy were orders and that the government had no worry about conjecture of any sort." The *Virginian-Pilot* told its readers that timing and strategy of the shift was for the tacticians, not the laymen, to explain, and while the former were not *doing* any explaining, the Norfolk paper urged its readers to remember that the "ceremonial always gives way to considerations of national safety."

Even newsmen attempting to question the President directly, during his press conference on 18 April, got nothing further. "Why six weeks ahead of schedule," one reporter asked. "Because the Navy is subject to [a] daily change of orders," Roosevelt quipped. While the President's jocular response elicited laughter from the assembled newsmen in Washington, at Norfolk, particularly at the Naval Supply Base, few saw any humor in the situation, as the base worked mightily to provision the fleet for the sortie. That key facility stepped up its activity to meet the demand, revising loading schedules accordingly.

On the morning of 20 April, the fleet—"fit for fight or frolic" VADM King had said at a luncheon the day before, paraphrasing RADM "Fighting Bob" Evans as the "Great White Fleet" set out on its momentous voyage in 1907—began standing out of Hampton Roads. *Yorktown*, as part of this general fleet movement, cleared the Virginia capes that morning in company with *Lexington* and *Enterprise*. The fleet transited the Panama Canal on the 27th (for *Yorktown* and *Enterprise* this was the first time that they had done so) and reached San Diego on 12 May, soon finding that the tension that had apparently prompted the urgent return had relaxed considerably.

SMOKER

U. S. S. YORKTOWN

Gonaives, Haiti

25 March, 1939.

Captain E. D. McWhorter,
Commanding Officer

Commander C. P. Mason,
Executive Officer

Typical entertainment on board ship was the "smoker," featuring selections by the ship's orchestra, "popular songs" and "familiar tunes," together with wrestling and boxing events, after which refreshments and cigarettes were served in mess compartments. The program cover illustrated here was for the smoker held at Gonaives, Haiti, on 25 March 1939. (Montalvo)

Soon after her arrival on the west coast, there were changes on board *Yorktown*; CDR Gerald F. Bogan relieved CDR Mason as executive officer on 1 June, a turnover followed a little over two weeks later when CAPT Ernest L. Gunther relieved CAPT McWhorter as commanding officer on 16 June. The fighting squadron assigned to the ship meanwhile exchanged its Grumman F2F-1s for newer Grumman F3F-3s and -2s, the last biplane fighters in the Navy. There was a change in the flag slate, too, as RADM Blakely got a temporary third star, relieving VADM King as COMAIRBATFOR, and broke his flag in *Yorktown*. RADM Halsey became COMCARDIV 1 and broke his flag in *Saratoga*.

For the next five months, *Yorktown* operated from San Diego, chiefly in the Los Angeles-Coronado area. After completing one particular training evolution, *Yorktown* dropped anchor off Coronado late on 31 August, and was lying there when war broke out in Europe with the German invasion of Poland on 1 September. On the other side of the continent, President Roosevelt directed the establishment, on 5 September, of a "Neutrality Patrol" to "report and track any belligerent air, surface or underwater naval forces approaching Atlantic coasts of the United States or the West Indies." The next day the Navy formed the patrol, to operate under COMATRON. On 8 September, the President then proclaimed a "limited national emergency" and directed an increase in the nation's armed forces.

That same day, 8 September, ADM Harold R. Stark, who had relieved ADM Leahy as CNO, wrote to ADM Claude C. Bloch, CINCUS, and broached the subject of a "Hawaiian Detachment"—the idea apparently triggered by the fear, within the Administration, that Japan would "seize the opportunity" in the European war "to get rid of the French and British interests in China." Less than a month later, on 5 October, the Navy established the "Hawaiian Detachment" under VADM Adolphus Andrews, COMSCOFOR, to test the capabilities of Pearl Harbor, T.H., as a force base.

Yorktown had been considered for assignment to this unit, but had been unavailable, for, within three weeks of the outbreak of war in Poland, she sailed for Bremerton, and an overhaul at the Puget Sound Navy Yard. With *Yorktown* known to be due for a yard availability at that juncture, ADM Stark suggested that *Enterprise* be sent instead. While her air group remained shore-based at San Diego, *Yorktown* remained at Puget Sound through the autumn and into the winter, clearing the Straits of Juan de Fuca on the morning of 21 December 1939 and arriving at San Diego on the morning of the day before Christmas, to spend the remainder of the year 1939 in port, preparing for the busy schedule of operations in the new year.

CAPT Ernest Ludolph Gunther, USNA 1909, was described by a classmate as a "handsome, dark-eyed lad from Tennessee, ... An impulsive, hot-blooded son of the south with a happy-go-lucky disposition ... Intensely fond of having his own way ... Quiet and gentlemanly in manner, but has proved, on several occasions, his ability to hold his own when angered ..." An expert rifle shot, Gunther earned a Navy Cross in World War I for his leadership in commanding *Jarvis* (Destroyer No. 38). Designated naval aviator on 9 March 1936, he commanded seaplane tender *Wright* (AV-1) and was prospective commanding officer of carrier *Wasp* (CV-7) before he became *Yorktown*'s second commanding officer. (NH 49222)

Yorktown, wearing the flag of RADM William F. Halsey, Jr., COMCARDIV TWO, transits the Panama Canal, 27 April 1939, Pacific-bound. Note the unique temporary bridge constructed over the flight deck to provide a centerline position from which to guide the ship through the locks of the isthmian waterway. (Montgomery)

VADM Charles A. Blakely, COMAIRBATFOR, and his staff, on board *Yorktown* on 29 March 1940. CAPT John H. Hoover (chief of staff and aide) and CAPT John J. Gaffney (SC) flank VADM Blakely; LTCOL Edward A. Craig, USMC, force marine officer, is seated at far right. At the left end of the second row is CDR Miles R. Browning, the brilliant if temperamental officer who headed the Fleet Aircraft Tactical Unit. (80-CF-8008-1)

Northrop BT-1 (BuNo 0637), coded 5-B-10, at Oakland Flying Field during a navigation and training flight *circa* 1940. The stylized "Lieutenant Wright" beneath the cockpit still indicates that this aircraft was normally flown by LT Bennett W. Wright, USN, the executive officer of Bombing Five. Note radioman on wing beside pilot, since the BT-1's poor forward visibility made it imperative that the rear-seat man direct him through crowded airport conditions on shore. (Larkins)

CHAPTER 2

An Indefinite Stay in Hawaiian Waters

THE OUTBREAK OF WAR in Europe, together with the declaration of a limited emergency in the United States, provided the incentive to step up the fleet's tactical training. The European conflict gave impetus to the development and installation of machine gun batteries in the fleet, and to training in anti-aircraft gunnery and in the wartime use of surface ships, submarines and aircraft.

For the first three months of 1940, *Yorktown* operated locally out of San Diego in accordance with the quarterly employment schedule, taking an active part in the laboriously planned slate of exercises which covered the operations of the ships ranging from battleships to the busy auxiliaries of the Fleet Train in minute detail. Twice during this period (12-21 January and 23 February-1 March) *Yorktown* operated a Marine fighting squadron, VMF-2. Commanded by MAJ Vernon E. Megee, USMC, VMF-2 performed very well during the exercises conducted off the coast of southern California, and its successful temporary deployment coincided with final preparations for the annual "Fleet Cruise" to take place that spring.

The idea of evaluating "full war strength operations" for *Yorktown*-class carriers had been first broached by CINCUS on 7 September, but by late February 1940, no opportunities had arisen to implement CINCUS' desires. VADM Blakely, though, suggested the "practicability of operating an increased complement of planes" in *Yorktown* during the upcoming Fleet Problem. He posited that the proposed five-squadron complement for that carrier would number 107 planes, only two shy of the projected "war complement" of four squadrons plus 50 percent spares. The plan also offered a chance to evaluate the "feasibility of operating five squadrons" from the ship, the number once contemplated for CV-5 and CV-6 and considered "necessary in some emergencies."

In view of VMF-2's successful temporary deploy-

ment on board *Yorktown*, and the fact that she would be the only carrier attached to one of the "warring" powers in Fleet Problem XXI (*Lexington* and *Saratoga* on the other), Blakely opined that the "presence of a second fighting squadron" in his flagship would be "very acceptable." The Marines liked the idea, as did COMBATFOR, VADM Charles P. Snyder, who concurred with COMAIRBATFOR's assessment "that many advantages are to be gained" in embarking VMF-2. When the squadron was hoisted on board the carrier at North Island its plane complement included 18 Grumman F3F-2s and one SBC-4, with three spare F3Fs. Among the pilots were two men destined to earn Medals of Honor in World War II: CAPT Henry Talmage Elrod, USMC, and 2dLT Gregory Boyington, USMC. *Yorktown*, with her augmented air group, then sailed for Hawaii on 2 April. All hands expected to return to the west coast about 17 May.

The scenario for Fleet Problem XXI supposed hostilities between two continental powers, BLACK and WHITE. *Yorktown* was assigned to the BLACK covering force, along with six battleships, two light cruisers, and 13 destroyers. *Lexington* and *Saratoga*, along with their supporting vessels, were assigned to WHITE. Part II of the Problem employed virtually all elements of the fleet except for submarines, patrol planes, and minecraft, and pitted two approximately equal fleets against one another, with one concentrated and the other divided. These exercises were designed to "afford training in making estimates and plans, in scouting and screening, in the coordination of types . . . to develop rapid and secure communications . . . employ standard and special fleet dispositions" and eventually exercise the opposing fleets "in decisive engagements."

For the first few days, as the opposing sides moved toward one another, *Yorktown*'s planes flew morning and afternoon searches, augmented by cruiser-based floatplanes the latter part of each day. At dawn on 4

Yorktown (top) lies alongside the station dock at NAS San Diego on 29 March 1940 while her air group taxies through the streets of North Island from the field at lower left, a few days before the ship's departure for Hawaiian waters to take part in Fleet Problem XXI. (80-CF-2115-10)

April, with WHITE fleet units known to be closing, *Yorktown* steamed to a point 50 to 75 miles northwest of the BLACK main body and launched her air group, putting up a strong combat air patrol over the fleet. Shortly after midday, one of her SBCs reported contact with three *Lexington* planes; almost simultaneously, a WHITE scout plane spotted two *Yorktown* aircraft. *Yorktown*, herself, had remained undiscovered by the searching enemy.

Unfortunately, at that juncture two VB-5 BT-1s became lost, requiring peacetime safety procedures to be instituted to bring them home—giving out radio bearings and making smoke so that the planes could spot the carrier visually. These measures, while put into effect to save the two planes and their crews, delayed the last flight of picket aircraft and the combat air patrol, seriously weakening *Yorktown*'s air defense

at a critical juncture. The two BT-1s found the carrier, all right, but so, too, did the "enemy," using the same homing procedure. And, as MAJ Megee wrote later, "the lost sheep brought with them an attack group from the *Lexington* which treated us to a dive bombing attack and practically ended the war . . ."

Indeed, while *Saratoga*'s planes were inflicting only light damage on the BLACK battle line, losing 33 aircraft to BLACK's "heavy and effective" anti-aircraft fire, planes from "Lady Lex" were tangling with *Yorktown*'s fighters, which downed 27 *Lexington* planes. Despite the valiant efforts of the defenders, though, the attackers managed to inflict 40 percent damage upon *Yorktown* and shoot down eight of her F3Fs. The BLACK fleet generally had weathered the storm, but not without cost. While BATDIV 1 was able to make 12.75 knots, BATDIV 2 could manage only 9.9.

Three Grumman F3F-2s of VMF-2 in flight over Southern California *circa* late 1939-early 1940. Operating from *Yorktown* during a minor joint exercise in January 1940, one division of the squadron's F3F-2s repeatedly flew inside a defensive Lufberry Circle of Curtiss P-36s, bringing their guns to bear at will, prompting VMF-2's CO to contend "that biplane fighters are definitely superior to the faster monoplanes" in fighter vs. fighter combat over a defended area. Nevertheless, the F3F-2's engine vibrations rendered the plane not a particularly steady gun platform, necessitating a close approach to the target to score hits in battle practice with fixed machine guns. (NH 83924)

With their Grumman F3F-2's behind them, the pilots of VMF-2 gather for an informal portrait at North Island, *circa* July 1940, after the squadron had embarked in *Yorktown* for Fleet Problem XXI. All but four of the men in this photo took part in the exercises in April and May. (L to R) 2dLT Gregory Boyington, CAPT Herbert P. Becker, CAPT Charles L. Fike, 1stLT Frank C. Tharin, 1stLT Ralph K. Rottet, 2dLT Robert A. Harvey USMCR, CAPT Henry T. Elrod, 2dLT William A. Millington USMCR, 2dLT Robert B. Fraser USMCR, 2dLT Robert E. Galer, 2dLT Winton A. Miller USMCR, 2dLT Charles N. Endweiss, 1stLT Richard D. Hughes, CAPT Bocker C. Batterton, 2dLT Everett H. Vaughan USMCR, 2dLT Freeman W. Williams, 1stLT John F. Dobbin, 2dLT Beverly B. Kramms, 1stLT Donald K. Yost, MAJ Vernon E. Megee (Squadron CO). Of this group, three would later be awarded the Medal of Honor: Boyington, Elrod (posthumously) and Galer. Note unusual and rare insignia, reminiscent of a Disney creature from *Fantasia*, visible on the F3F behind Boyington. (Bauer Collection, MCHC)

Two of *Yorktown*'s "adversaries" during Fleet Problem XXI; heavy cruiser *Portland* (CA-33) (L) and carrier *Saratoga* (CV-3) (R), the latter launching a Douglas TBD-1, in this view taken on 4 April 1940. Like *Yorktown*, *Saratoga* carries a distinctive stack marking (a vertical black stripe) to distinguish her from sistership *Lexington* (CV-2). (80-CF-362-3)

Yorktown's theoretical damage limited her to only 14.

For the final phase in Part II, the WHITE carriers unleashed destruction on the BLACK battle line, damaging *California* and *Maryland* (BB-46). The commander of the BLACK forces, however, not out of the fight *yet*, dispatched *Yorktown* to launch a strike on the WHITE ships. Her BT-1s roared down on *West Virginia* (BB-48) and *Louisville* (CA-28), and the TBDs of VT-5 scored hits on the latter, *Yorktown*'s planes causing 9 percent damage to the battleship and 66 percent to the cruiser. *Louisville* strove to turn the tables,

taking the vulnerable carrier under fire with her 8-inch guns three times, but due to the extreme range and the fact that she herself came under "damaging fire" from the BLACK battle line, umpires declared *Louisville* out of action "with accumulated damage of 122 percent." This carrier-vs-cruiser duel ended the aerial operations in Part II, and shortly thereafter the onset of bad weather compelled CINCUS to discontinue that part of the exercise.

A period of upkeep and logistics at Lahaina Roads, the deep-water anchorage off the island of Maui, then followed the conclusion of Part II. The games soon resumed in earnest with Part VI, scheduled to last from 19 to 25 April. The scenario for this phase supposed war between "two powerful maritime nations . . . whose interests lie in the Pacific." MAROON (an eastern power) and PURPLE (a western power), the latter enjoying a two-to-one carrier superiority.

Yorktown was assigned to the MAROON force's southern detachment, along with three battleships, six heavy cruisers, one light cruiser, and eleven destroyers. Early-on, MAROON minefields eliminated PURPLE's two seaplane tenders, thus sharply reducing the effectiveness of that power's search capability, but, its carriers undamaged, PURPLE's carrier-based planes took up the slack.

On the early afternoon of 21 April, a MAROON submarine,

ENS Eric A. Lohmann, A-V(N), USNR, exhibited poor technique on 4 April 1940 in trying to correct his plane's veering to the right after receiving the "cut" signal from the LSO, resulting in 5-B-14's careening into the starboard catwalk. Although the BT-1 (BuNo 0614) suffered damage (right landing gear fairing, right and center flaps, tailwheel fairing, and a fuel line connecting the after outlet of the right wing tank), neither Lohmann nor AMM2c George H. Tharp, his passenger, suffered injury. Among the men converging on the scene is a sailor in an asbestos suit, should his assistance be required in case of fire. (80-G-5036)

U.S. Fleet anchored off Lahaina, Maui, T.H., 12 April 1940, during a period of upkeep in between phases of Fleet Problem XXI; *Yorktown* is at far right, near *Saratoga* and *Lexington*. One can easily see why the Japanese who planned the attack on the fleet in 1941 wanted to catch it at Lahaina instead of Pearl Harbor. Ships sunk off Lahaina would have been most likely irretrievable; those in the shallow waters at Pearl could be salvaged. (80-CF-3703)

Salmon (SS-182) reported spotting a carrier, three cruisers and six destroyers, giving the enemy's position as being 270 miles away on a converging course. Patrol plane reports, near dusk, subsequently confirmed this and prompted the MAROON commander, VADM Andrews, to maneuver his force "so as to be very near the estimated position of the enemy carrier at daylight; to launch all aircraft from *Yorktown* at dawn to search the surrounding area and to attack with the greatest possible expedition." Andrews felt sure that the PURPLE forces were completely unaware of MAROON ships in their vicinity. Andrews also planned to send his six heavy cruisers after the PURPLE force if it was "in close proximity at daylight."

On the morning of the 22d, *Yorktown* launched her scouts to locate the "enemy" carrier—which proved to be *Lexington*. VADM Blakely, however, in directing the searches from *Yorktown*, had omitted one 30° sector to be covered, believing, on the basis of intelligence data he had received to that point, that the enemy carrier would be "almost underfoot" that morning.

At daybreak, *Yorktown* had also launched her two embarked fighting squadrons, VF-5 and VMF-2. The former, after 3.5 hours in the air, landed to fuel, while VMF-2 remained overhead, covering the operation, and then took off while the Marines dropped down into the landing circle, after having spent 4.2 hours aloft. No sooner had *Yorktown*'s LSO begun bringing VMF-2 on board when a squadron of *Lexington* bombers, summoned to the scene by the reports of a VB-2 SB2U, came over and attacked *Yorktown*, unmolested, since VF-5 had not reached an altitude at which to intercept! A half-hour later, another *Lexington* squadron arrived while VMF-2 was getting ready to launch, eluded Fighting 5, and caught the Marine F3Fs on

deck. Sighed "Ivan" Megee later: "Finis la guerre for *Yorktown*!"

A second search had been ordered after the first had failed to disclose *Lexington*'s presence in proximity to the MAROON southern force, but the later's plans had been seriously delayed. The surprise factor lost, PURPLE located MAROON's carrier "and a typical carrier duel followed." *Yorktown* was "sunk," but *Lexington*—found at last by *Yorktown*'s planes—suffered heavy damage.

Upon the conclusion of Part VI of Fleet Problem XXI, the fleet put into Pearl Harbor for "logistics, upkeep, and liberty" and to prepare "for return to normal bases." The BLACK-WHITE and MAROON-PURPLE "wars" over, the commanders and their staffs reviewed the data, recorded their impressions and readied themselves for the usual critiques, which were scheduled to be conducted in the Moving Picture Pavilion at the Submarine Base at Pearl Harbor—that for Part II on 6 May and for Part VI on the 7th.

Prior to the critiques' being held, however, CINCUS, ADM James O. Richardson, received a dispatch from the CNO on 29 April, four days after the fleet had arrived back at Pearl, warning that Italy's possible entrance into the European war in May could compel the retention of the fleet in Hawaiian waters—an implicit warning to Japan not to take advantage of the troubled European situation to move on French and British possessions in the Far East. Richardson, troubled, soon wrote on 1 May, asking that a final decision on the matter be deferred until it could be discussed in detail in Washington. On 4 May, however, CINCUS received word, by dispatch, of the "probable" retention of the fleet in Hawaiian waters "for a short time" after 9 May. CNO promised to send further word.

Few men perhaps realized the uncertainty hovering ominously over the proceedings at Pearl Harbor those early days in May. The critiques went off as planned, with the participants shedding light on a number of avia-

Grumman F3F-3 (BuNo 1445), photographed at the Grumman factory at Bethpage, Long Island, N.Y., on 29 December 1938. The plane carries the markings of Fighting Squadron Five, and, bearing the coding 5-F-1, is earmarked for assignment to the squadron CO. (Lucabaugh)

GHOST AVIATORS - APR. 22, 1940, FLEET PROBLEM XXI.

Cartoon which appeared in a contemporary BuAer newsletter reflecting the carrier "battle" of 22 April 1940, during Part VI of Fleet Problem XXI, between *Yorktown* and *Lexington* (CV 2), with the results depicted here: *Yorktown* sunk and *Lexington* badly damaged. (*Bureau of Aeronautics Newsletter No. 123* of 1 June 1940)

tion-related points. VADM Blakely, remarking on Part II, urged that more attention be given to the ability of a carrier to alter her defensive, or offensive, weapons by changing her squadrons—"a special complement of this nature might not only provide for the better performance of the task at hand, but would increase materially the ease of operation of the carrier air group"—thus increasing the efficiency of her operations. He posited that a better air group for *Yorktown* for Part II, for example, would have been *three* fighting squadrons, instead of two, one of the fighter units replacing the bombing squadron, the net effect being to increase the defensive power of the ship's combat air patrol. Along the same lines, Blakely urged that five-squadron complements be provided each of the fleet's four carriers, *Yorktown* having proved that this number could be operated from a ship her size.

By the same token, COMAIRBATFOR declared that Fleet Commanders "must realize that although carrier aircraft can perform a variety of tasks for the fleet they cannot be ready to perform *all* of these tasks at a moment's notice (thus echoing VADM King's complaint after Fleet Problem XX). After noting the increasing difficulties that a five-squadron air group could cause, the admiral observed that more extensive use of catapults to get planes airborne would permit the utilization of a larger number of planes. "It would appear," he concluded, "that whatever loss in flexibility . . . would be compensated for . . . by the presence of an additional squadron." The advantages which lay therein, the admiral declared, could be appreciated "if it is realized that if all four of our large carriers are increased to a five-squadron complement we would have the equivalent of one additional carrier in the fleet . . ."

Blakely did not limit his remarks on 6 May, how-

VADM Charles A. Blakely, USN, descended from a War of 1812 naval hero, served in the 2d Kentucky Volunteers during the Spanish-American War, before he received an appointment to the USNA, graduating in 1903. In 1910, while a lieutenant, Blakely observed the Harvard Aeronautical Society's Harvard-Boston Aviation Meet and reported perceptively that the "aeroplane" was not just useful as a "scouting machine." "I believe," he wrote, "that with the development of the aeroplane will come a machine that can be carried and flown from aboard ship . . ." After various tours of duty afloat and ashore, Blakely was designated a naval aviation observer in 1932, and commanded *Lexington* (CV-2) before—completing the senior course at the Naval War College. After further aviation training he was designated a naval aviator (at age 54!) in 1936. Commanding NAS Pensacola (1936–1937) he became COMCARDIV 2 in 1937, breaking his flag in *Yorktown* for the first time that September. He was regarded as "kind, gentlemanly, and very intelligent," and his directing VF-2 and VF-5 to evaluate two-plane sections within fighter squadrons paved the way for what would ultimately become the most successful naval fighter tactic ever devised, the "Thach Weave." Retiring on 1 October 1942, Blakely ultimately died on 12 September 1950 at San Diego. This informal photograph was taken in his cabin on board *Yorktown* between June 1939 and June 1940, when he was COMAIRBATFOR. The frigate *Blakely* (FF-1072) honors his ancestor, Johnston Blakely, as well as Charles A. Blakely. (NH 95346, Blakely)

training the aerial pickets deployed as the fleet's early warning, to appreciate the importance of early detection.

Finally, Blakely addressed the matter of communications, urging that the cumbersome system of "codes, calls, authenticators, etc." be investigated thoroughly to simplify it and thus aid in allowing clearer contact reports to be made. After noting that it had taken VS-5's commander 30 minutes to decode and clear garbles in one particular message, Blakely urged the use of plain language for contact reports. "The enemy already knows where he is," he observed wryly, "and the news should reach all our friends as soon as possible."

During the session the following day, VADM Blakely noted with pleasure that all of the air operations in Part II and Part VI had been carried out "without any injury to any personnel, loss of any planes or any accident other than a few, incident to hard landings or plane handling on deck." This, he concluded, was in spite of the ever present hazards of aircraft operations . . . augmented to some degree in fleet exercises by the increased tempo of operations . . ."

Deemed by VADM Andrews "one of the best and most instructive problems" the fleet had ever had, Fleet Problem XXI was now over. All that remained was for the fleet to begin the return to its west coast bases, something held in abeyance by the CNO, who had promised to send further word. And, as promised the "word"

ever, to only the number of planes on board carriers. He also addressed their tactical employment, disagreeing with then-current tactical publications which downgraded the importance of the combat air patrol. "I believe this situation is somewhat changed," he said, "and that the fleet can expect that it will be the exception rather than the rule if bombing attacks reach the fleet unmolested when *adequate* aerial pickets and combat air patrol are in the air." To be effective, COMAIRBATFOR stated, "a combat air patrol . . . must have considerable strength . . . preferably two or three squadrons." He also stressed the need to emphasize

came on 9 May, but it was not the hoped-for tidings: the fleet would remain at Pearl!

"The bombshell which landed in our midst on Tuesday," MAJ Megee confided to LTCOL Louis Woods in a letter written from on board *Yorktown* at Pearl Harbor on 9 May, "caused considerable grousing at the prospect of an indefinite stay in Hawaiian waters." Much discussion ensued from wardroom to crew's quarters; doubters pondered the statement, for public consumption, about the training that had to be conducted from the Hawaiian Islands. Weren't the operating areas off Long Beach or Coronado sufficient?

U.S. Fleet at Pearl Harbor, 3 May 1940, shortly before it was retained there indefinitely in the wake of Fleet Problem XXI. *Yorktown* is moored at berth F-2, Ford Island, with eight battleships moored singly or in pairs at the interrupted quays astern of her; two more battlewagons are moored alongside 1010 dock across the channel. Naval hospital, Navy Yard, fuel tank farm and Submarine Base are at left; Fleet Air Base is at center. (80-G-411119)

by the time it anchored at Lahaina after Part II of Fleet Problem XXI than it had been before, did not relish the thought of an indefinite stay at Pearl Harbor. Further communication from the CNO, which arrived in CINCUS' hands on 15 May, did not prove very illuminating in what it said in answer to the crux of the matter. Responding to Richardson's plaintive "how long," Stark only replied: "For some time." Quite naturally, the indefiniteness of the situation clearly rankled CINCUS. How *could* the fleet carry out its important training from Pearl Harbor? This was more than merely a rhetorical question: it demanded an answer.

For *Yorktown*, though, the length of time she would stay in Hawaiian waters—at least at the outset—was very short, for she sailed for Puget Sound on the morning of 18 May, in company with *Brooklyn* (CL-40), *Benham* (DD-397) and *Ellet* (DD-398), for a yard overhaul. She arrived at Bremerton on the afternoon of 25 May and entered drydock soon thereafter.

Late on the evening of 28 May, shortly before she left the drydock, *Yorktown* received a new executive officer, when CDR Arthur W. Radford, a future admiral and chief of the Joint Chiefs of Staff, relieved CDR Bogan. Radford, although considered by some of the junior officers to exude a "brilliant but chilly presence" looked forward to serving in *Yorktown*. CAPT Gunther was a "friend of long-standing" and he (Radford) knew many of the senior department heads well. And, too, *Yorktown* was known to be a "happy" ship. As the carrier, eased out into the stream by a bevy of chuffing yard tugs, emerged from drydock to set out for San Diego, Radford was sure he was going to enjoy his tour.

After conducting a full-power trial on the run down to North Island, *Yorktown* docked at NAS San Diego on the morning of 1 June, where she disembarked VMF-2, whose pilots had begun to wonder if they were going to be taking up permanent residence on board. Returning from San Diego to Pearl Harbor

Most knew that Pearl Harbor, in the spring of 1940, boasted of practically none of the fleet support facilities available on the west coast to take care of the fleet and its train. And, for the officers and men with families who followed the fleet, accommodations in the area were going to be hard to come by!

If any anticipated an improved international situation permitting a swift return to the west coast, startling events were occurring soon thereafter—again in Europe—to dash such hopes. Three days after the "bombshell" had triggered the grousing among the Marine pilots temporarily guests on board *Yorktown*, Hitler unleashed his *Blitzkrieg* against the Netherlands, Belgium and Luxembourg. Before four more days had elapsed, the German Army had smashed through the French lines at Sedan and was heading for the English Channel. Fearing that Japan would seek to profit from British, Dutch and French preoccupation with war on their doorstep, President Roosevelt steeled his resolve to keep the fleet in Hawaii as a deterrent to the militarists in Tokyo.

ADM Richardson, on the other hand, while he had evinced the thought that the fleet was better trained

VADM William F. Halsey, Jr., USNA 1904, *circa* 13 June 1940. After receiving his wings as a naval aviator at Pensacola in 1935, Halsey filled a succession of command billets afloat and ashore, commanding carrier *Saratoga*, NAS Pensacola, COMCARDIV 2 and COMCARDIV 1 before becoming COMAIRBATFOR. Although writing of a CINC of a fleet, that portion of Halsey's Senior Thesis at the Naval War College in 1933 proved remarkably prescient given what lay ahead for him in World War II. "He must be a presence that is felt throughout his command," Halsey wrote, "and he must be known and trusted down through the lowest rating. His subordinates must feel that he has their well being always close to his heart, and that they have a leader whom they will gladly follow in battle . . . his courage both moral and physical must be unquestioned." (Author)

Yorktown, her flight deck packed with a variety of planes (F3F-3s and -2s, BT-1s, TBD-1s, SBC-3s, an SB2U, JRFs, J2Fs and JRSs) as well as gasoline and stake-trucks, prepares to return to Hawaiian waters from San Diego in June 1940. Note the odd deckhouse fitted to the port side of the sky control platform, just above "pri-fly." Close scrutiny of this photo reveals an interestingly painted trio of TBD-1s, right aft, which reflect the orders received on 12 January 1940 decreeing that three VT-5 planes be painted in an experimental camouflage scheme for evaluation in Fleet Problem XXI. Originally, one plane's upper surfaces were painted solid dark green, one's upper surfaces were "lightly mottled" with dark green, and the third one's were painted dark green "well mottled" with aluminum. On all three, the fuselage markings and vertical tail surfaces were lightly mottled with aluminum, and the national markings obliterated by dark green on the upper surface, aluminum on the lower. This photo shows the planes as they appeared as repainted at Lahaina, dark gray paint having been substituted for dark green. (80-G-651042)

LT(jg) Thomas D. "Butch" Cummins overshot the groove as he returned to *Yorktown* from a gunnery hop on 23 July 1940, but in attempting to recover from that mistake, overcontrolled. His right wing fell more than he had anticipated and the Northrop BT-1 (BuNo 0640) then hit the deck, right wheel first, tail-high, and went over the side, crashing into the sea at a 30 degree angle. Destroyer *Perkins* (DD-377) (R) speeds to the scene; she rescued Cummins and his passenger, RM3c Donald MacKillop, but could not salvage the aircraft, which remained afloat for about 20 minutes before sinking irretrievably in deep water. Both men suffered bruised left elbows; Cummins (who would be killed on 14 November 1940 in the crash of another BT-1 near Pearl Harbor) a scalp wound and a bruised left shoulder. (80-G-5129)

"Any landing you can walk away from . . ." A landing mishap on board *Yorktown* on 3 September 1940 resulted in EM1c (NAP) C.M. O'Brien putting 5-T-11 (BuNo 0284) in the catwalk, its tailhook still snagging the cross-deck pendant. (RG 72, VTBD-1/L11-1 file, Box 5519, Vol. II via Doll)

Submarine *Salmon* (SS-182) passes *Yorktown* in Hawaiian waters, summer 1940. This photo shows two of the types of men-of-war that would become prominent in the conflict in the Pacific that was looming on the horizon: the aircraft carrier and the fleet submarine. (80-G-64785)

soon thereafter, with her flight deck packed with a full load of planes, ranging from disassembled Sikorsky JRS flying boats to her own air group, as well as other cargo, *Yorktown* then proceeded to Lahaina Roads where, on 13 June, RADM Halsey relieved VADM Blakely as COMAIRBATFOR, receiving the temporary rank of VADM in so doing.

For the better part of the next three months, *Yorktown* operated in Hawaiian waters, pursuing a regimen that saw the ship generally underway three to four days a week, sometimes longer, carrying out tactical exercises and type training. The change in operating schedules for the 1939-1940 gunnery year made necessary by the shift to Hawaii and the lack of target services, however, seriously affected this work. This turn of events prevented *Yorktown*, as well as *Enterprise* and *Lexington*, from carrying out all required gunnery exercises; only *Saratoga* completed them all. Generally, *Yorktown*'s operations were routine but her passing over a submerged submarine, *Shark* (SS-174), and damaging her conning tower during fleet tactical exercises out of Lahaina, highlighted the late summer.

During this time, something new had appeared in Hawaiian wa-

ters, a strange bedspring-like contraption seen on the superstructure of *California* early in August—a CXAM radar antenna. Ever since the 1930s, experiments in radio detection and ranging ("radar" for short) had been carried out, almost simultaneously, in the United States and Great Britain. The U.S. Navy's first primitive radar had been installed in the destroyer *Leary* in 1937 and, later, in the battleships *New York* (BB-34) and *Texas* (BB-35), where they were tested during Fleet Problem XX. The capabilities promised by the first crude design spurred further work, leading to the Navy's adoption of the first production radar for the detection of aircraft, CXAM, the first of which had been installed in *California*.

Initially, it had been intended to install a CXAM in *Yorktown* at Puget Sound in May, but the alteration had to be postponed until the ship's next interim docking period, scheduled for Pearl Harbor Navy Yard that September. Accordingly, the carrier moored in the Repair Basin on 16 September and emerged on the morning of 12 October, the installation of the CXAM

In this photograph, believed never before published, *Yorktown*'s new CXAM radar can be seen at her foremast, Pearl Harbor Navy Yard, 1 October 1940. This view is cropped from a larger photograph showing the progress of construction on the district oiler *YO-43*. (Author)

(Serial No. 6)—the first on board an aircraft carrier—having been accomplished, the antenna installed in the foretop, and displacing the four .50-caliber Browning machine guns that had been mounted there.

The new device installed at Pearl Harbor subtly transformed *Yorktown*'s appearance, as Radford noted: "The outward evidence of the installation was a huge antenna atop the foremast which looked like a huge bedspring. Naturally, it caused comment at a time when very few ships had similar installations." Soon, word spread on board *Yorktown* that she was now "equipped with an amazing device which could detect ships and planes, day or night, and give their distance from the ship . . ."

VADM Halsey had eagerly anticipated the installation of this new electronic marvel, and was not disappointed when he first witnessed its use as *Yorktown* proceeded to San Diego the third week of October, 1940. Halsey was "awestruck" when it located an opposing force in tactical exercises "out of sight over the horizon, at a distance of 35,000 yards," and helped the ship find her anchorage in a thick fog.

Yorktown's being the most well-equipped carrier in the Pacific perhaps lay behind her being considered for assignment to the Asiatic Fleet, in the event that a show of force was required in the Far East, together with a powerful group of cruisers and destroyers. This substantial reinforcement of a fleet long written-off in time of war with Japan would, however, be overshadowed by the needs of another theater—the Atlantic. The plan which proposed sending *Yorktown* to Manila would be, in time, replaced by another that addressed the matter of a different primary enemy—the Germans.

While her fate was being decided by others, though, *Yorktown* maintained her active schedule of operations. After a brief visit to San Diego (20 October-5 November), *Yorktown* returned to Hawaiian waters, and operated locally until returning to the Pearl Harbor Navy Yard on 29 November for a yard availabil-

Admiral James O. Richardson, *circa* September 1940, most likely pictured before his second visit to Washington to seek the fleet's return to west coast operating areas; he briefly used *Yorktown* as his temporary flagship at the Pearl Harbor Navy Yard in 1940. (Author)

ity. During the weeks which followed, the four machine guns that had been removed from the foretop during the CXAM installation were relocated according to the ship's preference, mounted on platforms constructed on the gallery deck level, at each corner of the flight deck, and the ship received a temporary degaussing installation, cables mounted externally on the hull to neutralize magnetic mines. Splinter protection was also fitted around all sky lookout positions, but not around any of the ship's guns. She was also dry-docked on 11 and 12 December, when the damage sustained in her brush with *Shark* three months before was inspected, and a coat of Mare Island shipbottom paints, formula 42-B (anti-corrosive) and 142 (plastic anti-fouling) was sprayed onto the ship's bottom. She then went back to the Repair Basin on the 12th.

While there, *Yorktown* embarked ADM Richardson, CIN-CUS, at 0914 on 16 December, who occupied *Yorktown*'s vacant flag quarters (VADM Halsey staying on shore when his flagship was in port) in the absence of his regular flagship, *New Mexico* (BB-40), until the morning of the 19th, when the ship moored at 1010 dock. By that time, Richardson had twice journeyed to Washington in unsuccessful attempts to dissuade the President from his course of action which saw the fleet's retention in Hawaiian waters as a deterrent to Japan. In later years, Radford, who accompanied the admiral on his walks, recalled how the carrier's four-starred visitor paced her flight deck as she lay in the Navy Yard. He seemed "rather moody and . . . preoccupied as though he had something very important on his mind which he could not discuss." Had Richardson seen the proverbial handwriting on the wall? Within a month and a half, he would be relieved by ADM Husband E. Kimmel, who would then inherit all of the problems with which Richardson had wrestled since early in 1940, and, ultimately, be buried by them.

CHAPTER 3

With a Bang and a Prayer and a Cheer

T HE YEAR 1940 had come and gone and the United States was not yet involved in the war then ravaging Europe, the Mediterranean and the Far East. On New Year's Day, 1941, the Honolulu *Star-Bulletin* posited that the millions of Americans looking apprehensively at 1941 could "take heart from the lessons of history." Many times in the nation's past she had battled for survival, emerging stronger from each crisis. The *Star-Bulletin* likened the anxiety felt by some on 1 January 1941 to the "dark days of 1918—days before the great American war machine began to move irresistibly forward, impelled by the magnificent strength and unity of the people at home. Those who stood steadfast in spirit through troublous times then will face 1941 steadfastly now." The new year, the paper editorialized, "will call for struggle and sacrifice but it will end with the nation united, strengthened, moving forward . . ."

New Year's Day, 1941, found *Yorktown* finishing out her yard availability, lying alongside 1010 dock, the circumstances of her presence there recounted in humorous verse by LT H.D. Scrymgeour, the officer of the deck, at the start of the mid-watch (0000-0400):

Twelve wire and manila with rat guard
Moored the *Yorktown*'s port side in Ten Ten Dock
At the vast Pearl Harbor Navy Yard
While all hands ran around the clock.

When they found themselves standing up straight,
Nineteen Forty One was born.
We hope she'll be blessed by a Fate
A lot kinder than "Forty Forlorn."

The Captain's enjoying some leave.
The executive has gone ashore.
The last watch of Forty's relieved—

HIS log's written. (Gosh, what a chore!)

Number three boiler is steaming main
For auxiliary purposes bare.
Though the yard engine failed to remain,
We still get some services there.

All the boats are as bright as a penny,
Their coxswains' keep them that way
And rather than too few, better too many,
In the water, so Confucious [sic] say.

Ships present: the *New Mexico* aft
with CINCUS as SOPA;
Other units of the U.S. Fleet; and craft
From the yard and district, here to stay.

The *Yorktown* has just entered the groove
With a bang and a prayer and a cheer!
In all things important we'll try to improve,
So it's, "Gangway! You big ol' New Year!"

That same day, the Navy Department announced that there would be no large scale war games held in 1941. The fleet would remain concentrated in Hawaiian waters "on the alert for any international development." At the same time, the press release noted, the fleet would continue its training.

This routine, governed by the "Quarterly Employment Schedule," commenced for 1941, for *Yorktown*, less than a week into the new year, when she got underway for operations off Oahu on 6 January. Returning to port on the morning of the 10th and mooring in berth F-9, off Ford Island, *Yorktown* remained there for a short time, getting underway on the afternoon of the 13th to return to sea. Over the days which followed she carried out flight operations, qualifying her pilots

Outfitted in their dress whites, the officers and enlisted men of Bombing Squadron Five pose for a portrait in front of one of the unit's Northrop BT-1s, in a hangar at NAS Ford Island, 4 January 1941. Senior chief petty officers and commissioned officers are seated in the second row. (Trott)

in deck landings. During these evolutions on 16 January an SBC-3 (5-S-5) flown by ENS F.L. Faulkner, A-V(N), USNR, crashed over the port quarter, the Curtiss supported precariously by the arresting cable as it dangled over the side. The carrier immediately stopped all engines and maneuvered to avoid damage to the plane, its anxious occupants inside. Fortunately, both Faulkner and ACMM (PA) J. Ulmer were rescued, but the plane sank during the attempted salvage.

Yorktown resumed flight operations, and carried out further qualifications and night landings on the 17th before she returned to the waters off Ford Island, mooring in F-10 at 0842 on the 18th. The next morning, *Neosho* (AO-23) moored alongside to transfer fuel oil and aviation gasoline to the carrier's tanks.

A few mornings later, on 25 January, CAPT Elliott Buckmaster, an able, conscientious and energetic officer, came on board, with orders designating him as the ship's new commanding officer. He embarked that day to commence the preliminaries to the turnover procedure with CAPT Gunther, to begin to learn all about the ship that was to be his to command in a few days. He was not unfamiliar with carrier operations, having been executive officer of *Lexington* before his most recent post, that of commanding officer, NAS Ford Island. He had long desired a carrier command.

At 0758 on 29 January, *Yorktown*—her future commanding officer embarked as a passenger—hauled in her lines from the interrupted quay moorings at F-10 and moved ponderously out into the channel, and shaped her course for the harbor entrance, passing the buoys abeam at 0905. Soon *Preston* (DD-379) and *Smith* (DD-378) fell in as plane guards and formed an inner antisubmarine screen. That afternoon, *Yorktown* be-

gan recovering her air group at 1445, the red-tailed F3F-3s and -2s, BT-1s, SBC-3s and TBD-1s, completing the recovery by 1604. Joined by *Flusser* (DD-368), *Drayton* (DD-366) and *Mahan* (DD-364) at 0645 on 30 January, *Yorktown* carried out flight operations throughout that day and the next, her dive bombers practicing their trade on a target towed by *Robin* (AM-3) on the morning of the 31st. Plane-guarded by *Preston* and *Smith* on 1 February, the carrier continued her routine exercises with her air group. On 3 February, VADM Halsey and his staff came on board from an *Enterprise* boat, to conduct the annual military inspection. This completed by 1140, VADM Halsey donned flight gear and climbed into the rear cockpit of an SBC-3 (5-S-15) to be catapulted off for the flight back to Pearl Harbor. Another SBC, 5-S-16, accompanied COMAIR-BATFOR's. By 1500, *Yorktown* was steaming up the entrance channel to Pearl Harbor, ultimately mooring by 1526 in berth F-9.

While *Yorktown* was preparing to receive her new commanding officer, there was another change of command at Pearl. On the morning of 1 February, on the broad quarterdeck of the fleet flagship *Pennsylvania* (BB-38), Husband E. Kimmel, given the temporary rank of admiral, relieved ADM J.O. Richardson as CINCUS. In addition, with the reorganization of the fleets and operating forces that had just been carried out, Kimmel also became CINCPAC. Over the next few months, the fleet's officers and men would become familiar with the new CINC, who would drive them hard to prepare them for war.

A few mornings later, at 0915 on 5 February, *Yorktown*'s crew mustered in whites beneath the light cumulus clouds that floated high in the blue canopy

CAPT Elliott Buckmaster, *Yorktown*'s last CO, had been appointed to the USNA from Virginia, and graduated with the class of 1912. Tall and vigorous, "Buck" (to his classmates) was said to combine the "amiable characteristics of the Southerner" with the "shrewdness of the Yankee," and when it came to doing things for others, the 1912 Lucky Bag States, "Buck" would fight with you shoulder to shoulder. He evidenced that trait early in his career when, while an ensign in the battleship *New Jersey*'s landing force during the occupation of Vera Cruz in 1914, he had gone to the assistance of a wounded sailor while exposed to heavy Mexican rifle fire, carrying him to a place of safety. Designated a naval aviator in 1936, after having commanded the first modern destroyer built for the Navy since the World War I emergency program, *Farragut* (DD-348), Buckmaster served as XO of *Lexington* (CV-2) (1938-1939) and commanded NAS Pearl Harbor (1939-1941) before he took command of *Yorktown*. This particular view was taken on 6 September 1940, four months before he became *Yorktown*'s CO. (NH 57377, cropped)

above Pearl Harbor, the officers and men drawn up in formation on the chrome-yellow striped, maroon-stained flight deck. There CAPT Buckmaster relieved CAPT Gunther as commanding officer, and assumed command, Gunther with orders to report to San Diego to take charge of the NAS there.

Yorktown resumed her participation in the intensive training soon thereafter, underway on 12 February and back to Pearl on the 19th. Underway again on the 26th, she carried out more qualifications for her pilots, and her air group bombed a sled target on the 27th. The following day, with *Dunlap* (DD-384) and *Fanning* (DD-385) as plane guards, *Yorktown* backed down at 1125 and landed 12 SBC-3s over the bow. On 2 March, VADM Halsey and his staff came on board, at sea, and remained on board for the remainder of the ship's underway training over the next few days. Only one deck landing mishap occurred during Halsey's time on board, when a BT-1 crashed at 1018 on 3 March, going into the water off the port side of the carrier. *Worden* (DD-352) headed for the scene promptly and recovered both men in the plane's crew, LT(jg) John J. Powers and RM1c O.A. Phelps, who had both sustained head injuries in the crash. The carrier's number one motor whaleboat ultimately brought back both men from *Worden* soon thereafter.

After more training evolutions on the 4th, including night exercises involving destroyer torpedo attacks on the battle line, *Yorktown* returned briefly to Pearl Harbor, mooring at F-2 from 5 to 12 March before she resumed her operations off Oahu on the latter date. On 17 March, the ship utilized her catapult, flinging off the first plane at 0801, followed seven minutes later by the launch of another aircraft without the assistance of the "cat." Tragedy soon visited the ship, however, during the launching of VT-5. As the planes were joining up in formation, just after take-off, two TBD-1s, 5-T-2, piloted by LT(jg) Frank M. Robinson, and 5-T-3, flown by ENS Kenneth L. Berry, A-V(N), USNR, collided at 1,000 feet, the latter attempting to join up too quickly. As onlookers watched, both torpedo bombers crashed 2,500 yards broad on the port bow. The destroyers in company all lowered boats, while the carrier lowered her no. 2 motor whaleboat and no. 2 motor launch; as the ship changed course to land another TBD-1 in a "deferred forced landing," those who watched the spot where the planes had crashed could see only debris. Recovering the bodies of Berry and Robinson, *Yorktown*'s boats returned to the ship. *Anderson* (DD-411), ordered to linger in the vicinity to search the area, only recovered small parts of the aircraft and pieces of clothing. *Yorktown*, after more exercises on the 18th, returned to Pearl Harbor the following day, sending a boat ashore with the remains of the two pilots killed in the collision on the 17th. As *Yorktown* moored in berth F-9, she half-masted her colors, a reminder that the naval profession can be a dangerous one in peace as well as in war.

During these underway training periods in the first three months of the year 1941, *Yorktown* was participating in the development of tactics which would, in time, revolutionize fleet air defense—those of "fighter direction." Prior to the advent of radar, the detection of an incoming enemy force—such as that which had bedeviled *Yorktown* in Fleet Problem XXI—was a matter of the enemy being spotted, visually, in time to intercept him. As we have seen, "early warning" consisted of an elaborate system of "picket" aircraft operating over and around the task force when it was operating within range of enemy aircraft. Even given this established procedure, the outer patrol could only pick up the incoming raid 25 miles out, not giving the CAP, orbiting over the fleet center, enough time to climb for altitude to intercept. Extending the CAP 10 to 15 miles out did not solve the problem. In addition, the prevailing doctrine called for the controller to be airborne to personally direct the interception—an obvious drawback since, in rapidly moving modern aerial combat, he could not see the whole picture developing from the confines of his own cockpit.

On the positive side, though, prevailing doctrine urged that the CAP attain an altitude advantage; that any opposition to an incoming attack was likely to disrupt the enemy's designs; and that interception be made as far from the fleet center as possible, to "increase the chances of knocking down the enemy" before he could press his attack home, thinning out his numbers before he even reached the fleet's anti-aircraft batteries.

Radar altered the picture by eliminating the need for aerial pickets, since the CXAM could tell distance, and, when its antenna was tilted, "slant range," and thus the height at which attacking planes were approaching. By late March, 1941, CAPT Buckmaster could report that combat air patrols had been "quickly and reliably" directed to intercept incoming raids in exercises. Fighting Squadron 5 in its Grumman F3F-3s and -2s (the precursors of the famous F4F "Wildcat") was pioneering the work of fighter direction doctrine.

This is not to say, of course, that all went smoothly. The development of tactics based on new technology takes time. Drawbacks existed since systems installed in ships not originally designed to have them meant less-than-optimum working conditions—radar plot, for example, being constructed in the corner of Air Plot, up in the "island" of the ship. The fighter direction officer (FDO) lacked adequate working space, a "trained team of plotters," and possessed no "central radar plotting room in which he could see the exercise unfolding," while the radar operators passed along their "unrelated and heterogenous ranges and bearings" via battle

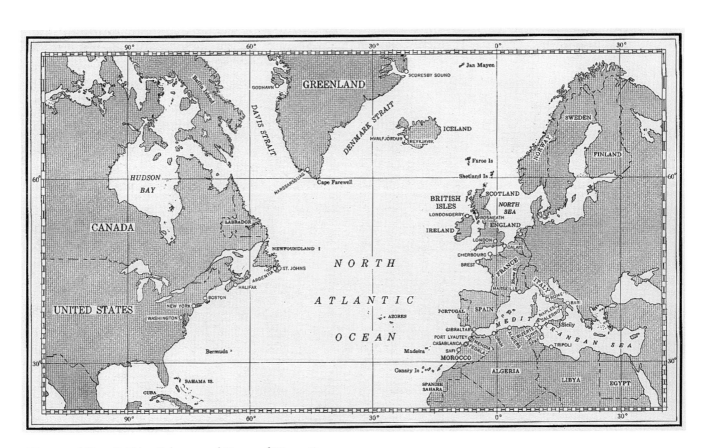

(Carter and Duvall, *Ships, Salvage, and Sinews of War*, p.3)

ADM Husband E. Kimmel, CINCPAC, flanked by CAPT Walter F. Delany (L), his operations officer, and CAPT William W. ("Poco") Smith (R), Kimmel's chief of staff, at Pearl Harbor, study a National Geographic Society map of the Atlantic Ocean. Transfer of *Yorktown*, battleships *New Mexico* (BB-40), *Mississippi* (BB-41) and *Idaho* (BB-42) in the spring of 1941 to the Atlantic Fleet took a sizeable strike force from the Pacific. Together with attendant light cruisers and destroyers, these heavy ships greatly enhanced the striking power being gathered to deal with the country that was, at that point, deemed the primary enemy to the United States: Nazi Germany. (NH 57100)

telephone to "air plot, conn, and sky control." *Yorktown*, like her sistership *Enterprise* later, would have to "make do" with these systems as installed. "Built in" facilities for fighter direction lay in the future.

While *Yorktown* was pursuing her rigorous scheduled evolutions in the Hawaiian Operating Area, however, elements of the U.S. Navy in another ocean were being moved steadily toward a wartime footing. The course of the "Battle of the Atlantic"—as it was then being called—was not looking favorable for the British, our blood allies from the First World War, and President Roosevelt sought, more boldly, ways to aid Great Britain in her struggle with Hitler, without actually entering the conflict, knowing full well that the country's armed forces were not fully ready to meet the serious emergency that would be imposed by war. On 2 January 1941, talks had commenced in Washington between American and British naval staffs, to determine joint strategy in the event of the United States' involvement in the Atlantic conflict. On 1 March, the "Support Force" was established in the Atlantic Fleet, basing initially on Narragansett Bay, operating out of Newport, R.I., and composed primarily of destroyers and patrol planes—earmarked for escort-of-convoy operations. American interests, the President and his advisors had concluded, lay in the Atlantic. Germany, not Japan, was the United States' primary enemy, and the defense of the United Kingdom was deemed "vital to the interests of the United States."

On 3 April 1941, while *Yorktown* was operating locally off Oahu, President Roosevelt met in Wash-

ington with ADM Stark and RADM Robert L. Ghormley, the latter in the city on a working leave from his post as the Special Naval Observer, London. In a conference prompted by the recent devastating foray of the German battle cruisers *Scharnhorst* and *Gneisenau* into the Atlantic, they discussed escorting transatlantic convoys to Britain. The three concluded that the Atlantic Fleet, as then constituted, would be "unable to provide the minimum ocean escort necessary" for such operations. There were no modern battleships, and, in terms of carriers, only *Wasp* (CV-7) was to be operational after mid-April, since *Ranger* was already due for an overhaul at that time.

"To provide a proper degree of safety for convoys in the western Atlantic and . . . an important striking force for catching raiders," the CNO stated, three battleships, a carrier, six destroyer leaders, a dozen destroyers, and four new light cruisers were urgently needed in the Atlantic. Unquestionably, such a transfer would require the utmost secrecy, and all concerned fully realized the "possible effect of the transfer as regards Japan." Nevertheless, "if we are to take an effective part in the Atlantic," Stark argued, the risks had to be taken.

Reflecting the above meeting, the CNO wrote a secret letter to ADM Kimmel. Dated 7 April, this missive informed CINCPAC of the impending transfer of certain units of his fleet from the Pacific, in response to the "existing and potential situation" in the Atlantic. The initial plan called for *Lexington* or *Enterprise* to depart Pearl Harbor in mid-May, after the movement of two battleships and simultaneous with the movement of a third. A little over a week later, though, on 15 April, ADM Stark sent a message to Kimmel which mirrored the President's hesitancy to commit modern battleships to the Atlantic theater—a reluctance possibly spawned by the Russo-Japanese non-aggression pact signed only two days before.

"Until the international situation clears," the CNO stated, the transfers indicated in his confidential letter of 7 April were to be "held in abeyance." In addition, he instructed Kimmel to substitute *Yorktown* for *Lexington*, with *Enterprise* to be the alternate in either case. To this, Kimmel responded on 16 April that *Yorktown* and the attendant destroyers, *McDougal* (DD-358) and DESDIV 18, would be ready to depart Hawaiian waters "approximately" 21 April.

Meanwhile, *Yorktown* had completed another stint of underway training and had returned to Pearl Harbor shortly after noon on 9 April for ten days of upkeep. Moored at berth F-2, off the southwest side of Ford Island, the carrier fueled to capacity from YO-24 on the 14th, and took on ammunition from a lighter on the 15th. Four days later, her crew loaded a large quantity of fresh fruits and vegetables, all items properly inspected for quality and quantity. That same day, 19 April, ADM Stark wrote a personal letter to ADM Kimmel, telling him that the shift of ships—which the CNO called the "first echelon of the `Battle of the Atlantic'"—was a matter neither to be discussed nor debated. "I'm telling you," Stark wrote, "not arguing with you" about the impending transfer.

After VADM Halsey's flag had been hauled down and broken on shore, *Yorktown* hauled in her lines at 0902 on 20 April and, assisted by the usual bevy of tugs required for the task, got underway from the mooring quays at berth F-2, everyone from CAPT Buckmaster on down believing the departure to be routine and merely the beginning of another cycle of intensive training with which the Pacific Fleet, under ADM Kimmel's unrelenting direction, was familiar. As *Yorktown* left the channel entrance an hour later, the destroyers *Worden* and *Dewey* (DD-349) took station as her plane guards.

That day and the next, the carrier conducted flight operations, in accordance with her prescribed schedule, evolutions marred by the loss of a TBD (5-T-6) on the 21st, and two of its three-man crew, when the Douglas' flotation gear activated in flight. Two men had bailed out of the aircraft, but one of these had apparently hit the stabilizer just as he pulled the ripcord on his parachute, knocking him unconscious, and the impact of his body tearing away part of the

stabilizer. The pilot did not bail out, and died in the crash. *Dewey* picked up the surviving crewman and soon transferred him back to his parent carrier.

Ordered to "cease present exercises," *Yorktown* sped off to join BATDIV 3 for tactical exercises, once again in accordance with her schedule, but then abruptly moved off in accordance with new instructions. *McDougal* and *Warrington* soon relieved *Worden* and *Dewey* as plane guards, joined a short time later by a third destroyer, *Jouett* (DD-396), and, finally, a fourth, *Somers* (DD-381). This completed the task group specified in the CNO's secret dispatch to ADM Kimmel of 15 April.

On the afternoon of 22 April, *Yorktown* received sealed orders which were to govern her future movements, and those of her screen of four destroyers. The secrecy, at the outset, spawned much speculation. "Rumors can spread faster on a ship than anywhere else," Radford writes. "By dinner time there were several versions of our probable future actions—the most popular of which had *Yorktown* proceeding to Manila . . ." to help defend the Philippines (as *had* been the scenario under WPL 44). By the next morning, however, all on board the five ships knew where they were heading—*Yorktown* and her consorts were Panama-bound!

Soon after receiving their secret orders, CAPT Buckmaster and CDR Radford met in the former's cabin "to talk things over." There was much work to be done: *Yorktown* had fueled to capacity at Pearl Harbor, and would thus have enough for the trip, as well as could top off the destroyers if the need arose; provisions, too, were in good shape. The comprehensive requirements for a ship *Yorktown*'s size transiting the Panama Canal, however, needed attention: trimming the ship fore and aft was something best done at anchor in calm waters—not underway at sea. Careful calculations about the trim of the ship when she left Hawaiian waters and fuel consumption had to be carefully measured, to ensure the identical trim, fore and aft, when the ship started through the canal. All protruding objects—boats, accommodation ladders, the gun platforms for the 5-inch guns—had to be rigged in.

Over the next few days, the passage proceeded uneventfully. En route, painters on board the carrier obliterated the prominent trademark of the ship, the black "Y" on her stack, with a coat of number five Navy Gray. CDR Radford instructed the medical officer at the outset to carefully monitor the living and working spaces on board to keep an eye on the humidity and temperature. The first few days were fine, but as the ship entered the more southern latitudes, the mercury rose accordingly, making crew's compartments "almost unbearable." "Operating in the tropics under conditions such as we experienced," Radford writes, "would be very debilitating if continued for any lengthy period of time."

Yorktown fueled the destroyers on 2 and 3 May, and took on board a sick man from *Warrington* on the latter day as well. The ships neared the Canal Zone, their arrival timed to occur well after dark so as not to arouse the suspicions of Axis operatives during the transit. Arriving off Balboa at 1935 on 6 May, *Yorktown* embarked her canal pilot, CAPT Luther, and his two assistants. A little over two hours later, *Yorktown* (anything which would reveal her identity, from the raised characters of the letters of the name across her stern to life rings and ship's boats having been concealed) entered Miraflores Locks. Suddenly, those on board felt a jar as the ship's prominent "knuckle" scraped across the lock entrance on the starboard side, to the consternation of CAPT Buckmaster, who sent CDR Radford to see what had happened. As Radford recalled later, information about the recent construction of an armored cover over certain elements of the lock machinery had not been provided the ship. Fortunately, no serious damage—only a long dent and some scraped paint—resulted.

Clearing the Gatun Locks at 0413 on 7 May, *Yorktown* slowed to drop her pilots a little over an hour later. CAPT Luther, escorted to the accommodation ladder by CDR Radford, informed the carrier's executive officer that he (Luther) had been thinking, for some time, of retiring from the business—the big ship's nocturnal transit of the isthmian waterway had convinced him that perhaps retirement was a wise decision. He would delay no longer. "Your fine ship," he declared to Radford, "will be the last one I take through."

At 0544, the darkened *Yorktown* took departure from the Canal Zone and stood out, falling in astern of the four destroyers which formed her antisubmarine screen at 0608. Less than three quarters of an hour later, though, lookouts on board the carrier spotted a Japanese freighter, hull down on the opposite course. Did the merchantman sight *Yorktown* and her screen and thus render academic all of the secrecy that had accompanied the voyage thus far?

Indications are that perhaps she may *have* glimpsed the ships but did not identify them correctly, for some time later (on 2 June), Japanese diplomatic representatives in Panama were asked to find out whether or not *Lexington* had passed through the Canal, Atlantic-bound. *Yorktown*'s transit had apparently escaped the notice of the Japanese, for on 6 June their consul (Izawa) reported to Ambassador Nomura Kichasaburo (who would, in turn, relay the information to Tokyo) that only one Pacific-to-Atlantic ship movement occurred in May, that of a "four-funnelled destroyer"—probably one of the 15th Naval District's "flush-deckers" assigned to that command for local patrol duties. Significantly, though, the Japanese nest of spies operating from the consulate on Oahu no longer reported *Yorktown*'s presence at Pearl Harbor.

Yorktown's apparently successful secret movement Atlantic-ward encouraged OPNAV, who later radioed CINCPAC that "small groups . . . can apparently make the transit without publicity." While *Yorktown* had been making her way east, task groups were being formed on 23 April to carry out "Neutrality Patrols" to base upon the recently established (7 April) NOB at Bermuda. *Wasp* set out from Hampton Roads on 26 April to inaugurate the operations, while *Ranger*, which had arrived at NOB Bermuda shortly after its activation, set out for her initial patrol on 9 May.

Yorktown, having reported, by dispatch, for duty in the Atlantic Fleet on 7 May, reached Bermuda on the morning of the 12th, dropping her hook in Murray's Anchorage at 0726, to begin

NOTHING is to be written on this side except the date of writing and the signature of the sender. Sentences not required should be crossed out by sender. IF ANYTHING ELSE IS ADDED, THE POST CARD WILL BE DESTROYED.

I am well

~~I have been admitted into the hospital as~~ ~~sick~~ ~~serious~~ ~~wounded~~ ~~not serious~~

Am getting on well. ~~Hope to return to duty soon.~~

I ~~have received your~~ ~~Letter, date~~..............,.....
~~Telegram, date~~...............
~~Parcel of~~....................

Letter follows at first opportunity.

~~I have received no letter from you~~ ~~for a long time.~~ ~~lately~~

(Signature only) *C R Ware*......,..................

Date .... *May 11, 1941*...................................

Postcard sent by LT(jg) Charles R. Ware, of Scouting Squadron FIVE, to his grandmother on 11 May 1941 reflects the security-consciousness that surrounded *Yorktown*'s transfer to the Atlantic. (Urban)

ten days of upkeep. *Wasp* soon joined her, later that day, *Yorktown*'s crew cheering their new Atlantic cousin as she anchored nearby. *Yorktown* received mail upon arrival, loved ones reporting the upheaval the dramatic secret departure had caused, and the ship's officers and men were soon contacting their families, omitting, of course, where the ship *was*. Some of her bachelor officers who had left automobiles on the dock at Pearl Harbor were busily seeking to dispose of them "at long range." The large number of used cars, Radford learned later, temporarily depressed the market in Honolulu!

Shortly after *Yorktown* arrived in Bermuda, CAPT Buckmaster invited CDR Radford to accompany him in the ceremonial call on the island's governor, an invitation that the exec accepted with alacrity. A quick trip in the captain's gig soon put them ashore, where Buckmaster engaged a carriage for the trip to the governor's house. Spic and span in their best blue uniforms, the two officers set out in the back of the open-topped carriage, "exclaiming at the beauty of the day and the lovely Bermuda countryside." As their picturesque conveyance jolted jauntily down the main highway to Hamilton, the capitol, continuous heavy traffic rumbled the other direction—trucks engaged in the construction of the American base there—and generated clouds of fine white dust. Buckmaster and Radford soon remove their blouses and put on their raincoats, tucking the blouses underneath the raincoats. "Regardless of precautions," Radford recalled later, "the white dust covered the horse, our driver, our carriage and we ourselves." Looking like "two snow men" the captain and his exec alighted from the carriage, the horse looking like a "snow white charger" and the driver resembling a dwarf from "Snow White." "It took several well-manned whisk brooms," according to Radford, "and almost a bath to make us presentable." The ensuing call was pleasant, but the two men returned to the ship via a different route; they sent a message directing the captain's gig to come around to Hamilton. They thus avoided another picturesque—but (as they had found

RADM Arthur B. Cook, USNA 1905, was designated a naval aviator in 1928. Among his tours of duty afloat and ashore, he had commanded carriers *Langley* (CV-1) and *Lexington* (CV-2), as well as headed the Navy's Bureau of Aeronautics, before becoming COMAIRLANT/ COMCARDIV 3. A contemporary once wrote that "Cookie" (as Cook was known to his Naval Academy classmates) "Frightens his own eyes out of his head with the fury of his language." He is seen here inspecting *Wasp* (CV-7) at Hampton Roads on 21 July 1941. (80-G-463407, cropped)

out to their chagrin) *dusty*—trip. Radford was in no hurry to repeat the experience!

Yorktown's crew not having enjoyed liberty for a long time resulted in some serious difficulties while the ship lay at Bermuda. Permitted to send one watch on liberty from 1200 to 1800, *Yorktown*ers soon discovered that the pubs did not open until 1700. After killing time around Hamilton for several hours—wandering around or riding bicycles—the sailors would make a run on these establishments, consuming as much as they could. The combination of "errors in judgment of capacity" and "a very long and rough ride back to *Yorktown* in an outer anchorage" Radford recalled in later years, produced some "pretty sad looking sailors." Truculence and fighting once the men got back to the ship increased the number of "masts" (a sort of court where punishment is awarded) "every morning for a while." Gradually, *Yorktown*ers learned to gauge their capacity and learned from experience.

While in port, *Yorktown* assumed a more warlike color, as the ship's force painted her in the somber overall dark gray (Measure One) finish specified on 22 March for ships assigned to patrol duty in the Atlantic. This scheme, determined to be the most effec-

A Vought SB2U-3 of VMS-1 in flight, 7 June 1941. Planes of this USMC squadron operated off *Yorktown* during the ship's second neutrality patrol (29 June-12 July 1941), during which time the squadron was redesignated to VMSB-131. Half of this SB2U-equipped unit operated alongside VMO-1, equipped with Curtiss SBC-4s and the SB2U-equipped VS-41. (NH 95310 via Grossnick)

A Douglas SBD-3 of VS-5, coded 5-S-14 and painted in the overall light gray scheme specified for U.S. Navy aircraft in December 1940; with a practice bomb rack visible beneath the right wing, VS-5 transitioned from Curtiss SBC-3s during June, 1941, while *Yorktown* was operating at sea with elements of *Ranger*'s air group. (McDonnell-Douglas/Gann, HG80-296)

A Grumman F4F-3 (BuNo 2527), coded 42-F-8, taxies on the ramp at NAS Norfolk in the spring of 1941, painted in a transitional paint scheme; while retaining the colored tail surfaces (green, for *Ranger*), this VF-42 plane bears the white codes specified for the light gray scheme like that worn by 71-F-17, a *Wasp* aircraft, in the right background. BuNo 2527 was lost on 7 May 1942, along with its pilot, ENS John D. Baker, A-V(N), USNR. (Scarborough)

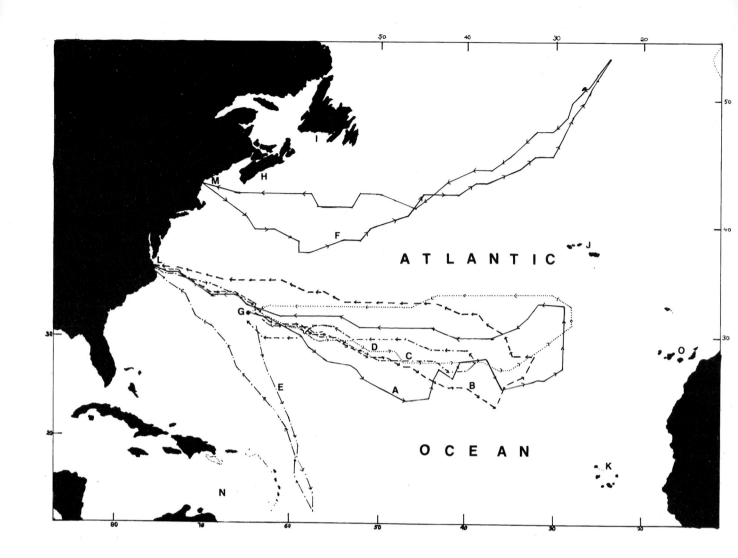

Yorktown's Operations in the Atlantic, May–November 1941
(Arrows indicate direction of voyage)

(A) Neutrality Patrol No. 1, 31 May–14 June 1941
(B) Neutrality Patrol No. 2, 29 June–13 July 1941
(C) Neutrality Patrol No. 3, 30 July–10 August 1941
(D) Neutrality Patrol No. 4, 15 August–27 August 1941
(E) Neutrality Patrol No. 5, 29 August–6 September 1941
(F) Convoys "Cargo" (eastbound) and CT-5 (westbound), 26 October–8 November 1941
(G) Bermuda

(H) Nova Scotia
(I) Newfoundland
(J) Azores
(K) Cape Verde Islands
(L) Hampton Roads (Norfolk)
(M) Casco Bay
(N) Caribbean Sea
(O) Canary Islands

tive low-visibility finish under various lighting conditions encountered, was already worn by *Wasp* and *Ranger*, and *Yorktown*'s crew mixed the black striping paint usually used to paint the ship's waterline with the regular number five Navy Gray paint to arrive at the prescribed shade.

Further changes were in the wind in other aspects of the ship's routine, too. At 0631 on 23 May, *Yorktown* got underway and cleared the harbor a half-hour later, screened by *Gwin* (DD-433) and *McDougal*, to rendezvous with *Ranger*, which was just returning from her first neutrality patrol. Between 0855 and 1939, *Yorktown* brought on board the Grumman F4F-3s of VF-41 and Vought SB2U-2s of VS-41. Three *Yorktown* squadrons, VF-5, VS-5 and VB-5, soon went over to *Ranger*, in which they would make one Neutrality Patrol cruise before they returned to the United States to re-equip with more modern aircraft. Of the squadrons which *Yorktown* had brought with her from the Pacific, only VT-5 remained embarked.

This "cross-decking" completed, *Yorktown* returned to Murray's Anchorage shortly after noon,

44

where, soon thereafter, the two carriers exchanged air group material. Still later that same day, at 1600, RADM Arthur B. Cook, Commander, Aircraft, Atlantic Fleet (COMAIRLANT) and COMCARDIV 3—an energetic, sometimes fiery man of "impulsive" and enthusiastic temperament—broke his flag in *Yorktown*.

Four days later, on 27 May, and less than week after *U-69* had torpedoed and sunk the American merchantman *Robin Moor* on 21 May, President Roosevelt addressed the nation, declaring a state of "unlimited national emergency." He also announced that the operations of the Neutrality Patrol would be extended, and disclosed, for the first time, that units of the Pacific Fleet had been transferred to the Atlantic. The next day, on the 28th, CDR John J. ("Jocko") Clark relieved CDR Radford as executive officer. *Yorktown* stood out at 1000 on 31 May with COMAIRLANT's flag at the main, to begin her first patrol into the central North Atlantic, to conduct surveillance of the trade routes and good weather areas in that region. *Vincennes* (CA-44), *Gwin* and *Sampson* (DD-394) accompanied her, and indicative of the sharing of naval knowledge with the British, *Yorktown* embarked a British naval observer: CDR Ernest H. Shattock, accredited to the British Embassy in Washington as Assistant Naval Attaché (Air).

The next morning, at 0432, *Yorktown* launched her first patrol, three TBD-1s and two SB2U-2s, and over the next two weeks maintained a regular schedule of searches and patrol flights, her pilots compiling 1,200 hours of flight time as the ship steamed 4.550 miles, ranging almost to the Cape Verde Islands. They spotted neither U-boats nor merchantmen.

The only serious mishap for the air group occurred early in the cruise. On the morning of 4 June, LT Joe Taylor, who had only recently assumed command of VT-5, was bringing his TBD-1 (5-T-13) (BuNo 0359) in for a landing when something went wrong—perhaps he had eased the throttle back just before getting the "cut" from the landing signal officer, a dangerous practice. The TBD settled and hit the ramp, continuing across the deck, damaging the last .50-caliber machine gun in the after port gallery as it did so, and crashed into the sea. *Sampson* reached the scene immediately, and fished Taylor and his radioman, CRM (PA) Harrison S. Nobbs, from the water, but the third man in the crew, AMM1c B.W. Brooks, went down with the plane—*Yorktown*'s first fatality of the Battle of the Atlantic.

Yorktown eventually brought her inaugural patrol to a close at Hampton Roads on 14 June, flying off her air group to NAS Norfolk before her arrival in port. She remained in port for two weeks of upkeep and logistics before she embarked another *Ranger* squadron, VF-42 (also equipped with Grumman F4F-3s); VS-41 (for its second cruise); and two USMC squadrons from the 1st Marine Aircraft Wing at Quantico: VMO-1 (equipped with Curtiss SBC-4s) and half of VMS-1 (equipped with Vought SB2U-3s), the leathernecks spelling Navy squadrons on Neutrality Patrol duties while the latter re-equipped with newer planes. *Yorktown* left VT-5 at Norfolk when she departed Hampton Roads on the morning of 29 June in company with *Stack* (DD-406) and *Wainwright* (DD-419). *Vincennes* soon joined the formation, as did another group of warships—*Quincy*, *Mustin* (DD-413) and *Hammann* (DD-412).

The second cruise covered 5,030 miles, the second longest voyage conducted by the ships of TF-2 since its Neutrality Patrols began (*Wasp*'s initial cruise of 5,292 miles between 26 April and 12 May ranked first) and the pilots and aircrew of the *Yorktown* air group spent 1,190 hours aloft on flights ranging from searches and patrols to target-towing by the utility unit J2F-4s and combat air patrol exercises by VF-42. During the course of these flight operations, the ship lost two planes—a VS-41 SB2U-2 on 3 July and a VMS-1 SB2U-3 (BuNo 2079) on 6 July—with pilots and passengers being rescued by plane guard destroyers in each instance.

Few contacts with passing ships relieved the monotony of the voyage and the Marine pilots, in their off-duty hours, became proficient at four-handed cribbage. On 1 July, though, a report from VMS-1 and VS-41 scouts disclosed a "man-of-war" 15 miles distant at 1025. One section of VMO-1's SBCs took off within five minutes to investigate and ultimately identified the stranger as *Winslow* (DD-359). Nine additional reports came in from *Yorktown*'s scouts, and cruiser-based Curtiss SOCs from *Quincy*, during the voyage, mostly of freighters whose positions, heading, and descriptions were duly logged in. Detaching *Hammann* and *Mustin* and the two cruisers at 0400 on 10 July, *Yorktown* proceeded on to Norfolk in company with only *Stack* and *Wainwright*. Lookouts' sighting a "periscope" at 1314 on 11 July enlivened the final leg of the cruise, until closer investigation revealed that the object in question was "apparently a stick of wood." Two days later, the carrier and the two destroyers reached Hampton Roads, anchoring there late on the afternoon of the 13th.

While *Yorktown* had been at sea on patrol, a task force landed Marines at Reykjavik, Iceland, on 7 July, and President Roosevelt simultaneously announced that an executive agreement between the United States and Iceland had been reached, allowing for the stationing of American forces to occupy the country. Now tasked with keeping open the sea lanes between the United States and Iceland, the Navy soon established TF-16 to support the Marines and escort convoys to that new American base. As part of the build-up, *Wasp* sailed from Norfolk on 27 July with U.S. Army fighters on board.

Three days later, on 30 July, *Yorktown* cleared Hampton Roads, too, heading out into the Atlantic in company with a new group of escorts—the light cruiser *Brooklyn* and the destroyers *Eberle* (DD-430), *Grayson* (DD-435) and *Roe* (DD-418)—and new orders: to "operate as under war conditions, including complete darkening of ships when at sea." The carrier's air group for this cruise consisted of only three squadrons: VF-42, VS-41, and VT-5, and the utility unit, and it put in 842.3 hours of flight time during the 3,998-mile voyage. *Yorktown* again utilized her J2F-4s for target-towing duties, too, for her own anti-aircraft practice and that of her escorts as well. Generally, the patrol was without incident, five ships being sighted. Two of these were British—the light cruiser HMS *Despatch* and the merchantman under her escort.

Winding up the voyage at Grassy Bay on 10 August, *Yorktown* and her screen did not linger long in Bermuda's waters, for they resumed their patrol on the afternoon of the 15th. During the course of this cruise, *Yorktown* and her consorts steamed another 4,064 miles, the carrier pilots and aircrew amassing 1,188.3 hours in the air and the ship probing further eastward into the central North Atlantic than she had ever done before, winding up the voyage at Bermuda at 1831 on the 27th. There was still work to be done, however—no rest for the weary. The carrier and her consorts—*Brooklyn*, *Grayson*, *Eberle*, and *Ericsson* (DD-440)—weighed anchor at 0702 on the 29th, steering southeasterly, ultimately skirting the Virgin Islands and steaming almost as far as Trinidad, hunting down a "rumored German cruiser" operating in those parts, before they turned northward and shaped course for Hampton Roads. During the course of the voyage, they noted only the presence of friendly merchantmen along the way—the Greek *Argos*, the British *Henzada* and the American *Trimountain*. Ultimately, *Brooklyn* and *Eberle* leaving the formation "on duty assigned" at 1800 on 4 September, *Yorktown* arrived back in Hampton Roads on the afternoon of the 6th, with *Grayson* and *Ericsson*, for a well-deserved respite from her Atlantic labors.

While *Yorktown* had been operating in the Atlantic, the matter of her overhaul was being taken up. Originally, she was to have commenced it at Pearl Harbor on 4 August, but since her transfer to the Atlantic Fleet had come about, it had been rescheduled to start on 6 October at Norfolk. The operational situation in the Atlantic, however, prompted CINCLANT to query COMAIRLANT on 29 August: "At a time when the services of all ships are urgently needed, what if any are the compelling reasons for the *Yorktown* to be out of service for a scheduled 2 months period beginning October 6?"

Yorktown alongside Pier 7, NOB Norfolk, on 9 September 1941. Her camouflage at this time is Measure 12-Graded System: the lowest color being sea blue, the next ocean gray, and the topmast haze gray. The mainmast appears to have remained black, to hide discoloration from stack gasses. Close examination reveals the CXAM radar above her foremast fire control position, and that the once-prominent flight deck markings, "Y K T N" at each end, have been obliterated; some deck striping, however, remains. (80-G-454535, cropped)

On 31 August COMAIRLANT replied, citing the 3,000 man-hours of work required by rebricking six boilers, as well as the "additional work of military importance" that could be accomplished on a "not to delay" basis, but obligingly cut the overhaul to three weeks. A few days later, while *Yorktown* was on her way back to Norfolk, CINCLANT radioed CNO on 2 September telling him of the reduction of the ship's availability to the period 6 to 27/29 October 1941. To paraphrase "Ernie" King, *Yorktown* would have to do the best she could with what she had.

Two days before *Yorktown* made port at NOB Norfolk, however, an event occurred which would, within a month, change dramatically the orders under which she, and the rest of the Atlantic Fleet, would operate, and ultimately further delay the already once-postponed availability. On 4 September, the destroyer *Greer* (DD-145), shadowing a German U-boat 175 miles southwest of Iceland, suddenly found herself under attack from her exasperated quarry, *U-652*, which fired two torpedoes. Fortunately, both missed, as did *Greer*'s depth charges when the destroyer counterattacked.

On 11 September, President Roosevelt, in a nationwide address, condemned the Germans' "deliberate" attack on *Greer*, declaring: "The time for active defense is now . . . Upon our naval and air patrol . . . falls the duty of maintaining the American policy of freedom of the seas—now. That means," the President continued, "very simply and clearly, that our patrolling vessels and planes will protect all merchant ships—not only American ships but ships of any flag—engaged in commerce in our defensive waters." If German or Italian warships entered "American Defensive Waters" they did so "at their own peril." This meant that the Navy's mission was "shoot on sight."

By the end of the month, the Navy was to patrol, cover, and escort, and to report or destroy any German or Italian naval forces encountered. "So far as the Atlantic is concerned," wrote ADM Stark to a friend, "we are all but, if not actually, in it. The President's speech of September 11 . . . put the matter squarely before the country and outlined what he expected of the Navy. We were ready for this . . ."

Yorktown remained in port for over a week, preparing to sail northward to Argentia, Newfoundland, where a base had been established in mid-July, and from whence the U.S. Navy's escorts in that theater were operating. Before she left port, LCDR William E.G. Taylor, USNR, visited the ship. Taylor, an American who had recently returned from England, had served in the Royal Navy's Fleet Air Arm and had seen action in the Norwegian campaign before he had received his USNR commission. During his time in the British Isles, he had worked in the areas of fighter direction and the use of radar to effect interceptions.

Taylor was spending the month of September, 1941, on temporary duty with the Atlantic Fleet's three fleet carriers—*Yorktown*, *Ranger* and *Wasp*—lecturing the fighter squadrons "on combat tactics and fighter direction," as well as the use of search radar. Taylor eventually returned to Washington and reported to BuAer on what the ships contemplated doing in those areas. *Yorktown*'s installation particularly impressed him. "The radar equipment aboard *Yorktown*," he later said, "was superior to any . . . used in the British Navy and at least as good as the Royal Air Force shore-based search radar." As to the comparative abilities of the men operating the equipment, Taylor praised them. While radar operators were largely "under training," he recalled, ". . . the main radar enlisted man and the main radar officer aboard ship were both very well trained and versed in the operation of the equipment."

There were, of course, precious few opportunities to practice the craft of fighter direction, except in drills, when there was little likelihood of an adversary's planes showing up in the peculiar wartime conditions prevailing in the Atlantic. Nonetheless, other operations could be carried out, and *Yorktown*'s air group had—despite its heterogenous character (the group's composition varying on almost every patrol)—flown searches and conducted patrols in a realistic training environment. With the increasing tempo of the Battle of the Atlantic, and the more aggressive role given the U.S. Atlantic Fleet, *Yorktown* would soon head into the Navy's most active theater.

For this cruise, VB-5, which had exchanged its BT-1s for the newer Douglas SBD-3 (and a few -2s), rejoined the ship at Norfolk. The SBD was a "great improvement" over what the *Yorktown*ers had been equipped with, capable of greater range, speed, and better performance in a dive, with the perforated flaps (pioneered in the BT-1s which had equipped VB-5) making the new SBD "much better as a dive bomber." Scouting Five had also received SBDs, turning in their biplane SBCs. Before it returned to sea, however, VS-5 remained shore-bound, slated to take part in the U.S. Army's General Headquarters (GHQ) maneuvers between 10 and 30 September.

The Army's "long-standing neglect of ground-support aviation" for its troops meant that it had to call upon the Navy for help. Consequently, LCDR William O. Burch, Jr. led VS-5 down from Norfolk, and his squadron (along with *Lexington*'s VB-2) made its

Part of two of *Yorktown*'s squadrons at NAS Norfolk on 13 September 1941, the day before the carrier deployed to Casco Bay, Maine, and Argentia, Newfoundland. In the foreground are 15 of the 18 TBD-1s assigned to VT-5, while a dozen of VB-5's SBD-3s are in the background; further beyond them are five F4Fs and three SB2Us. All planes visible, except the TBD-1s, are painted in overall light gray. The torpedo planes, however, in advance of instructions to do so, have their uppersurfaces painted blue gray. Later, the folding wing sections on the TBDs would be painted to match the uppersurface scheme to lessen the visibility of the planes from the air when parked on a carrier deck. (80-CF-55215-7, Doll)

temporary base at Lake Charles, Louisiana, at a facility many of VS-5's sailors referred to as a "cow pasture." Other USN and USMC units involved in the large-scale war games were *Wasp*'s VF-72 and *Lexington*'s VB-2 and four USMC squadrons (VMF-111, VMSB-131 and -132, and VMO-151).

Despite the bad weather (a hurricane warning on one occasion prompted VS-5 to shift from Lake Charles to Jackson, Mississippi) and low ceilings, not to mention opposition from the RED force, Scouting Five and Bombing Two SBDs executed their missions "perfectly," "destroying" bridges and attacking the main RED airdrome. In addition, the Navy planes wreaked havoc among the RED armored forces, and their reconnaissance flights yielded "most valuable information concerning the disposition and movement of the mass of the Armored Force" which proved of the utmost importance to the commander of the Third Army (BLUE force) as he planned to meet the RED "enemy."

On 15 September, GEN Herbert A. Dargue, commanding general of the [BLUE] Third Air Task Force, passed on a "well done" to his "brothers in the Naval Air Service." Four days later, Dargue declared "We have the Reds on the go . . . due in large part to the fine cooperation of the naval units based on Lake Charles . . ." Subsequently, LTGEN Delos C. Emmons, USA, Commanding General, Headquarters Air Force Combat Command, praised the USN and USMC squadrons as having "carried out their tasks in a most creditable manner with contagious enthusiasm . . . deserving of high commendation." LTGEN

Charles Codman (L), a correspondent for the *Saturday Evening Post*, embarked in *Yorktown* on 14 September 1941 and spent three weeks on board her, and on board *Ranger*, observing life at sea; he flew a simulated dive bombing mission as observer in a Bombing Five SBD flown by ENS Robert D. Baer, A-V(N), USNR. This photo of Codman, seen here on board *Ranger*, shows him with LCDR William E. G. Taylor, USNR (R), who also spent some time in September on board *Yorktown* as well. (Author)

Emmons called their cooperation "under the most unusual circumstances" exemplary, and their performance of duty "uniformly excellent." LT(jg) Charles R. Ware, of VS-5, summed up the experience: ". . . a lot of fun with the Army—quite rugged though—living in tents, mud, rain, dust, flying in all sorts of weather. With the help of our dive bombing squadron our side won!"

Yorktown cleared Norfolk on the afternoon of 14 September, and headed for Argentia. Four days later, OPNAV informed the Norfolk Navy Yard of the cancellation of the October availability for the carrier. *Yorktown*, her presence required in these northern waters, reached her destination on the afternoon of the 22d, and operated from that place until 10 October. She then carried out routine flight operations (when the fog and cold rain permitted it) and training from Casco Bay, officers and men alike enjoying the warm hospitality of Portland, Maine, as their duty allowed. During this period, on 25 September, RADM Cook—who had used *Yorktown* as his flagship since the spring—transferred his flag back to *Ranger*, which had just emerged from a period of repairs and alterations at the Norfolk Navy Yard. RADM H. Kent Hewitt (COMCRULANT), wore his flag in *Yorktown* during her passage from Argentia to Casco Bay between 10 and 14 October, before he shifted to the light cruiser *Philadelphia* (CL-41).

In the meantime, while *Yorktown* was operating locally in Casco Bay, the U.S. Maritime Commission had answered a British plea for shipping by transferring six modern freighters to the British Merchant Marine. Getting the half-dozen

ships eastward across the Atlantic, however, required escorts, as did getting a troop convoy westward. Accordingly, on the afternoon of 25 October, *Yorktown* heaved up her anchor and stood out, following in the wakes of *Philadelphia, Savannah* (CL-42), and *New Mexico,* and passed the Portland lightship abeam at 1637. Their mission was to provide ocean escort for a convoy of the six merchantmen—*Empire Egret, Empire Pintail, Empire Fulmar, Empire Pigeon, Empire Peregrine,* and *Empire Oriole*—which had only recently exchanged the stars and stripes for the "Red Duster." Nine American destroyers rounded out the goodly company.

The experience of covering these freighters, a convoy only given the codename "Cargo," would be the first for the task group commander, RADM Hewitt, but it was for that precise reason—to *give* him the experience—that ADM King, CINCLANT, had assigned him charge of the operation. It was valuable training that other flag officers in the Atlantic Fleet had had, beginning with RADM David M. LeBreton in the occupation of Iceland in July, 1941.

RADM H. Kent Hewitt, USN, as Commander, Cruisers, Atlantic, *circa* autumn, 1940. Hewitt briefly flew his flag in *Yorktown* in October 1941, and commanded the task force, of which *Yorktown* formed a part, in escorting convoys in the North Atlantic in late October and early November, 1941. (NH 49129)

The business of convoying ships was not one to be entered into lightly. As the year 1941 dragged on, chances of incidents between German and American warships multiplied as the former became more heavily involved in a "shooting war." On 17 October, *U-568* torpedoed the destroyer *Kearny* (DD-432) as she had gone to the assistance of convoy SC-48 in its battle with a "wolf pack." *Kearny* made port, where she was repaired, but she had taken casualties (11 dead, 22 injured)—the first inflicted by the Axis on the U.S. Navy in the Battle of the Atlantic.

While *Yorktown* and her escorts sailed on, shepherding the convoy, U-boats were prowling nearby. On the afternoon of 28 October, one of the destroyers in the screen picked up a submarine contact, and thinking that her lookouts had spotted what appeared to be a periscope, attacked with six depth charges. Accordingly, the convoy executed an emergency turn to starboard. Two more emergency turns followed another sound contact less than 30 minutes later, but no depth charges roiled the sea. The "noises" were attributed to marine life, and not submarines.

Still later, the convoy's speed dropped to 11 knots while engineers toiled on board *Empire Pintail,* repairing an engine casualty. For over five hours the ships maintained this comparative snail's pace, until, upon completion of the repairs, they increased speed. During the night, American RDF intercepted strong German radio signals, indicating that U-boats were nearby, perhaps stalking the convoy. The bearings indicated a "trailer" astern, sending out "homing" signals to attract other boats to the vicinity. Hewitt sent a destroyer astern to sweep the area, to destroy the submarine or force her under.

There are indications, though, that while U-boats were indeed operating in that area, *Yorktown* and her charges may have escaped their attention. The westward-bound convoy ON-28, though, which included in its company the Navy oiler *Salinas* (AO-19), did not fare so well. *U-74* spotted it at 1704 on 27 October. As ON-28 plodded onward, it gradually attracted more U-boats.

After 29 October had passed uneventfully, *Yorktown* and *Savannah* fueled the destroyers the next day, covered by an inner air patrol of SOCs from the light cruisers. One aircraft mishap, however, marred flight operations on the 30th when LT(jg) Powers of VB-5 made a bad landing and his SBD went over the side. Unhurt, Powers and RM3c Everett C. Hill swam free; *Hammann* picked them up unhurt. By mid-day, *Yorktown* had completed recovering planes and was proceeding to fuel *Sims* (DD-409) when *Anderson* reported a submarine contact.

Going to general quarters, *Anderson* surged ahead to develop her contact, dropping a standard pattern of six 600-pound depth charges at 1225. Five minutes later, *Morris* (DD-417) dropped an "embarrassing barrage." As other ships in the vicinity, though, soon began reporting porpoises and blackfish, COMDESDIV 3 in *Anderson* opined over the TBS that, in view of the fish sightings, the contact was false. Soon thereafter, however, *Anderson*'s men saw what looked like an oil slick. A bucket lowered into the midst of it disclosed the presence of "oil, water, and burnt TNT." That ship then picked up a "very good contact"—propeller noises—at 1305, close aboard. She attacked at 1311 with a second pattern of six depth charges.

A short time later, *Hughes* (DD-410), also in on the hunt, picked up a contact and requested *Anderson* to develop it, which she did, dropping another pattern at 1409. Securing from general quarters at 1421, the latter, in company with *Hughes*, tried to develop further contacts, or obtain evidence of a kill, but without success. The day ended with the convoy still intact, proceeding on to the "Mid-Ocean Meeting Point" (MOMP) a few days away.

Elsewhere at this juncture, though, other Allied convoys did not enjoy such good fortune. U-boats had doggedly trailed the above-mentioned ON-28, but achieved little success because of the escorts which aggressively depth-charged their adversaries and prevented them from carrying out their attacks. The enemy submarines, did, however, manage to torpedo one ship, *Salinas*, on 30 October. Her assailant, *U-106*, considered her target as "sunk" but the Navy oiler, a tough Newport News-built ship, survived to make port under her own power. The next morning, *U-552* made contact with HX-156, outward-bound from Halifax, and torpedoed and sank *Reuben James* (DD-245), with heavy loss of life, the U.S. Navy's first warship loss in the war with Germany.

Yorktown and her consorts, meanwhile, still having evaded attacks by German submarines, proceeded on, unmolested, but not relaxing vigilance. Engine repairs on board *Empire Oriole* had reduced the convoy speed to 12 knots for an hour on the 31st, and a scout plane report of "suspicious bubbles" only two miles away, a short time after the ships had resumed their regular speed, prompted some evasive steaming. The next day, 1 November, *Hughes* picked up a sound contact at 1137, the report of which caused an emergency turn by the convoy; *Hughes* discovered her quarry, though, to be only fish, and the assemblage of ships resumed its course, unaware that *U-96* was crossing their path and *U-568*—*Kearny*'s erst-

while assailant—their wake, neither submersible apparently stalking convoy "Cargo."

On the morning of 2 November, *Yorktown* reached the MOMP, LT Vincent F. McCormack of VF-42 commenting "that the meeting point was based on the British conception of mid-ocean," and RADM Hewitt's escort force exchanged "Cargo" for CT-5, a westbound convoy that had departed the Clyde on 30 October screened by an anti-aircraft cruiser and six destroyers. CT-5 consisted of eight British transports—*Andes, Dutchess of Atholl, Orcades, Oronsay, Reina del Pacifico, Sobieski, Warwick Castle*, and *Durban Castle*—which had embarked among them over 20,000 men, most of whom were bound, ultimately, for the Middle East. They were to shift to U.S. Navy transports at Halifax for the voyage to Suez, via Cape Town, South Africa.

With all these lives at stake, there was certainly no relaxing the lookouts on the return trip, as *Yorktown* and her convoy steamed back across that stormy stretch of U-boat infested Atlantic, when "the scale of U-boat effort was probably the greatest and the scope of their patrol the widest spread of the whole Atlantic campaign up to that time." Destroyers picked up three echo contacts on the afternoon of the 2d, at the outset of the voyage westward. *O'Brien* (DD-415) reported "torpedo tracks" at 0550 on the 3d, and *Yorktown* went to general quarters; turning into the wind, she launched aircraft to provide cover for the convoy while it took the usual precaution of executing emergency turns to put the menace astern. Later that same day, *Walke* (DD-416) made contact with what she determined to be a submarine, dropped depth charges, but could not determine whether or not her attack had been a success.

Yorktown's planes continued to conduct patrols overhead as the weather permitted over the days which followed, while the destroyers maintained a vigil with their echo-ranging gear. The weather worsened considerably; all ships had rough going. *Yorktown* pitched into the sea, bringing up tons of green water as she lifted her head in the heavy swells. Ultimately, on 6 November, eight additional destroyers arrived to take the convoy to Halifax; *Yorktown*, along with *New Mexico* and seven destroyers of the original nine (two being detached to proceed independently) then parted company with the eight troopships which they had chaperoned across the dangerous seas, and headed for Casco Bay on 7 November, reaching that haven on the 9th. In retrospect, it appears now that CT-5 and "Cargo" had benefitted from the skillful use of cryptographic intelligence. The Admiralty, having captured

Looking aft from light cruiser *Philadelphia* (CL-41) one can see (L-R) *Reina del Pacifico, Oronsay, Yorktown*, and *Orcades* as troop convoy CT-5 plods across the choppy North Atlantic toward Halifax, early November 1941. This rare panorama is the only one that shows *Yorktown* (barely visible through the haze) at sea during 1941. (Author)

two U-boats by that point (*U-110* and *U-570*), had gained invaluable knowledge of then-current German codes (which the enemy mistakenly considered impenetrable), and were using the invaluable information thus gleaned to route convoys around known U-boat concentrations. In this fashion the Americans and British frustrated the U-boats into November, 1941.

For the rest of the month of November, *Yorktown* operated locally out of Casco Bay, carrying out flight operations, and gunnery exercises for her 5-inch, 1.1-inch and .50-caliber batteries, as well as "periscope recognition runs" with the submarine *S-21* (SS-126). Underway at 1120 on 30 November in company with *Lang* (DD-399), the carrier then sailed for Norfolk, mooring to the north side of Pier 7, NOB Norfolk, after an uneventful passage down the eastern seaboard, on the afternoon of 2 December.

The next morning, *Yorktown* began transferring her air group ashore to NAS Norfolk; *Yorktown*ers looked forward to a well-deserved rest, their ship having steamed over 17,000 miles during 1941 in safeguarding American neutrality in the Atlantic. She was also due for an overhaul, but the materials needed for it would not be on hand at Norfolk Navy Yard until 2 January 1942.

The bridge was to be substantially altered, to bring it more in line with the improvements in design for *Hornet* (CV-8), refinements themselves brought about

as the result of operational experience in the *Yorktown*-class ships. *Yorktown* was slated to have FD radar installed, as well as two power-driven Mk.II 1.1-inch mounts, and foundation work for ultimate installation of 40mm guns, and Mk.44 directors to accompany the new automatic guns. Oerlikons were to be installed, as was a permanent degaussing installation. The work to be performed was extensive, and would have resulted in *Yorktown*'s emerging from the yard in far better shape than when she went in.

While *Yorktown* had been at Casco Bay, though, the international situation between the United States and the Axis had worsened. On 17 November, a joint congressional resolution allowed the arming of American merchantmen so that they could enter the war zones; that same day, a special envoy from Japan, Kurusu Saburo, arrived in Washington to confer with Secretary of State Cordell Hull; and on 20 November Ambassador Nomura presented the American government with Japan's "final proposal" for peace in the Pacific, countered by an American proposal with a week's time, on 26 November. The next day, the 27th, with United States-Japanese relations deteriorating inexorably, ADM Stark sent a "war warning" to the commanders of the Pacific and Asiatic fleets. One was not needed in the Atlantic, for the Fleet in that ocean had been at war for all intents and purposes since the spring.

To those who read the newspapers around Nor-

Refueling a Douglas SBD-3 of VB-5, coded 5-B-7, on *Yorktown*'s flight deck on 13 November 1941. Note 325-pound depth charge attached to the bomb crutch beneath the SBD's belly, as well as the aircraft's overall light gray finish, and mounting brackets for a "camera gun" just below the windscreen. (80-CF-5526-1)

Nevertheless, though, against that ominous backdrop there were other events those days of a much happier nature: the lanky, Australian-born ENS Leslie L. B. Knox, A-V(N), USNR of VF-42 wedding Miss Louise Francis Kennedy on Saturday, 6 December, at Our Lady of Victory Chapel at NOB Norfolk; and a Scouting Five cocktail party at the officer's club at the NOB in honor of the newly-married LT and Mrs. Roger B. Woodhull, the previous Friday afternoon.

Yorktown lay in port on the morning of 7 December 1941, observing Sunday routine. The usual mooring lines held her in place, and her hull rubbed lazily against the camels that lay between the ship and the pier; the usual gangways were rigged, watched diligently by Marine

folk in those days, it was clear that the situation in the Far East was becoming more alarming. Headlines in the Norfolk *Virginian-Pilot* hinted at the imminence of war in the Pacific; noting that President Roosevelt had cut short a visit to Warm Springs, Ga., and returned to the capitol, the *Virginian-Pilot* headlines on 1 December declared "War Across the Pacific Looms; British Send Troops and Warships to Orient." The next noted how "Roosevelt, Hull, [and] Stark" were mapping plans "despite Tokyo's hint of backing down."

sentries. Early that afternoon, *Yorktown*'s radio room picked up a "flash" message telling of a Japanese air attack upon Pearl Harbor. As the "word" spread, reactions varied. Hadn't the newspapers that morning told of President Roosevelt's sending a direct appeal to the Emperor of Japan, in a "last move" to prevent an open break between the United States and Japan? LCDR William O. Burch, Jr., commanding officer of Scouting Five, asked one of his pilots who had called to tell him the news: "How do you know it was the Japanese?"

Three VS-5 SBDs, NAS Quonset Point, R.I., 14 November 1941, in the standard blue gray (upper) and light gray (lower) color scheme for naval aircraft. Markings (squadron number, mission letter and individual plane number, such as 5-S-7) are in low-contrast black. Individual plane numbers also appear on the leading edge of the wing just inboard, on each side, of the prominent ribs near the center section. (80-CF-55215-16)

ENS Arthur J. Brassfield (left), VF-42's engineer officer, oversees work on a Grumman F4F-3A of the squadron at Casco Bay on 13 November 1941. Brassfield is wearing the green winter working uniform prescribed for aviators, and leather flight jacket; the crewman is clad in dungarees, and wears a "watch cap" on his head. Note that even at this late date the plane's color scheme is still overall light gray, and that propeller blades are natural metal. A Douglas SBD is in the background, carrying a depth charge. (80-G-64709)

On board *Yorktown*, though, the "word" spread fast. In one berthing compartment a sailor ran through yelling that the "Japs" had attacked Pearl Harbor. Soon everyone who could do so gathered around radios where, in silence, they listened to the news that came in. Unknown on board was the extent of the damage: four battleships, a minelayer and a target ship sunk; four battleships, three cruisers, three destroyers, a seaplane tender and a repair ship damaged in varying degrees. Over 2,000 sailors had been killed; over 900 wounded.

Down in a berthing compartment, one enlisted man, James Xanders, thought "Boy, you are going to get to fight a war—*Yorktown* will be right in the middle of it." Some voiced the opinion that that war would be over "before we can get to the Pacific and get in it." Others evinced the hope that the war would last long enough so that they, too, could get a crack at the Japanese.

The outbreak of war left little doubt as to what *Yorktown*'s future employment would be. On 8 December—the day upon which the United States declared war on Japan—an OPNAV dispatch directed to CINCLANT to "expeditiously assemble BATDIV 3, *Yorktown*, and one modern destroyer squadron, at Norfolk [and] prepare them immediately for transfer to the Pacific Fleet." Further, OPNAV desired that the carrier embark her "full plane complement plus appropriate spares . . ." with the exception of torpedo planes, whose numbers were to be reduced from 18

to 12, so that the six remaining planes could be replaced by dive bombers.

Yorktown prepared energetically and purposefully for war over the following days, with "wartime security" being established on board at 1300 on the 7th.

Unbeknownst to the *Yorktown*ers, the conflict in the Pacific had started out very badly for the U.S. Navy. The loss of the "backbone of the fleet," the battleships, forced the Navy to adopt a policy of the "strategic defensive" until forces could be mustered to take the war to the enemy. While the battle line may have been crippled, though, "a very powerful striking force of carriers, cruisers, and destroyers," survived. "These forces," an early CINCPAC estimate of the situation declared, "must be operated boldly and vigorously on the tactical offensive in order to retrieve our initial disaster."

For *Yorktown*, the first order of business had been the twice-postponed overhaul, but the "exigencies of the service" militated against one as extensive as had been planned. On the morning of 12 December, *Yorktown* shifted to the Norfolk Navy Yard, where her .50 cal. Brownings were replaced by 20mm Oerlikons, mounted as follows: on the port side—five forward and five aft, on the gallery deck level, replacing the .50s that had been mounted there; two on the starboard side, aft; two on the main deck, at the fantail, and two mounted in tubs on the foc'sle. Due to the lack of time, eight guns were installed outboard of the island between frames 71 to 81 and frames 83 to 93, in a space once occupied by two 40-foot motor launches and the boat crane. The saluting battery also went at the same time. In addition, the closed surface rangefinder was removed from atop the pilot house;

Beneath and above the exhortation taped on the fuselage: "Speed work on this plane, it may sink a Japanese ship," three men indeed appear to be busy, working on a Torpedo 5 TBD-1 coded 5-T-1, in what may have been an obviously posed example of early wartime propaganda photography. Contemporary tactical organizations list 5-T-1 as BuNo 0319, flown by the VT-5 CO, LCDR Joe Taylor. This view was taken between 7 and 16 December 1941, when the air group from *Yorktown* was ashore at NAS Norfolk. (80-PR-3644, Doll)

splinter protection "for all exposed battle stations" was installed (20 mm, 1.1-inch and 5-inch mounts), only the .50-caliber batteries on the starboard side forward and aft not getting the protection of ballistics shielding. Her CXAM radar was also altered to improve its detection and recognition capabilities. The boiler rebricking, though, had to wait. There was simply no time.

Yorktown then moved back to Pier 7, NOB Norfolk, on the morning of the 16th; there, at 0855 that day, she commenced hoisting on board her air group from NAS Norfolk—VB-5, VS-5, VT-5, and VF-42—as well as an important cargo: nine SBDs (a -1, four -2s and four -3s) and 20 F4Fs (six -3As and 14 -3s), urgently needed in the Pacific theater. All planes loaded, the carrier moved out into Hampton Roads. Underway at 2108, *Yorktown* stood out, passing Cape Henry abeam to starboard at 2228, and followed in the wakes of the four destroyers assigned to operate with her as her screen. All were familiar from the North Atlantic—*Hughes* led the formation, followed by *Walke*, *Sims*, and *Russell* (DD-414).

Designated as TG 18.5, the five ships sailed down the east coast, bound for the Canal Zone, darkening ship each evening and sounding general quarters each morning. They sighted no other ships until *Walke* spotted one at 1535 on the 18th, 15 miles away. Going to general quarters, the destroyer maneuvered to investigate, and discovered the stranger to be the Standard Oil tanker *Esso Aruba*, en route from Artiba to New York.

On 21 December, TG 18.5 reached its initial destination, Cristobal, *Yorktown* commenced flying off thirteen F4F-3s of VF-42 at 0627 to cover the carrier's passage. Picking up her pilot, Mr. J. Munden, and his three assistants, at 0714, the carrier commenced her Pacific-bound transit, en-

While *Yorktown* was undergoing final preparations to sail for the Pacific, the destroyers that would escort her and fight alongside her wrapped up accelerated refits as well. Here, *Russell* and *Sims* complete theirs alongside a pier at Norfolk Navy Yard, 16 December 1941; they would sail with *Yorktown* later the same day. Both destroyers have received the very individualistic Measure 12 (modified) camouflage; 20-millimeter Oerlikon MGs have replaced the .50-caliber Brownings (one of the new guns is visible to the left of *Russell*'s Mt.52). Air search radars have been fitted as well (*Sims'* can be seen at center, top). (19-N-26675)

tering Gatun Locks at 0830 and clearing the Miraflores Locks a little over eight hours later before she moored at Pier 18, Balboa, at 1726. There she disembarked a draft of men who had inadvertently accompanied the ship to war, being drafted to load provisions during the rush to ready *Yorktown* for sea at Norfolk, and commenced taking on board aviation gasoline and fuel for her depleted bunkers.

At 0600 the following morning, *Yorktown* began making preparations for getting underway, and began edging away from the dock at 0800, five men (one of whom who had been AOL since 16 December) missing the sailing of the ship. Steaming various courses and speeds to conform to the channel, *Yorktown* left Balboa in her wake, dropping her pilot at 0910 and proceeding out into the Pacific, joining up with *Hughes, Walke, Russell* and *Sims,* and *Trenton* (CL-11) and *Richmond* (CL-9) that had been added to their group at Balboa.

For ships that had recently operated in the Atlantic, where the danger of U-boats constantly lurked about them, submarine-consciousness was high. *Walke* illustrated this a half-hour after *Yorktown* had dropped her pilot, when the destroyer, operating off the carrier's port bow, picked up a submarine contact at 0940 and dropped depth charges. Again, at 1123 and 1141, screening destroyers reported contacts and

roiled the sea with depth charges, while Curtiss SOCs from *Trenton* and *Richmond* alternated in providing inner air cover. Later that day, between 1513 and 1540, *Yorktown* then recovered those planes from her air group that she had sent ashore on the 21st. In all probability, the "submarines" the destroyers had so aggressively depth-charged were whales, since the U.S. Navy's effective anti-submarine measures put into effect soon after Pearl Harbor had caused the Japanese to pull back the nine I-boats they had originally deployed up and down the west coast at the outbreak of hostilities, by the middle of December.

The next eight days passed without any major incidents, although on the 23d a VS-5 SBD-2, flown by LT Charles R. Ware, crashed on take-off, for the only aircraft mishap of that leg of the voyage to the (*Russell* rescued Ware and his RM2c James E. Roll). *Yorktown* encountered a whale on the 24th; no damage to the ship resulted (the whale's reaction was not recorded), and the task force celebrated Christmas at sea on the 25th. Ultimately, TG 18.5 reached its destination, San Diego, on 30 December, *Yorktown* sending off her air group to base at North Island before she moored at the station dock at 1137. Morale on board the carrier was high—all hands were eager for action.

Cover and first page of *Yorktown*'s "Morning Press" for Christmas Day, 1941. The talks between President Roosevelt and British Prime Minister Churchill in Washington, and the gallant defense of Wake Island were the lead items of interest. (Lindsay)

MORNING PRESS

U.S.S. YORKTOWN   DECEMBER 25, 1941

WASHINGTON   President Roosevelt and British Prime Minister
                Churchill extended Christmas greetings tonight in
brief talks from the South Portico of the White House in Washington.
The President asked all Americans to arm their hearts for the suffering and the labor necessary to achieve ultimate victory in the present
world conflict. Churchill requested that the people of the far flung
British Empire put aside their cares and worries for a day and give
to their children the happiness of Christmas that is possible in a
free country.

        The Navy Department released a dramatic account of
the battle of Wake Island which is destined to go down in history as
one of the most courageous stands ever made by a military force.
After announcing that the island apparently now has fallen to the
Japanese, the Navy revealed that the Wake Island force which hammered
back at the Japanese for fourteen days consisted of only four hundred
Marines. The Navy account of the Wake Island defense described that
even though the Wake Island defenders were subject to assaults from
sea and air they repeatedly beat off Japanese landing forces. The
account ended with the word that Japan had landed an invasion force
yesterday. The Wake Island radio then went silent.

        The Navy announced that the last American Ship
which had been caught in Far Pacific waters at the outbreak of the
Japanese war has arrived at a west coast port. The ship was the
tanker Fitzsimons. The Navy said the safe arrival of the Fitzsimons
left the passenger liner President Harrison as the only American
ship to fall into Japanese hands.

UNDATED   The Japanese attack on the Philippine Islands was
             intensified tonight as forces were landed at two more
points on the coast. A decisive battle was believed developed at the
point of heaviest attack on Lingayen Gulf when Commander-in-Chief,
General Douglas MacArthur and his staff took the field.

        At the same time it was announced that consideration
was being given to the withdrawal of the Government's military headquarters from Manila so that the capital could be declared an open
city. The announcement was made as the Japanese intensified their
air attacks on Manila and began to bomb non-military areas.

        The Japanese were estimated to have no less than
100 troop ships in Philippine waters, heavily protected by Naval and
air forces.

        At Hongkong, the British and Canadian Garrison con-
tinued to stand off heavy Japanese attacks while Chinese forces on the
mainland reported progress in their division operations against the
Japanese rear.

        The British authorities reported that a naval and
air battle occurred off the northern coast of Borneo. There were no
details of the action and the outcome was not given.

        On the Malaya sector, the Japanese offensive remained
at a standstill with only patrol activity reported.

CHAPTER 4

The Morale of the Fleet Demands It

WHILE *Yorktown* HAD BEEN AT SEA, en route to the Pacific, plans were being made to employ her. On 24 December, a CINCPAC estimate declared that available forces, "well-suited for this work," could be sent to raid Japanese positions; a "judicious choice of objectives" would "help to improve our relative strength." Acknowledging that the U.S. Navy could not "afford to accept losses on a ship for ship basis" it nevertheless had to "take some risks in order to strike the enemy a blow from time to time. The morale of the Fleet and of the nation demands it."

After most Americans had been led to believe throughout 1941 that the U.S. Navy could easily handle the Japanese, the enemy's stunning triumph at Pearl Harbor proved an unpleasant shock. The litany of defeat continued over the next few weeks, and did nothing to further Allied confidence. Guam fell on 10 December and Wake Island, after a gallant defense, two days before Christmas, while in the Far East, the Asiatic Fleet had fallen back to the "Malay Barrier," its main weapon, its substantial force of fleet submarines, performing with far less success than had been hoped.

Two days before *Yorktown* reached San Diego, she had been designated as flagship for TF-17, the ocean escort for a convoy being gathered and loaded to sail to Samoa. On the day after the carrier's arrival, RADM Frank Jack Fletcher, the man designated as commander, TF-17, emplaned at Pearl Harbor for San Diego, arriving the same day. At 1030 on New Year's Day 1942, Fletcher broke his flag in *Yorktown.*

The mission entrusted Fletcher was to see that the 2d Marine Brigade, formed on 24 December and 4,798 men strong, reached Samoa intact, to bolster the woefully weak defenses there and complete the airfield at Tutuila. Embarked in the former Matson liners *Monterey, Matsonia* and *Lurline* and supported by the cargo ship *Jupiter*

Sandy-haired Iowa-born RADM Frank Jack Fletcher, known in his USNA days as a "strenuous son of the middle west," of "sunny disposition," and nicknamed "Flap-Jack" or "Fletch" by his classmates, graduated from the Academy in 1906, and after the required two years of sea duty, was appointed ensign in 1908. During the period between the outbreak of war in Europe in 1939 and the attack on Pearl Harbor, Fletcher served in command billets at sea— COMCRUDIV 3 (September 1939-June 1940) and COMCRUDIV 6 (June 1940-December 1941), before becoming COMCRUSCOFOR on 31 December 1941 and breaking his flag in *Yorktown* the following day. Awarded the Medal of Honor in 1914 for his performance of duty in evacuating refugees from Vera Cruz, Fletcher later received the Navy Cross for service in command of *Benham* (Destroyer No. 49) in World War I. For his services in command of TF-17 at Coral Sea and Midway, he received the Distinguished Service Medal. Regarded by his staff as "affable and considerate," Fletcher nevertheless could be "stern and demanding when the occasion required." In the context of his times, Fletcher carried out his duty in a modest and workmanlike fashion. The Navy commemorates his service, and that of his uncle, ADM Frank Friday Fletcher (the latter for whom the World War II *Fletcher* (DD-445) was named, in the *Spruance*-class destroyer *Fletcher* (DD-992). (Author)

(AK-43), the ammunition ship *Lassen* (AE-3) and the oiler *Kaskaskia* (AO-27), the 2d Marine Brigade sailed on the morning of 6 January 1942, the sortie commencing at 1045. These Marines, under BGEN Henry L. Larsen, USMC, constituted the first American expeditionary force to leave the United States following the declaration of war. *Yorktown, Louisville, St. Louis* (CL-49) and the destroyers *Russell, Walke, Hughes* and *Sims* comprised the ocean escort.

As *Yorktown* and her charges proceeded toward Pago Pago, CINCPAC, ADM Chester W. Nimitz, deemed the time ripe for an offensive against the Japanese. COMINCH, ADM King, had urged CINCPAC's "thorough consideration" of a raid against the Gilberts. Early-on, Wake, the Marshalls—as well as the Gilberts—had all come under consideration as potential targets, although planners initially eliminated the first place because of uncertainty over the fate of the men captured there on 23 December.

CINCPAC and his staff harbored three objectives to guide their planning: to inflict damage on the enemy, first and foremost, sufficient to deny him the use of his bases in the Mandated Islands; to divert his attention and draw off forces which he could deploy elsewhere, in other operations; and to boost the morale of not only the fleet but of the nation—both thirsty for a victory after the drought of defeat. While ADM Nimitz weighed these options, *Enterprise*, as the flagship of TF-8, together with her screen, sailed from Pearl Harbor on 11 January to operate to the northward of TF-17, screening the 2d Marine Brigade's progress toward Samoa.

Meanwhile, only one day out of San Diego, troubles of one kind or another began vexing *Yorktown's* VF-42. ENS Edgar R. Bassett, A-V(N), USNR, put 42-F-9 into the barrier on the 7th, ENS William S. Woollen, A-V(N), USNR, was taking off at 1417 on the 8th when his aircraft, 42-F-1, lost power and plunged into the sea; *Russell* picked him up. At 1617 on the 12th, ENS Walter A. Haas, A-V(N), USNR, crashed in 42-F-3; *Walke* picked him up. "Another fighter hit the drink," RM3c James H. Cales of VS-5 wrote in his diary, "makes 3 planes so far this trip." Misfortune did not stop there. PVT Edward Allen, USMC, reported a man overboard at 2040. PVT Everett Chapman, USMC, threw over a life ring while *Yorktown* signalled for *Walke* to conduct a search. A muster soon revealed the missing man to be Sea2c William H. Reckhouse; *Walke* came up empty-handed.

LT Harlan R. "Rocky" Dickson (L), of VB-5, and ENS William E. "Pappy" Hall (R), of VS-5, pose during Crossing-the-Line ceremonies, 14 January 1942. Dickson's "binoculars" are fashioned from Coca Cola bottles taped together, while Hall, attired in diver's dress and fur-lined flying helmet, wields a sword in the best swashbuckling tradition. (Traynor, via Sawruk)

Bad weather resulted in cancellation of flight operations on the 13th as *Yorktown* and her consorts neared the equator. Drills kept the ships busy. "Cool but sticky," Jim Cales observed of the prevailing heat and humidity,"On [a] clear day you seem to eat air instead of breathe it."

Flying operations resumed the next day, 14 January, but so, too, did VF-42's problems. ENS Richard L. Wright, A-V(N), USNR, took off in 42-F-14 only to make a water landing when his engine failed. *Walke*, which still had Walt Haas on board from 12 January's rescue, picked up Wright.

LT(jg) Stanley W. "Swede" Vejtasa (L) and LT(jg) Earl V. Johnson (R) flank a grinning LCDR William O. Burch, Jr., VS-5's skipper, during the Equator crossing. (Traynor, via Sawruk)

ram her starboard quarter—rang down emergency flank speed and full right rudder. *Kaskaskia* then stopped to recover her hose and fittings, dragging in the water, maneuvering to keep the hose and lines clear of her propellers, and ultimately recovered her equipment by 1819, to resume the voyage. *Kaskaskia's* commanding officer theorized that uncoupling the quick-release of the after fuel hose to the carrier, done without order from the oiler, necessitated stopping the ship's port engine to avoid fouling her screw, with the resultant loss of steering control. Fortunately, later fueling-at-sea evolutions (this was *Yorktown's* first) would be much smoother.

At 0830 on 19 January, *Yorktown* launched planes for inner air patrol and to search the 150-310° sector, 150 miles out; throughout the day the force proceeded on its way toward Samoa. The carrier recovered her first flight at noon, and the second, which she had launched at 1155, at 1325. Later, at 1500, Fletcher detached *Matsonia, Lurline* and *Monterey,* escorted by *Walke* and *Hughes,* to proceed independently to Pago Pago at 20 knots. The next morning, *Yorktown* put 13 planes aloft, eight for search, three for inner air patrol, and two of the utility unit's J2Fs for flights to Samoa for mail (one of the latter returning on board within a half-hour of takeoff).

Yorktown then put 12 planes aloft to provide inner and intermediate air patrol for the transports, at 0730, recovering them at 1045; at 1230, Fletcher received word that the three Matson liners had reached Pago Pago, those ships immediately commencing the disembarkation of the Marines in all available boats. Unloading soon began, too, to be carried out on a round-the-clock basis until completed. Soon thereafter, Fletcher detached *Lassen, Jupiter* and *Kaskaskia* to proceed to Pago Pago, escorted by one destroyer and six *Yorktown* planes.

Over the next few days, *Yorktown* and her screen lingered in the area, patrolling, and covering the unloading and disembarkation phase of the operation, occasionally glimpsing the verdant mountains through the poor visibility conditions. With *Louisville* and *St. Louis'* planes providing inner air patrol,

Despite the growing difficulties being experienced by the fighter squadron, shipboard routine went on. Even in wartime, when circumstances permit, sailors conduct the time-honored rituals surrounding the crossing of the equator. Some of *Yorktown's* officers put on a "Neptune Party" on the sunny flight deck during the 1200-1600 watch, initiating "Pollywogs" into the domain of King Neptune.

On the 17th, *Yorktown* experienced some anxious moments. Shortly after noon, *Kaskaskia* began preparing her special sea details to get ready to fuel *Yorktown,* and the first line went over at 1304, the oiler commencing pumping at 1443. Shortly thereafter, ENS Haas and ENS Wright rode "bosun's chairs" back to their ship (*Kaskaskia's* war diarist noting that "no orders accompanied [their] transfer"). At 1630, *Kaskaskia* approached too close, and then sheered out, apparently to correct her course, before she veered in again. The two ships scraped sides; the carrier sustained some damage to a motor launch and to her side, while the oiler lost a boom in the exchange. Soon, the two ships again scraped sides, causing additional damage to both; the oiler sheered out again, parting the fuel hose forward. At 1649, with *Kaskaskia* clear of *Yorktown,* the former commenced a turn to port, going full speed astern to back clear; *Yorktown,* believing a collision imminent—that the oiler was going to

Yorktown conducted daily search missions with her planes, and daily flight operations, including exercising her aircraft at bombing towed sleds. Daily flights to Pago Pago by the ship's J2Fs continued, exchanging mail and dispatches.

Meanwhile, at Pearl Harbor, ADM Nimitz had decided how to employ the two task forces he had at sea in the South Pacific, TF-8 and TF-17. On 24 January, Nimitz ordered Halsey, in TF-8, to raid the Marshalls and Gilberts "after the unloading phase" of the Samoan operation had been completed, with TF-17 to make its attack in conjunction with TF-8. Nimitz directed Fletcher's force to depart Samoan waters "as soon as [the] troops were disembarked." At 1427, TF-17 formed its cruising disposition and began standing northwestward. At 1600, *Yorktown* launched 15 planes, three for intermediate air patrol and ten to search designated areas around the task force; the last two planes were J2Fs being transferred to Pago Pago. With the last of the transports unloaded and the Marines of the 2d Brigade deployed in defensive positions around the island, and Tutuila assuming the aspect of a "large, teeming military post," TF-17 was heading for the Gilberts, heading for action, *Yorktown*'s planes aloft during the daylight hours, probing the cloudy skies and braving scattered rain squalls.

Planners for the raids on the Mandates accorded Jaluit and Makin priorities as targets, for intelligence estimates had reckoned the former as the "seat of government in the Marshalls" as well as the center of defense and "apparently the most developed" spot in the islands. Makin, the northernmost isle of the Gilberts chain, and a British protectorate before the war, had been taken early on 10 December by the 51st Naval Garrison Unit, and a seaplane base completed by the following day. Intelligence estimates placed "a portion of Airron 24" (actually the 24th Air Flotilla), as well as "probably a tender and some four-motored seaplanes" there. Mille, as far as anyone knew, boasted

CDR Curtis S. "Curt" Smiley, USNA 1923, led the *Yorktown* Air Group in the strike on Jaluit, and later planned and directed its operations at Lae-Salamaua. He is seen here reading orders to command the seaplane tender *Pocomoke* (AV-9) on 4 May 1943. (80-G-200962)

a Navy "base detachment" but little else. *Enterprise* and TF-8 were to concentrate on the Marshalls.

While her sistership headed for her assigned areas to the northward, and both carriers had eluded detection by the Japanese commerce raiders, *Aikoku Maru* and *Hokoku Maru*, then winding up their somewhat lackluster raiding career and en route to Truk, *Yorktown* and her consorts approached their objectives at 25.5 knots in the pre-dawn darkness on 1 February 1942, beneath a high overcast. Apparently undetected, they reached a point midway between the islands her planes were to attack. At 0415, screened only by *Louisville* and *St. Louis*—the four destroyers having been detached the night before to form a scouting line—*Yorktown* went to flight quarters.

LCDR Robert G. Armstrong, commanding Bombing Five, enjoyed the honor of being the first man off the ship, as his SBD cleared the bow ramp at 0452. The rest of the attack groups, and the fighters (which would be retained over the task force as a combat air patrol) took off "without incident." The setting moon, obscured by clouds, produced an excellent visible horizon but caused diffuse light conditions which made the rendezvous very difficult to effect.

The murky weather principally affected the Jaluit-bound attack group—17 SBDs and 11 TBDs—led by *Yorktown*'s air group commander, CDR Curtis S. Smiley, who later reported: "All planes did not effect rendezvous and some proceeded independently to the objective. It was impossible for the group and squadron leaders to determine whether all planes were in the formation on departure." A light rain squall, encountered soon after take-off, forced the ragged formation to descend to 500 feet before they ran into "intermittent squalls of varying intensity." A half hour out from the ship, the Jaluit group ran into a "particularly heavy squall" which scattered them even more. "Upon emerging," wrote Smiley later," the group formation had broken up and thereafter was never assembled in larger units than sections . . ."

LCDR Bill Burch, flying the SBD nominally assigned to the CYAG, leads the attack on Makin, 1 February 1942; CRM Oliver W. Grew sits at the ready with the single .30-caliber flexible mount in the after cockpit. Photographed by PhoM2c J.V. Pflaum, in ENS Thomas A. Reeves' SBD. (Tailhook MN 01004, Vejtasa, via Lawson)

Things got worse before they got better. As the SBDs and TBDs neared Jaluit, now scattered into sections or individual aircraft, they encountered a fierce thunderstorm; sheet lightning and torrential rains forced the hard-pressed pilots to resort to instrument flying to make a landfall at their objective. Some came in at 50 feet; some at 11,000.

Armstrong, who at one point had managed to form a group of seven planes, pushed over at 9,000 feet through the heavy cloud cover. His windscreen and telescopic sight fogged during the dive, throwing off his aim; his bomb plunged into the water almost 100 feet off the port quarter of what he determined to be a large "merchant or tender-type vessel [seaplane carrier *Kanto Maru*] in the middle of the anchorage." LT John L. Nielsen, flying wing on Armstrong, missed with his bomb; LT John J. Powers, Armstrong's other wingman, had circled for 20 minutes before he started down to make his attack. On the way down, his windshield and sight fogged, too, and although he could not make out his target distinctly, he estimated its position and made allowance for Armstrong's and Nielsen's drops; he then released his bomb (he missed, too) and retired to the northeast, strafing a building as he did so.

As Armstrong then led his section toward the supposed seaplane facilities at Emidjii Island (a place which did, apparently, contain stocks of diesel fuel, aviation gasoline and bombs), he noted very little activity "neither guns, personnell, nor gunfire . . ." at Jaluit. He and his two wingmen strafed a ship at what they took to be a seaplane base, Armstrong noting his tracers passing through and ricocheting off the water beyond as he bore in at 50 feet above the wavetops. Continuing on up the atoll, Bombing Five's commander noted no signs of any more military activity at Jaluit, observing nothing except "occasional thatched huts among the palm trees."

In contrast to the importance which intelligence estimates had bestowed upon Jaluit, it looked like it contained few installations of note.

LT Sam Adams and one of his wingmen, ENS "Duke" Berger, A-V(N), USNR, both failed to score a hit with their bombs, too. Adams' other wingman, ENS David R. Berry, A-V(N), USNR, elected another target, releasing his bomb at what looked like a barracks, and although LT Adams' radioman, RM1c G.H. Mansfield, later reported that Berry's bomb had hit, the ensign didn't see it. On retirement, Berry saw three bursts of anti-aircraft fire far away, and snickered.

Although hampered by the weather, which prevented a coordinated attack, all of the pilots on the Jaluit strike "showed considerable initiative and perseverance in selecting objectives and pressing home their attacks, both by bombing and strafing." The weather prevented high-altitude bombing, forcing some of the TBDs to make glide-bombing approaches. Others, however, LCDR Taylor among them, not finding targets and facing a dwindling fuel supply, jettisoned their ordnance into the sea.

LCDR Bill Burch, VS-5's CO, led the nine SBDs assigned to attack Makin; they initially flew at 1,000 feet and encountered rain squalls en route. Less than an hour after leaving the ship, at 0630, Makin came into view. Reversing course, VS-5's first division began climbing to bombing altitude, 12,000 feet, using the clouds to cover their approach and drawing near the island from the northwest. Each carrying a 500-pound bomb, the SBDs circled the south side of the atoll to attack from out of the sun.

Ahead lay two Kawanishi H6K4 Type 97 flying boats from the Yokohama *Kōkutai* moored in the lagoon just off Butaritari, tended by gunboat *Nagata Maru*—a force in line with the intelligence estimate. A third Kawanishi, earmarked for a rest and repair period, had taken off before dawn on a reconnaissance flight over Howland and Baker Islands.

Knowing that sights would fog if his men went to high altitude, Burch brought them in at 12,000 feet, knowing, too, that they could expect no fighter opposition. As they neared their objective, VS-5's CO discerned a ship and two four-engined flying boats in the lagoon. Deciding to tackle the "seaplane tender" first, Burch pushed over at about 0658, coming down out of the sun. LT(jg) "Swede" Vejtasa, bringing up the rear, saw that as the "skipper" did so, a burst of antiaircraft fire smudged the sky directly ahead of the CO's plane. "Miles off," snorted Burch.

As the *Yorktowner*s had circled Makin, they could see that the enemy had apparently spotted them. Riding behind Burch in the SBD normally assigned the CYAG, CRM Oliver W. Grew saw that it appeared that the ship was trying to get underway. PhoM2c Pflaum, in ENS Thomas A. Reeves' S-2, noted a "large cloud of black smoke" issuing from her stack and turbulence in the water beneath her stern as she looked to be heading for shallow water. The base commander at Makin, meanwhile, radioed that nine enemy aircraft, initially identified as "fighters," were attacking.

Burch's 500-pound bomb hit *Nagata Maru* squarely on her after well deck. RM2c John Hurley, LT Stockton B. Strong's radio-gunner, saw "a sheet of flame 100 feet high" reaching skyward; fragments and debris splashed into the water around the ship out to "about 150 yards" away, as LT Roger B. Woodhull observed from his vantage point in the cockpit of B-1. Fires broke out immediately.

Next in line, Birney Strong dropped his bomb and pulled out; his radioman, Hurley, swore his pilot got a hit; LT Turner Caldwell and LT(jg) Frederic L. Faulkner, likewise confirmed what looked like another direct hit from Strong's 500-pounder. Taking their intervals in almost textbook fashion (Vejtasa observing

the other planes to be "well-spaced in the dive following the captain [Burch]"), the other SBDs loosed their loads on the hapless former freighter. Vejtasa, the last to dive, saw that smoke and flying debris nearly obscured the target from view. Nevertheless, he squinted into his telescopic sight and aimed for *Nagata Maru*'s bow, releasing his 500-pounder at 2,500 feet. His attention distracted by the sight and windshield which immediately fogged up, he did not observe where his bomb hit. With at least one direct hit aft

Smoke rises from the two Kawanishi flying boats torched off the shores of Butaritari islet by Scouting Five's SBDs at Makin, 1 February 1942, photographed by PhoM2c J.V. Pflaum. (Tailhook MN 01005, Vejtasa, via Lawson)

(Burch's), *Nagata Maru* had suffered considerable damage from near-misses, particularly along her port side at the waterline.

Regaining altitude as they pulled out, Burch's SBDs wheeled over Makin in a large circle, and bore in again for a second run in the face of the "desultory and ineffective" anti-aircraft fire. His two forward-firing .50-calibers charged, Burch opened up on the left-hand Kawanishi riding placidly at anchor in the lagoon off Butaritari. His bullets struck home quickly, torching the plane's massive fuel cells. The fire soon reached the bomb load slung beneath the parasol wings, and the resulting explosion tore the big flying boat apart.

The other eight pilots shifted their sights to the second flying boat. Although ENS Walton A. "Crash" Austin, in a borrowed VB-5 mount, noted his tracers hitting home, the Kawanishi did not catch fire. The SBDs wheeled around for a third pass, Burch and his wingmen going after *Nagata Maru*, Scouting Five's CO radioed Turner Caldwell, leading the second section: "Get that plane."

The base commander at Butaritari had ordered the flying boat to take off and retire from the area to get out of danger, seeing what had befallen the first plane on the water. Scouting Five's next strafing attack, however, caught the Japanese aircrew in the midst of take-off preparations. As the SBDs roared in, antiaircraft

guns on board *Nagata Maru* opened up, but, as Vejtasa could see, the fire was "erratic and ineffective."

ENS Reeves, in S-2, came across the lagoon, following Burch and Strong, to strafe *Nagata Maru* from her stern and port quarter. He drew fire all the while, one particularly close burst noticeably jarring Reeves and his passenger, Pflaum, the latter thinking that they were drawing fire from the second anchored seaplane, too.

LT Harlan T. Johnson, XO of VT-5 and pilot of one of the two TBDs to land in the lagoon at Jaluit.

ACMM C.E. Fosha, LT Johnson's bombardier.

RM1c J. W. Dalzell, LT Johnson's radio-gunner.

ENS Herbert R. Hein, Jr., A-V(N), pilot of the other TBD to ditch at Jaluit.

AOM3c J. D. Strahl, ENS Hein's bombardier.

Sea1c Marshall E. Windham, ENS Hein's radio-gunner.

Turner Caldwell, meanwhile, fired two sighting-in bursts, aware of the fact that one brave Japanese sailor had apparently reached one of the flexible 7.7-millimeter mounts "aft of the wing" (probably in one of the plexiglas "blisters" high in the fuselage) and was firing at him. Caldwell put about twenty rounds on target and stopped the return fire as the flying boat's fuel tanks exploded in a "large ball of fire." "Fritz" Faulkner added to the damage a few moments later. Five of the nine-man crew of the Kawanishi died in their attempt to get aloft.

Their mission completed, Burch and his men headed for home. In their wake lay *Nagata Maru*, heavily damaged but with her fires out; four men had been killed and twenty-six wounded in the bombing and strafing attacks. Two flying boats burned fiercely. Sea1c Frank B. Wood, Vejtasa's radioman, summed up the raid: "In all I would say that our raid was very successful for what was on the island."

The planes assigned to Mille, led by Scouting Five's XO, LT Wallace C. Short, Jr., found neither bad weather nor targets! His five SBDs encountered "no hampering adverse weather" but found little to either expend ordnance or ammunition on: only a small warehouse looked worth attacking. The pilots and radiomen of this group found no evidence, from the air, that this atoll

LT George Bellinger, XO of Bombing Five, was among the pilots lost in the Jaluit strike; he is seen here as an ENS at Pensacola in March 1935. (USN)

was being used as a base, although a swath cut through a palm grove hinted at some kind of construction—perhaps a nascent airfield. They saw a pile of lumber, but no heavy machinery. The paucity of targets frustrated LT(jg) A.L. Downing, A-V(N), USNR, in 5-B-7. Undecided as to what to bomb, he finally selected a "couple of small tanks" as his target. Observing no fires after his bomb had exploded, he concluded that he had "destroyed the natives' supply of fresh water," and caused considerable confusion among the populace, who fled "in all directions."

An hour after the four destroyers had meanwhile joined *Yorktown* and the two cruisers, the Makin attack group began coming on board shortly after 0800, followed soon by the Mille group, neither of which

had suffered any losses. At about that time, a radio message crackled into the earphones of the men monitoring the air group, at 0815: "This is 77V44-77V44 and 76V44 are landing at Jaluit—are landing alongside one of the northwestern islands of Jaluit. That is all." The "77V44" signified the TBD flown by LT Harlan T. "Dub" Johnson, the tall, blond-haired executive officer of Torpedo Five, while "76V44" denoted that flown by ENS Herbert R. Hein, A-V(N), USNR. Both planes landed in the water, their crews taking to their rubber boats, and the men made land soon thereafter, to be hidden by local natives. However, the arrival of a Japanese patrol two days later cut short their freedom and all six became prisoners of war.

Meanwhile, as the Jaluit attack group, decimated by the weather, straggled back to the ship, commencing recovery at 0858, *Yorktown* re-armed and serviced an anti-torpedo plane patrol drawn from the SBDs of the returned Makin and Mille groups. She had no sooner turned into the wind and launched them, however, when a heavy rain squall lashed the task force with winds that gusted up to 50 knots and sheets of rain that reduced visibility to 100 yards. Stragglers from the Jaluit group, some with only two gallons of gasoline remaining in their tanks, landed on *Yorktown*'s rain and spray-slicked deck amidst these appalling weather conditions.

The day's events were by no means over. One of the VS-5 SBDs that had been launched on anti-torpedo plane patrol, 5-S-2 (BuNo 4567), flown by ENS T.A. Reeves, A-V(N), USNR, crashed at 0940 during a heavy squall, close aboard on *Hughes*' port quarter. While the destroyer stopped to keep the plane in sight in the poor visibility conditions then prevailing, Reeves and his radioman, Sea2c Lonnie C. Gooch, took to their rubber boat; COMDESDIV 3, CDR Frank G. Fahrion, in *Hughes*, directed *Walke* to pick up the crew.

Walke slowed and began circling, and spotted the

downed airmen in their raft at 0947, 500 yards away. The destroyer lowered her motor whaleboat and recovered Reeves, who was suffering from a severe scalp wound, and the apparently uninjured Gooch, radioing the report of the successful rescue at 1003. After her own pharmacist's mate treated Reeves' head injury, *Walke* later transferred both men to *Louisville* for further medical attention.

On board *Yorktown*, meanwhile, the cost of the raid on Jaluit was being totalled up. Johnson's and Hein's TBDs were accounted for, but what of those flown by LT Jack C. Moore, and his crew of two; and LT Francis X. Maher—"Navy, born and bred" and possessing a "practical [and] imaginative mind"—and his two crewmen? Two SBDs were also lost: that flown by LT George L. Bellinger, (Bombing Five's tall, quiet, and capable exec) and his radioman, RM1c D. MacKillop, last seen en route to Jaluit. LT(jg) Myron P. Fishel, A-V(N), USNR, and his radioman, RM1c L.W. Costello, had not been seen since their departure from the ship.

Deeply concerned over the men and planes that had not yet returned, RADM Fletcher directed *Russell* to proceed ten miles astern, on course 270° (T) to "direct or assist any planes lost or downed in an extremely heavy rain squall" then swirling through the area. They soon had something to look for.

LT(jg) Thomas B. Ellison, flying 5-T-2, sighted a TBD in the water on his way back to *Yorktown*. His bombardier, AOM1c E.M. Whaley, saw a man standing in the rear cockpit of the ditched torpedo plane, waving; the radioman, RM3c E.W. Jones saw it, too, and threw a smoke bomb to let those down below know that they had been seen. Ellison, meanwhile, reported the sighting. A few moments later, LT Albert B. Furer, in 5-T-3, also groping his way back to the ship on the ship's homing beacon, sighted a TBD, too. Furer, a USNA classmate of Jack Moore's, saw the downed TBD's flotation bags inflated, and his radioman, RM3c G.C. Aulick, told Furer he thought *he* saw the crew nearby in a rubber boat. Furer, too, immediately reported his sighting, giving his position as being only 20 miles from *Yorktown*. Five minutes later, Furer glimpsed a destroyer, *Russell*, which asked for bearings to the downed "Devastator" which he provided. Continuing back to the ship, Furer landed with ten gallons of gasoline remaining; Ellison had had only two sloshing in his TBD's tanks.

Steering the course given her by LT Furer, *Russell* proceeded through the moderate swells, her lookouts scanning the stormy gray sea in visibility that ranged from several miles to 500 yards, while *Hughes* and *Sims* were receiving orders to join *Russell* in her search. The first ship, though, reached the prescribed distance astern of the task force at 1037 but found only an empty sea—no trace of the TBD reported by the two VT-5 pilots. Undeterred, however, *Russell* kept up the search, joined soon thereafter by *Hughes* and *Sims*, the destroyermen briefly glimpsing each other in the scud—*Hughes* trailing five miles astern of *Russell*, *Sims* four miles off the latter's starboard quarter.

At 1105, however, *Russell's* SC radar obtained a contact on an aircraft closing from ten miles away: one of the three Kawanishi Type 97 flying boats that had taken off from Jaluit after the *Yorktown* Air Group had departed earlier that morning. *Sims* and *Hughes* soon picked up the intruder, too, only moments before the Japanese sighted them at 1110, glimpsing two of the three ships through the patches of cloud that hung over the sea like a shapeless, ragged gray mass.

Russell challenged the Kawanishi, and seeing the plane approaching on an "attack course," commenced firing at 1110 with 5-inch and 20mm guns, maneuvering to keep her batteries unmasked. Several 5-inch bursts blossomed around the big flying boat as its pilot turned the aircraft into the shelter of the heavy rain clouds. *Russell* ceased fire and, over the TBS, warned *Sims* that the flying boat was headed in her direction.

Sims, though, had been tracking the Kawanishi all along, and noted the enemy's climbing left turn. She matched the flying boat's movements, turning to keep her batteries unmasked and trained skyward in the direction of the plane, and working up to 35 knots. At 1114, a stick of bombs harmlessly straddled *Sims'* wake, 1,500 yards astern, and the destroyer noted the Kawanishi beginning a wide right turn, presumably to make another approach. *Sims'* guns crashed out at 1125, and the destroyer's 30 rounds of 5-inch in the vicinity of the Kawanishi convinced the enemy pilot that keeping his distance was wise; the Japanese plane soon lost contact.

Hughes reported the incident to *Yorktown* and requested air support, her plea received on board the carrier at 1126. The destroyer then anxiously radioed *Yorktown* again at 1141, inquiring if "air coverage had been sent in response to their request," following this a few moments later (1144) with another transmission reporting that the patrol plane was ten miles north of them. After one more search of the vicinity, the Kawanishi banked and headed for home at 1145, unable to regain contact; almost simultaneously, the three destroyers reluctantly gave up their

One of the more unsung fighting squadrons of World War II: *Yorktown*'s VF-42. Pilots of this unit pose informally in front of one of their Grumman F4F-3s in this picture taken on 6 February 1942, en route to Pearl Harbor after the Marshalls-Gilberts Raid. Seated (L-R): LT(jg) B.T. Macomber, A-V(N), USNR; LT(jg) A.J. Brassfield; LT(jg) R.M. Plott; LT(jg) W.N. Leonard; LT C.R. Fenton (XO); LCDR O. Pederson (CO, later *Yorktown*'s AGC); LT V.F. McCormack; ENS W.S. Woollen, A-V(N), USNR; ENS L.L.B. Knox, A-V(N), USNR. Standing (L-R): LT(jg) E.D. Mattson; ENS R.L. Wright, A-V(N), USNR; ENS H.B. Gibbs, A-V(N), USNR; ENS W.W. Barnes, Jr., A-V(N), USNR; ENS J.D. Baker, A-V(N), USNR; ENS E.S. McCuskey, A-V(N), USNR; LT(jg) R.G. Crommelin; ENS J.P. Adams, A-V(N), USNR; ENS E.R. Bassett, A-V(N), USNR; ENS W.A. Haas, A-V(N), USNR. Knox and Baker would be lost on 7 May 1942, at Coral Sea; Bassett on 4 June, at Midway. McCuskey and Adams had just scored the squadron's first "kill" on 1 February, when they teamed to destroy a Kawanishi Type 97 flying boat of the Jaluit-based Yokohama *Kōkūtai*. (Leonard)

search, too, having found no trace of the missing TBDs, and set course to rejoin TF-17 at 36 knots. En route, lookouts in *Hughes* spotted what looked like two oil slicks at 1212, but nothing more. The sea had swallowed up the *Yorktown*ers.

Yorktown, meanwhile, had picked up the intruder that the destroyers were engaging at 1117, bearing 270° (T), 32 miles distant. The carrier changed course for flight operations, and, at 1120, scrambled six F4F-3s of VF-42 to investigate, under LT "Mac" McCormack. They were unsuccessful in finding the snooper, though, returning to the ship shortly before 1300, orbiting the carrier while she launched a relief patrol of six "Wildcats" under the squadron's exec, LT Charles R. Fenton. McCormack's six F4F-3s then landed.

Yorktown's CXAM picked up another intruder at 1307, bearing 082° (T), 32 miles distant. Going to general quarters, the carrier recovered the last of McCormack's CAP and changed course, readying

herself for the arrival of the latest "snooper," who soon proved to be another Type 97 flying boat, emerging from the low-hanging clouds only 15,000 yards from *Yorktown* at 1313. This Kawanishi was also from the Yokohama *Kōkūtai*, basing in the Marshalls, but would meet a fate quite different from the sister aircraft that had encountered the destroyers a short time before.

The carrier and her consorts held their fire to avoid hitting the combat air patrol, whose third section, composed of ENS E. Scott McCuskey, A-V(N), USNR, and ENS John P. Adams, A-V(N), USNR, soon made contact with the Type 97. The seaplane crossed *Yorktown*'s bow at 1315, just as McCuskey and Adams were heading in the same direction in which the other two sections had been vectored. With his guns already charged, McCuskey closed at full throttle, test-firing his four .50-calibers as he came, and dived under the cloud, coming up to find himself confronted by the sight of a big four-engined seaplane bearing the "big red ball" insignia. "Coming in too fast to fire," McCuskey passed only a few feet under the flying boat's hull; he then pulled up into a wingover and instituted a high side run from ahead on the beam.

Before he triggered his guns, he noted that Adams had slipped in astern of the big Japanese plane and was already firing. McCuskey then opened fire, too, seeing his tracers "hitting in the vicinity of the starboard wing root." Suddenly, a "flash like a bolt of lightning shot across the top of the wing."

Observers below noted that the flying boat "exploded in midair and broke into many fragments" two minutes after she had crossed Yorktown's bow. In the skies above, McCuskey jerked back the stick to avoid the wreckage, and quickly glanced back to see "what appeared to be engines falling along with other objects." He could only recognize "a part of a wing that slowly fell into the sea like a falling leaf." Letting out a couple of war whoops, the excited McCuskey reported: "We just shot his ass off!"

At 1325, Yorktown changed course and landed aircraft, the flight deck crew according "Doc" McCuskey and "Johnny" Adams a reception they wouldn't forget. As they arrived in VF-42's ready room, someone told them to report to the bridge immediately for a little ceremony. The riggers in the parachute loft had made appropriate presents for the first man to down a Japanese plane; since McCuskey and Adams shared that honor, they shared the presents: McCuskey a colorful jacket and Adams a fez.

RADM Fletcher contemplated sending another raid against Jaluit that afternoon, but the badly overdue planes from the first strike on that island meant that a second raid would have necessitated night recovery, probably in poor weather conditions. He considered other objectives, but decided to continue retirement from the area since heavy rain storms had already caused the loss of two planes not even involved in raids—Reeves' SBD and an SOC from Louisville that had been launched on inner air patrol. In addition, Yorktown's aerologist noted the presence of an "extensive trough . . . spread over the area in those latitudes . . ." Further, Fletcher considered, on the basis of reports submitted to him by the returning pilots and radiomen, that "no objectives of any real military value were known in the vicinity." Weighing all the options, Fletcher elected to withdraw and refuel his destroyers, to prepare for further operations in concert with TF-8 in what would hopefully be improved flying weather. Before he could carry out this intention, though, VADM Halsey directed him to with-

The earliest wartime photo yet discovered of Yorktown was taken as she entered Pearl Harbor on 6 February 1942, after the Gilberts/Marshalls Raid. Taken from Enterprise, this view shows clearly the Measure 12-Graded System camouflage; absence of hull number; the prominent external degaussing cable, and the crew mustered in whites on the flight deck—as they would be on their next (and last) return to Pearl three months later. Saratoga (CV-3) is visible in the background, undergoing repairs after having been torpedoed by I-6 off Oahu on 11 January 1942. Three Pacific Fleet carriers were thus in Pearl Harbor at one time, only Lexington being at sea with TF 11. Also note the tubs for the 20mm battery, visible at far right, for the guns that Enterprise at that point had not yet had installed. (NH 95551).

draw "not later than the ensuing night." TF-17 headed back to Pearl Harbor.

Singling out the younger and less experienced pilots in the air group for praise, CAPT Buckmaster subsequently reported that the conduct and spirit of all had "upheld the highest traditions of the service." Although the amount of damage inflicted upon the enemy had not been great, the men who carried out the attacks did so in the face of appalling circumstances, even after most had become separated from their leaders. Torpedo Five mourned the loss of its men, as did Bombing Five, the latter particularly saddened over the loss of its likeable exec, George Bellinger.

That evening, as *Yorktown* retired with her screen under the cloak of heavy rainstorms and the gathering darkness, McCuskey, "feeling quite pleased," was trying to go to sleep in his bunk when "Johnny" Adams knocked on his door. "Come in and pull up a seat," McCuskey said, soon observing Adams to be "unusually quiet for such an exciting day." McCuskey then attempted to draw out his squadron mate: "What's the trouble?"

Slowly raising his head to reply, Adams asked quietly: "How many men do you think were aboard the Jap aircraft?" Then, after a little discussion, wherein they arrived at a figure of perhaps seven or more, it suddenly dawned on McCuskey what had so concerned his friend. "We had been involved in the killing of human beings." McCuskey reflected many years later, "instead of just shooting down an aircraft." What chance did those seven, or more, men, in their lumbering, vulnerable, volatile flying boat have against two nimble and heavily armed fighters whose pilots now sadly pondered their fate.

On 6 February, *Yorktown* reached Pearl Harbor, the day after *Enterprise* and TF-8 had arrived, and as she stood up the channel, returning to the port that she had departed that April day in 1941, the officers and men mustered in whites on the flight deck beheld the still very visible signs of destruction from the Japanese raid of 7 December—"a distressing and unforgettable sight," as "Jocko" Clark recalled later. ENSs McCuskey and Adams saw it, too, and they soon lost whatever concern they had had for the comparatively defenseless crew of the flying boat they had shot down. This, after all, was war.

Yorktown off-loaded the planes carried from Norfolk (except those which she had taken over to fill losses), spending four days at Berth F-9 before she shifted to the Pearl Harbor Navy Yard on the 10th for a brief availability. When asked if he wanted to

William Hipple, a 28-year-old war correspondent who had begun his journalistic career at age 15, embarked in *Yorktown* at Pearl Harbor on 15 February 1942, covered the 10 March 1942 Lae-Salamaua Raid, and disembarked at Tongatabu on 25 April 1942, whence he proceeded to Australia to cover General MacArthur's headquarters. On assignment for the Honolulu *Star-Bulletin* and Associated Press (AP), Hipple's articles in the May 1942 *Star-Bulletin*, "At Sea on a Carrier" give glimpses into *Yorktown*'s daily routine during the time he was embarked. He proved his mettle as a war correspondent, consequently, on Guadalcanal (contracting Malaria in the process), covering the Battle of Santa Cruz (26 October 1942), waded ashore with the Marines at Tarawa (in the first wave), accompanied Navy strikes on Manila (November 1944) as well as Army Air Force bombers on raids over Tokyo, and finished World War II as a top *Newsweek* correspondent, "widely recognized in his craft as an accurate observer and a writer of unusual force, clarity and vividness . . . " This particular view was taken on 29 April 1945 on board the amphibious command ship *Rocky Mount* (AGC-5), while he was covering the Tarakan landings. (80-G-359925)

make any changes in the installation of the 20mm Oerlikons that had been so hurriedly shipped at Norfolk, CAPT Buckmaster said no, he was content with things the way they were. The ship's force had made their own modifications in the magazines to handle the Oerlikon ammunition, and *Yorktown*'s commanding office said that would suffice for the duration.

While *Yorktown* lay at Pearl Harbor, planning was proceeding on what offensive actions the Pacific Fleet could undertake next. On 11 February, ADM Nimitz—who had assessed the initial Pacific raids as "well conceived, well planned and well executed"—decided to employ TF-8 and TF-17 as one force, TF-13, "to make a strong coordinated raid" on Wake and Eniwetok or Marcus, CINCPAC deeming that "as strong an aggressive raid as can be undertaken" at that time. Superstitious people balked at the projected 13 February departure (a Friday) and the designator, however, prompting Nimitz to alter both: TF-*16* would sail on Monday, *16* February.

On board *Yorktown* there were some new faces. At noon on 12 February, "Jocko" Clark, who "had set high standards" and driven the ship hard during the eight months he had been on board, having received promotion to captain, was relieved by CDR Dixie Kiefer, a stocky, thinning-haired, extroverted bachelor whose dynamic personality and infectious positive spirit would make itself felt in the coming months. On the 15th, LT Forrest R. "Tex" Biard, who had been one of the last Japanese language students to leave Tokyo before the outbreak of war, joined Fletcher's staff as assistant combat intelligence officer, accompanied by two radiomen from FRUPAC and assured by LCDR Joe Rochefort that he would be back "in two weeks." The same day, Mr. William Hipple, a 28-year-old war correspondent on assignment for the Honolulu *Star-Bulletin* and the Associated Press (AP), also came on board, for transportation, on his way to join the AP Bureau in Australia.

Yorktown cleared Pearl Harbor on the morning of 16 February, in company with *Louisville, Astoria* (CA-34), the oiler *Guadalupe* (AO-32), and four destroyers: *Sims, Anderson, Hammann* and *Walke*. Around noon of the day of departure, however, CINCPAC received a dispatch from ADM King, disagreeing with Nimitz's proposed joint raid on Wake and Marcus. "Occasional raids on the Mandates," King believed, "are sufficient" and suggested that CINCPAC deploy his fleet "to meet suspected threats of enemy forces." To that end COMINCH suggested sending TF-8 or TF-17 to Canton Island, leaving one task force to raid Wake and Marcus. Consequently, Nimitz sent TF-17 to the former place; TF-8 to attack the Japanese bases.

Yorktown, signals two-blocked at her yards indicating that flight operations are in progress, is seen here soon after departing Pearl Harbor for the South Pacific; oiler *Guadaloupe* (AO-32) is in the background. "We roll down the deck," Bill Hipple wrote of a takeoff in a VT-5 TBD-1 like the one abreast the island in this photo. "The takeoff is so easy I can't realize we're in the air. No rocking, no bumping. Easy bank to the left. Carrier sliding away. It looks like a tennis court . . ." (80-G-640553, cropped)

Eight days later, on 24 February, CINCPAC ordered TF-17 to join TF-11 in response to VADM Wilson Brown's request for a second carrier to raid the Japanese base at Rabaul, New Britain.

During the time between *Yorktown*'s departure from Pearl to her being ordered to the South Pacific, however, operational casualties continued to take a toll of her main battery when VB-5 and VS-5 each lost an SBD; the former on 21 February when LT John L. Nielsen's mount lost power in the groove and splashed astern of the ship. *Walke* immediately rescued Nielsen and RM2c D.W. Straub; neither man had suffered any injuries. LT Elbert M. Stever and RM3c W.A. Fontenot were not as fortunate on the 24th when their "Dauntless" crashed on takeoff. Stever suffered a fractured left arm and a lacerated lip; Fontenot, contusions on his left leg and right hip. As had been the case on the 21st, *Walke* rescued the crew.

Further word on how *Yorktown* would be deployed soon came. On 2 March, COMINCH directed VADM Brown "to use his combined forces to make an attack on the New Britain-Solomons Area" about 10 March, to cover the arrival of an Army convoy at Noumea, New Caledonia. To carry out those orders, Brown conferred with his staff and *Lexington*'s commanding officer, CAPT Frederick C. Sherman, on the evening of 5 March, to plan strikes on Rabaul and Gasmata.

Soon after TF-17 and TF-11 met on 6 March, Frank Jack Fletcher, accompanied by CAPT Spencer S. Lewis (chief of staff); CDR Gerard S. Galpin (operations officer), and CAPT Buckmaster and CDR Murr E. Arnold, *Yorktown*'s air officer, journeyed over to *Lexington* in *Yorktown*'s number two motor launch to meet with their opposite numbers. Although Brown had favored a moonlight air strike against Rabaul and Gasmata, the fact that *Yorktown*'s pilots lacked the necessary night flight qualification forced the adoption of a dawn mission. Cruisers and destroyers would follow up the air strike with a shelling of the enemy installations. On 6 March, RADM John G. Crace, RN, commanding the ANZAC Squadron, conferred with Brown in *Lexington*, and OpOrder No. 5-42 was distributed.

The Japanese, however, had emptied the nest that Wilson Brown had hoped to catch full of shipping. Unbeknownst to the Allied force, a convoy commanded by RADM Kajioka Sadamichi had quit Rabaul on 5 March, bound for Lae and Salamaua, settlements on the northeastern coast of New Guinea. "SR" Operation was to be a preliminary to the planned seizure of Tulagi, in the Solomons, and Port Moresby. Kajioka's ships remained undetected until the afternoon of 7 March, when an RAAF Lockheed "Hudson," homeward-bound from a photographic reconnaissance flight, reported what appeared to be five or six transports, escorted by cruisers and destroyers, 56 miles northeast of Buna.

Splashing ashore in a heavy rainstorm at 0100 on the 8th, Japanese South Seas Force troops landed at Salamaua. Within six hours, they had overcome the resistance offered by the "small but stout-hearted" detachment of the New Guinea Volunteer Rifles and RAAF men and occupied the airfield that lay south of the town. The invaders found the 1,200 meters by 80 meters-wide airstrip soft but usable; interrogation of a POW revealed that a "Hudson" had taken off that morning. Only one bomb crater—and that on the outer edge of the runway—marred its otherwise pristine appearance.

Meanwhile, Special Landing Force sailors under CDR Miyata landed at Lae. They brushed aside slight resistance and captured not only the gravel-surfaced airfield but the telegraph station and the town. Like the Salamaua field, Lae's measured 1,200 feet in length, but was only 30 meters wide. CDR Miyata's sailors found evidence that demolition crews had been at work, though; about 40 holes marred the 15-meter taxiway, craters 1.5 meters deep and, in some cases, five meters wide.

Far from the unfolding Japanese occupation of Lae and Salamaua that Sunday, Bill Hipple attended the divine services on *Yorktown*'s hangar deck. "The metal side curtains were up," he later described the setting, "exposing to our view the blue sea, the wisps of clouds, and nearby warships. Now and then [the chaplain] would stop his sermon as planes on patrol roared low alongside," an incongruous setting "for a message of peace, hope, and faith." As Hipple and his fellow worshipers listened, LCDR Frank R. Hamilton, ChC, USN, had begun his sermon with words from Psalm 107: "Thy way, O Lord, is in the sea and Thy path in the great waters. They that go down to the sea in ships and do business in great waters, they see the works of the Lord and His wonders in the deep." At another point in the service, the newsman noted the words of the Navy Hymn, "Eternal Father, Strong to Save," that sought the Lord's protection of "the men who fly through great spaces of the sky . . . in darkening storms or sunlight fair; Oh hear us when we lift our prayer for those in peril in the air . . . " On the eve of the missions planned for Rabaul and Gasmata, seeking such solace was most appropriate.

In the meantime, the industrious Japanese found the damage to the airstrip at Lae by no means irreparable, estimating that the craters could be filled by 1600 that day. Using their own landing craft and commandeered Australian lighters, Japanese unloading operations proceeded with such swiftness that they estimated that *Kongō Maru* could be unloaded by the 10th, *Ten'yō Maru* (which had air base equipment on board) on the 11th, and *Yokohama Maru* by the 12th.

On the heels of the landing force, the engineers—according priority to readying the Lae field—followed. In spite of the foul weather, the Airfield Construction Unit quickly began filling in craters, removing obstacles, and bringing ashore its heavy equipment. The original estimates had been close; by 1800 on the day of the landings, Lae was almost in business to handle fighter aircraft.

The bad weather over the beachhead and the approaches to the seized settlements prevented Type 96 *kansens* from the 24th Air Flotilla at Rabaul from flying cover during daylight on the 8th. Thus, RAAF "Hudsons" could make six passes over Salamaua; one Lockheed's bombs landed close aboard *Yokohama Maru*. Antiaircraft fire and aircraft from seaplane carrier *Kiyokawa Maru*, however, drove off the "Hudsons" before they could cause any further trouble, and artificers from the convoy commander's flagship, light cruiser *Yūbari*, soon made temporary repairs to *Yokohama Maru*'s damaged bow. Four USAAF B-17s were to fly up from Townsville to participate in the attack, but one suffered engine trouble and the other three could not find the target because of the heavy cloud cover.

Word of the occupation of Lae and Salamaua, meanwhile, had prompted what RADM Crace later called a "complete change of plan" for the force heading toward Rabaul and Gasmata. The Japanese landings seemed, to CDR C. Turner Joy, VADM Brown's operations officer, "an answer to prayer" since now the enemy could be hit when he was the most vulnerable—before he could consolidate his gains. Consequently, the admiral modified OpOrder 5-42 by dispatch to address a strike on the enemy's shipping off Lae and Salamaua. Accomplishing the desired objective, though, was easier said than done. Proceeding up the north coast of New Guinea, the most direct route, exposed the task force to the seemingly ever-vigilant search planes of the enemy that had foiled the first attempt to pound Rabaul on 20 February.

While VADM Brown and his staff wrestled with how to surprise the Japanese, RADM Kajioka was grappling with problems of his own. Although everything seemed to be going well, the lack of friendly fighters undoubtedly worried him. He radioed Rabaul at 2200 on the 8th:

SINCE OUR LANDING THIS MORNING AND DESPITE BAD WEATHER CONDITIONS ENEMY AIRCRAFT HAVE ATTACKED OUR TRANSPORTS SIX TIMES X ALTHOUGH ENEMY AIRCRAFT ARE FEW THEY HAVE CAUSED CONSIDERABLE DAMAGE BY REPEATED BOMBING ATTACKS FROM BASES NEARBY AND PRESENT CONSPICUOUS OBSTACLE TO ATTAINMENT [OF] OUR OBJECTIVES.

LAE AIRFIELD WAS COMPLETELY ROLLED TODAY AND IN CONDITION [TO] RECEIVE SHIPBOARD FIGHTER TYPE AIRCRAFT X THEREFORE HOPE FIGHTER AIRCRAFT WILL BE SENT FORWARD TO LAE AIRFIELD AS SOON AS POSSIBLE.

An inspection team sent down from Rabaul, though, seemed more pessimistic about Lae's readiness to receive the Mitsubishi A5M4 Type 96 *kansens* which Kajioka so urgently wanted. No less than an hour after the admiral's optimistic assessment, the inspectors reported at 2300 on the 8th that despite the Lae field's hard surface, it was not yet ready. "By picking up and removing large pieces of gravel and rocks, and then rolling it with six rollers," 800 meters of the airstrip could be used by fighters and land bombers. Unloading delays and intermittent rain made it im-

possible to predict a time of completion on the 9th. If the large pieces of gravel were removed and the field rolled, the inspectors believed, a test landing of a Type 96 carrier fighter could be conducted on the 10th.

On the morning of 9 March, the commander of the Rabaul-based 24th Air Flotilla force directed that fighters patrol over Lae and Salamaua from 30 minutes after sunrise to 45 minutes before sunset on the 9th. At 0730 on the 9th, believing that Lae's field was, in fact, operational, he directed the air base people there to spread T-shaped panels on the ground to signify that the field was ready.

At 1000 on 9 March, the South Seas Air Force headquarters at Rabaul exhorted its men:

AIRFIELD CONSTRUCTION UNIT SHALL TO THE BEST OF THEIR ABILITY COMPLETE LAE AIRFIELD READINESS AS DESIRED BY THE STAFF 24TH AIR FLOTILLA.

The *kansens* based at Surumi, 200 miles from Lae, set out as ordered on the 9th but encountered bad weather incident to the seasonal monsoons. The flight leader radioed Rabaul that it was thus impossible to carry out his orders. At 1300, the fighters began the return flight. Had the pilots flown lower, they might have seen the panels on the ground and have seen for themselves that Lae—the airstrip enlarged and rolled—was indeed operable as a fighter base. At 2000 on the 9th, Kajioka again radioed Rabaul that the field was ready. Communication delays, however, resulted in that word not reaching the Commander, 24th Air Flotilla, until 0600 on the 10th.

In the meantime, last-minute planning continued in TF-11. In view of the Japanese air activity over the northern route to Lae and Salamaua, Brown and *Lexington*'s CAPT "Ted" Sherman opted to launch a strike from the *southern* side of New Guinea, from the Gulf of Papua. That, however, meant that the strike group would have to fly over the Owen Stanley range, and few white men, other than for gold or Gospel, had ever been near those "towering mountains, thick rain forests, and terrible swamps," while stone-age tribes inhabited the nearly impenetrable jungles. Those who knew the area deemed the Owen Stanleys as wild, unexplored territory, with its loftiest peak, Mount Victoria, towering 13,200 feet above sea level; more often than not, clouds cloaked the jagged peaks. None of the charts available on the ships revealed anything about the interior other than the shoreline; coral shoals (their existence covered only by "old and somewhat doubtful charts") studded the waters in which two valuable aircraft carriers were to be hazarded.

Last-minute intelligence-gathering flights, to Townsville and Port Moresby, however, netted valuable information. CDR William B. Ault, *Lexington*'s Air Group commander, returned from the latter place reporting that Aussie bush pilots had told him of a 7,500 foot altitude pass between Mounts Chapman and Lawson, but that it could only be used between 0700 and 1100 daily, before or after which clouds would prevent passage. With the opening of that proverbial window of opportunity, Brown directed that the raid take place the following morning, with all fuel and ordnance loads carefully calculated.

To cover his flank to the east, as well as to be in a position to intercept any Japanese move toward Port Moresby, and simultaneously cover the arrival of troops at Noumea, Brown detached a surface force to operate off Rossel Island, in the Louisiade Archipelago. He placed the heavy cruisers *Astoria*, *Chicago* (CA-29), *Louisville*, and HMAS *Australia*, and destroyers *Anderson*, *Hammann*, *Hughes*, and *Sims*, under the vigorous and very capable RADM Crace.

The Japanese, meanwhile, continued their unloading operations with seemingly little to fear. Type 96 and Type 1 *rikkōs* had bombed the RAAF fields at Port Moresby, Wau, and Bulolo, while Type 97 flying boats, as well as *rikkōs*, had been searching, north of the Solomons and the Coral Sea, for American carriers. They had sighted none. Except for ground fire from the guns defending the RAAF airdromes, the reconnaissance flights had been unopposed by RAAF planes, leading the Japanese to conclude that they had completely destroyed Allied air power in the region.

TF-11's avenue of approach had been well-chosen. The Japanese had no inkling of the presence of the most formidable carrier task force sent to sea by the U.S. Navy that began girding itself for battle before dawn on the 10th, as it stood toward the Gulf of Papua. On board *Yorktown*, general quarters sounded at 0545, and the sight of her crew moving to their stations moved Bill Hipple to observe: "You would have seen a stirring and unforgettable sample of the spirit of our Navy at war." Resounding words and phrases tritely recited by an after-dinner speaker came alive before his gaze as he sensed a "spirit of determination . . . everywhere" on board. To the visiting newsman "an air of excitement" pervaded the ship.

Hipple visited VF-42's ready room, and heard "Red" Bassett (who normally kept his shipmates in stitches) being ribbed by his shipmates, who joked how cannibals would make a meal of the stout Pennsylvanian. "Oh, no," Bassett replied, "I have it planned that if I'm forced down, I'll prey upon their superstitions, become a great white god, and live the life of Reilly . . . "

Bassett's friends, however, knew that worry lurked beneath "Red"'s cheerful demeanor. A fortune-teller had predicted that he would not survive his 28th birthday, a milestone that fell on the day of the strike. Obsessed by the thought of being forced down and not being prepared for it, Bassett had accumulated fish hooks and line, a hunting knife, a flashlight, a revolver and extra ammunition and oil to keep it serviced; patching equipment for his raft and extra compressed air tubes for his life jacket; quinine; extra rations, and a waterproof cigar lighter. He also boned up on how to deal with sharks. Finally, the day before he had added cuff links, uniform buttons, and trinkets to trade with the natives. He stuffed everything in the battered and bulging gas mask container he took with him to whatever plane was assigned him. One of his shipmates thought Bassett "looked like a tribal chieftain." Like other VF-42 pilots, Bassett purloined a meat cleaver from the wardroom pantry to hack his was through the jungle if necessary.

Hipple later watched in fascination as *Yorktown*'s flight deck crew prepared and spotted the planes for launch. Chalked on some of the bombs were slogans like "Get a Load of This," or "A Present from F.D.R." Men had chalked wives' or girlfriends' names, or expressions like "Heads Up Below," "Another Cloud for the Rising Sun," or "Don't Laugh—This is Over Your Head," on the planes.

There were last minute changes in plan: LT "Mac" McCormack, VF-42's flight officer, found that his plane would not start. Exercising the prerogative of a senior, he "bumped" ENS "Willo" Woollen and took the junior officer's F4F-3 for the mission. Settling himself in the cockpit, McCormack noticed a meat cleaver in the map case.

At 0749, shortly after the task force entered the Gulf of Papua, *Lexington* turned into the wind and began launching her air group; at 0803 *Yorktown* commenced putting her planes aloft. "Lady Lex" completed the evolution by 0822 having put 52 planes—including the SBD-3 flown by CDR Ault—into the air in a little over a half hour. To give her fighters more fuel for the flight, *Lexington* recovered those that would accompany the strike and topped off their tanks. By 0849, all of *Yorktown*'s planes were on their way.

All told, there were now 104 planes droning toward the unsuspecting enemy. From *Lexington*, 18 SBD-2s and -3s of VS 2 under LCDR Robert E. Dixon; 12 SBD-2s and -3s of VB-2 under LCDR Weldon L.

Hamilton; 13 Douglas TBD-1s of VT 2 under LCDR James H. Brett, Jr., and, as escort, eight Grumman F4F-3s under LCDR John S. Thach. CDR Ault paced the rest, having been entrusted by Brown with the responsibility of initiating or aborting the strike.

Yorktown's 52 planes followed: 17 SBD-2s and -3s of VB-5 under LCDR Bob Armstrong; 13 SBD-3s of VS-5 under LCDR Bill Burch; 12 TBD-1s of VT-5 under LCDR Joe Taylor; and ten F4F-3s of VF-42 under LCDR Swede Pederson. To provide cover for the task force, each carrier put up six fighters for CAP while *Lexington* contributed five SBDs and *Yorktown* four for an anti-torpedo plane patrol.

CDR Ault, finding optimum flying conditions at the key pass, orbitted that point halfway across the peninsula to direct and coordinate the passage of both groups. He began broadcasting weather and other operational data to the planes and the task group in the Gulf of Papua. As VF-42's fighters came out of the clouds and flew toward the gap in the mountains, Art Brassfield and Walt Haas both had "visions of never finding our way back."

At Lae and Salamaua, with the important exception of the delay in sending planes from Rabaul to base at the former's field, all continued to go well. Rain clouds had blanketed the area since midnight, and only one predawn alarm had occurred when a "Hudson" had near-missed *Ten'yō Maru* off Lae.

Bob Dixon led his troops up from the south and passed slightly to the east of the ships before peeling off to the left to initiate the attack. Scouting Two began to put teeth in the expression "Remember Pearl Harbor" when they pushed over above Lae at 0922, and the transports *Ten'yō Maru* and *Kokai Maru* and armed merchant cruiser *Kongō Maru* lying offshore. Fire from the four 8-cm. high-angle guns of the 3rd Special Base Force splashed an SBD; the four escorting F4Fs then strafed the battery and put it out of action.

As the first SBDs, the pilots plagued by fogging windshields and telescopic sights, had dropped their bombs, an urgent message went out from the Commander of the Occupation Force:

ENEMY IS OVER LAE MAKING TORPEDO AND DIVE BOMBING ATTACKS

Six minutes after VS-2 had provided the curtain-raiser, VT-2 and VB-2 arrived in the wings. The latter split into two six-plane divisions, the first scoring two close-misses out of six bombs dropped near the mine-layer *Tsugaru*. The second division, hampered like the first by fogging windshields and bomb sights, near-missed transport *China Maru*.

Torpedo Two fared little better. Three TBDs bore in on *Yokohama Maru* and *China Maru* off Salamaua. One Mk. XIII torpedo punched into *Yokohama Maru* and she began to settle. Two fired against *China Maru*, however, missed; one blew up on the beach. The rest

Ten'yō Maru heads inshore off Lae. *Kokai Maru* is visible just off the settlement, which is itself obscured by the cloud to right of center. (NH 95432)

Scouting Five SBDs flying at 16,000 feet, bound for Lae; Japanese ships in Huon Gulf are making smoke in the distance. This and other pictures of VS-5's operations on 10 March are most likely the work of PhoM2c Walter C. Goldie, the squadron photographer. (NH 95435)

Douglas SBD-3s of Scouting Five over Lae during the action of 10 March. Taken from approximately 6,000 feet, this view shows the Markham River delta (L); close scrutiny reveals three Japanese ships close inshore: *Ten'yō Maru* and *Kokai Maru* off Lae proper, *Kongō Maru*, smoke rising from her, visible below *Kokai Maru*. Only *Kokai Maru* would survive the attacks this day. *Ten'yō Maru*'s wreck would be visible offshore into the 1960's. (NH 95431)

Armed merchant cruiser *Kongō Maru* settles by the stern off Lae; the largest of the ships sunk on 10 March, she had been completed in 1935 and had been converted to an auxiliary warship in 1941. (NH 95434)

at her), but did not observe its run.

The situation in which Kajioka found himself must have given him an uncomfortable sense of *deja vu* and confirmed his worst fears of what could befall his force should it remain unprotected by fighter aircraft. He may have vividly recalled the considerable damage, all out of proportion to their meager numbers, wreaked on his ships off Wake Island three months before by USMC "Wildcats" from VMF-211. Once again, Kajioka's flagship *Yūbari* would be the target of American pilots eager to ply their trade of destruction and avenge Pearl Harbor.

Kajioka's ships scattered for open water. *Yūbari*, *Tsugaru*, and destroyers *Yūnagi*, *Oite*, and *Asanagi* put up a "moderate" amount of small-caliber antiaircraft fire, and maneuvered hard, making smoke to cover their movements.

Some 25 miles east of Lae, seaplane carrier *Kiyokawa Maru* and destroyer *Mochizuki* lay at Hanisch harbor; the former's air unit consisted of Nakajima E8N2 Type 95 and Mitsubishi F1M2 Type 00 seaplanes. One Type 95, its ash-gray tail bearing the yellow code R-18, attacked VS-2's SBDs but ended up being splashed by a *Lexington* F4F. Sea1c Otomo Takumi and PO3c Gasai Shigeo, the seaplane's crew, perished.

On board *Yorktown*, meanwhile, "Tex" Biard and his intercept team—RM1c P.E. Seward and RM2c W.W. Eaton—were busy. Seward and Eaton, sure that they had been monitoring the proper local area enemy circuits which the ships at Lae and Salamaua would use, and listening accordingly, picked up the word of the air raid alarm almost as soon as word had arrived from the air groups about to carry out their attack. Using a radio borrowed from one of *Yorktown*'s officers, Biard tried to tune in on the ships being hit.

While the Japanese reeled under the blows struck by *Lexington*'s men, the *Yorktown*ers were not far behind. Bob Armstrong led VB-5 down to commence the attack on ships off Salamaua at 0950, splitting his squadron into three divisions; he led the first, Sam Adams the second, and Bill Guest the third.

of Torpedo Two headed out over Huon Gulf. Three of that group headed for Lae, where one pilot's "fish" holed *Kongō Maru*. *Kokai Maru* took a hit, too; *Ten'yō Maru*, shaken up by her bout with VS-2, managed to emerge unscathed from an attack by five TBDs. One TBD pilot fired his torpedo against a "destroyer" (it may have been *Tsugaru*, which easily evaded the "fish" fired

Although vexed by fogged sights and windshields, Armstrong's six SBDs bracketed *Yūbari* with 500- and 100-pound bombs, bouncing shrapnel off her sides and showering her with spray that rained down on her decks like a summer cloudburst. Adams' division did likewise; the pilots claimed three direct hits on *Yūbari* and three "probables" with their six 500-pounders and six 100-pounders. Guest's troops dropped their 500-pounders on the flagship, too, but wisely saved their smaller ordnance after shaking up *Yūbari*. They holed *Asanagi*, putting her boilers out of commission; another bomb hit *Yūnagi* amidships, damaging her main engines. His planes also strafed a nearby "gunboat"—probably the minesweeper *No.2 Tama Maru*—and set her afire.

Bill Burch split VS-5 into two divisions and pushed over at 1005 above Lae. Burch, with seven planes, hit *Kokai Maru* and *Kongō Maru* while his aggressive and highly competent exec, Wally Short, took six planes to tackle *Ten'yō Maru*. Burch's pilots scored "at least two direct hits" on each of the ships—Burch getting one himself—while determined strafing with the SBDs' fixed .50-calibers stopped the anti-aircraft fire coming from their decks. Short's division, meanwhile, roughed up the third ship, with Short, too, scoring a direct hit, leaving her "on fire and sinking when beached." In return, anti-aircraft fire only made "superficial" fragment holes in the tail section of one SBD. As VS-5 cleared the area, its targets lay "beached and burning." ENS Samuel J. Underhill, A-V(N), USNR, on his first combat mission, had "missed by a mile" with his bomb, but RM3c James H. Cales, his radio-gunner, "got off a few rounds with [his] thirty caliber onto the deck of a CA."

At 1020, Joe Taylor led Torpedo Five over to Lae and up the coast, and found *Kiyokawa Maru* with

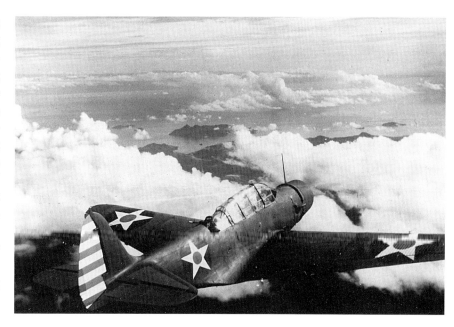

LCDR Joe Taylor leads VT-5 toward Salamaua in plane no. 1, a TBD-1 (BuNo 0319), pictured in the series of photographs taken by PhoM2c F.J. Meers on 10 March. Note matte finish of the upper surface camouflage paint, full-chord national insignia on the wings, and retention of only the individual plane number (1) on the side of the fuselage, with the squadron number (5) and mission letter (T) omitted for security purposes. (Author)

Lead formation of VT-5 heads out over Huon Gulf while Japanese ships—possibly the auxiliary vessel *Noshiro Maru* and the auxiliary minesweeper *Hagoromo Maru* —make smoke in an attempt to cover their maneuvers. Plane no.1 (BuNo 0319) is flown by LCDR Joe Taylor, plane no.2 (BuNo 0354) by LT Leonard E. Ewoldt, plane no. 3 (BuNo 0376) by ENS Francis R. Sanborn, A-V(N), USNR. (Author)

four planes on her deck, and the nearby *Mochizuki*. Operating as high-level bombers since the attack planners had doubted that a "Devastator" could make it over the Owen Stanleys with a Mk. XIII (thus leading to the decision to arm *Lexington*'s TBDs with

A pair of TBD-1s, each carrying two 500-pound bombs, over Huon Gulf, radio-gunners with their flexible-mount .30-caliber machine guns at the ready. Smoke below is from Japanese ships—perhaps *Noshiro Maru* and *Hagoromo Maru*—sortiing off Salamaua (L). (NH 95439)

torpedoes and *Yorktown*'s with bombs, to thus ensure that at least half of the "Devastators" could contribute meaningfully to the attack), Taylor's TBDs, each armed with a pair of 500-pound bombs slung side-by-side beneath the belly, commenced their runs from 13,000 to 14,000 feet.

"The lack of qualified and experienced bomb sight operators," however, "considerably handicapped" Torpedo Five and led to poor results. Only one bomb of the 24 dropped apparently landed near enough to the converted freighter to do any damage, although one close miss from one of the first division's planes apparently sprung some plating enough to open *Kiyokawa Maru*'s engine room to the sea and stop the ship dead in the water. Fragments from other near misses holed the ship's side.

One TBD, with a photographer in the middle seat, missed *Kiyokawa Maru* as the tyro bombardier toggled the bombs at the wrong time. Fortunately, PhoM2c F.J. Meers proved better at taking pictures than he was at dropping bombs; the photos he took are the only ones to show the attack on *Kiyokawa Maru*. Meers, how-

ever, had to listen to the pilot cuss him out for almost the entire return trip.

While *Lexington*'s TBDs had made their runs unmolested, *Yorktown*'s met one of *Kiyokawa Maru*'s Type 95s, its tail bearing the yellow code R-22, as Sea2c Uemura Hideo and PO2c Aoshima Masaburo bravely tackled six "Devastators." RM1c Angus M. Shirah, Jr., RM3c Eugene W. Jones and RM3c Don D. Allen, however, handled their .30-calibers with accuracy and skill, holing one of the Nakajima's floats. When R-22 returned to its parent ship later, it turned turtle soon after landing, forcing Uemura and Aoshima to swim for it.

The fighters of VF-42, like those from VF-3, drew fire away from the dive bombers—as VF-3 had done for the SBDs and TBDs of the *Lexington* air group. Swede Pederson's pilots strafed ships and shore installations at low level and dropped fragmentation bombs. Pilots of the four F4F-3s accompanying the

LCDR Joe Taylor's radio-gunner, CRM(PA) Harrison S. Nobbs, goggles down, searches the skies from the third seat of BuNo 0319. Nobbs's .30-caliber Browning machine gun is fitted with a ring-and-bead sight and armor plate. (NH 95442)

planes at Salamaua strafed boats in the water attempting to rescue men from the sinking *Yokohama Maru*.

After expending all of the bombs and torpedoes, the two air groups cleared the area, their return shepherded by Bill Ault. And, as a *Lexington* pilot had been the first on the scene, one of their number would be last to leave. LT(jg) Joseph G. Smith lingered and assessed the results as best he could before heading for home.

Having reported the completion of his squadron's attack at 0945, LCDR Dixon of VS-2 arrived over the task force an hour later. At 1046, his weighted beanbag plopped onto *Lexington*'s flight deck. Dixon's laconic message had been one of the first indications of what had occurred in the raid; he reported three large transports off Lae hit by VS-2's bombs, that there had been no air opposition and only scattered antiaircraft fire. He also reported the presence of other ships at Salamaua and in the roadstead.

"Lady Lex" commenced recovery operations at 1057, and except for a brief delay caused by repairs to a parted arrestor cable, completed the evolution before noon. The *Lexington* air group had only lost one aircraft.

On board *Yorktown*, her men had eagerly followed the action coming in via the radio much like sports fans listen to ball games and root for the home team. To Bill Hipple, the banter indicated that "the planes were having great success." As he observed *Yorktown*'s air group take their landing intervals, he noted: "They came near the carrier and flew around. The planes had personality—they seemed to fly jubilantly now, their motors seemed to purr . . . one by one, the planes came down, coming to a jaunty halt on the flight deck" as the arrestor gear caught the cross-deck pendants.

Pilots and aircrew alighted from the planes, happy and smiling ("Red" Bassett had beaten the jinx!) " . . . as calm as if they'd just returned from a routine patrol flight." By 1201, all planes of the attack group had been recovered, the men reporting three cargo ships hit and beached off Lae, a seaplane tender stopped east of Salamaua, a light cruiser hit at least four times, two destroyers stopped by 100-pound bombs, one large transport listing heavily and another sunk off Salamaua.

Seaplane carrier *Kiyokawa Maru* (top) increases speed off Hanisch Harbor; destroyer *Mochizuki* (below) cuts a graceful "S" as VT-5 deploys to attack. (NH 95443)

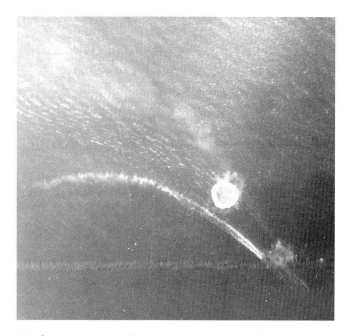

Kiyokawa Maru, carrying one Nakajima E8N2 Type 95 reconnaissance seaplane ("Dave") and three Mitsubishi F1M2 Type 00 observation seaplanes ("Pete"), all apparently painted in the early wartime color scheme of AN2 light gray, is near-missed by bombs from a VT-5 "Devastator" on 10 March; one misses almost a ship-length astern, the other splashes close aboard the port quarter. (NH 95444)

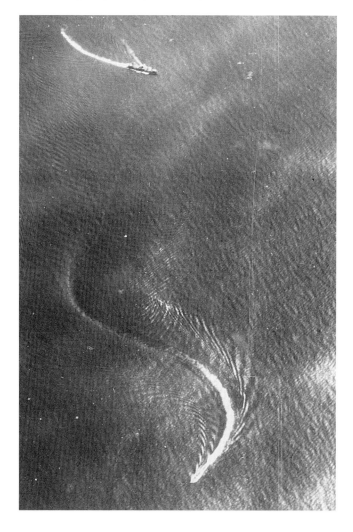

"When we finally landed," LT(jg) Floyd Moan of VB-5 confided later to his diary, "everybody from the lowest ensign to squadron commander was unanimous in the opinion that we should have gone back and finished up the job, confident that not many of us would miss the second time . . . " Elated *Yorktown*ers convinced Fletcher that they should go back. Brown, however, reasoned that the attack had caused "decisive and complete" damage to the shipping off Lae and Salamaua. Floyd Moan complained in his diary that not going back indicated "It doesn't seem to me that we are trying very hard to win this war." Yet he was willing to give his senior officers the benefit of the doubt. "Of course," he allowed, "there might be other considerations of which I know nothing, but it seems to me, with slightly greater risk, that we could have achieved a major victory than merely a fairly successful raid."

Although spotted by a prowling Japanese flying boat, TF-11 cleared the area unmolested. USAAF B-17s and RAAF "Hudsons" later raided the two settlements, the latter engaged by *Kiyokawa Maru*'s seaplanes, but the major damage had already been inflicted. By noon, local time, on 10 March, four Mitsubishi A6M2 Type 00 fighters—ferried into Rabaul by the small carrier *Shōhō*—would be over the settlements: too few, too late.

Unfamiliarity with Japanese ship types and the rudimentary nature of anti-shipping tactics complicated the assessment of damage, while smoke screens and radical maneuvering generated confusion as to "numbers, location, and damage." *Yorktown*'s squadrons' bombs having instantaneous fuses (rather than delayed-action) limited the damage from a direct hit; only one-third of *Lexington*'s bombs had had instantaneous fuses. VT-2's torpedoes ran erratically; VT-5's lack of training proved detrimental to its high-level bombing efforts.

The Japanese considered the Americans' abilities in bombing and torpedo attacks as being of a "low order" but also admitted that there had been too many attacking planes to deal with and that shipboard anti-aircraft defense was not adequate. Moreover, the shipping off the beachheads lacked a support force. The Japanese claimed 11 planes shot down—ten more than were actually destroyed. Only one SBD, with its two-man crew, had been lost.

Pitting two carrier air groups against one target had not only proved feasible (a concern of VADM Brown's on the eve of battle) but devastating. The pioneering pilots, bombardiers and radio-gunners of *Lexington*'s and *Yorktown*'s planes sank *Kongō Maru*, *Ten'yō Maru*, and *Yokohama Maru*, while *No. 2 Tama Maru* (which had suffered 5 dead and 10 wounded) sank two days later. Near-misses and strafing accounted for damage to *Yubari* (which soon returned to Japan for repairs to her generators and shafting, and which had suffered her exec and 13 men killed and 49 wounded— more casualties than she had suffered off Wake), *Oite*, *Yunagi* (29 dead, 38 wounded), *Asanagi* (18 dead, 47 wounded); *Kiyokawa Maru* and *Kokai Maru*. *Tsugaru* had taken a direct hit near her stack and weathered four near misses; her crew counted 50 holes, port and starboard. Eleven *Tsugaru* sailors had been killed, 13 wounded. All told, 130 men had died, another 245 had been wounded. Of the 18 ships off Lae and Salamaua that March morn, 17 suffered damage to one extent or another. Declaring that his ships had been on "strict alert," RADM Kajioka blamed the devastation on the delay in moving fighters forward to Lae.

The lack of Japanese aerial opposition had certainly enabled *Lexington*'s and *Yorktown*'s aviators to attack their targets with minimal hindrance. "It was a cinch," one SBD pilot told Bill Hipple,"a dive bomber's field day." The newsman later called the raid "dangerous and difficult," carried out in a "magnificent" manner, the product of "careful planning and meticulous attention to detail." This "bold and successful stroke," Hipple declared, "definitely delayed the Japanese southward drive." While VADM Brown considered the raid as "highly successful," ADM Nimitz downplayed it, noting that it had not dislodged the enemy from New Guinea; CINCPAC doubted that the Japanese advance would be greatly retarded.

Soon thereafter, however, Japanese planners posited that future operations in that area would need the support of at least one carrier division. The Lae-Salamaua raid forced an already overextended enemy to postpone his projected moves toward Tulagi and Port Moresby for a month until he could gather more amphibious shipping to cover the losses incurred on 10 March and marshall air support. American carriers constituted a dangerous variable in the enemy's future invasion equations.

Although his admirals may have disagreed on the impact of the Lae-Salamaua Raid on the Japanese, President Roosevelt harbored no such uncertainty. "It was by all means," F.D.R. declared proudly to British Prime Minister Winston Churchill on 17 March, "the best day's work we have had."

CHAPTER 5

To Destroy Enemy Ships . . . At Favorable Opportunities

THE U.S. NAVY's carrier situation by late March, 1942, did not allow much room for flexibility of deployment: *Saratoga* had been torpedoed off Oahu by *I-6* on 11 January; *Lexington* needed repairs and alterations, as did *Enterprise*, both ships having been at sea a great deal since even before the start of hostilities. *Hornet* was on her way from the east coast, the exigencies of war denying her a proper "shakedown" such as her cousins *Yorktown* and *Enterprise* had enjoyed in the piping days of peace; *Wasp* would soon be sailing for the British Isles to operate with the Home Fleet. *Ranger* too was in the Atlantic, as was *Long Island* (AVG-1), the Navy's first "escort carrier." This left *Yorktown* the only U.S. Navy fleet carrier in the South Pacific. Hers was a lonely watch.

Brown departed with *Lexington* and TF-11 on 16 March, six days after the Lae and Salamaua strike and shortly after transferring newer planes to *Yorktown* (one of which, an F4F-3, crashed shortly after taking off *Lexington*, its pilot, ENS Haas, being forced to take his second swim since the outbreak of war). With TF-17 now on its own, operating directly under COMINCH, Frank Jack Fletcher waited patiently for the enemy to move southward. Some members of his staff pressed him to launch an attack on Rabaul—Wilson Brown's elusive goal—to hit Japanese shipping there. Fletcher did not agree, Brown's experience fresh in his mind. He harbored a healthy respect for land-based air. If he pressed on after being sighted, he reasoned, he felt sure he would find Rabaul empty of the shipping he sought. Then what? His force would be

subject to enemy air attack, "with no worthwhile objectives for our planes."

Possible courses of action with regard to the Japanese in that theater were not the only concerns, however, with which Frank Jack Fletcher had to wrestle. Being at sea for over a month, the force soon found fresh provisions running low, especially on board the destroyers. Predictions were being made that the supply situation would be particularly critical around 1 April, the day upon which the storeship *Bridge* (AF-1) was due to arrive at Noumea, New Caledonia. The situation on board the larger ships in TF-17, *Yorktown* and her cruiser consorts, was not much better—a sailor on board *Astoria* complained in his diary: " . . . chow is getting poorer by the day . . . I'd rather get killed in action than keep this up . . ."

Fletcher, keeping in mind the fitness of the men under his command, accordingly radioed COMINCH and COMANZAC (VADM H. Fairfax Leary) of his intention "to operate in the Coral Sea" until TF-17 returned to Noumea "about the first of April for provisions."

At that juncture, however, Army planes based in Australia reported spotting TF-17 "228 miles south of Rabaul" on 29 March. Leary informed Fletcher of the sighting, as well as CINCPAC, by dispatch. Nimitz' headquarters marveled at TF-17's proximity to the enemy, "so far within the air search range of enemy forces." Since Japanese shipping had been previously sighted south of Bougainville, CINCPAC's staff posited that TF-17 was "in excellent position to strike."

Left: Marching past a line of VB-5's SBDs parked along the edge of the flight deck, *Yorktown*'s band precedes the "big T-boned steak" billed as "the only one in captivity," guarded by four Marines bearing bayonet-tipped Garand rifles, during part of the "*Yorktown* Jamboree" on 10 April 1942 in the Coral Sea. The tail of the parked VF-42 F4F-3 (BuNo 3999) (R) is that of an ex-VF-3 aircraft transferred to *Yorktown* from *Lexington* on 14 March 1942. Plane no. 10 was nominally assigned to ENS Edgar R. Bassett, A-V(N), USNR. (NH 95570, Naval Institute Photo Library)

Below: CCS C.E. Callaway and CCS H.L. Sims oversee serving of cafeteria-style meals circa April 1942; in the foreground, "Red" Hicks, with SC3c T.E. "Ace" Dison at his left, dishes up spaghetti mixed with what appears to be canned sausage. All fresh meat would be gone by the second week of April. Only sailor clearly identifiable is Sea2c V.J. Roma (fifth from right). (80-G-12508)

Unfortunately for Fletcher, the "TF-17" spotted by the Army must have been enemy ships, for his own force was not in the position attributed to them by the Army pilots, whom the admiral deemed "notoriously incorrect as to types." Fletcher thus sent a dispatch to Leary, giving his true position, and told CO-MANZAC of his plans to replenish at Noumea. It was a conditional declaration of intent, though, for Fletcher went on to state that if the Japanese moved southward, he would "turn around" and head back to attack them.

Leary's original dispatch to Fletcher—the erroneous sighting of his force—had not reached CO-MINCH, prompting ADM King to fire off an abrasive interrogatory message to Commander, TF-17: "Your [message] not understood if it means you are retiring from [the] enemy [in] vicinity to provision..." CTF-17 responded by explaining his plans for victualling and refueling, but it did little to assuage King, who reminded Fletcher in another dispatch that the situation in that theater required "constant activity of a task force like yours to keep the enemy occupied. Requirements for [the] use of other task forces like yours make it necessary to continue your active operations south of the equator until your force can be relieved." De-

spite another message by Fletcher, attempting to clarify the situation further, the incident had sown seeds of doubt in King's mind about his far-distant subordinate's aggressiveness.

On 30 March, intelligence from Leary's planes pointed to the enemy's "definite move to the southward," indicating "considerable shipping . . . in the Shortland Islands area..." Fletcher started north, fully intending TF-17 to attack the Shortlands on 6 April. The Japanese, though, pulled out, leaving nothing but "two small schooners" in that area—hardly worth the effort. Thus left with "no worthwhile objectives" south

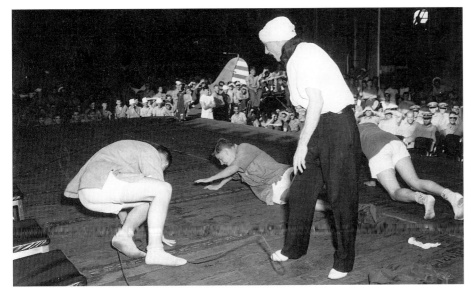

On the amidships elevator that serves as the stage for the show, "The Swami of Granby Street" (CEM Walter G. Fox, USN) has hypnotized three sailors into believing that they are swimming, much to the obvious delight of the officers and enlisted men watching this part of the "*Yorktown* Jamboree" on 10 April 1942. SBD in background (center) bears a black "S" on the fin, indicating the plane's assignment to Scouting Five. (80-G-12561)

Sea1c John E. Underwood of VF-42 serves the winners of the "Last T-Bone Steak in Captivity" during the *Yorktown* Jamboree on 10 April 1942. (80-G-12560)

While the *Yorktown* orchestra plays swing tunes, two sailors, Sea2c Pete Montalvo and F3c Sid Flum, do the "jumping jive." Note sailors ringing the open elevator pit and ringing the elevator itself; and airplanes triced up in the overhead, visible above the two men jitterbugging; these appears to be (from front to back) two SBD-3's and an F4F-3. (80-G-12559)

of Rabaul, Fletcher canceled the projected raid on the Shortlands on 4 April, and TF-17 resumed its routine of marching and countermarching across the Coral Sea.

The watchful waiting continued into the second week of April, and *Yorktown* began experiencing shortages of foodstuffs. LCDR Hamilton, the ship's chaplain, sought to alleviate the monotony of shipboard existence by staging a "Jamboree" on 10 April, auctioning off the last steak on board. Placed in a glass case the prized beef was borne by a mess attendant as part of an elaborate and colorful parade, guarded solemnly by four Marines with bayonet-tipped M-1 Garands. The winners of the auction sat at a table set upon the makeshift "stage"—no. 2 elevator, which had been lowered to within a few feet of the hangar deck—and a buxom "waitress" (a VF-42 sailor, John Underwood) served the winners. At other points in the program, *Yorktown*'s orchestra—acclaimed as the "best dance band in the fleet" by those men Bill Hipple talked to—performed swing tunes for the assembled crew, while

F3c Sid Flum and Sea2c Pete Montalvo did the "jumping jive." CEM Walter G. Fox, a *Yorktown* "plank owner," billed as the "Swami of Granby Street" and "Red Skelton's Brother" performed feats of hypnotism on volunteers from the audience.

It was all good fun, and the "Jamboree" left lasting and fond impressions in the minds of those who witnessed it or participated in its hi-jinks, but the realities of the lonely tedium of patrolling the Coral Sea soon intruded back into the *Yorktown*ers' lives.

For VF-42, their problems were becoming alarming. The rubber gasoline tanks of the F4F-3s (designed to be self-sealing in the event of a bullet's penetrating it) started deteriorating on 7 April in the aromatic gasoline being used in that theater. These "leak proof tanks . . . going sour" alarmed Fletcher. Reduced to only a dozen operational F4F-3s within a week, he radioed CINCPAC that if any more were incapacitated he would retired to the recently established "intermediate operating base" at Tongatabu, in the Tonga

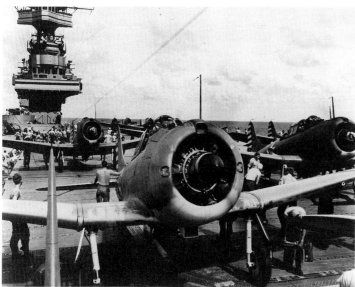

Left: Bombing Five SBD-3s spotted forward on the flight deck, during operations in the Coral Sea in April 1942. Note weathered paint finish and individual airplane number (3) on cowl; VS-5's planes carried their individual plane numbers on the leading edge of the wing. Both squadrons carried their plane numbers aft of the fuselage star as well. (NH 95571, via Naval Institute Photo Library)

Right: BOSN Chester E. Briggs, Jr., the *Yorktown*'s Air Department Boatswain, directs a just-landed TBD-1 during the ship's operations in the Coral Sea in April 1942, the "Devastator" having just returned from an antisubmarine sweep (two 325-pound depth charges are carried side-by-side beneath the plane's belly) and the hookman disengaging the plane's arrestor hook from the cross-deck pendant. (Author)

A very weathered SBD-3 of VS-5 gets the signal to take off, April 1942 in the Coral Sea. Note that plane 18 does not have a star beneath the port wing, and the difference in size of that insignia she carries beneath her starboard wing with that of the plane immediately behind her, the latter being much larger. BOSN C.E. Briggs, Jr., is identifiable at left (arms folded across his chest, behind the officer waving the plane off). (80-G-10152)

Islands. Happily, CINCPAC almost simultaneously ordered TF-17 to make for Tongatabu for "provisions and upkeep."

Fletcher's predicament thus solved, his force headed for the Tonga Islands, as ordered, and put into that port on the morning of 20 April, anchoring in Nukualofa Harbor shortly after noon. *Yorktown* with two F4Fs poised on her flight deck catapults, finding *Bridge* and the destroyer tender *Dobbin* (AD-3) awaiting them, the former with much-needed provisions and the latter with bombs for the carrier's air group. The next day, at 0600, *Bridge* commenced issuing provisions to *Yorktown* and the ships that had accompanied her, and for the remainder of the day carried out this vital revictualling task, issuing 578.3 tons of stores in 11 hours and 15 minutes. The cruisers *Astoria* and *Portland* each loaned the carrier one of their ship-unit SOCs for use as utility planes, while a small part of the air group, flown ashore, stayed at the airfield on Tongatabu, utilizing the facilities constructed by *Bridge*'s shipfitters and carpenter's mates. Two days later, *Walke* arrived with VF-42's eagerly awaited gasoline tanks.

There, too, a Consolidated PB2Y-2 "Coronado" of VP-13, the squadron flying a regular courier service between Pearl Harbor and Australia, touched down on the harbor on the morning of 24 April. Among the passengers who alighted from the big flying boat was LCDR James H. Flatley, Jr., whose personality and abilities far belied his diminutive stature, and who held orders to take over VF-42. His arrival surprised his USNA classmate Charley Fenton, who had been given the reins of command when Oscar Pederson became Air Group Commander with Curt Smiley's detachment. Flatley's orders were *bona fide*—Fenton's orders

detaching *him* from VF-42 had been routed to *Ranger*, the ship to which VF-42 had nominally been assigned, in the Atlantic! A flurry of dispatches soon followed to get to the bottom of the matter.

Curt Smiley bid farewell to the ship at Tongatabu, relieved as CYAG by "Swede" Pederson, as did Bill Hipple, his transportation completed. *Yorktown*ers enjoyed the respite at the South Sea isle which resembled, to at least one *Yorktown* officer, something right out of Nordhoff and Hall, but the sojourn was all too brief. By 22 April, ADM Nimitz believed, on the basis of intercepted message traffic, that the Japanese were planning a seaborne assault on the New Guinea area, directed at Port Moresby, at the end of April or the first week of May. To parry this thrust, CINCPAC had begun directing forces into the area.

Consequently, *Yorktown* weighed anchor at 0909 on 27 April and stood out, again bound for the Coral Sea. At the same time, TF-11, now under RADM Aubrey W. Fitch, a friend and classmate of Frank Jack Fletcher, was hastening toward the area, Fitch's flag in the recently refitted *Lexington*. Diverted to join TF-17, "Lady Lex"—now bristling with 1.1s that had replaced her 8-inch mounts—would arrive in *Yorktown*'s vicinity on 1 May, southwest of the New Hebrides. Their presence in the area was unknown to the Japanese.

Two days out of Nukualofa, *Yorktown* lowered her no. 3 motor launch at 0930 on 29 April, for the short trip over to *Sims*, which had come out from Suva with

Two Scouting Five SBD-3s pass low off *Yorktown*'s port side during operations in the Coral Sea in early April 1942, as seen from the photographer's vantage point between two VF-42 F4F-3s. The SBDs carry their individual plane numbers on the after fuselage (10 on the upper plane and 15 on the lower) while each plane carries a distinctive "S" on the fin. Markings are otherwise standard for this time period: red-centered stars in six positions, with 13 red and white stripes on the rudder. Size of underwing insignia differs, though, that on number 15 being almost full-chord. The F4F-3 markings are of interest, too. Contrast the 13 rudder stripes on plane no. 12 (R) with that of no. 10 on page 80; color scheme on the F4F at left features an overlap of the uppersurface color onto the lower wing at the leading edge, with the individual plane number (18) on the leading edge, outboard of the taped-over outer gunport. No numbers appear on the cowl, while the prop blades are natural metal with no warning stripes. Also note what appear to be painted-on gunports just outboard of the number (18), giving the impression of the plane mounting 4 guns in the wing! (80-G-16044)

nine ensigns on board for transfer to the carrier. Five were only embarking in *Yorktown* for transportation to *Lexington*; three held orders to VB-2; two to Scouting Two. All were on board and the launch hoisted by 0950. *Yorktown* soon worked up to 22 knots to resume her place in the cruising disposition, heading for her rendezvous with TF-11.

In the meantime, as Fletcher's flagship probed deeper into the Coral Sea, the task force formed around *Enterprise* and *Hornet* sailed from Pearl Harbor. Fletcher mapped out his battle plan—OpOrder No. 2-42—and divided up his force into three parts: an attack group (TG 17.2) under RADM Thomas C. Kinkaid in *Minneapolis* (CA-36); a support group (TG 17.6) consisting of two Australian cruisers, HMAS *Hobart* and HMAS *Australia*, and one American, *Chicago* (CA-29) and two destroyers under RADM John G. Crace, RN; and an air group (TG 17.5), consisting of *Yorktown*, *Lexington* and four destroyers, to be under RADM Fitch's command. Fletcher's objectives were well-defined: "To destroy enemy ships, shipping and aircraft at favorable opportunities" to check the enemy's advance into the "New Guinea-Solomon Areas." On 1 May, *Yorktown* fueled from *Neosho*.

In view of the impending showdown with the Japanese in the Coral Sea, CAPT Buckmaster attended to some urgent personnel matters. Feeling that *Yorktown*'s air group needed all of the experienced pilots it could get, he retained LCDR Flatley (who had received new orders to command the forming VF-10) in VF-42 as the squadron's XO, and kept LT(jg) Stanley W. Vejtasa and LT(jg) Faulkner (who had been directed to VS-10) in their old unit, Scouting Five. In addition, Buckmaster also retained the five ensigns slated to go to *Lexington* as replacement pilots; four—including ENS Davis E. Chaffee, A-V(N), USNR—went to VB-5; one went to Scouting Five.

Vejtasa figured in an event that transpired soon thereafter. Fletcher, unwilling to have to rely wholly on long-range, land-based aerial reconnaissance, had the carriers conduct daily search and patrol flights to augment the Australia-based Army planes operating from Darwin, Glencurry and Townsville, and Navy PBYs from Noumea, based on the tender *Tangier* (AV-8). One of *Yorktown*'s local flights turned up potential trouble.

At 1517 on 2 May, in the course of a patrol by two Scouting 5 SBDs, LT(jg) "Swede" Vejtasa, and his radioman, RM2c Leon Hall, spotted a wake, five miles away to starboard. It was *I-21*, four days out of Truk with orders to patrol off Noumea, travelling on the surface, with its deck awash, only 32 miles from the

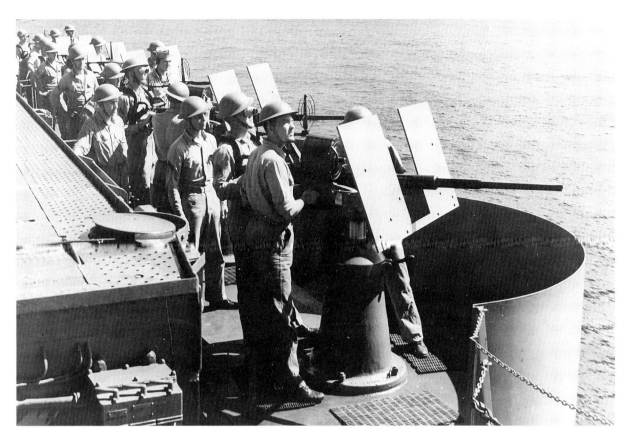

Marine-manned 20-mm. Oerlikon battery, located just aft of 5"/38 guns numbers two and four, responsible for Sector II of *Yorktown*'s AA defense (port bow). The gun assemblies are of the "mechanical mount" type, served by a crew of three (clockwise): the loader, who placed magazines on the gun and unshipped them when empty; the gunner (a sergeant in this case) who is strapped to the shoulder rests on the after end of the weapon, who elevated, trained and fired the gun; and the trunnion operator (obscured by the shield) who raised or lowered the column on which the gun was mounted. The Leathernecks appear to be wearing the M-1917A1 steel helmet. Note non-skid rubber matting on deck. (80-G-29129)

Peaceful view of the forward end of *Yorktown*'s island, *circa* April 1942. Visible are the forward 5"/38 cal. guns (L), with the outriggers deployed. The ship's CXAM "bedspring" radar antenna is turned at a right angle to the camera. (80-G-464630, Reilly)

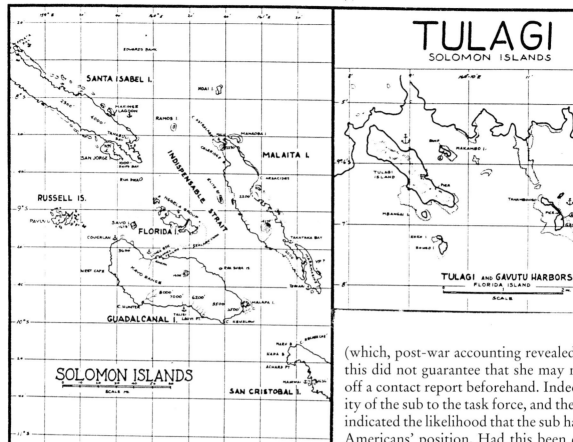

SOLOMON ISLANDS

TULAGI
SOLOMON ISLANDS

TULAGI and GAVUTU HARBORS
FLORIDA ISLAND
SCALE

task force. Evidently having spotted the planes, *I-21* dove, leaving a turbulent swirl in her wake. Vejtasa and his wingman, ENS H.N. Ervin, A-V(N), USNR, made three up-sun passes—determining the I-boat's probable course and speed—before returning to the carrier without breaking radio silence, to report the sighting by message drop, the weighted bean-bag plopping onto *Yorktown*'s deck at 1536.

At 1602, the carrier turned into the wind and launched three TBDs under LT(jg) Ellison, each plane carrying a pair of Mk.17 depth bombs, fused to explode at a 50 foot depth. Thirteen minutes later, Ellison spotted *I-21*, again on the surface, two or three miles away, and deployed his section to attack. Again the submarine frustrated the Americans by diving, and the three TBDs expended their ordnance to no avail. Soon, 11 SBDs were airborne from the carrier, each carrying a 500-pound depth charge with anti-submarine fuses. These scoured the area, but eventually returned to the ship, empty-handed, at 1825. CAPT Buckmaster optimistically concluded on the basis of the TBD pilots' reports that the submarine had been damaged or sunk.

Even if they had sunk the Japanese submarine

(which, post-war accounting revealed, they had *not*) this did not guarantee that she may not have gotten off a contact report beforehand. Indeed, the proximity of the sub to the task force, and the RDF bearings, indicated the likelihood that the sub had disclosed the Americans' position. Had this been done, the Japanese would have had the first "definite indication" of the American presence. As events turned out, however, the submarine captain only reported being attacked by planes—but not what kind. TF-17 continued on its way, on into the night, its existence unknown to the Japanese.

On 3 May, Fletcher refueled his destroyers from *Neosho*, as he prudently sought to have his ships "consistently kept in readiness for action on short notice" whenever they could take 500 barrels of fuel. He planned to top off the other ships the following morning, upon the rendezvous with the forces under Fitch and Crace. At 1900 that day (3 May), however, Fletcher received information from COMSOWESPAC (Leary), whose planes had spotted five or six ships off the south coast of Santa Isabel Island at 1700 the previous day, the vessels believed to be standing toward Tulagi, in the Solomon Islands. The same dispatch disclosed the presence of two Japanese ships off-loading at Tulagi.

As Fletcher put it, word of the Japanese landing operations proved "just the kind of report we had been waiting for two months to receive . . ." His prudent fueling operations now paid handsome dividends, enabling him to fight a strong force in TF-17—*Yorktown*, four heavy cruisers and six destroyers. Unable to wait for Fitch and Crace, Fletcher purpose-

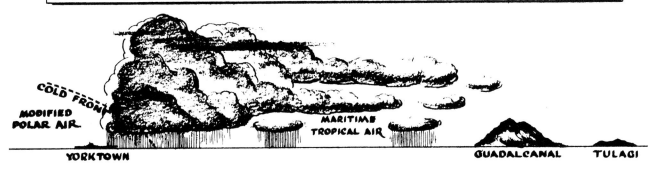

CROSS SECTION OF THE ATMOSPHERE, 1100 (-11) 4 MAY 1942

The skillful use of weather cloaked the approach of the *Yorktown* Air Group to Tulagi on 4 May. This drawing, extracted from the Naval War College Analysis of the Battle of the Coral Sea, shows the cloud cover enjoyed by *Yorktown*'s fliers as they headed toward Guadalcanal.

fully sped north, detaching *Russell* to guard *Neosho*, *Yorktown* proceeding at a pace calculated to take her within range to launch a strike at daybreak on the 4th. At 2100 on 3 May, Fletcher gave the order to attack the Japanese ships at Tulagi.

He could not have asked for better weather to cloak his approach. A frontal zone, extending east to west, covered the island of Guadalcanal and the area 70 miles to the south, effectively shielding the advancing TF-17 from prying eyes. At 0701, *Yorktown* began launching her air group, starting with a six-plane CAP over the task force. Joe Taylor's 12 TBDs came next; then 13 SBDs under Bill Burch; and 15 SBDs under Wally Short, who now had a squadron of his own. Each squadron proceeded on its separate way, to coordinate at their destination, through the squalls which blanketed the area ahead of them.

Scouting Five flew a sweep to the northward to see if any shipping was coming from that direction; Burch only saw a single ship—what looked to him like a destroyer—heading north, before he reached Tulagi, just in time to catch sight of the other two squadrons' arrival. From 20,000 feet, the Scouting Five commander saw what looked like three cargo ships in the harbor; at 0845 he divided his squadron into two divisions (one of six planes and the other of seven), assigning one ship to each division and directing Wally Short of Bombing Five to take the third.

At 0850, the first of Taylor's TBDs dropped down through the scattered cumulus clouds from over the lush green hills ringing the harbor, each plane with an Mk.XIII torpedo slung beneath its belly, set to run at a depth of 10 feet. Spreading out and descending to an altitude of 50 feet above the waves, three "Devastators" attacked the transport *Azumasan Maru* (the ship that had carried the "air base equipment" to Tulagi) but

scored no hits, two of the Mk.XIIIs churning past that vessel and exploding on the beach beyond. Seven TBDs then attacked a "nest" of ships—the large minelayer *Okinoshima* and the destroyers *Yūzuki* and *Kikuzuki* and, the pilots reported, of the six torpedoes released, three made hits on what looked like a "light cruiser," but which was, in fact, *Kikuzuki*. However, one of the

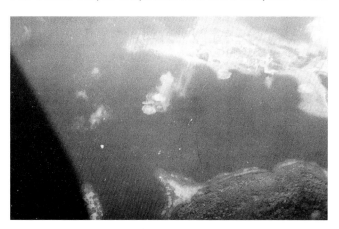

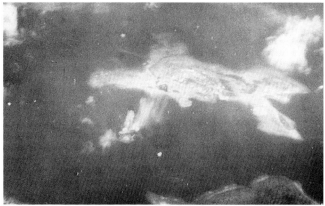

Bombs straddle *Koei Maru* off Tulagi on the morning of 4 May 1942. Incredible as it may seem, the ship was able to get underway and escape; *Yorktown* pilots counted five near misses around this particular vessel. (80-G-20532 [upper]; 80-G-20533 [lower]).

87

Bomb crutches empty, Douglas SBDs of *Yorktown*'s air group head back to the ship after a strike on Tulagi harbor on 4 May 1942. Note thick cloud cover. (80-G-20515)

pilots in this group of seven could not release his "fish" and had to retire with it still hanging beneath the plane. The last two planes of VT-5 claimed two hits on a cargo ship (*Koei Maru*). Having completed their runs, the TBDs headed back to the carrier. While they had encountered "heavy" anti-aircraft fire from all ships in the harbor that had guns to shoot with, only one of their number—5-T-11 (BuNo 0286), flown by ENS George E. Bottjer, A-V(N), USNR, took any hits.

As Torpedo Five began their attack runs, and then released their Mk.XIII's at four to five hundred yards out, Bill Burch was leading Scouting Five down over the harbor. Coming down from 20,000 feet, and the cold air prevailing at that altitude, the SBDs hit a layer of moister, warmer air, that fogged the windshields and telescopic sights and forced Burch and his pilots to adopt a less satisfactory method. As he put it later: "It is like putting a white sheet in front of you and you have to bomb from memory. If you start down, watching anti-aircraft fire, with your sight well fixed, and then hit 8,000 feet and somebody puts a sheet in front of you, you feel sort of bad about it. You try to stick your head out over the side of the cockpit, and aim down the side of the target ship. That's not very accurate bombing."

Nevertheless, Scouting Five claimed four "sure" hits and one "probable" of the 13 bombs dropped, knocking apart the "nest" which contained *Kikuzuki*.

Wally Short quickly parceled out the targets for his pilots and divided VB-5 into three five-plane sec-

tions. At 0900, the first division attacked what looked like a cargo vessel (*Tama Maru*) but scored no hits "and no misses closer than 30 feet." Short then spotted a Mitsubishi F1M2 from *Kiyokawa Maru*'s detachment, piloted by Sea1c Fugawa Kijiro, attempting to get airborne from off Makambo Island, and splashed him forthwith.

The second division of VB-5, meanwhile, pushed over from between ten and eleven-thousand feet and attacked what looked like a "large seaplane tender"—but what was actually the large minelayer *Okinoshima*—as she got underway and attempted to clear the harbor. They claimed one hit and "several near misses." The third division divided up: one group (three planes) headed for *Okinoshima*, claiming one sure hit and one possible of the three 1,000-pounders dropped. The other two SBDs attacked *Tama Maru* and the destroyer *Yūzuki*, but failed to score any hits.

The Japanese had been at work unloading their ships for nearly an hour when the *Yorktown* air group showed up to begin its task of interrupting the enemy's latest consolidation of his beachhead, and the dramatic arrival of the planes bearing the red-centered blue and white stars triggered euphoria among the watching Solomon Islanders. The beating of a signal drum at the coast-watching station at Aola, on the north coast of Guadalcanal, soon accompanied the dull booming of explosions and the staccato hammering of machine gun fire, summoning the harried coastwatchers to see the invaders getting their come-uppance!

Yorktown's air group then returned to their ship, intact, the first plane coming on board at 1001. Re-arming and gassing the planes proceeded swiftly; more 1,000-pound bombs and torpedoes came up from the magazines, were trundled across the deck and shackled beneath the bellies of the SBDs and TBDs, respectively; more belts of ammunition for the fixed guns. The speed at which the re-arming crews turned to their tasks impressed Bill Burch, as he later observed (perhaps with slight exaggeration) he hadn't even had time to "get a cup of coffee" during the comparatively short time he was on board.

CAPT Buckmaster turned *Yorktown* into the wind a little over an hour after the first planes had returned from the first strike; at 1106, Wally Short led Bombing Five's SBDs off for the second attack on Tulagi; followed at 1134 by Scouting Five and Torpedo Five at 1150, the last-named squadron now taking only eleven planes due to the damage suffered by 5-T-11 on the first raid.

Each squadron proceeded independently of the other, the SBDs scouting ahead to the west and northwest of Tulagi to report targets for the TBDs but being hampered in their mission by the SBDs' poor radio performance—incident to too-long periods of disuse while operating under strict radio silence. As *Yorktown*'s planes began arriving, they saw *Azumasan Maru* where they had left her, earlier, with *Koei Maru* standing out; a destroyer (*Kikuzuki*) had been beached. The SBDs scouting to the northwest noted *Okinoshima* and a destroyer (*Yūzuki*) heading in a northwesterly direction, and a column of three "gunboats" (actually minesweepers), northeast of Savo Island, heading west.

VS-5 began attacking the fleeing *Okinoshima* at 1240, and claimed "two sure hits and one probable" with its 1,000-pounders. "Heavy and accurate" anti-aircraft fire, however, damaged two planes. PO1c Kurazawa Takashi tried to intercept the *Yorktowners* but Sealc Lovelace M. Broussard, "Swede" Vejtasa's radio-gunner, splashed the second *Kiyokawa Maru* machine. Their bombs gone, Scouting Five turned-to

LT(jg) William N. Leonard of VF-42 (seen here at NAS Kaneohe, May 1942), encountering Mitsubishi F1M2 type 00 observation seaplanes in combat over Tulagi, sketched the strange planes from memory when he returned to *Yorktown*; his drawing proved remarkably accurate. (Photo: Leonard; drawing: Enclosure E to CO, USS *Yorktown* 054 of 11 May 1942; insets: author)

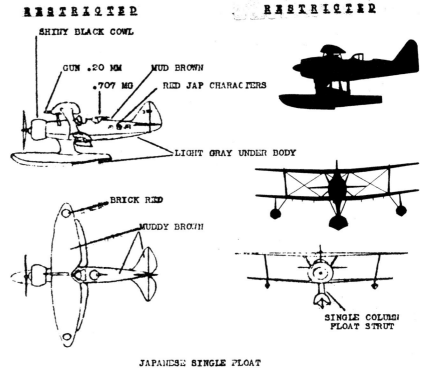

RESTRICTED   RESTRICTED

SHINY BLACK COWL

GUN .20 MM   MUD BROWN

.707 MG   RED JAP CHARACTERS

LIGHT GRAY UNDER BODY

BRICK RED

MUDDY BROWN

SINGLE COLUMN FLOAT STRUT

JAPANESE SINGLE FLOAT

FIGHTER ENCOUNTERED OVER TULAGI BY VF-42

AIRCRAFT, 1430, 4 MAY, 1942.

Drawn from memory by:

Lieut(jg) Leonard, USN.

Enclosure (E).

and strafed small launches in Tulagi Harbor, sinking "several" and damaging "some."

Torpedo Five split into two divisions. The first, of six planes, attacked *Okinoshima* (believing her to be a "heavy cruiser") from off her starboard bow, starting their approach from 10,000 yards out. The large mine-layer brought all of her anti-aircraft guns that could do so to bear on the TBDs as they charged through the heavy fire; *Okinoshima* increased speed and began turning to starboard. The TBDs closed to two to three thousand yards, at which time they released their torpedoes, but scored no hits. A Nakajima E8N from *Kiyokawa Maru*'s detachment attempted to intercept VT-5's first division, but the TBD gunners "chased him back to harbor" and scored damage that prompted the intrepid pilot to land off Makambo Island, covered by shore-based anti-aircraft guns.

The second division then attacked five minutes after the first, going after the same "heavy cruiser," and closed the range still further in hopes of getting a hit. *Okinoshima* dodged all five torpedoes from this group, too, turning to port and evading the Mk.XIIIs dropped from 1,000 to 1,500 yards away, all the while keeping up a steady anti-aircraft fire.

Both sections of Torpedo Five then strafed small launches in Tulagi Harbor, with "indeterminate" results, before the squadron rendezvoused for the return flight to *Yorktown*. As they left the area, though, one plane, flown by LT Leonard E. Ewoldt, became separated from the rest of the squadron.

Bombing Five, meanwhile, after scouting to the west and northwest of Florida Island, sighted a trio of what they identified as "gunboats" five miles east-northeast of Savo Island. The first division—five planes—attacked the "gunboat" bringing up the rear and destroyed her. "One direct hit" with a 1,000-pound bomb not surprisingly "blew the ship to pieces" and three close misses shot up geysers of water around her.

The second division shifted their sights to the second craft in column and repeated the accuracy that had destroyed the first; another direct hit blew her to atoms. The third division attacked the lead craft, which, seeing the disaster that had befallen the other two astern, executed evasive tactics, turning sharply to avoid the bombs; three 1,000-pounders splashed around the fleeing vessel, as she escaped. The fourth plane in the last division then set his sights on the nearby *Okinoshima*, his bomb hitting "close aboard within 20 feet of the forecastle, port side." The first and second divisions then strafed the last "gunboat," leaving her "in a sinking condition" near Vatilau Island. Japanese records revealed the destroyed pair to have been converted trawlers, the

auxiliary minesweeper *Wa 1* and *Wa 2*. Later in the war, targets such as these would have called for the expenditure of only a 5-inch rocket.

The report of Japanese seaplanes attacking planes of VB-5 and VT-5 prompted the quick scramble of four F4F-3s of VF-42, led by LT(jg) William N. Leonard, at 1340. ENS Bassett flew as Leonard's wingman, while LT(jg) McCuskey (section leader) and ENS Adams made up the second section. They proceeded directly to Tulagi, intently scanning the skies over that island for signs of the reported enemy planes. Finding none, they continued on a northwesterly course, following the coast of Florida Island until Leonard and Bassett, flying at 4,000 feet, spotted three single-float seaplanes flying in a loose formation 2,500 feet below them, northwest of Tulagi. Leonard picked the second, pushed over and attacked.

WO Kageyama, however, flying an F1M2 from *Kamikawa Maru*'s detachment, boldly pulled up and came straight at him. Leonard's .50-calibers chattered simultaneously in reply, and Kageyama pulled up, straining for altitude, but, apparently mortally wounded, abruptly dived into the water.

At about this time, the third plane in formation entered the battle, and ENS Bassett engaged him in a sharp dogfight. Leonard, seeing his own victim crash into the waters below, suddenly found that the other Japanese floatplane had come around and secured an advantageous position on his tail! In a tight turn, though, the enemy pilot could not effectively bring his guns to bear, and Leonard applied full power, his F4F-3 pulling away from the surprisingly nimble floatplane. "From a safe distance," Leonard then initiated a second attack on his worthy antagonist who, like the first, soon confronted him with the sight of an opponent growing larger in his gunsight, head-on. Both planes fired, but the heavier .50-calibers hammered at the floatplane with telling effect; the enemy plane "ducked under, pulled up, began emitting white vapor, and then suddenly dived into the water." While Leonard had been shooting down the *Kamikawa Maru* F1M2 flown by WO Uemura, Bassett's quarry escaped over Tulagi.

Leonard then grouped his four F4Fs near the destroyer they had seen near Tulagi, making knots in a northwesterly direction, and ordered a strafing attack. Identifying their target as a "new two (2) stack destroyer . . . of the *Asasio* [sic] class" (but actually the considerably older *Yūzuki*), Leonard, Bassett, McCuskey and Adams pressed home their attacks vigorously: "two runs from astern down the fore and aft axis of the ship, then two runs from abeam, with the point of aim for the first at the waterline, and for the

Seen through wisps of cloud, the Japanese destroyer *Yūzuki* attempts to flee Tulagi during the *Yorktown* air group attack on 4 May 1942. Successful as she appears to be in evading destruction, four VF-42 F4F-3s later carried out a devastating low-level strafing attack, killing her commanding officer and nine other men, and wounding 20. (80-G-20540)

second on the bridge." Intermittent anti-aircraft fire greeted the first two runs before the strafing—carried out from 3500 feet down to 150 or 200 feet away from the ship—seemed to silence the guns. The F4Fs' tracers appeared to start fires on deck; their bullets evidently holed a fuel tank for, after the first strafing run "a thick, brown oil slick developed," marking the ship's track. When the four F4Fs of VF-42 broke off their attacks, *Yūzuki* continued on her way, but having suffered LCDR Tachibana Hirota, her captain, and nine other men dead, and 20 wounded.

At about the same time the four VF-42 "Wildcats" were dogfighting floatplanes over Tulagi and strafing *Yūzuki*, *Yorktown* was turning into the wind to launch the third strike—this one only composed of SBDs from VS-5 and VB-5. Upon arrival over Tulagi, the VS-5 pilots saw *Azumasan Maru* and "a number" of launches in the harbor; at 1530, the first SBDs pushed over at 9,000 feet, making their dives from down wind at 70 degrees. Encountering "light and inaccurate" anti-aircraft fire from the ship, Scouting Five claimed one hit and "several near misses" before strafing several launches and a "gunboat."

The paucity of targets confronted VB-5, too. They ignored *Koei Maru*, about five miles northeast of Savo Island, and a beached "gunboat" off Vatilau Island—the same one they had bombed and strafed earlier, during the second attack—before they saw an oil slick. Bombing Five's SBDs then followed the slick to its source—*Yūzuki*—but left her alone in favor of bigger game, *Okinoshima*.

At 1545, Bombing Five's first division pushed over, attacking *Okinoshima* from the west; the second division then attacked from the south. Two of the nine

bombs dropped "landed very close" to the target, and the remainder within 50 yards, and their quarry appeared to slow down, putting up only a "weak and inaccurate" anti-aircraft fire in her own defense. Her sharp maneuvers to avoid the bombs, though, had saved her once again, and she remained afloat, though damaged.

While all of these events were unfolding during the third attack, LT Ewoldt of VT-5 was facing an unenviable predicament. Having gotten separated from the rest of the squadron after they had finished their attack on *Okinoshima*, he had attempted to form up with returning planes but couldn't catch them, and lost them in the clouds blanketing the area. Plagued by a bad radio—it could send but not receive—the pilot couldn't find *Yorktown* and after groping around the clouds, his fuel supply dwindling to zero, he decided to "ditch," radioing word of this at 1605.

After a perfect water landing, Ewoldt scrambled from the cockpit to help his radioman, RM3c Raymond A. Machalinski, break out the raft, as the "Devastator"—not equipped with flotation gear—rose and fell in the swells 40 miles off Guadalcanal, rapidly filling with water. They had no sooner broken out the rubber boat when the TBD suddenly lurched down by the nose, tossing Ewoldt and Machalinski into the sea, not only before they had time to inflate the boat but before they could extract the emergency rations from the plane. It was a struggle, but eventually they managed to inflate the boat and climb in; Ewoldt figured the current was taking them toward Australia.

Ewoldt and Machalinski, though, were not the only men from *Yorktown*'s air group in trouble. LT(jg) McCuskey and ENS Adams of VF-42 were in some of their own. McCuskey, lost, elected to land at Cape

91

Henslow, on the south coast of Guadalcanal, unaware that Adams knew the way back to the ship. Adams, his wingman, stayed loyally with him, landing there, too. Both planes were out of fuel. Greeted cautiously but in friendly fashion by the local natives, the two pilots set up housekeeping.

At 1640, shortly before the first of Bombing Five's planes, returning from the third strike, began landing on board *Yorktown*, RADM Fletcher ordered *Hammann*, CDR Arnold E. True in command, to proceed north to Guadalcanal to attempt the rescue of the two VF-42 pilots, 42 miles away. If *Hammann* could not find the men, she was to rejoin the task force at a point 325 miles south of Cape Henslow. Fletcher also detached *Perkins* (DD-377) to try and locate the TBD crew.

Hammann consequently steamed north at her best speed, 30 knots, and arrived less than two hours later. She closed the beach and reconnoitered until, at 1810, the destroyermen spotted a small patch of white—a tent fashioned from a parachute—against the dark background of the jungle, near the beach, two miles east of the cape. As the ship edged as close as she dared to the strange coastline, she spotted both of the planes. At 1820, *Hammann* put a motor whaleboat over the side with a crew of five men, under 25-year-old ENS Robert P.F. Enright, USNR.

Enright soon discovered, as his boat neared the uncharted shore at dusk, that they could only approach to within 150 yards of the beach. Heavy breakers rendered a landing impossible. Seeing that the boat could come no closer, McCuskey and Adams set out seaward in their rubber boats, only to be thrown back by the thundering surf. COX George W. Kapp, Jr., perceiving their predicament, then took a line and plunged into the water, swimming to a point where both pilots could reach him, and the men in the boat soon pulled rescuer and rescued out to them.

However, the pilots then told the boat officer, Enright, that they had not been able to destroy their planes, although they *had* managed to destroy "confidential gear" (the ZB homing device in McCuskey's plane). Having been instructed to destroy the aircraft, Enright attempted to do so with small arms fire which, from 150 yards in a bobbing whaleboat, in gathering darkness, did not work. McCuskey then volunteered to take pyrotechnic material ashore and try it himself. He struck out for the shore, but became entangled in the line; freeing himself, he continued on through the breakers to gain the beach, unaware that the line he had cast off had fouled the boat propeller. BM2c Albert S. Jason dove in, and,

with hacksaw and knife, managed to clear the screw, but not before the boat had drifted down the strand, away from where McCuskey had landed. Worn out by the strenuous exertion, meanwhile, McCuskey had collapsed on the beach.

A half-hour passed as the rain-pelted men in the boat anxiously scanned the shore through the squalls. Finally, Enright, Adams, and the enlisted men, saw a Very's star arcing into the sky. COX Kapp, for the second time, plunged into the water and headed toward the shore, but had to abandon the attempt, being dragged, nearly exhausted, into the boat. Jason, though, although tired from his exertions in unfouling the boat propeller a short time before, nevertheless took a line and struck out for the beach.

McCuskey and Jason then tried, unsuccessfully, to set fire to the planes, but abandoned any further attempts "in view of the need for haste" and made their way back to the boat through the pounding breakers. Ultimately, the odyssey over, the whaleboat reached *Hammann*'s side at 2118, almost three hours after it had set out on its rescue mission.

CDR True attributed the finding and recovery of McCuskey and Adams to a "succession of most fortunate circumstances," and commended the "skill and judgment with which the boat was handled by Ensign Enright." *Hammann*'s commander also praised, lavishly, the two enlisted men who had risked their lives in the "heavy surf on an unknown shore in complete darkness and rain." Without *their* courageous and continued efforts, the rescue of the two pilots "would probably not have been effected." The next day, their maladies probably induced by exhaustion and exposure, Kapp and Jason were placed on the sick list with catarrhal fever.

Although *Perkins* returned to the task force not having found LT Ewoldt and RM3c Machalinski, the two men she had been seeking were very much alive and well. They drifted for three days in their rubber boat, subsisting on rainwater gleaned from passing squalls, and were scrutinized and left ("they saw our condition was bad," Machalinski surmised later, "and were sure we had plenty of sharks for company") by what was most likely Japanese destroyer *Ariake* on 7 May. The two *Yorktown*ers then paddled to Guadalcanal; met by "natives with pierced noses and filed teeth," Ewoldt and Machalinski received fine treatment from missionaries and coastwatchers and eventually sailed for Efate, New Hebrides, in a 45-foot schooner with a seven-man Chinese crew. After an eleven-day voyage, they fell in with destroyer *Paul Jones* (DD-230), and ultimately returned to Pearl!

CHAPTER 6

Scratch One Flat-top

B Y THE ACCOUNTING of *Yorktown*'s aircrews, the three raids on Tulagi had netted a handsome "bag": two destroyers, a light cruiser, a cargo ship, and four gunboats sunk; a destroyer, a heavy cruiser, a cargo ship, and an aircraft tender damaged. Four floatplanes had been destroyed. The *actual* bag, however, was far less impressive, considering the prodigious expenditure of 22 torpedoes and 76 1,000-pound bombs, and 12,570 rounds of .50 caliber and 7,095 rounds of .30 caliber ammunition: destroyer *Kikuzuki*, three minecraft, and four barges sunk, and varying degrees of damage inflicted on *Yūzuki*, *Okinoshima*, *Azumasan Maru*, and *Koei Maru*. The raids had only cost damage to six SBDs and two TBDs; one TBD and two F4Fs had been lost.

From a practical standpoint, the Tulagi raids had provided *Yorktown*ers with invaluable refresher training and combat experience, something that there had been little time for since 10 March. However, the raids also provided the Japanese with the first definite indication of an American presence in the region, and it soon became obvious, from the enemy's efforts to find the carrier force whence the raiders had come on 4 May, that the *Yorktown*ers had bestirred a proverbial hornet's nest.

ADM Nimitz' estimate of the situation, based on the careful analysis of the intelligence available to him and his staff, that had led to the dispatch of *Yorktown* and *Lexington* to the Coral Sea, was proving correct: the Japanese were at sea in considerable force, having put in motion Operation "MO," an attempt to take Port Moresby. Eleven troopships, covered by the small carrier *Shōhō* (whose air unit consisted of 13 Mitsubishi A5M4 Type 96 and A6M2 Type 00 *kansen*s and six Nakajima B5N2 Type 97 *kankō*s), four heavy cruisers and one destroyer. Another task force, formed around fleet carriers *Shōkaku* and *Zuikaku*, with a screen of heavy cruisers and destroyers, steamed close enough to the invasion force to support it.

At 0808 on 5 May, a patrolling SBD sighted a submarine—one of four that had cleared Truk on 30 April—only 150 miles from the task force. Three TBDs, however, armed with depth bombs, sent in search of the submersible, could not find him. More trouble, though, loomed within a half-hour. On her way back to the task force with McCuskey and Adams embarked, *Hammann* spotted a Japanese flying boat in the distance.

Yorktown's CXAM picked up an aircraft only 25 miles distant at 0825, and the carrier launched two sections of F4F-3s, led by LT McCormack, to investigate. They proceeded out on the bearing given them, 275°, for the 25 miles, when the leader spotted their quarry two miles away on the starboard beam. As McCormack swung his F4F around to investigate, the others—LT(jg) Arthur J. Brassfield, ENS Haas, and LT(jg) Edward D. Mattson—fell in astern. As he drew nearer, McCormack discerned twin rudders . . . four engines . . . and the unmistakable red markings on the wings and fuselage—a Kawanishi Type 97 flying boat (a type of plane with which the *Yorktown*ers were becoming quite familiar) from the detachment of the Yokohama *Kōkūtai* based at Tulagi.

Since the section leader's inspection had carried him over the enemy plane, the honor of making the first attack went to Brassfield—the former Missouri school superintendent—the next pilot astern. As McCormack turned to parallel the Kawanishi's course, Brassfield "attacked from above and forward of the starboard beam," lacing his tracers into the flying boat. McCormack then started down from the port beam in a 60-degree dive, and depressed the trigger, his four .50-calibers hurling a lethal dose of metal into the Type 97's big wing. The flight leader maintained his firing

93

run, marveling at how slowly the majestic plane moved across ahead of him as his tracers struck home.

McCormack carried out his attack as close as he dared, and then sharply pulled out above the Kawanishi. He glanced over his shoulder and noted smoke pouring from two of the four engines. ENS Haas then made his pass, his .50-calibers hammering home, from the same angle McCormack had chosen. Just as Haas completed his attack, though, the Type 97, all four of its engines now smoking, "nosed over sharply into about a 20° glide." LT(jg) Mattson was about to make his first attack, and Brassfield his second, before the latter pulled up short, the flying boat obviously doomed. Afire "all along the center wing section and seemingly throughout the inside of the fuselage," the Kawanishi continued in the glide straight into the sea, exploding upon impact; "a huge column of flame and smoke shot up and continued for some time," after which only small bits of wreckage remained floating in the Coral Sea. There had been no parachutes; no return fire.

The whole encounter, McCormack later reported, had "lasted barely thirty seconds." There had been no time to send out a contact report—the Japanese would still not know where TF-17 was. Fletcher, though, could not be sure that his great good fortune at remaining undetected still held, and deliberated upon how best to carry out his plans.

While Fletcher mulled over the best course of action to take, and a little over an hour after *Yorktown*'s planes had dealt with the latest "snooper," *Neosho* rejoined TF-17 at 0932 on the 5th, and as the ship steamed slowly on a southeasterly course, fueled *Astoria* and then *Yorktown*.

On board the carrier, a small group of men was planning to leave. CM Uriel H. Leach bade farewell to the ship that had been his "home" since she'd been commissioned; APC Arthur H. Walton, too, soon made the precarious trip in the bosun's chair to the oiler alongside, as did ACMM(PA) Kenneth T. Woodruff, who, like Leach, was a *Yorktown* "plank owner." There were four others: ACRM(PA) Harrison S. Nobbs—long the radioman for VT-5's skipper, LCDR Taylor; RM1c George H. Mansfield, detached from VB-5; BKR3c

RM1c George H. Mansfield, one of the seven men transferred from *Yorktown* to *Neosho* on 5 May 1942, held orders directing him to report to NAS Pensacola, to take flight training to become a pilot. (USN)

Leonard Q. Smith and SK3 Charles H. Tyler. As Tyler took departure from the storekeepers' "gang," he shook hands all around, while his shipmates "told him how lucky he was, and that we would like to trade places with him." Once these men were embarked, and *Yorktown* had topped off her bunkers, *Neosho* then resumed her place in the cruising disposition.

Fletcher's tactical dispositions for TF-17 were nearly ready by day's end on 5 May. He considered sending either Kinkaid's attack force or Crace's support group (or both) to attack enemy shipping (at day or night as opportunity offered." He contemplated shifting his flag to a cruiser to lead the attack himself, leaving his classmate "Jake" Fitch in command of the air group, but demurred when faced with the "entirely inadequate" communication and administrative facilities prevailing in that course of action. For the remainder of 5 May, all of Fletcher's forces available to him—TF-17, TF-11 and TF-44 (Crace's support group) steamed within visual signalling distance of each other, a goodly company of combatants, girded for battle.

Having gathered all of the forces under his tactical command, Fletcher now began to implement his operation order: at 0625 on 7 May, he detached Crace's support group to intercept any Japanese movement through the Louisiade Archipelago. TF-17 then proceeded warily northward, skirting the edge of a frontal zone, hunting for the enemy; at 0700 Fletcher placed OpOrder 2-42 in effect. He also detached *Neosho*, with *Sims* to escort her, to one of the prearranged fueling rendezvous points, her presence with the task force not immediately required.

Fletcher's adversary, VADM Takagi Takeo, commanding the 5th Carrier Division (*Zuikaku* and *Shōkaku*), did not like the situation in which he found himself on 7 May. For the previous two days, his force had been marking time, marching and countermarching, Takagi relying upon cruiser-based reconnaissance floatplanes and land-based aircraft to carry out searches unaware that a Rabaul-based flying boat had spotted TF-17 at mid-morning on the 6th. Such were the communication difficulties plaguing the enemy

Oiler *Neosho* (AO-23) fuels *Yorktown* on 1 May 1942; a similar scene took place four days later as the former, in addition to fueling the flattop, received passengers from the carrier; note rough water between the two ships. (80-G-464653)

that Takagi did not learn of this intelligence until the next day! On the morning of the 7th, one of his search planes, apparently standing off from a distance so as not to be intercepted and shot down—a common fate that had befallen other snoopers—spotted *Neosho* and *Sims*, which became, due to the distance, a carrier and an escorting cruiser. Takagi, elated at his good fortune, ordered a "full out attack"—36 Aichi D3A1 Type 99 carrier bombers ("Val") and 24 Nakajima B5N2 Type 97 carrier attack planes ("Kate"), escorted by 18 *kansens* (A6M2 Type 00 fighters), took off from *Zuikaku* and *Shōkaku*, commencing at 0815.

Upon arrival over the target, however, the Japanese pilots discovered that the "carrier" and "cruiser" were in fact an oiler and a destroyer. Wisely withholding torpedoes, the Japanese ravaged the two ships with dive bombers only; three bombs out of the four dropped against her struck *Sims* in swift succession. Seven bombs ripped into *Neosho*, while eight churned up the sea close aboard, and one Type 99 dive bomber crashed the oiler aft. Four *Yorktown*ers would perish in *Neosho*'s travail—Nobbs, Mansfield, Smith and Tyler.

Although depriving Fletcher of an invaluable auxiliary, as well as sinking the destroyer with her, it appeared that the Japanese had unwittingly tipped their hand, and lost the chance to surprise TF-17. However, fortune still smiled at them, for *Neosho*'s report of her plight, received on board *Yorktown* at 1051, only mentioned her being attacked by aircraft—but not what *kind* (land-based or carrier-based?).

Fletcher, not knowing where Takagi's force was, had ordered a search sent aloft at first light on the 7th, to search an arc of 120°; embracing the Louisiade Archipelago and the Coral Sea to the north and east of the Louisiades. Bad weather caused one of the scouts to return to the ship, but two of the carrier's planes encountered Japanese aircraft engaged in similar missions.

LT John L. Nielsen, flying 5-B-2, came across a floatplane that looked like a "Type 97" (carrier attack plane) with floats: it proved to be an Aichi E13A Type 00 seaplane ("Jake") from seaplane carrier *Kamikawa Maru*. Nielsen spotted the strange plane at 0815 in the course of his search. LT(jg) Ogata Eiichi, the pilot and plane commander, unhesitatingly engaged Nielsen, who climbed and turned toward his bold adversary, making one pass from above with his fixed guns before he made a diving turn. Ogata turned toward Nielsen as the latter climbed, but unwittingly set himself up for the SBD to make a high-side approach. Nielsen opened fire with his fixed .50-calibers, his bullets "going directly into the forward cockpit" of the Type 00 before the *Yorktown* pilot broke away with only 15 yards to spare to avoid a collision. The twin-float Aichi spiraled down, out of control, and exploded on impact off Misima Island, killing Ogata and his crew. Shortly thereafter, ENS Lavell M. Bigelow, A-V(N), USNR, in 5-B-12, sighted an E13A from heavy cruiser *Furutaka*, commanded by the observer, WO Matsumoto Chuichi, and after a few minutes of dogfighting and avoiding the return fire from Matsumoto's gunner, shot him down, too.

Soon after Nielsen had eliminated his Aichi, he spotted six Japanese ships and promptly got to work encoding the contact report for his radioman to send back to the ship. In so doing, however, the system of pegs and holes necessary to enable him to report what he had seen had not been aligned properly. On board *Yorktown*, his coded report, when decrypted, disclosed the presence of two carriers and four cruisers. Elated at having found the Japanese carriers he was seeking, Fletcher immediately ordered *Yorktown* and *Lexington* to launch strike groups to attack the enemy formation reportedly 225 miles to the northwestward. Blanketed by the towering clouds of an almost stationary frontal zone extending some 100 miles from east to west (the same cloud cover that had furnished such an effective cloak to *Yorktown*'s approach to Tulagi on the 4th), both American carriers launched planes: 50 from "Lady Lex" and 43 from *Yorktown*, Fletcher certain that the ships his scout had spotted were two of the three carriers he knew to be in the area. By 1030 all had formed up and were heading for the enemy—their take-off duly reported by a "snooper" from *Kinugasa*.

Only a short time before, however, COMSOWESPAC replayed an earlier sighting report, by an Australia-based B-17, of a force consisting of one aircraft carrier, ten transports and 15 other vessels of an unidentified type. This report did not reach Fletcher until after the strike groups had been briefed and had left on their mission. Quick work on the charts showed the reported position from the B-17 as some 60 miles south of the one given by LT Nielsen in 5-B-2. Were these forces, when combined, the sought-after enemy carrier group? The monitoring of Japanese radio traffic, however, revealed that the 5th Carrier Division was not a part of the immediate Port Moresby occupation force.

LT John L. ("Johnnie") Nielsen (seen here as ENS at NAS Pensacola, 27 February 1940) had served for almost two years as an enlisted man before attending the USNA. Although Nielsen, the eldest of five sons of a minister, "caught hell" for his inadvertently erroneous sighting report on 7 May, his heroism in the carrier action the following day earned him the Navy Cross. (Author)

The recovery of the search group soon dispelled the mystery, as Nielsen explained that he had sighted two *cruisers* and four *destroyers*—not two carriers and four cruisers! The revelation of Nielsen's error—for which he "caught hell"—prompted swift rectification. *Yorktown* radioed the corrected composition of the enemy force in plain language. "We could have gotten along with this," LCDR Flatley later complained, "and it undoubtedly warned the enemy of our appearance eliminating the element of surprise." He was unaware that a *Kinugasa* snooper, lingering near TF-17, had already reported the strike group's departure!

While *Yorktown*'s and *Lexington*'s respective groups were en route to their new target, a Kawanishi flying boat showed up, lurking near TF-17. *Yorktown*'s CXAM picked up the Type 97, though, and the ship vectored out two F4F-3s, flown by LT(jg)

Richard G. Crommelin and ENS Wright to intercept. After flying by instruments for the first eight miles, Crommelin and his wingman broke through the clouds and saw their quarry seven miles away, "flying at about 1,500 feet, skirting the scattered clouds." The flying boat, evidently having spotted her pursuers, then turned and headed for shelter, but not before Crommelin and Wright had each managed to carry out one firing pass, each answered by the Kawanishi's gunners.

The three planes then played a deadly game of hide-and-seek. Although Crommelin lost sight of Wright, and the Type 97, several times, he fired short bursts whenever the enemy came within his sights. Crommelin attempted persistently to locate the flying boat until, finally, "the enemy plane . . . made the mistake of getting out into the open again." He attacked from above and on the Kawanishi's port beam, his wingman from above and from the rear. Early in this simultaneous attack, the Type 97 "exploded and plunged into the water in flames from an altitude of about 1,000 feet." Again, there were no parachutes.

In the meantime, while Crommelin and Wright were relentlessly hounding the flying boat to his doom, the *Yorktown* and *Lexington* strike groups found their objective. *Lexington*'s planes, arriving first, sighted *Shōhō*, loosely screened by the heavy cruisers *Kako*, *Aoba*, *Furutaka* and *Kinugasa*, and the destroyer *Sazanami*, north of Misima. In contrast to the weather over their own task force, TF-17's fliers found bright sunshine and unlimited visibility, the Japanese warships arrayed like toy ships on a bright blue board; their white wakes stood out vividly from a good distance away and betrayed the enemy's presence.

While it appears now that both strike groups from the American carriers conducted their attacks almost simultaneously, each side unaware of the other's presence in the excitement and confusion of battle, it did not seem that way at the time. *Lexington*'s three squadrons, VS-2, VB-2, and VT-2, pushed over or swept in while the screen appeared to draw away from the carrier. The cruisers fired everything from their eight-inch main battery rifles to small-caliber machine guns

LCDR Joe Taylor (L), CO of VT-5, and LCDR William O. Burch, Jr. (R), CO of VS-5, stand in front of a VT-5 "Devastator" at NAS Ford Island, 6 June 1942. Taylor and Burch (both USNA 1927) each earned a Navy Cross for leading his squadron through the Lae-Salamaua strike and the Battle of the Coral Sea. Each would later earn a third award of the Navy's highest decoration: Taylor as air officer of carrier *Franklin* (CV-13) and Burch as exec of carrier *Ticonderoga* (CV-14). (80-G-13043)

them to bomb "by memory" at Tulagi, the SBDs of VS-5 and VB-5 scored hits in rapid succession. Bill Burch scored first, according to his wingman, "Swede" Vejtasa, who later declared: " . . . the skipper laid one right in the middle of her flight deck." The SBDs then pulled out of their runs astern and to leeward of *Shōhō*, using high speed and retiring low over the water to open the range.

Jim Flatley, commanding the VF-42 escort, meanwhile tried to "coach" Torpedo Five from his Olympian vantage point high above the unfolding action, seeking in vain to divert planes from the already doomed carrier to other, undamaged, targets. Perhaps eager to score a hit after the disappointing day at Tulagi, though, Joe Taylor led VT-5 in "on the deck" to attack *Shōhō*, too. Unhindered by fighters or much anti-aircraft fire, his planes maintained formation, the first division composed of Taylor, LT(jg) Ellison, CAP E.J. Williamson, LT Furer and ENS F.R. Sanborn, A-V(N), USNR; and ENS Bottjer. All made their runs from the starboard bow, and "at such close range as to make it almost impossible to miss." All ten TBDs dropped their Mk.XIIIs, all pilots claimed hits.

Six minutes after *Yorktown*'s planes had commenced their attacks, the order went out on board *Shōhō* to abandon ship. Within five more minutes, though, the carrier sank, taking with her all but 255 of her 800-man crew and having suffered hits from at least 13 bombs and seven torpedoes before the keeping of records of such massive destruction became superfluous. To Bill Burch, watching from his SBD, *Shōhō* "just ploughed herself under." LCDR Robert E. Dixon, commanding *Lexington*'s VB-2, reported laconically, "Scratch one flattop."

All the while, Jim Flatley and his fighter pilots had been watching the action from 10,000 feet, waiting up-sun of the enemy to be ready to deal with enemy fighters if they attempted to attack the TBDs. Thus far, outside of the anti-aircraft fire (which Flatley considered to be "weak and sporadic" from his vantage point) *Yorktown*'s fliers had encountered no opposition.

in a valiant, but futile, attempt to stop the charging men from "Lady Lex." The barrage proved ineffective—the screen was simply too full of holes. One early hit knocked out the after elevator, another wrecked the steering gear; *Shōhō* had no choice but to steer a straight course.

By the time Scouting Five found *Shōhō*, it appeared to Bill Burch that only one small fire was burning, astern, and the ship's speed unimpaired. It appeared that *Shōhō* had eluded one group, and was turning into the wind to launch planes: two Mitsubishi A5M4 Type 96 *kansens* and three Type 00s under LT Notomi Kenjiro. One "Zero" and two Type 96s were already aloft.

As Burch prepared to push over in his dive, he heard the voice of his USNA classmate, Joe Taylor, crackling through his earphones, imploring him to wait. Burch told him that *Shōhō* was launching planes, and that he (Burch) was "not going to let them get off." Accordingly, Scouting Five's commander pushed over and dove on *Shōhō*, the carrier a "dead pigeon" in his telescopic sight. Unhindered this day by the fogged windscreens and sights that had compelled

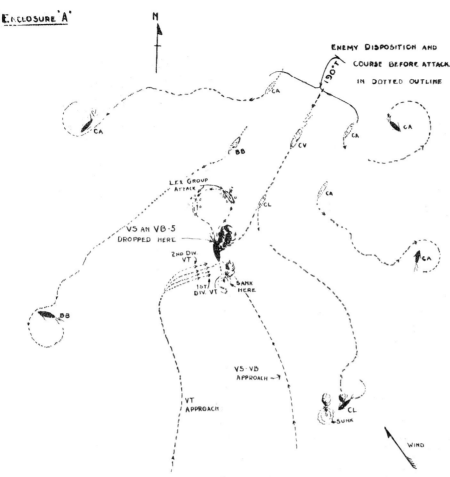

N

ENEMY DISPOSITION AND
COURSE BEFORE ATTACK
IN DOTTED OUTLINE

CA

CA

190 T

CA

BB

CV

CA

LEX GROUP
ATTACK

CL

VS AN VB-5
DROPPED HERE

CA

2ND DIV
VT ?

1ST
DIV. VT

SANK
HERE

BB

VS - VB
APPROACH →

CL
SUNK

VT
APPROACH

WIND

LT(jg) Arthur L. Downing, A-V(N), USNR, of VS-5 sketched the "disposition and movement of enemy ships" on 7 May: he believed that the enemy screen was comprised of a battleship, three heavy cruisers and one light cruiser; in fact, it consisted of four heavy cruisers and a destroyer—illustrating the difficulty of estimating the size of an enemy force by aerial observation. Nevertheless, the attack it shows resulted in the sinking of Japanese carrier *Shōhō*. (Enclosure A to CO, *Yorktown* "Air Operations of *Yorktown* Air Group against Japanese forces in the vicinity of the Louisiade Archipelago on May 7, 1942")

DISPOSITION AND MOVEMENT OF ENEMY SHIPS

At that juncture, however, at least four of the mixed bag of Mitsubishis—Type 96s and Type 00s—swept in, well below Flatley's five F4Fs, going after VT-5. Although they came in at an altitude well below what Flatley expected, he took his men down to deal with this newly developed opposition. Flatley picked out a Type 96 not more than 100 feet above the water, and came in from above at an angle of 60°, walking his bullets across the water until they hit metal; the fixed-gear Mitsubishi splashed into the sea. Before the engagement was over, two more enemy planes would be shot down—both by the former Philadelphia pharmacist, ENS Haas—one of which proved to be the first "Zero" downed by a U.S. Navy or Marine Corps fighter pilot in World War II.

In this, VF-42's first encounter with enemy fighters, the American pilots came away with an appreciation for their adversaries' maneuverability. The old-fashioned "dog fight" did not work with the Japanese, whose "steep wingovers, rolls, and loops at low altitude" marked them as tough customers in aerial com-

bat. Jim Flatley warned that "chasing tails" was not satisfactory, and "must not be employed" as a tactic when opposing Japanese fighter aircraft. Noting that the Japanese were "extremely clever acrobats" and apparently had found some method of overcoming the effects of "blacking out," Flatley went on to note that their planes could outclimb his own; he had tried to overtake a retiring Japanese fighter in a fruitless pursuit. "He [the enemy pilot] climbed rapidly away without any difficulty" leaving the "Wildcat" far behind. The Americans were learning that the Japanese were not just a bunch of stereotyped amateurs.

Yorktown's air group, having administered the *coup de grâce* to *Shōhō* and decimated her combat air patrol, returned to the ship between 1309 and 1338. Damage was slight: only three TBDs had taken hits (minor "bullet and shrapnel holes in wings, tail, and fuselage"), but one SBD did not return. ENS J. Windsor Rowley, A-V(N), USNR, had attempted to dogfight a Japanese plane after his attack on *Shōhō*, but in so doing had become separated from the rest of VB-5. Facing fuel starvation, Rowley came across Crace's ships, circled them, and then set course for Port Moresby. He ran out of gas before he could do so, though, and he was forced to make a water landing. Rowley and his gunner, ARM3c D.C Musgrove, then broke out their rubber boat and rowed ashore, where natives aided them and helped them start on their way back to friendly hands.

The day's activity, however, was far from over, as *Yorktown*'s radar picked up an unidentified plane only 18 miles from the ship at 1653. Fighters vectored out to intercept did not make contact, although lookouts on board *Yorktown* could visually identify an "enemy seaplane" at 1659. The snooper eluded a second section of fighters vectored out to intercept him, and went off the radar screen at 1717, 27 miles away from the ship.

Undoubtedly, this snooper had pinpointed the exact position of TF-17, for, at 1747, the American radar picked up a large incoming formation of enemy aircraft—27 dive and torpedo bombers—18 miles distant, attempting to get in a strike against *Yorktown* and *Lexington* in the waning hours of daylight and in the squally weather then prevailing. They had been launched around 1615 to find the American task force.

Forewarned, *Lexington* (controlling the fighter direction circuits) vectored out fighters to intercept—VF-2 would take up a position further out from TF-17, VF-42 close in. *Yorktown* launched additional fighters to lend a hand, Flatley's among them, to investigate radar contacts to the westward of the ship.

Lexington's FDO told Flatley to take his three two-plane sections (he actually had seven planes with him) "to effect an interception" but told him precious little else. Flatley and his men flew on through the heavy squalls, and soon discerned, through a curtain of rain, several fires burning brightly below on the water—traces of Japanese planes downed a short time before by the F4Fs of VF-2.

Flatley, thinking he was searching for a patrol plane in view of the four contacts with snoopers that day, opened up on the radio and asked *Lexington*'s fighter

As seen from the TBD-1 (BuNo 0354) (5-T-)2 flown by LT(jg) Tom Ellison on 7 May, Japanese small carrier *Shōhō*, her steering gear wrecked by an early hit, steams unerringly to oblivion off Misima Island, in this view snapped by RM3c E.W. Jones, Ellison's radio-gunner. On the original print at least three "Devastators" are visible, and *Shōhō* can be seen taking water over the bow, giving credence to LCDR Bill Burch's assertion that *Shōhō* "just ploughed herself under..." after taking multiple bomb and torpedo hits. (80-G-17047)

In this view believed never before published, smoke and explosions signal the death throes of *Shōhō* on 7 May; a "Devastator" is visible at left, most likely from VT-5. (Author)

director what type of planes they could expect to contact—not having been informed en route. Before the answer came, though, Flatley spied several planes below in the murk, heading the opposite direction. LCDR Paul Ramsey, commanding VF-2, soon came on the radio in answer to Flatley's query: they were looking for enemy fighters. At that instant, the last two planes in the VF-42 formation broke, and, on their own initiative, attacked the planes that the leader had assumed, up to that moment, were *Lexington*'s.

ENS Leslie L.B. Knox, A-V(N), USNR, the squadron navigator, and his wingman, "Willo" Woollen, correctly discerned the unfriendly character of the aircraft passing beneath them—six Type 97 carrier attack planes from *Shōkaku*—and drove into the fray, Knox bagging one of the Nakajimas almost immediately, while Woollen broke up one section, chased a Type 97 through the rain squalls but could not down the seemingly indestructible enemy torpedo bomber. Flatley then took the remainder of the airborne VF-42 planes into the fray, carrying out high-side approaches on another group of enemy planes—a half-dozen Aichi Type 99s from *Zuikaku*. LT(jg) Brainard T. Macomber, A-V(N), USNR, closed in astern of one of the bogies, and fired a two-second burst. As the Aichi burst into flames, Macomber pulled up to avoid him. Bad weather limited the rest of the encounters to fleeting ones in the squalls and low visibility that ranged from zero to two miles. For Knox, who later downed a second *kankō*, the battle fought in the murk over the Coral Sea on 7 May proved to be his last: the lanky Australian-born pilot, married only a day over five months, disappeared during the melee.

Then, in the words of the character in *Alice in Wonderland*, things got "curiouser and curiouser." At 1850, less than a half-hour after sunset, three enemy aircraft flew close by *Yorktown*'s starboard side, "showing lights" and making "no sign of hostility," even blinking in morse code with an Aldis lamp "..-..-.." Crossing to port, over the carrier's bow, their actions roused the suspicions of LT(jg) Macomber, who was still waiting to land. Too many planes in the circle, as well as a deck crash temporarily fouling the deck, had forced Macomber to orbit the ship; he, too, saw the running lights of the strange planes, and their blinking Aldis lamp, and, suitably curious, gave chase. He closed in on one of the planes, whose tail light betrayed its existence in the dark sky to the east but, his gunnery affected by the slipstream, switched his gunfire to one of the other planes which was showing all of its running lights, provoking an almost blind fire from the enemy's rear seat man, green tracers arcing out into the night. One of the three then turned beneath Macomber, the F4F pilot noting the distinctive tapered, pointed wingtips and the red ball insignia on the wing in the failing light in the western sky. Not wanting to lose the ship, and having only two guns working, Macomber turned 180° to return to *Yorktown*. At 1858, *Yorktown*'s landing signal officer, LT Norwood A. "Soupy"

Campbell, began bringing VF-42's "Wildcats" on board in the inky blackness, but soon discovered he had pilots in the landing circle who seemed unfamiliar with U.S. Navy doctrine. Three enemy planes again appeared, perhaps the same three as before but still obviously lost in the confused night. This time, *Yorktown*'s gunners opened fire with every gun that could be brought to bear, tracers criss-crossing the sky in a "lot of night fireworks." As *Yorktown*'s communication officer, LCDR C.C. Ray, later recalled the experience: "A night carrier action against an attacking air group is a bunch of confusion and not much else." In the melee, ship's gunners claimed at least one of the three Japanese planes that had attempted to land on board, but only succeeded in holing the F4F flown by ENS W.W. Barnes, Jr., A-V(N), USNR.

ENS John D. Baker, A-V(N), USNR, who had returned to the ship with Flatley, broke away from the section leader to engage the enemy planes. Apparently disoriented in the confusion, he became lost. *Yorktown* established radio contact with him, making ". . . every effort . . . to get him on the radar screen and back to the ship." At 1930 *Yorktown* landed the last of her combat air patrol, with two planes—Baker's and Knox's—missing. Still unable to pick up Baker on radar by 2028, *Yorktown* gave him a course to the nearest land, Tagula Island, but whether or not he made it is not known. He was never found.

Keeping tabs on the Japanese radio transmissions, meanwhile, Fletcher's intelligence officer and his Japanese linguist, LT Biard, could determine that the Japanese attack force had been cut up by *Lexington*'s and *Yorktown*'s fighters. As Bill Burch later recalled, "Tex" Biard told of hearing one transmission from one plane, the man asking his carrier to turn on the searchlights since "his pilot was dead and he was flying the ship from the rear cockpit." LCDR Ray opined that the Japanese apparently had not done much in the way of night flying from carriers "because the air was full of their conversation trying to get home and aboard." Takagi, presaging a bold move by RADM Raymond A. Spruance in the Battle of Midway, a month later, and VADM Marc Mitscher in the Battle of the Philippine Sea two years hence, ordered his carriers to turn on their searchlights to guide the battered strike group home. Even so, the last planes did not come on board until after 2300, and Takagi soon found out he had suffered the loss of nine planes (one *kanbaku* and eight *kankōs* in combat. Eleven Aichis and seven Nakajimas reached their own flight decks safely.

Radio interception of the enemy's transmissions had

earlier told the Americans that the Japanese carriers "were in the vicinity" but did not pinpoint their exact location to everyone's satisfaction. At 2200, RADM Fitch advised Fletcher that *Lexington*'s radar had pinpointed "an enemy carrier or carriers" about 30 miles away at 1930—two and a half hours earlier! *Yorktown*'s radar had not shown this, but *had* picked up a circling plane—later tracked and believed to be one of *Yorktown*'s missing fighters—25 to 30 miles distant.

Fletcher pondered his next move. Earlier that day, after the two air groups had polished off *Shōhō*, he decided to steer westward during the night, expecting the Japanese to pass through the Jomard Passage by morning, headed for Port Moresby, in force, probably accompanied by a carrier. The sighting of enemy planes, and the resultant discovery that Japanese carriers were only 30-odd miles distant, altered the situation accordingly.

Radio intercepts placed the Japanese to the east, as did material from FRUPAC, on Oahu. Did Frank Jack Fletcher have a golden opportunity thrust into his hands on a silver platter? Fletcher put the matter squarely to the pilots. Did they want to risk a night attack in the horrendous weather blanketing the Coral Sea, perhaps ending up jettisoning their bombs into the ocean, as the Japanese pilots had done, and thus having no ordnance to drop when the enemy *was* found? As one of the pilots recalled later, the aviators advised against it and Fletcher did not insist. Perhaps both parties, the admiral and his airmen, remembered the Jaluit strike and the planes lost directly to the inclement weather—just three months before. Had a strike been carried out on the night of 7 May, Turner Caldwell reflected, "some of us would have been lost," having neither "the doctrine nor the training for night combat."

The admiral weighed the remaining possibility. Primarily a cruiser sailor, Fletcher knew the advantages of using these ships to strike a blow on the enemy and then retire. Yet the aviation angle could not be neglected. Given the proximity of the enemy carriers, Fletcher considered it "inadvisable to detach

LCDR James H. Flatley, Jr., (seen here 7 July 1942 while CO of VF-10) earned a Navy Cross for showing "the highest qualities of leadership, aggressiveness and complete disregard for his personal safety" in the Battle of the Coral Sea. He scored VF-42's first "kill" of the battle when he splashed a Mitsubishi A5M4 Type 96 *kansen* on 7 May 1942. (80-G-64814)

cruisers and destroyers, or even destroyers alone" for a night surface engagement. Night battle practice in the U.S. Navy in the pre-war years had been primarily defensive in nature, not receiving the emphasis it should have—as events in the then not-too-distant future soon proved.

Fletcher knew he had to retain some destroyers to provide antisubmarine protection for the valuable carriers. And, should the attack force be unable to rejoin by daylight, this turn of events would place his own forces in double jeopardy—the cruiser/destroyer force without air cover and the carriers bereft of the cruisers' and destroyers' anti-aircraft guns that could prove the deciding factor in repelling an enemy air attack. "All things considered," Fletcher later wrote, "the best plan seemed to be to keep our force concentrated and prepare for a battle with enemy carriers [the] next morning." It proved a wise decision.

Such preparations were taking place in Bombing Five's ready room, as the squadron flight officer, LT "JoJo" Powers lectured the pilots on "point of aim" and "bombing technique." In his discourse, Powers advocated a low-level release point to ensure greater accuracy, but stressed the dangers inherent in such technique: enemy antiaircraft fire, a too-low pullout from which no recovery was possible, and getting caught in one's own bomb blast. Those who knew Powers would not have been surprised at his unconventional pet theories; indeed, it appears in the 1935 *Lucky Bag* that the dark-haired New Yorker, "entirely unencumbered with any peculiarities" and "markedly positive," could never be trusted to respect "conventionalities." Powers' were not the theoretical ramblings of a classroom tactician, but those of a man who fully intended to, and did, practice what he preached.

Elsewhere on board *Yorktown* men stood their watches or tried to catch what sleep they could. "Everyone knew that tomorrow would be a long, hard day," a *Yorktown* sailor recalled in later years of the night before the Battle of the Coral Sea, "and we would find out just how good we were as man-of-wars men."

Mitsubishi A6M2 Type 00 carrier fighters prepare to take off from carrier *Zuikaku*; *kansen*s from this ship, flown by PO1c Iwamoto Tetsuzo, PO1c Ito Junjiro, and Sea1c Mae Hichijiro intercepted Scouting Five's SBDs as they attacked *Shokaku* on 8 May 1942. (Author)

Explosions of bombs close aboard *Shōkaku* on 8 May send geysers of spray towering above the carrier as she maneuvers desperately to avoid the attacking planes from *Yorktown* and *Lexington*. (Author)

CHAPTER 7

No Higher Honor than to Have Commanded Them in Battle

A T 0025 ON 8 MAY, "Jake" Fitch proposed to Fletcher that a 360° search be carried out as early as practicable, with a radius of 200 miles in the northern semicircle, 125 in the southern. In addition, he suggested that attack groups be placed in condition of readiness one, and that fighter and anti-torpedo plane patrols be sent aloft 15 minutes before sunrise. Fletcher obligingly replied: "As usual, I agree with you thoroughly. I will change course to west. Set your own course." Soon thereafter, Fletcher dispatched *Monaghan* (DD-354) to look for survivors of *Neosho* and *Sims*, as well as to transmit radio messages from a point well away from the task force.

Fitch had been well justified in opting for the 360° air search, since land-based reconnaissance planes from Australia and PBY's from Noumea had not located the elusive enemy carriers whose presence in the area had been pinpointed by radio interceptions. Fitch, as Commander, Air, ordered the cruisers of TF-17 to launch planes for an inner-air patrol while soon thereafter directing *Yorktown* to "launch and maintain four plane combat [air] patrol and eight scouts as anti-torpedo plane patrol." *Yorktown*, however, proved slow in executing the order, eliciting an interrogatory message from Fitch: "Why have you not launched combat and anti-torpedo patrol?" at 0720.

Uncertainty had existed on board as to whether or not the attack group would be sent aloft *before* the anti-torpedo patrol—hence the delay—and while the carrier respotted her flight deck, *Lexington* launched her scouts, reporting at 0730 that 12 had been sent aloft to look for the Japanese carriers. *Yorktown*, her deck finally ready, commenced putting four F4Fs and eight SBDs airborne at 0745.

Lexington's dozen SBDs fanned out to cover their assigned sectors, groping through the clouds; the bad weather that had so far shielded the Americans from detection had now seemingly shifted sides, protecting the Japanese from prying eyes. Then at 0828, *Lexington* informed *Yorktown* of electrifying news which she had just received from one of her scout planes: "FOLLOWING RECEIVED FROM ONE SCOUT X CONTACT 2CV 4CA 3DD X POSITION OF SCOUT UNKNOWN X AM TRYING TO CONTACT NOW." LT(jg) Joseph G. Smith, in 2-S-2, had made this sighting report, confirmed at 0833 by another: "CONTACT 2 CARRIERS 4 CRUISERS MANY DESTROYERS BEARING 006 DIST (ANCE) 120 SPEED 15 at 0820." Fitch radioed Fletcher at 0847: "2 CARRIERS, 4 CRUISERS, MANY DESTROYERS BEARING 028 DISTANCE 175 MILES."

Interestingly enough, at about the same time, a Japanese "snooper"—PO1c Kanno Kenzo—had found TF-17. Ten minutes before Fitch's message had arrived, RADM Fletcher had informed his classmate "Believe we have been sighted by enemy carrier plane . . ." The monitoring of Japanese radio traffic soon revealed that Kanno had sighted TF-17 only minutes before *Lexington*'s plane had spotted the enemy's carrier task force.

The enemy's position now known, all preparations proceeded apace for the launching of the attack groups. As "JoJo" Powers quit Bombing Five's ready room, he exhorted those around him to remember that "the folks back home are counting on us." "I am going to get a hit," he declared emphatically, "if I have to lay it on their flight deck." No one could know for sure that Powers' cheerfully confident declaration of intent would become his epitaph.

While her flight deck came alive with the noisy,

CDR Walter G. Schindler, gunnery officer on RADM Fletcher's staff, earned a Silver Star for his "cool, efficient performance of duty" as an observer on combat missions at Coral Sea. "A rear seat gunner has better than an even chance against a single fighter approaching from high astern," he reported from experience, "But he must have practice." He is seen here in December 1943 as a CAPT, when he received his decoration from Secretary of the Navy Knox. (Author)

ENS John H. "Yogi" Jorgenson, A-V(N), USNR, of VS-5, *circa* November 1941, found himself the object of attention of PO1c Iwamoto, PO1c Ito, and Sea1c Mae, from *Zuikaku*'s air unit, after the attack on carrier *Shōkaku* on 8 May 1942, but survived to make it back to TF-17. For his "extraordinary heroism and devotion to duty," Jorgenson received the Navy Cross. (Author)

LT John J. "JoJo" Powers, USNA 1935, had served as a watch and division officer in *West Virginia* (BB-48), *Augusta* (CA-31) and *Utah* (AG-16) before he underwent aviation instruction at Pensacola, where this photo was taken on 10 April 1940. Receiving his wings on 27 November 1940, he joined VB-5 soon thereafter, and remained with the squadron until his death on 8 May. "A hilarious rebel," a USNA classmate called him, "his own man." (80-G-415496)

purposeful activity of launch, engines roaring to life and pilots and aircrew manning their planes, *Yorktown* sent a signal snapping crisply up her flag hoists, imparting information to TF-17: "Two enemy carriers, bearing 028. Distance 175 miles." Between 0900 and 0915, *Yorktown* launched her air group: six F4F-3s of Fighting Forty-two (two to cover the SBDs and four to escort the TBDs); 24 SBDs of Scouting and Bombing Five; and nine TBDs of Torpedo Five. *Lexington* followed suit soon thereafter.

In his operation plan, Fletcher had specified that in the event of an air battle, tactical command would be in the hands of "Jake" Fitch, a naval aviator. At 0908, while *Yorktown*'s planes were rolling down the deck and struggling with full loads of gasoline and ordnance to clear the bow ramp, Fletcher turned the conduct of the impending battle over to Fitch, whom some considered to be one of the most experienced carrier admirals in the U.S. Navy. Another flag signal soon snapped up *Yorktown*'s halyards, "CTG 17.5 [Fitch] assume tactical command of the fleet."

At about 1032, *Yorktown*'s planes first sighted Takagi's task force, identifying it as containing "an *Ise*-class" battleship, two carriers, six heavy cruisers, and four light cruisers or destroyers moving at 20 knots beneath the broken layer of clouds that lay at two to three thousand feet. For about 17 minutes, *Yorktown*'s SBDs circled over the Japanese ships like hawks wheeling above their prey, waiting patiently for the slower torpedo planes to catch up. *Zuikaku* headed for a nearby rain squall during that time, while *Shōkaku* turned into the wind and commenced launching planes. Bursts of anti-aircraft fire began to blossom in the skies. Then, at 1057, Joe Taylor—having been guided to the scene by the homeward-bound LT Smith of VS-2—radioed his Academy classmate Bill Burch: "OK Bill, I'm starting in . . ."

As Scouting Five now pushed over, *Shōkaku* began maneuvering, taking evasive action. She commenced turning to port as the "Dauntlesses" began screaming down in their dives, and then reversed course sharply to starboard. The TBDs of Torpedo Five, boring in at 200 feet to prevent enemy fighters from attacking them from underneath, had begun their approaches in a loose echelon of divisions, the planes in each division forming a column. The volume of anti-aircraft fire, though, forced Taylor and his men to adopt highly individual tactics, with "every pilot on

ARM2c Everett C. Hill of VB-5, LT "JoJo" Powers's radio-gunner, who perished with his pilot in the crash of their SBD after the attack on *Shōkaku* on 8 May 1942. (Author)

ENS Davis E. Chaffee, A-V(N), USNR, an Ohio native, graduated *cum laude* from Baldwin-Wallace College in 1938; awarded his aviator's wings on 1 October 1941, he was to have reported to Bombing Two in *Lexington* but was retained on board *Yorktown* on the eve of the Battle of the Coral Sea to serve in Bombing Five. He was awarded a posthumous Navy Cross. (Author)

Sea1c John A. Kasselman, like his pilot, ENS Chaffee, hailed from Ohio; he turned 23 years old less than two months before the Battle of the Coral Sea in which he was lost. (Author)

his own to determine the best position for attack." Droning in at between 100 and 110 knots, the big "Devastators" dropped down to 50 feet, the pilots releasing their torpedoes at ranges between 1,000 and 2,000 yards in the teeth of an anti-aircraft barrage of "terrific intensity." Despite claims to the contrary by VT-5's pilots, all of the torpedoes dropped missed, as *Shōkaku* combed the wakes and evaded them. Three of the Mk.XIII's ran erratically.

While Joe Taylor was leading his "Devastators" on the "deck," Bill Burch—his plane the target of an "ace" from the Sino-Japanese War—was leading the SBDs of Scouting Five through swarms of "Zero" fighters and considerable anti-aircraft fire, and the moist air over the target which fogged windshields and telescopic sights. LT Caldwell, VS-5's XO, encountered "Zeroes" as soon as he pushed his SBD over into the dive. Riding in the rear cockpit was CDR Walter G. Schindler, RADM Fletcher's gunnery officer, who was along for his fifth combat mission, in the capacity of an observer, in as many days (three at Tulagi and one against *Shōhō*). "Butch" Schindler—recalling free gunnery training in his USNA days—unshipped the single .30-caliber Browning and blazed away whenever a

"Zero" came within range. The first "Zero" slid past, unable to stay on Caldwell's tail when the pilot opened his dive brakes; Caldwell released his bomb (which missed) and pulled out, only to find another Mitsubishi astern. Once more, Schindler fired his Browning and drove off the attacker, although the Japanese pilot managed to score several hits on the "Dauntless." For the rest of the time over the Japanese task force, "Butch" Schindler kept the enemy at bay, later getting credit for a "Zero."

One VS-5 pilot who was not so fortunate to get away relatively unscathed was ENS John H. Jorgenson, A-V(N), USNR. As Jorgenson pulled out of his dive, and closed his diving flaps, anti-aircraft fire hit his left wing. Recovering from the spin caused by the hit, Jorgenson soon discovered three "Zeroes" on his tail. Bullets from his antagonists' 7.7mm and 20mm guns tore into the "Dauntless," peppering the fuselage and wings. Some passed over the pilot's right shoulder, tearing away the rear part of his telescopic sight; others thudded into his seat armor; another wrecked his cockpit instruments; three grazed his right leg. His radioman/gunner, Sea1c Anthony W. Brunetti, meanwhile kept up a steady fire from his single .30-

caliber machine gun, trying to keep the enemy planes at a respectful distance.

Bombing Five encountered the same hot reception. As LT John Nielsen glanced over at his roommate, "JoJo" Powers, before he pushed over into his dive, he saw a sight he never forgot, and which illustrated his friend's ability to find humor in any situation— Powers was "making monkey faces." The "Zeroes" and anti-aircraft fire met them on the way down; Powers' plane was hit and caught fire, but he bravely pressed on. Nielsen, meanwhile, had pulled out of his dive and glanced behind him to see how his roommate had fared. Powers' bomb hit squarely amidships, but his plane crashed into the Coral Sea moments later, carrying the unforgettable Powers and his radioman, ARM2c Everett C. Hill. For pressing home his attack almost to *Shōkaku*'s flight deck, as he had promised, Powers received, posthumously, the Medal of Honor.

As the *Yorktown* SBDs pulled out of their runs, the "Zeroes" of the combat air patrol jumped them, carrying out their attacks until the "Dauntlesses" joined up and presented them with a more formidable defense. Nevertheless, another VB-5 plane went down, flown by a young ensign who had been with the squadron less than fortnight and who had been treated like everyone's kid brother—ENS Davis Chaffee; both Chaffee and his radioman, Sea1c John A. Kasselman, were killed. Bombing Five claimed three fighters downed in return; Scouting Five claimed two shot down and seven damaged. Bombing Five had outdone their Scout shipmates, though, in one respect: they had scored two hits on *Shōkaku*, rendering her temporarily incapable of flight operations: a hit near the bow damaged the bow ramp and ignited gasoline storage tanks, while an explosion ripped through an engine repair workshop. *Lexington*'s SBDs added a third hit after the *Yorktown*ers had finished their attack.

The SBDs, lacking fighter cover (their escorting F4Fs, flown by LCDR Fenton and ENS Harry B. Gibbs, A-V(N), USNR, having lost track of them en route due to the cloud cover, the SBDs' high rate of climb and the F4Fs' high fuel consumption), ran into trouble with the defending Japanese fighters. The TBDs of VT-5, however, had a comparatively easier time on the way out, due to the efforts of their four escorts. F4Fs flown by LT(jg)s Leonard, McCuskey and Woollen, and ENS Adams which downed one of the "Zeroes" harassing the "Devastators." "Close radio liaison" between the F4F pilots and the TBDs aided them immeasurably; the latter's pilots and radiomen picked out the targets and the fighters went after them, providing an "air tight defense."

While the Japanese had used the cloud cover, so did the *Yorktown*ers upon retirement from the scene. Although what had been estimated as a 15 to 18-plane combat air patrol had been put up over the Japanese carriers, *Yorktown*'s retiring planes flew into two large cumulus clouds, the presence of which proved a godsend; as *Yorktown*ers later admitted, these clouds aided in keeping losses to a minimum.

As *Yorktown*'s planes departed the area, *Shōkaku* was afire, at the bow and aft of her island. Seeing that, Bill Burch ruminated, "If she was all right after that (the *Yorktown* Air Group's attack), she was tougher than any other carrier I've ever seen; including our own." As it turned out, *Shōkaku* did survive, but after suffering heavy damage topside (her flight deck disabled) and casualties (109 dead, 114 wounded). She could still make top speed, however, and the misses apparently did not affect her underwater hull; her gunnery department still functioned. The repairs, in homeland waters, that TF-17's fliers had inflicted would keep *Shōkaku* out of action for some time. Her flight deck temporarily out of commission, she directed the planes from her air group to land on board her sistership *Zuikaku*.

The murky weather conditions prevailing in the sky around the Japanese task force rendered any hope of the *Yorktown* group joining up for the trip back to the ship a vain one. The planes of VS-5, VB-5, VT-5 and their VF-42 escorts all made their way back as best they could; almost miraculously, all that had survived the anti-aircraft fire and fighters over the enemy force, did. En route, the returning American and Japanese groups passed each other (the Japanese attack on TF-17 will be discussed presently), and a few aerial engagements occurred between isolated antagonists. In one, LT(jg) Leonard of VF-42, while escorting the damaged SBD-3 flown by ENS Harry A. Fredrickson, A-V(N), USNR of VB-5, encountered a lone *kanbaku*, and claimed a "probable" shooting up the Type 99 but not seeing it splash. His victim (Fredrickson saw it crash) was none other than LCDR Takahashi Kakuichi, commander of the *Shōkaku* Air Group and one of the Japanese naval air arm's more colorful, dependable, and aggressive individuals who had proved his mettle in combat. LCDR Fenton and ENS Gibbs encountered two returning Aichis and, Fenton lacking the fuel to verify whether or not his quarry splashed, claimed a "probable" kill. LT(jg) Woollen and ENS Adams teamed up to flame a Nakajima Type 97, the one flown by the gallant PO1c Kanno Kenzo, who had guided the *Shōkaku* and *Zuikaku* attack groups to TF-17.

Simultaneous to TF-17's planes attacking Takagi's carriers, the Japanese strike force, 69 planes in all, guided by PO1c Kanno's reports as he eluded detection and maintained contact with the American carriers, was boring in on TF-17. Air activity over the American task force had consisted of the maintenance of a combat air patrol, the first of which, *Lexington's*, had been launched at 0625. At 0804, *Yorktown's* radar picked up an unidentified plane and the ship vectored out fighters to intercept, but did not make contact, the bogey disappearing from the radar screen seven minutes later. A second report, at 0831, sent another group of fighters hunting for the snooper, and while they did not make contact it was generally agreed that the plane was friendly, since it was heading on a retirement course away from the formation.

Yorktown's combat air patrol overhead changed at 0941, as she launched four F4F-3s piloted by McCormack, Brassfield, Mattson and Haas, the carrier landing the previous four to be reserviced. At 1008, *Yorktown* alerted *Lexington* to the presence of a "bogey" 12 miles away, after lookouts had visually identified the snooper as a Kawanishi flying boat "flying at a low altitude." This only elicited *Lexington's* response: "Roger . . . should be our returning scouts." She had evidently not seen the Type 97, but radioed the leaders of *Yorktown's* combat air patrol sections, given the call signs "Wildcat Orange" and "Wildcat Brown" to "orbit at 10 miles. Keep formation in sight."

McCormack and Haas headed over to investigate the stranger, vectored by *Yorktown*, which, about that time, also told the SBDs of Scouting Five, still aloft since earlier that morning as the anti-torpedo plane patrol, to be alert for an air attack expected to arrive shortly.

McCormack and his wingman soon found the "snooper." Through the static in *Yorktown's* radio room came the message: "Bogey ahead looks like [a] bandit seagull," ("seagull" being fighter-director lingo for seaplane). A "tallyho" came next as McCormack initiated the attack "from above and slightly forward of the starboard beam, then high side port, then high side starboard," raking the seaplane with his four .50 calibers. Haas duplicated McCormack's tactics as the enemy pilot attempted "S" turns, and dove, once pulling up into a 45° climb for a few seconds in attempting to evade his pursuers. After the first pass, McCormack and Haas could both see that the big parasol-winged Type 97 was smoking. As Haas bore in, the Japanese plane blew up, almost in his face, and its burning fragments fell into the sea. McCormack's jubilant war whoops cut off an interrogatory message from *Lexington* asking how many planes he was up against. The two "Wildcat" pilots then returned to their station, climbing up 7,000 feet to watch, to wait, and to listen.

At that juncture, *Yorktown's* and *Lexington's* radars were tracking the incoming attack groups from *Shōkaku* and *Zuikaku*, which were closing in almost simultaneously as the American planes heading out to attack the carriers whence they had come. At 1055, *Yorktown* signalled *Lexington*: "Many bogeys. Aircraft bearing 135. Distance 68. Have you got them?" "Affirmative," *Lexington* responded, code-named "Romeo." "We have it." At about the same time, *Yorktown* picked up Joe Taylor's "OK Bill, I'm starting in" which was initiating the attack on *Shōkaku*. *Yorktown* now vectored Brassfield and Mattson "to orbit about 15 miles" in the direction from which the Japanese planes were coming. Haas and McCormack climbed still farther.

Events picked up speed rapidly as RADM Fitch, in *Lexington*, directed *Yorktown* to launch additional planes for the combat air patrol; *Lexington* simultaneously turned into the wind and began putting aloft the remainder of her combat air patrol, too. *Yorktown* recalled all of her fighters to the vicinity of the ship and launched four more "Wildcats" from VF-42: one section consisting of Flatley and his wingman, Crommelin, the other composed of Macomber and Bassett. *Yorktown's* division had only been told that an attack was expected—nothing more. As soon as VF-42's executive officer and his men cleared the ship, the fighter director in *Lexington* ordered them to "proceed to a point ten miles distant from the carrier and to circle there at 2000 feet." At 1059, *Lexington*, directing the task force fighters, then sang out: "Hey, Rube," gathering in all combat air patrol planes over the carriers to protect them. *Yorktown* again alerted her own anti-torpedo plane patrol, the eight SBDs of Scouting Five under LT Roger B. Woodhull and his USNA classmate, LT Stockton B. Strong.

Yorktown, meanwhile, had been at general quarters since 0545, and the effect of over five hours running "closed up" can be imagined in the tropical heat. Soon after his ship had picked up the incoming Japanese strike on her radar, CAPT Buckmaster eased the condition of readiness on board ("Affirm") to allow the ventilation of the ship below decks "as [the] air was becoming very foul." Men stood by openings, however, ready to close them quickly if required. With the report of the enemy planes only 40 miles away, though, it was time to close-up again for action. At 1100, CAPT Buckmaster reset condition "Affirm."

CAPT Buckmaster awaited the incoming attack planes on his bridge, in the open. To assist him in fight-

While *Shōkaku* maneuvers to avoid the SBDs attacking from above, irregular wakes in the foreground attest to the erratic Mk.XIII torpedoes carried into battle by the lumbering TBDs of VT-5. (80-G-17030)

C. Campbell, A-V(N), USNR, and his radioman ARM3c Franklin Delano Richeson, were the first to go down, their SBD spinning into the Coral Sea. Likewise shot down within the first sickening moments were LT(jg) Earl V. Johnson, A-V(N), USNR, ENS Edward B. Kinzer, A-V(N), USNR, and ENS Samuel Jackson Underhill, A-V(N), USNR; all of their radiomen—ARM2c Leon Hall, Sea1c Charles S. Bonness and ARM3c Woodrow A. Fontenot, were killed as well.

In the furious moments that followed, the remaining four SBDs, flown by Woodhull, Strong, Vejtasa and ENS Walton A. Austin, A-V(N), USNR, fought for their lives. The latter two pilots, schooled in fighter tactics by Scouting Five's CO, Bill Burch, put these into practice against the "Zeroes" that tormented them. Vejtasa scored hits on a particularly aggressive antagonist who came at him, head-on.

Scouting Five's "splendid example of courage and devotion to duty" did not stop the incoming torpedo planes, but only proved a momentary annoyance, since the covering "Zeroes" man-handled the SBDs with frightening ease. The Type 97 carrier attack planes then split into two groups: four from *Zuikaku* heading for *Yorktown*, while the remainder, drawn from both ships' (*Shōkaku* and *Zuikaku*) groups, headed for *Lexington*.

In this dramatic confrontation between incoming Japanese planes and defending American fighters—divided up piecemeal and stacked and dispersed to different altitudes—the combat air patrols from both U.S. carriers found themselves unable to hit the enemy *en masse*. At 1108, LCDR Flatley's four F4Fs were vectored out on a 020° course, 15 miles out, and told to climb and "intercept an attack approaching above 10,000 feet." Seeing empty expanses of sky, Flatley broke radio silence in frustration at 1119: "I am at 10,000 feet astern of the ship. Give me something to do."

His answer came soon enough: "Return to ship," came crackling in his earphones, "it is being attacked . . . as quick as possible. We are being attacked by

ing the ship, three officers and CQM (AA) Earnest E. Parton, stood nearby—LT(jg) C.B. Gill on the port wing of the bridge, along with Parton; LT(jg) John E. Greenbacker and ENS Norman L. Tate (the latter less than six months out of the Navy Academy) on the starboard, each man to watch for the approach of enemy planes and torpedoes and to sing out the bearings of enemy aircraft. The ship's navigator, CDR Irving D. Wiltsie, stood ready in the conning tower with the steering, main engine, and whistle controls; the executive officer, CDR Kiefer, stationed himself in Battle II, on the after end of the bridge platform, 120 feet from the pilot house, so that he could assume command if a bomb hit the bridge and killed the captain.

Radar tracked the enemy planes at 29 miles and closing, at 1106; five minutes later they were only 15 miles away. At 1112, the fleet course was changed, and speed increased to 20 knots; one minute later, orders came down to increase speed to "flank," 28 knots. At about the same time, COMDESRON 2 in *Phelps* heard the report over the TBS: "Our planes have sighted (the) enemy and are going after them."

After the incoming strike outdistanced the poorly positioned section of VF-2, it ran into the two sections (eight SBDs) of Scouting Five under LTs Woodhull and Strong. The speed at which the enemy approached, however, took the Americans by surprise—they apparently expected the enemy's torpedo planes to have the same slow speed that afflicted the TBDs with which they are familiar. Six "Zeroes" then jumped the eight SBDs as the latter attempted to wade into the 18 carrier attack planes (8 from *Zuikaku* and 10 from *Shōkaku*). In the swirling melee, ENS Kendall

Pilots and rear seat men of Scouting Squadron 5; although taken on board *Enterprise* in July, 1942, this picture shows many of the men who had been with the unit through the early wartime campaigns on board *Yorktown*. ACRM W.E. Glidewell and LT Turner F. Caldwell, Jr. are seated in front, Caldwell having relieved LCDR William O. Burch, Jr., as CO by this time. Second row (L-R): LT Roger B. Woodhull; ARM2c A.W. Garlow; ENS Pfautz, A-V(N), USNR; ARM2c H.J. Wilger; ENS W.E. Brown, A-V(N), USNR; ARM2c Fives; ENS Lawrence G. Traynor, A-V(N), USNR; ARM1c J.H. Cales; ENS Elmer Maul, A-V(N), USNR; RM3c Harding. Third row (L-R): ARM2c E.C. Strickland; ENS E.A. Conzett, A-V(N), USNR; ARM2c A.W. Brunetti; ENS John H. Jorgenson, A-V(N), USNR; ENS H.E. Buell, A-V(N), USNR; ARM2c F.B. Wood; ENS Walter W. Coolbaugh, A-V(N), USNR; ARM1c C.A. Jaeger; LT(jg) Hugh W. Nicholson, A-V(N), USNR; ARM2c Kustula. Rear row (L-R) ENS Walton A. Austin, A-V(N), USNR; LT Stockton B. Strong; ENS Barker, A-V(N), USNR; ARM3c E.J. Monahan; ENS H.N. Ervin, A-V(N), USNR; ARM2c E.W. Adams; LT(jg) A.L. Downing, A-V(N), USNR; ARM1c Jones; ENS Richey, A-V(N), USNR; ARM2c Broussard; ENS Estes, A-V(N), USNR; RM3c Starney; ENS Burnett, A-V(N), USNR. (NH 95553)

torpedo planes and everything . . ." Flatley quickly took his sections back to the task force—but the battle was passing them by.

A minute before Flatley's exasperated voice had come on the radio, *Yorktown* had sighted the four planes of the *Zuikaku* attack unit approaching. Coached over the flight deck loudspeakers by LCDR Davis, the gunnery officer, from his exposed position above the pilot house, and with the doctrine impressed upon them that "it is the individual responsibility of every gunner that enemy planes do not approach . . . unfired upon," *Yorktown*'s gunners opened fire as range allowed: the heaviest guns, the 5"/38's, opening at eight to ten thousand yards; one of the 5-inchers even having an extra hand in the ammunition train: CDR Ralph J. Arnold, (SC), *Yorktown*'s supply officer. The 1.1's opened up at 4,000 yards and the 20-millimeters and .50 calibers at 2,000. ENS Tate and LT(jg) Gill, on the port wing of the bridge, called out the bearings of the incoming

strike. CAPT Buckmaster ordered "right full rudder" and "emergency flank speed."

One *Zuikaku* Nakajima, aflame and with its torpedo still shackled beneath its belly, plunged into the sea between the carrier and the heavy cruiser *Chester* (CA-27), in the screen, while the other three maintained their attack, dropping their torpedoes which, due to CAPT Buckmaster's skillful maneuvering, all missed, passing close aboard to port. *Lexington*, though, being a much larger ship, answered her helm more slowly, and, when faced by a determined and well-orchestrated attack, this almost proved her undoing. Two 800-kilogram aerial torpedoes hit the big carrier—both on the port side—but failed to slow her down! LCDR Harry B. Jarrett, *Morris*'s commanding officer, marvelled at how *Lexington* could maintain 25 knots with two torpedoes in her.

The Japanese, though, would not afford *Lexington* the relative luxury of a breather in between tor-

land as an aiming point. These deadly missiles exploded in the sea, sending up towering geysers of water that reached skyward and then tumbled down in sheets of spray. Fragments from this exploding ordnance "pierced the shell in four or five places," dented it in "numerous" spots, cut a coil of the prominent external degaussing cable at frame 18, and severed a gasoline line two frames farther aft.

One of the Aichi Type 99's that had penetrated the veritable umbrella of anti-aircraft fire hurled up by the carrier and her consorts, released its bomb and then escaped from the maelstrom of steel. At about 1127, this missile penetrated the flight deck, making a hole about 14 inches in diameter, 23 feet forward of number two elevator, and about 15 feet inboard of the island. It went through number three ready room, glancing off the bottom of a safe as it did so, its path deflected as it plummeted downward, through the hangar deck and second deck, angling toward the starboard side before it hit a beam and a stanchion and angled back to port, piercing the third deck. An instant before it reached the fourth (armored) deck, directly above the head of the ship's engineer officer, LCDR John F. Delaney, it exploded in a high-order detonation in compartment C-402-A, an aviation storeroom.

Five levels below the main deck, in a crew's messing compartment, C-301-L, the engineering repair party, led by LT Milton E. Ricketts, had awaited the call to action they knew would come if the ship's machinery was hurt. Ricketts, in charge of "repair V," was a "plank owner," having been among those assigned to *Yorktown* to fit out and commission her. Outside of a previous tour in *Ranger*, Ricketts had spent his entire naval career in *Yorktown*. A classmate of "JoJo" Powers, he had been regarded by his friends at Annapolis as "easy going, even tempered, and generous to an extreme." In another two months, he would celebrate his 29th birth-

LT Ema Tamotsu, seen here relaxing on board *Zuikaku* circa April 1942, would lead that carrier's *kanbaku*s in the attack against *Yorktown* on 8 May. (Prange, via Wenger)

LT Milton Ernest Ricketts, USNA 1935, awarded a posthumous Medal of Honor for heroism during the Battle of the Coral Sea on 8 May 1942. (NH 95297)

day. Tragically, when *Zuikaku*'s dive bombers commenced their attack at 1124, he had less than five minutes to live.

The blast from the exploding bomb in C-402-A spent itself upward, partly through a six-foot hole it tore in the deck of C-301-L, hurling shrapnel and devastating the surrounding area, doing considerable damage on the third deck and demolishing an adjacent bulkhead in a laundry storeroom, and causing fragment damage to the second deck. It also damaged bulkheads between the third and fourth decks, in varying amounts, from an area which extended from frame 100 to frame 129 (a distance of some 116 feet), and blew a door off its dogs and hinges at frame 101 (thus marking the "forward extent of the damage"). The force of the explosion also hurled a double door, which had been tightly dogged, 40 feet aft! Lighter bulkheads suffered proportionately, being crumpled or demolished outright. Fires started immediately among the crated supplies in C-402-A, "expeditionary stores," target sleeves and bundles of rags. Dense black smoke filled the immediate area and, due to the fact that the bomb, on its downward flight, had severed "general lighting, battle lighting, and power cables," darkness "reigned" in the compartment.

The exploding bomb decimated the repair party, most of whom had been either sitting on deck or standing in C-301-L. Concussion, shrapnel and flame shot through the compartment, mutilating several men beyond recognition; a few men survived; those who did, unprepared with flash-proof clothing, suffered horrible burns. LT Ricketts, shocked, burned, and bleeding, mortally wounded, opened the valve of a nearby fireplug and partially led out a fire hose, his strength ebbing rapidly. He started to direct a heavy stream of water at the blaze licking up from the compartment below, through the jagged hole in the deck, but soon crumpled, dead, having expended

Lexington recovers her air group on the afternoon of 8 May; a TBD-1 has just landed and is taxiing forward, out of the arresting gear, while a "Wildcat" from VF-2 approaches in the "groove" astern. (80-G-16806)

After respotting her planes aft to clear the flight deck, forward, *Lexington*'s officers and men gather among the clutter of fire hoses and parts from cannibalized aircraft. (80-G-16811)

his last energy to save the ship that had been his home for over four years. Yet even as he was taking this action—which would earn him the posthumous award of the Medal of Honor—others were converging on the scene of destruction on the third and fourth decks.

BOSN Edmund B. Crosby, the assistant to the ship's first lieutenant, CDR Aldrich, took a repair party to the scene of the damage, and CARP Boyd M. McKenzie, another of Aldrich's assistants, was the first to enter the darkened, wrecked, smoke-filled compartment. "Smoke, debris, and live electrical cables hanging about" rendered progress "exceedingly difficult" but the men carried on. Among the living in C-301-L was EM1c L.R. Brooks, who, although burned and severely shocked, refused to go to sick bay for treatment; he carried on his duties of damage control, disregarding his own condition. Another man who ignored his own wounds was Ptr3c William Carpenter, who had immediately proceeded to the compartment after the bomb had hit, and "guided two injured men to safety" before re-entering the compartment, sustaining severe burns in so doing.

LT(jg) Edward A. Kearney, MC, USN, the ship's junior medical officer, arrived soon thereafter from dressing station number one and, "as soon as he could enter" began immediately examining the bodies, directing the rescue of those who showed signs of life "and immediately rendered medical attention which undoubtedly saved the lives of several men who were seriously burned or otherwise severely injured."

Not only had the blast caused much devastation in the immediate area, but the concussion caused a flareback in three boilers, leading to the mistaken impression that fire had broken out in that compartment. Boilers 8 and 9 were shut down, as was number 7; noxious gases and dense smoke filled firerooms 8 and 9, forcing the men therein to abandon their posts. Soon thereafter, though, WT1c Raymond C. Davis bravely entered the smoke- and gas-filled boiler rooms to investigate the extent of the damage. It would be largely through his efforts that the super-heat boilers were back on the line about thirty minutes later.

Topside, the ship fought on against the brief but fierce attack from the skies. Moments after the bomb pierced the flight deck and started its deadly flight downward toward Ricketts' men, two more bombs landed in the water, exploding close aboard on the port quarter, dishing in the shell from frames 101 to 113, "16 feet below the waterline" and pushing in the lower edge of the armored belt, opening a seam through which "Mr. Delaney's juice"—fuel oil—escaped into the sea. Two, or perhaps three, additional bombs exploded off the starboard quarter, literally raising the ship's stern clear of the water, the cascading spray from the great splashes from the near-misses washing gun crews around the gun tubs.

CAPT Buckmaster, knowing his ship was hit, called down to Main Control and asked what speed was available, eliciting the response: "24 knots." Buckmaster then asked if the ship should slow to re-

LT(jg) Scott McCuskey, A-V(N), USNR, of VF-42, unable to reach *Yorktown* because he was low on fuel, landed his F4F-3 (BuNo 2531), F-2, on board *Lexington*. Gassed and spotted first so that McCuskey could return to his own carrier, his "Wildcat" (R) sits on *Lexington's* flight deck as fires below gain headway and ultimately prevent further flight operations. While BuNo 2531 went down with "Lady Lex," McCuskey would be rescued by one of the screening ships, and ultimately returned to *Yorktown*. (80-G-16802)

pair damage, and drew the spirited reply: "Hell no! We'll make it." "At no time did the speed drop below 24 knots," the commanding officer later reported, "until signalled from the bridge."

As the fury of the Japanese attack spent itself against the ships, there still remained the combat above TF-17. Flatley had gone to the rescue of the four SBDs of VS-5 on the disastrous anti-torpedo plane patrol, but soon found himself heavily engaged and separated from Crommelin, Macomber and Bassett. The leader had promptly attacked a "Zero" on his first pass, with Crommelin following. As his wingman initiated his attack, he lost sight of Flatley, and never regained visual contact.

Over the moments that ensued, Crommelin attacked three other fighters in a melee before finding a "Zero" on his tail. Evading his pursuer only momentarily, Crommelin pulled up and inadvertently returned to the area in which there were three other "Zeroes," one of which promptly got on his tail. He finally evaded him, but his adversary had gotten the best of him. As he identified two "friendly" planes, Crommelin checked his instruments, finding all normal. As he continued climbing, however, he noted oil leaking from the gun inspection plate on his left wing. "Shortly thereafter," he later recounted, "oil began streaming from the trailing edge of my left wing, indicating a broken oil line . . ." Throttling back, he levelled off and "began flying among the scattered clouds looking for the carrier."

Meanwhile, at 1131, *Yorktown's* radar went out,

and she so advised *Lexington*, which did not acknowledge on the fighter circuit. By visual signal and TBS, *Yorktown* then informed her consort. Reasoning that *Lexington's* fighter circuit radio transmitter had been knocked out, *Yorktown* then broadcast to all fighters; "Radar out. Protect the fleet."

A carrier without her radar is blind in modern aerial combat. With the CXAM antennae now inoperative, RE Vane M. Bennett, "radio material officer for special super-frequency equipment" and the radar operator during the action, "immediately and correctly diagnosed the trouble as being located in the antenna array." He then unhesitatingly proceeded to the foremast, accompanied only by RM1c Alvin A. Attaway, who volunteered to assist Bennett in the task at hand. Both men soon reached the lofty platform and, initially "exposed to machine gun fire and fragments" from their own anti-aircraft fire, went to work putting the vital CXAM back in commission. Almost an hour of determined labor lay ahead of them before they would do so.

Shortly before *Yorktown* broadcast the word to "protect the fleet" to her airborne fighters, Dick Crommelin's engine "sputtered three or four times and then froze" just as he sighted *Lexington*. His oil pressure dropped to "zero" prompting him to radio Flatley at 1133: "Engine is going out. I'm going to make a forced landing." Seeing a destroyer and a cruiser, Crommelin picked out a point ahead of them and radioed: "I am making a forced landing directly ahead of you." To Flatley's "Good luck," Crommelin lowered his flaps

In this view taken from *Chester* (CA-27), about 1745 on 8 May 1942, *Lexington*, burning, abandons ship while her screen stands by; the heavy cruiser *Minneapolis* (CA-36) is in the immediate background, with *New Orleans* (CA-32) and a destroyer at right. In the far background can be seen *Astoria* (CA-34) and *Yorktown*. (80-G-32331)

and "made a fairly smooth water landing." Climbing out of his sinking F4F, he broke out his rubber boat and shoved off, the F4F-3 remaining afloat for "approximately 30 seconds" before it plunged toward the bottom of the Coral Sea. Soon, *Phelps* (DD-361) lay alongside, and brought Crommelin on board.

Other returning *Yorktown* fighter pilots were having trouble, too. Earlier, while being vectored back to the formation at the outset of the attack on the task force, "Wildcat Orange"—LT(jg)s Brassfield and Mattson—had spotted melee of F4Fs engaging a half-dozen "Zeroes" and evened the odds—momentarily.

Another enemy fighter section pounced on the newcomers, and forced them to fight for their lives. Brassfield, skidding and throttling back his F4F, sent a short burst into a "Zero" that had overshot, and claimed a "kill" before he dove and claimed a *kanbaku*. Recovering from his attack on the dive bomber, however, he noted three "Zeroes" above him, who pushed over and dove on him. One of their shells damaged his instruments, hitting the panel clock and shattering its face, showering him with glass; another grazed his left leg. "Mat" Mattson's experience was much the same: while attacking enemy fighters from astern, he soon discovered "one or more on his fail firing at him." Each time, he sought haven in a nearby cloud—as Brassfield had done—and emerged on one occasion to wing a "Zero."

At 1135, Brassfield radioed tersely: "Request permission to land aboard. Hurt . . ." "Permission granted," came the carrier's response. Soon, *Yorktown*'s "Wildcat Brown" section requested permission to "pancake" (land on board) to replenish ammunition. "Soupy" Campbell, the LSO, soon deftly guided

Yorktown's combat air patrol back to their home deck, bringing in six between 1135 and 1141, as well as a solitary *Lexington* orphan, ENS Edward R. Sellstrom, A-V(N), USNR, of VF-2.

Among those brought on board were Brassfield and Mattson. The former's F4F-3 required a major overhaul; those who looked over his damaged "Wildcat" counted at least 10 holes in the fuselage, "five of which had passed through the emergency fuel tank" to be stopped by the armor; one bullet had holed the main fuel tank, and one had gone through the vacuum tank, in addition to the one that had damaged the instrument panel. Mattson's "Wildcat," too, looked somewhat worse for wear: 30 small-caliber hits in the tail and fuselage.

At 1231, *Yorktown* commenced bringing on board her attack group. Only one of the TBDs had suffered any damage (a bullet hole in its right wing), but 18 SBDs made it back to the carrier with varying degrees of damage—three of which required major overhauls due to numerous 7.7mm and 20mm hits from "Zeroes" machine guns. The remainder, repair crews soon found out, had taken anywhere from one to 26 hits.

One pilot who brought his crippled SBD back to the carrier was LT(jg) Floyd E. Moan. His fuel tanks riddled with 22 holes and his flats inoperative, Moan got the "cut" from "Soupy" Campbell and came in. Unfortunately, his plane missed the wires and barrier and crashed into the island "in full flight." Deck crews scrambled to pull Moan and his gunner (both men had been wounded in the attack on *Shōkaku*), Sea2c Robert J. Hodgens, from their crippled "Dauntless." Both survived, but their plane, deemed "a total wreck," was "later pushed over the side."

One pilot whose battered plane could *not* make it back to the ship was ENS Jorgenson, of Scouting Five. Unable to lower his landing gear and having suffered damage to his wings, Jorgenson—wounded in the right leg—landed near the destroyer *Aylwin* (DD-355) at 1248, electing to ditch rather than foul the barrier. The ship maneuvered and took Jorgenson and his radioman, Brunetti, on board at 1259.

By 1300, about the time *Yorktown* had completed taking on board her air group, the "black gang" had cleared the smoke from the affected areas in the machinery paces, and had gotten boilers seven and eight back "on the main steam line." They got boiler nine back in business within 15 minutes.

Weighty matters confronted Frank Jack Fletcher about that time, too. To pursue or not to pursue: that was the question the admiral turned over in his mind. Should *Yorktown* gather *Lexington*'s undamaged aircraft, form them into a strike group with her own, and launch them to go after the undamaged Japanese flattop? RADM Fletcher contemplated this at the outset, as did CAPT Buckmaster, but CTF-17 seemed hesitant. "In view [of] enemy's fighter plane superiority and [his] undamaged carrier," Fletcher proposed retirement to regroup, at 1315. "What do you think," he queried his classmate, Fitch, who responded at 1324: "Affirmative." Fletcher accordingly ordered that as soon as all planes had been recovered, or that hope had been given up for their return, TF-17 was to proceed south-southwest "at best practicable speed."

Yorktown's planes had all returned by 1344, but not *Lexington*'s. At 1400, *Yorktown* picked up seven unidentified torpedo planes closing the ship from off the starboard beam, at 4,000 feet. Although on the correct return bearing, none of the incoming aircraft made the right recognition signal—even after being challenged 20 times. *Yorktown* opened fire, taking no chances, and fortunately scored no hits, as the seven soon identified themselves as "friendly."

Lexington, still proceeding well under her own power, recovered her stragglers, but her litany of misfortune continued. Her radar went out at 1410, followed by her YE homing antenna. *Yorktown* resumed fighter direction tasks, her circuits briskly crackling with reports by planes in the air, and on the situation below, and of planes circling and climbing, some still trying to get back to home base. *Lexington* asked for help from *Yorktown*: "If you see anything circling or climbing vector it to base . . ."

At this juncture, returning pilot reports all indicated that one of the Japanese carriers seen that morning had not been damaged, while radio intercepts re-

vealed that some *Shōkaku* aircraft had landed on board her sistership. Amidst all of this, RADM Fitch estimated that a *third* Japanese carrier had entered the fray. Should Fletcher launch another strike?

He had not completely abandoned the idea up to that point, but circumstances compelled him to reject it. Not counting *Lexington*'s air group, *Yorktown* could only muster eight F4F-3s, 12 SBDs and six TBDs. Only seven torpedoes were serviceable. Another option presented itself. Having had ample experience with cruisers over the years, Fletcher considered sending a surface attack against the Japanese, but the thought of sending out the strike force, without air cover, to probably be detected and subjected to a "strong carrier air attack before dark" militated against it.

As the decisions were being made as to whether or not to continue the battle, *Yorktown* continued to function as fighter director, as well as assumed the duty of trying to guide two stragglers from *Lexington*'s air group home. One of these was "Lady Lex" group commander, CDR William B. Ault (who had played such a vital role in the Lae-Salamaua strikes), who radioed *Lexington* at 1449: "Can you hear me and do you have me on the screen? I have gas left for about 20 minutes." *Yorktown* responded (*Lexington* being unable to): "I can hear you. You are not on [our] screen." The following transmissions reflected the taut drama unfolding:

1451 CLAG to *Yorktown*: SHALL I CIRCLE X DO YOU WANT ME TO GAIN OR LOSE ALTITUDE X I HAVE GAS LEFT FOR ABOUT 20 MINUTES

1452 *Yorktown* to CLAG: YOU ARE NOT ON THE SCREEN X TRY TO MAKE NEAREST LAND

1453 CLAG to *Yorktown*: NEAREST LAND IS OVER 200 MILES AWAY X WE WOULD NEVER MAKE IT

1454 *Yorktown* to CLAG: YOU ARE ON YOUR OWN X GOOD LUCK

CLAG to *Yorktown*: PLEASE RELAY TO 00V56 [*Lexington*] WE GOT ONE 1,000 POUND BOMB HIT ON A FLAT TOP X WE HAVE BOTH REPORTED 2 OR 3 TIMES X ENEMY FIGHTERS X AM CHANGING COURSE TO NORTH X LET ME KNOW IF YOU PICK ME UP

Yorktown to CLAG: ROGER X YOU ARE ON YOUR OWN X I WILL RELAY YOUR MESSAGE X GOOD LUCK

From CLAG: OK X SO LONG PEOPLE X WE GOT A 1,000 POUND HIT ON THE FLAT TOP.

Shortly before the final exchange of messages between the doomed *Lexington* air group commander and *Yorktown*, a more immediate and dramatic event occupied the attention of TF-17. At 1443, a serious explosion rocked *Lexington* and touched off uncontrollable fires below decks. Immediately prior to that time, although it had been known that *Lex* had suffered "two or more torpedo" hits and several bomb hits," she appeared to be "steaming easily and having no apparent trouble." Less than ten minutes after the explosion, about the time that *Yorktown* was sadly advising Bill Ault that he was on his own, *Lexington* signalled: "Fire is not under control." Soon thereafter, another signal snapped up *Lexington's* halyards: "This ship needs help."

RADM Fletcher now resumed tactical command of TF-17, and *Yorktown* assumed control over all of *Lexington's* radio circuits, calling in all of the latter's planes that were still in the air: six F4Fs and ten SBDs. By 1622, observers could see that *Lexington* was being abandoned, and that cruisers and destroyers lingered nearby, picking up the carrier's officers and men, while two cruisers and two destroyers remained guarding *Yorktown*, standing some distance away. Among the men picked up was "Doc" McCuskey of VF-42, who had landed on board *Lexington* after the battle.

While *Yorktown's* combat air patrol orbited overhead, *Lexington's* orderly abandonment proceeded apace. All his men off, CAPT Frederick C. Sherman took a last tour of his old command and then went over the side, shinnying down a rope to a motor whaleboat from the heavy cruiser *Minneapolis*. Joining RADM Fitch on board that ship, Sherman watched the "magnificent but sad sight" of his "burning and doomed ship." Her captain thought it "too bad . . . she had to perish in her hour of victory," but considered that end "more fitting than the usual fate of the eventual scrap heap or succumbing to the perils of the sea." *Lexington* "went down in battle," Sherman wrote later, "after a glorious victory." To CAPT Buckmaster, watching *Lexington* explode and burn, the sight of that carrier's death throes must have been poignant, too, since he had once been that ship's executive officer. There was no time for sentiment, however. Fletcher, to hasten *Lexington's* end, directed *Phelps* to sink the carrier with torpedoes. The destroyer fired five, of which at least three hit, and "Lady Lex" sank, practically on an even keel.

The *Lexington* pilots and radioman on board *Yorktown*, like orphans who had watched their home burn down, had lingered on deck for a time, watching the sad spectacle unfold on the horizon, before they went below, the officers repairing to the wardroom.

They shed no tears, but neither did speech come easily to them—no one knew what to say. At that moment, with morale at low ebb and spirits depressed, *Yorktown's* ebullient XO, Dixie Kiefer, strode into their midst with four bottles of Four Roses. "I wish I could do more," he said, "but at least there's enough here for each of you to have one good drink." To young ENS Arthur J. Schultz, Jr., A-V(N), USNR, of VS-2, Kiefer's producing the bourbon at that instant "couldn't've been timed better." The mood of the *Lexington* aviators changed—they began to feel a little bit better; someone understood their plight. There was hope after all.

Yorktown recovered her own combat air patrol shortly after sunset, and proceeded on course to clear the area, steaming at 14 knots in the gathering darkness. The ghastly task of removing the bloody and blackened corpses from C-301-L had been carried out, supervised by 1stMus Edgar L. Oakley, a bandsman and the senior stretcher bearer. With all of the corpsmen engaged in treating the wounded, Oakley had personally seen to the removal of the bodies to the after mess hall and thence to the propeller repair room on the 01 deck, a task that required intelligence and courage, and at which he worked until far into the night. Dixie Kiefer considered Oakley's conduct and efforts "beyond the call of duty."

"Due to the mutilated condition of the bodies, to the fact that we expected to be engaged in battle the following day, and for reasons of morale," CAPT Buckmaster decided that the slain should be buried at sea that night. Preparing the remains to be committed to the deep continued into the small hours of the next morning, and at 0200, LCDR Hamilton, *Yorktown's* chaplain, began the service; one by one, the dead, sewn into weighted canvas bags, splashed into the Coral Sea. The service concluded at 0240.

Yorktown maintained the flying-off of patrols to cover the retirement of TF-17. One plane, on 9 May, spotted what appeared to be a Japanese task force, and reported it as such. Alarmed at this turn of events, and limited in what action he could take by the comparatively small strike force he could launch, Fletcher ordered CDR Schindler to fly to Australia and report the sighting, the admiral not willing to give away his position by breaking radio silence. LT(jg) Hugh W. Nicholson, A-V(N), USNR, who had been slightly wounded in the foot the previous day while over *Shōkaku*, drew the duty of piloting the plane, a wear-weary SBD, no.12, and the two men climbed in and set off for Australia. strike mission, meanwhile, took off to bomb the "pursuing Japanese."

Nicholson and his passenger reached Townsville,

where Schindler attempted to reach GEN Mac-Arthur's headquarters by telephone. Unable to get through, he finally managed to get in touch with VADM Leary, COMANZAC. A hastily assembled strike force, consisting of B-17s, B-25s, and B-26s, took off from their Australian fields, but the "Japanese task force" proved to be a reef, which, from high altitude, resembled the wakes of moving ships. Such was the anxious state-of-mind prevailing at the time!

Unbeknownst to Fletcher, the enemy was, in fact, *far* away. After having *Shōkaku* damaged on 8 May, VADM Takagi had turned north, to regroup his force. Operation "MO" had stalled, and the invasion force had not transited the Jomard Passage after all, but had been ordered north on the morning of the 7th, after it had been spotted. ADM Yamamoto, though, when he heard of Takagi's decision, firmly ordered his subordinate to resume the battle: "to strike to the utmost to annihilate the remaining units of the enemy force." By the time Takagi's ships came around, however, TF-17 had outdistanced them. On 9 May, Japanese floatplanes based at Deboyne Island scoured the seas to the southward, but were "unable to follow the movements of the enemy."

The Japanese lost no time at home, however, in glorying over what they thought was a "smashing victory," indeed, "one of the greatest naval battles of all time." Japanese readers had just digested the banner headlines announcing the fall of Corregidor when their newspapers boldly proclaimed another victory—in the Coral Sea.

At 1720, Tokyo time, Imperial Headquarters

TIMES & ADVERTISER, WEDNESDAY, MAY 13, 1942

Crosses in the Wake of Allied Blockade

Macabre cartoon in the *Japan Times & Advertiser* for Wednesday, 13 May 1942, showing Uncle Sam tearfully erecting gravestones in the Coral Sea for his lost ships, one of which, U.S.S. *California*, was the figment of an over-eager Japanese propagandist's imagination! *Saratoga* was, in fact, *Lexington*, and it is obvious that the Japanese considered *Yorktown* as sunk, too. (*Japan Times & Advertiser*, May 13, 1942).

crowed: "Before the might of the ever victorious Imperial Japanese Navy forces, two enemy aircraft carriers, and a battleship, were sunk, and another enemy battleship and an A-class cruiser were severely damaged" in the Coral Sea. "Two American carriers, *Saratoga* and *Yorktown* sunk," a headline proclaimed; "Japan wins again," declared the *Japan Times and Advertiser* on 9 May. To the Japanese, the Battle of the Coral Sea was not "just another naval battle" but an event which marked "another emphatic step in the inevitable march of the Japanese Empire toward the destruction of the old and the building of a new and better world order . . ."

Japanese naval commentators scorned American tactics as "idiotic," and predicted that the battle spelled the doom of the U.S. Navy. Over the ensuing days, articles and editorials continued to call the battle a stunning victory for Japan, and chided the Americans and their Allies for hiding the truth from their people. Emperor Hirohito praised ADM Yamamoto in an Imperial Rescript, and a noted Japanese painter of seascapes, Ken Matsuzuye, depicted the death throes of "*Saratoga*" and *Yorktown*, presenting it to the Navy Ministry on 12 May. The caption which accompanied a photograph of the painting assured the reader that "the American-British combined fleet was thoroughly destroyed and the Pacific is now practically made safe from the Allies' major naval operations."

So confident were the Japanese in the belief that they *had* rendered the U.S. Navy powerless to stop them in the Pacific, that on 12 May, ADM Yamamoto issued the orders for "MI" Operation, the seizure of Midway—the key atoll located at the extreme western end of the Hawaiian chain—as well as for subsidiary assaults on Kiska and Attu, islands in the Aleutians. In so doing, ADM Yamamoto wished to lure out the U.S. Fleet and destroy it.

Although the Japanese exercised the utmost secrecy in planning the thrusts against Midway and the Aleutians, ADM Nimitz' extraordinary intelligence advantage—the broken Japanese naval code—allowed him to know the projected movements of the Combined Fleet in each operation in great detail. The Japanese strength, in both ships and aircraft, as well as the direction from which the offensive would be launched, and the approximate time of attack, all passed before Nimitz' gaze, enabling him to shape measures to meet the unsuspecting enemy.

On 15 May, meanwhile, TF-17 returned to Tongatabu. At Pearl Harbor on the 18th (19th in the Tonga Islands, west of the International Date Line), ADM

Nimitz and his staff discussed courses of action open to the Pacific Fleet in countering the "expected Jap offensive in the Hawaiian area and in Alaska . . ." All present generally believed that the Japanese were not only going to attempt to take Midway, but to raid Hawaii as well. Although Nimitz could not be sure of the exact timing for the operation, he wanted "everything possible to be done" by 25 May. Among the preparations he enumerated: the reinforcement of Marines at Midway—already underway; the stationing of four additional submarines off Midway; staging Army B-17s from the island to bomb enemy carriers when they came within reach; conducting searches with Midway-based PBYs, and employing TF-16 (*Enterprise* and *Hornet*)—plus *Yorktown*, if she could be ready in time.

Summoned back to Pearl Harbor at its "best sustained speed" TF-17 cleared Tongatabu, fully fueled, on 19 May, bound for Hawaii. *Yorktown* trailed a thin banner of oil in her wake from her leaking port fuel tanks.

During the passage back to Pearl Harbor, CAPT Buckmaster worked on his report of the recently concluded Battle of the Coral Sea. On 25 May, as his ship proceeded through the heavy swells driven by an east northeasterly wind, Buckmaster signed his recounting of events, concluding that the conduct of the "entire ship's company and air group" was "worthy of the highest traditions of the naval service." Realizing fully that "we were but beginning a long and arduous task," he writes, "every Officer and Enlisted Man had contributed to the ship's performance in battle." He praised their "tireless energy, unquenchable enthusiasm, and high courage," each man "giving of himself full measure to the successful accomplishment of their mission." Reading these words 42 years later, one senses the pride in his crew that swelled Buckmaster's breast as he wrote: "I can have no higher honor than to have commanded them in battle."

His crew had reciprocated the regard and affection. On the evening of 15 May, soon after the ship had put into Tongatabu, movies were about to be shown on the hangar deck. As was customary, the Chief Master at Arms barked, "Attention!" as the captain entered. What followed, however, was *not* customary: all hands spontaneously cheered and applauded, according Elliott Buckmaster a standing ovation and thus thanking him for bringing them through the Battle of the Coral Sea. Wrote one *Yorktown*er in later years: "At that time I don't think there was a member of the crew that would not have volunteered to go to sea with CAPT Buckmaster in a row-boat."

CHAPTER 8

Ready to Give a Good Account of Herself

THE BATTLE OF THE CORAL SEA once again delayed the Japanese' planned thrust toward Port Moresby. At first glance it looked like an unequal outcome to the contest: small carrier *Shōhō* for carrier *Lexington*, oiler *Neosho* and destroyer *Sims*, but Frank Jack Fletcher's men had not only deprived the enemy of the use of *Shōkaku* and *Zuikaku*, as well as of valuable planes and aircrew, but of *Shōhō*, too, which also had been allocated to the projected "MI" Operation. ADM Yamamoto, however, felt confident that "MI" could proceed on schedule supported primarily by the veteran *Akagi, Kaga, Sōryū* and *Hiryū*, and small carrier *Hōshō*.

On 27 May 1942 (26 May east of the date line), the Japanese Striking Force, almost arrogantly confident, stood out of the Inland Sea, bound for the central Pacific. Their mood contrasted vividly with the anxiety felt in the sortie Pearl Harbor-ward several months before. Appropriately for the enemy, 27 May was "Navy Day," a date upon which Japanese sailors toasted the glory of Imperial Japan and of Admiral Togo, victor over the Russians at Tsushima. "Navy Day this year," proclaimed the *Japan Times and Advertiser* that morning, "means more than it ever has ever meant before," but did not only call to mind Tsushima ("Japan's greatest naval victory prior to the present war") and the "naval heroes of today who have brought the nation even greater glory than in the past." Navy Day, 1942, was the occasion to hail Japan's new world position and to rededicate the nation's naval might to establish and protect a "new world order which will enable the peoples of East Asia to develop their own destinies free from the shackles of Anglo-American exploitation." Navy Day, 1942, boasted the *Advertiser* "is the climax for which all the Navy Days of past years have been a preparation." Britannia no longer ruled the waves, the Japanese proclaimed, and Britain's "auxiliary, the United States, has likewise had her Navy prac-

tically destroyed . . ." Japan, the editorials read, stood as "the premier naval power in the world."

That same day (26 May at Pearl Harbor) the mood in CINCPAC headquarters differed vastly from that prevailing in Tokyo. In evaluating the carrier situation, ADM Nimitz and his staff noted that *Yorktown* had been damaged, and required replacements of planes in her damaged air group. "It is possible," a CINCPAC estimate of that date theorizes, "that she [*Yorktown*] can be placed in service four days after her arrival [in] Pearl." If "adequate temporary repairs" could not be effected there, however, *Yorktown* "would be sent to Bremerton at once" for repairs at Puget Sound. The use of TF-17 in the impending action was a big "if." *Yorktown*'s disposition was to be determined by 28 May.

At 1026 on 27 May, *Yorktown* began launching her flyable planes—42 in number—and, at 1352, stood into Pearl Harbor, 101 days from her departure in mid-February, a time only broken by the two brief periods at anchor at Tongatabu. As she steamed up the channel and passed Ford Island, her crew mustered (as in her previous arrival from the strikes on the Gilberts) in dress whites in the bright Hawaiian sunshine, and the oil from her leaking tanks staining the waters in her wake, all hands who could do so turned out on shore and "cheered ship." Rounding Ford Island, she moored in the Repair Basin (Berth 16), Pearl Harbor Navy Yard, to commence battle damage repairs.

Urgent business confronted the yard force in making *Yorktown* fit for sea. RADM Fitch had estimated her damage to be "moderate" but requiring "about ninety days" to repair. At the outset, though, no one at Pearl Harbor knew exactly what the nature of their work was to be.

At 0720 on 28 May, tugs assisted *Yorktown* into dry dock number one; the caisson was positioned behind her and the dock then pumped out, leaving the carrier high and dry on keel blocks. ADM Nimitz himself personally inspected *Yorktown*'s dished-in shell plating, and left no doubt as to his expectations, when he told the inspection party emphatically: "We must have this ship back in three days." Reflecting Nimitz' inspection of the carrier that day, the CINCPAC "Graybook" contended that *Yorktown*'s damage was "not enough to prevent operations on the evening of the 29th."

Yorktown soon teemed with the cacophonous turmoil of a yard overhaul, workmen and ship's force toiling to meet Nimitz' deadline. Amidships in the damaged compartments, workers replaced "demolished and damaged structure" with materials of "equivalent weight, strength, and section modulus"; cut away "damaged portions of bulkheads" and installed "new beams and stanchions." In the way of the near-misses, workers found frames and transverse flooring to be substantially intact, requiring only that the shell cracks be caulked and the leaky seams and rivets caulked and welded.

To ensure the ship's watertight integrity, "all watertight doors and hatches below the main deck were repaired and tested for watertightness." The report of the repairs effected asserted "all essential watertight boundaries on [the] second deck and below were restored." As the "Graybook" recounts: *Yorktown*'s underwater damage was "slight" and she would be able to leave on the 30th in TF-17. Her presence gave the Americans a "much better chance to be successful at Midway the first week of June."

Although he had suspended liberty from 1830 on 26 May until "further orders," Nimitz allowed it for the men of TF-17 and TF-16, reasoning correctly that they needed it after their long time at sea. *Yorktown* sailors headed for the familiar "houses" and bars of Hotel Street, in Honolulu, before returning to the noisy ship. If a man came back suffering from the effects of too much of a night on the town, he found himself hustled into a shower to be sobered up quickly and hustled into one of the working parties laboring round-the-clock to provision the ship—fresh food in abundance was a treat to *Yorktown*ers used to canned meats and spaghetti.

Cobbling up an air group for *Yorktown* went on simultaneously, replacement squadrons drawn, in the main, from the *Saratoga* Air Group. LT Wally Short's VB-5 was chosen to stay with the ship, his dozen veteran pilots augmented by eight replacements. Much work lay ahead of them in working on the planes that would be assigned to them. The COMCARPAC (formerly COMAIRBATFOR) administrative unit at Ford Island, after surveying all available planes, came up with the best to equip Bombing Five: five were originally from VB-5; six came from VS-5; five came from *Lexington*'s orphaned VS-2; one had originally been CYAG's plane (BuNo 4547) and two came from the "pool" at Pearl Harbor. All needed twin mounts fitted in the rear cockpits to take two .30-caliber machine guns—effectively doubling the rearward-facing firepower. And, to avoid confusion once the squadron got to sea, COMCARPAC redesignated VB-5 to "VS"-5—a seemingly arbitrary decision that irritated *Yorktown*ers and ultimately caused a great deal of confusion over the ensuing decades as to which squadron—VS-5 or VB-5, actually participated in the Battle of Midway.

Short's men worked to near-exhaustion, and after the end of one particularly grueling day, the squadron commander took them to the officer's club at NAS Kaneohe to unwind. They arrived in their work clothes, sweat- and oil-stained khakis, *sans* neckties. Short ordered a round of drinks. The bartender, though, refused to serve them—the men were "out of uniform." For Short, the irritating effrontery of the barkeep was nothing compared to the anti-aircraft fire he had faced over

Yorktown rounds Ford Island, 27 May 1942, en route to the Repair Basin at the Pearl Harbor Navy Yard. Her sailors, as in her previous return from the Marshalls-Gilberts Raids, are wearing their dress whites. The harbor tug *Hoga* (YT-146) is in foreground, while just to the right of the carrier's stern is a reminder of 7 December 1941, the mainmast of battleship *Arizona* (BB-39). (80-G-21931)

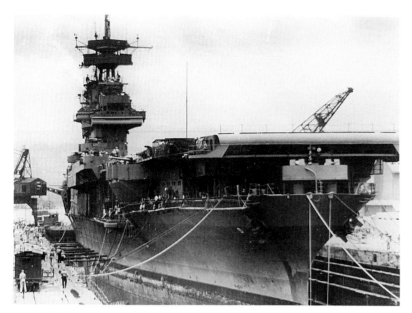

Shoho and *Shokaku*. So, he assumed the bartender's duties himself, while the displaced barman beat a hasty retreat to call upon higher authority—a captain who ordered Short to cease and desist immediately!

The fighting squadron earmarked to go to sea in *Yorktown*, VF-3, had its own unique headaches. Commanded by LCDR John S. "Jimmy" Thach, one of the finest fighter tacticians in the Navy, VF-3 consisted largely of inexperienced pilots fresh from the Advanced Carrier Training Group, leavened by old hands such as MACH Tom F. Cheek (NAP). While VF-6's pilots enjoyed rest and recreation at the Royal Hawaiian, 16 of *Yorktown*'s VF-42 pilots travelled from Ford Island to Kaneohe, a detachment earmarked for temporary duty in VF-3 which, at that point, had more planes than pilots. These planes, however, were new—the heavier Grumman F4F-4. Although the plane had two more guns, the increase in fire-power was largely illusory—the six guns each carried fewer rounds per gun than the -3s. In addition, the wing-folding feature, while fine for the mainte-nance crews and plane-handlers, was a decided handicap—it made the plane heavier and less maneuverable. All in all, some of the older hands could per-haps have been forgiven had they longed for the comparatively more ma-

neuverable F4F-3!

As on board ship, a good executive of-ficer constituted a valuable asset. LCDR Donald A. Lovelace, who had served under Thach in VF-3 during *Lexington*'s early war cruise, had been slated to return to the west coast to take over the newly formed VF-2. Aware that something bit was in the offing, though, Don Lovelace tendered his services to Thach to serve as XO of VF-3. Thach accepted his friend's offer with alacrity and apparently delegated to Lovelace the responsibility of conducting a crash course in the "beam-defense" maneuvers Thach had devised to allow the Grummans to even the odds against the formidable "Zeroes" that had faced them.

Of the 16 VF-42 pilots sent to Kaneohe, 13 had been on board *Yorktown* since February, and faced no imme-diate prospect for a rest. They were somewhat appre-hensive about the new CO and XO—apprehensions which the personable Thach and Lovelace soon put to rest. The small cadre of VF-3 pilots, and the "new" vet-erans of VF-42, began to prepare for the impending battle.

Torpedo Three, another ex-*Saratoga* squadron, was

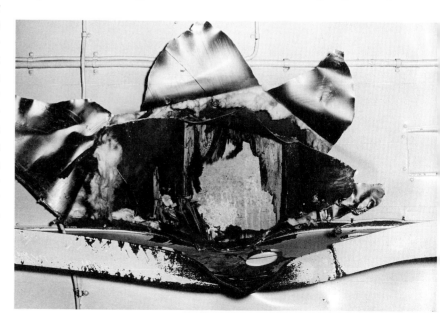

Impact hole from the bomb hit on the flight deck at Coral Sea, showing torn plating, splintered planking, and shredded insulation. (NH 95572)

selected to replace VT-5 for *Yorktown*'s air group. Like Thach, VT-3's commanding officer had tasted combat too—formerly the XO of VT-6 in *Enterprise*, LCDR Lance E. "Lem" Massey had distinguished himself in the early Pacific raids; the squadron considered itself fortunate that it had a "C.O. that had seen action . . ." "Intelligent, fair and well-liked by all of his command," Lem Massey enjoyed the confidence of his men and despite the comparative inactivity of the squadron's existence at Kaneohe, managed to maintain morale at a high level. Torpedo Three, left shipless by the torpedoing of *Saratoga*, had stood "pre-dawn to after-dusk alerts," with all planes manned and fully armed. Three months of relative inactivity passed until Massey took command and finally obtained permission to carry out training flights, with all planes still on alert status. Ground training, upkeep and maintenance of the 15 TBD-1s assigned VT-3 kept all hands busy. Then, in late May LCDR Massey had attended a conference in Pearl Harbor; he returned with the news that the squadron, less a small cadre who would remain behind to take delivery of the new TBF-1s scheduled to arrive soon, would be embarking in *Yorktown*. No one had any idea of the nature of the deployment, but all hands were "elated to go to sea again after the months of monotony on shore. Morale was high and all hands were confident of our invincibility against the lowly Jap."

Unlike VT-3, VB-3, under LCDR Maxwell F. Leslie, had had one period of active carrier operations. They had spelled Scouting Six—which had suffered the heaviest losses in the *Enterprise* Air Group in the early Pacific raids—on board *Enterprise* during the voyage to Japan covering *Hornet* with the embarked Doolittle raiders. Like VT-3 though, they had been operating out of NAS Kaneohe, practicing their craft.

Yorktown's fitness for the task at hand had not been all that had been in question. Upon Fletcher's return from the Coral Sea on 27 May, Nimitz had summoned him for an immediate meeting and the two men conversed about what TF-17 had done since late March. Fletcher convinced CINCPAC of his aptness for the task, but the latter asked TF-17's commander

Sailors clear away debris from the wreckage caused by the blast when the bomb exploded and holed the 3d deck on 8 May; this view is looking forward and to starboard from frame 110, centerline, in compartment C-301-L. (NH 95573)

Wreckage in aviation storeroom, compartment C-402-A, from the bomb detonation on 8 May; view is looking aft and to port from frame 109, centerline. (Author)

to commit his impressions to paper anyway, to "confirm his verbal statements." This he did, and what emerged, interspersed with pertinent passages drawn verbatim from his forthcoming action report on the Battle of the Coral Sea, amounted to what Fletcher called "an informal account of the 101 days away from Pearl Harbor." The lengthy missive, given to Nimitz on the 28th, corroborated the oral statements made

123

View of repairs to the outer shell of the hull below the waterline on the port side after yard workmen had caulked, welded, and patched it, Pearl Harbor Navy Yard, 29 May 1942. (19-N-110004)

Fragment damage to the hull on the starboard side, near frame 42, caused by the explosion of a bomb close aboard the ship at Coral Sea. Shadow is from yard workmen on scaffolding above, 29 May 1942. (Author)

by Fletcher to CINCPAC the previous day.

In his covering letter to ADM King on the 29th, Nimitz wrote that matters pertaining to Fletcher "had been cleared up to my satisfaction, and, I hope, to yours . . ." Fletcher had done a "fine job," CINCPAC declared, and exercised "superior judgement" in the previous months. Nimitz had found him to be an "excellent seagoing, fighting naval officer," and avowed his intention to retain him as a task force commander. In addition, Nimitz also asked that a Distinguished Service Medal be awarded Fletcher, and reiterated his

request that he be promoted to the rank of vice admiral. Fletcher would remain at the helm of TF-17.

In the same vein, Nimitz also described *Yorktown's* status to King, noting that she had been docked "for inspection and repair of a minor leak." When she cleared Pearl Harbor the next day, he went on, she would have a "full complement of planes and will in all respects be ready to give a good account of herself." "We are actively preparing to greet our expected visitors with the kind of reception they deserve," Nimitz concluded optimistically, "and we will do the best we can with what we have."

And what Nimitz had was one task force, TF-16, comprised of *Enterprise* and *Hornet* and their screening cruisers and destroyers, which had already departed Hawaiian waters. It was led by RADM Raymond A. Spruance, who had replaced a bed-ridden Bill Halsey. A second, formed around *Yorktown*, was readying itself for sea. Shortly before that carrier was to sail on the morning of 30 May, ADM Nimitz visited her. While no one recorded exactly what the admiral told CAPT Buckmaster, LCDR Ray recounted that Nimitz apparently "told the captain to announce to the crew that he was sorry he couldn't send us back to the Coast, that we had work that had to be done, and when the Midway affair was over he would send the *Yorktown* back to the West Coast for liberty and he did not mean peanuts."

On the morning of 30 May 1942, then, TF-17 sortied from Pearl Harbor, led by the plucky *Hammann; Morris, Anderson, Russell* and *Hughes* followed, all five destroyers wearing the irregular, splotchy blues and grays of their Measure 12 (mod.) camouflage; then came the heavy cruisers in their weathered blue warpaint, *Astoria* and *Portland*. Finally, at 0939, came *Yorktown*, still bearing her weatherbeaten Measure 12, blue and gray, paint job she had worn since her Atlantic days. She stood out proudly, like the lady she was. On deck, her band played "California, Here I Come."

Beneath clear skies, TF-17 headed northwesterly, a fresh northeasterly breeze whipping the sea into whitecaps. Early that afternoon, all ships of the force—including *Yorktown*—fired anti-aircraft gunnery practices, with 5-inch and automatic weapons, at towed sleeves or sled targets. LCDR Davis, *Yorktown's* gunnery officer, who had been anxious to see what his "revamped" gun crews could do, evidenced displeasure with the ship's "score," and he let his division officers know it in no uncertain terms. *Yorktown* had survived the Battle of the Coral Sea, he warned, but she would need "more hits per gun per minute" and "might need them very soon."

As LCDR Davis was admonishing his officers, CAPT Buckmaster's voice began coming over the ship's loud-speaking system. The captain imparted the news to his officers and men of what lay ahead, where *Yorktown* was going, and what would be required of her. *Yorktown* was heading for Midway, he said, and outlined the situation as it existed at that time. He then told the crew what ADM Nimitz had told him, that the ship would be sent to Bremerton when the battle was over—and not just for two weeks! "That announcement," recalled "Jug" Ray, "restored morale 100%." "We could see that beautiful Puget Sound and its secure Navy Yard . . . could visualize loved ones coming to meet the ship—and old timers could regale newer members of the crew with stories of *Yorktown*'s 1939 overhaul in Bremerton," remembered then-LT John Wadleigh, who wondered, along with his roommate, LT William R. Crenshaw, "what Bremerton would be like as a wartime boom town."

LT Wallace C. Short, Jr., began the war as XO of VS-5 but fleeted up to become CO of Bombing Five, which he led in the Battle of the Coral Sea. He is seen here on board *Yorktown*, 14 January 1942. (Traynor, via Sawruk)

That afternoon, while *Yorktown* and her consorts steamed northwestward, ADM Nimitz addressed a gathering at Memorial Day exercises at Pearl Harbor. During his speech, Nimitz declared that "the course before us holds long periods of intense preparation, arduous labor, and even danger—perhaps future disappointments . . ." before ultimate victory would be achieved. Only the comparative few who had been privy to all of the elaborate preparations for Midway's defense could have known how close to the truth Nimitz was in his statements. The Memorial Day speech reflected all that had been involved in getting Midway, and the task forces steaming northwestward to support it, ready to parry the impending Japanese thrust.

That afternoon, *Yorktown* began bringing on board her air group. Awaiting the new squadrons were some old hands; CAPT Buckmaster retained some skilled people—ordnancemen, mechanics, plane handlers, pharmacist's mates and cooks—from "The Mighty Y's" old squadrons that had been left behind: VF-42's men would service VF-3's new "Wildcats" (some of which were being flown by the cadre of veterans from the well-travelled Fighting Forty-Two); VT-5's would keep up the familiar TBD-1s of VT-3; VS-5's would maintain VB-3's SBDs.

Fighting Three flew in, led by "Jimmy" Thach, and as the CO taxied his F4F-4 up to the deck to be spotted forward, eager plane-handlers—unfamiliar with the intricacies of the new

LCDR John S. ("Jimmy") Thach (who inherited the nickname of his older brother James, who preceded him at the USNA), is seen here at NAS Kaneohe, May 1942, with some of his pilots: (L-R) MACHs (NAPs) Tom F. Cheek and Doyle Barnes, LT(jg) Nels L. A. Berger, A-V(N), USNR, ENS Robert A. M. Dibb, A-V(N), USNR, LCDR Thach, LT(jg) Charlie N. ("Tex") Conatser, A-V(N), USNR; both Berger and Conatser, formerly SBD pilots with VB-5, were on temporary duty with VF-3. (Cheek, via Lundstrom)

Grumman F4F-4 (BuNo 5171), plane no. 1 of VF-3, assigned to LCDR John S. Thach, CO of the squadron, flown on combat air patrol by LCDR Thach during the second Japanese attack on *Yorktown* on 4 June (Tomonaga's torpedo planes), during which engagement he downed the strike leader (Tomonaga). This photo illustrates the wing-folding process which plane-handlers on *Yorktown* had to learn quickly—their previous experience having been with the non-folding wing F4F-3s. View taken 29 May 1942. (80-G-66154)

folding wings—tried folding the wings of plane no. 1, only to break the flaps in so doing. Thach patiently explained how to do it the *right* way after leaping down from his cockpit, and no further mishaps occurred. Tragedy, however, soon visited the ship and robbed VF-3: LCDR Lovelace, flying plane no. 13, came on board without incident; after a hookman disengaged the F4F-4's tailhook from the cross-deck pendant, he taxied forward. ENS R.C. Evans, A-V(N), USNR, was meanwhile making his approach. Evans came in "hot" and cleared the barrier; motor snarling, his F4F-4 crashed atop no. 13, the propeller slashing through the exec's cockpit—Lovelace died within minutes of the accident.

A true leader should have the capacity of instilling subordinates with confidence which surmounts setbacks; Thach, though deeply grieved by the loss of his friend, gathered his men after all had come aboard and gotten settled in, and told them they could not dwell on the past—they had a big task ahead of them and had to devote their energies and strength to that job. Defending the task force, Thach told them emphatically, was paramount—even to the extent of ramming a torpedo plane to bring it down. LT(jg) William N. Leonard, a VF-42 veteran, after Lovelace's death became VF-3's XO; the preparation of the squadron's F4F-4s continued, crude bore-sighting ar-

Two Grumman F4F-4s of VF-3 at NAS Kaneohe on 29 May 1942. At left is no. 5 (BuNo 5167); at right is no. 10 (BuNo 5149), flown on combat air patrol during LT Kobayashi's dive bombing attack on *Yorktown* on 4 June, by LT(jg) Arthur J. Brassfield, who shot down four Aichi Type 99s. (80-G-61533)

"An eager, happy-go-lucky group of individuals," VT-3's pilots at NAS Kaneohe, 29 May 1942: Despite a light rain, LCDR "Lem" Massey* points to a chart, with his XO, a hatless LT Patrick H. ("Pat") Hart*, standing beside him. Kneeling (L-R): ENS David J. Roche, A-V(N), USNR*, MACH John R. Baker (NAP), and LT(jg) Donald E. Weissenborn, A-V(N), USNR. Standing in front (L): ENS Carl A. Osberg, A-V(N), USNR* (.45 at hip)(R); LT(jg) Richard W. Suesens, A-V(N), USNR* (ordnance), ENS Oswald A. Powers A-V(N), USNR*, LT(jg) Fred W. Herriman, A-V(N), USNR (assistant operations); standing, rear (L-R): CAP Wilhelm G. ("Bill") Esders (NAP), ENS Wesley A. Osmus, A-V(N), USNR** (behind ENS Roche), MACH Harry L. Corl (NAP)***, LT(jg) John N. Myers (personnel), ENS Leonard L. Smith, A-V(N), USNR*, MACH John W. Haas (NAP)*, ENS Gerald L. Stablein, A-V(N), USNR, ENS John W. Armitage, A-V(N), USNR, ENS Charles W. Schneider, A-V(N), USNR (looking up). Not present (perhaps the photographer?): LT(jg) Curtis W. Howard* (operations). (* indicates killed in action in Battle of Midway; ** executed by Japanese while POW in Battle of Midway; *** killed in action at Eastern Solomons, 24 August 1942). (Esders)

rangements were devised and gunsights calibrated.

The men topside on board the destroyers screening *Yorktown* had watched these landings with professional interest. *Anderson* had noted the fatal deck crash in her log, while observers in *Morris*, a ship that had operated with *Yorktown* many times, did not like the looks of the landings on board the carrier. This particular group of aviators, "Beany" Jarrett later commented, looked definitely "green."

While *Yorktown* and TF-17 was steaming to join it, TF-16 had not been idle; it had begun flying searches to augment those being carried out from Midway and Johnston Islands, and provide security for itself as *Enterprise* and *Hornet* and their screens passed out of the areas covered by Hawaii-based planes. *Hornet*

launched the forenoon search on 1 June; fog cancelled those scheduled for that afternoon. On 2 June, *Enterprise*'s planes carried out the forenoon search, but bad weather ("cold and wet as hell," commented an *Enterprise* pilot) compelled them to return early. Rain and fog cancelled the afternoon searches, too.

At 1600 on 2 June, TF-17, having fueled from the oilers *Cimarron* (AO-22) and *Platte* (AO-24) on 1 June, rendezvoused with TF-16 and RADM Fletcher, senior to RADM Spruance, assumed tactical command of the strike force as it steamed north of Midway, on courses designed to keep "well clear of the Hawaiian chain" and to avoid Japanese submarine activity. As events would prove, Nimitz' timely dispatch of these two task forces resulted in their not being detected by

Yorktown en route to Midway, as seen from *Portland* between 30 May and 4 June. The carrier's Measure 12 camouflage is clearly discernible, as are the groups of life rafts slung directly below the island—eight groups of two, as well as on the lower part of the stack, at least four rafts visible here. (80-G-32585)

LCDR Lance E. Massey, CO of VT-3, in the cockpit of the Douglas TBD-1 (BuNo 0343) which he had flown while XO of VT-6 (6-T-2) but which had been transferred to VT-3 by the time this picture was taken on 24 May 1942. Note the sinking ship superimposed on the "rising sun" emblem beneath the cockpit windscreen, one of the earliest examples of that kind of marking. BuNo 0343 was later coded T-8 and lost in the Battle of Midway; its pilot was ENS D.J. Roche, A-V(N), USNR. Massey, who had earned a DFC by this time for his performance of duty while XO of VT-6, would later be awarded (posthumously) a Navy Cross for his leadership of VT-3 at Midway. He was flying T-1 (BuNo 0285) that day. (80-G-66074)

the picket submarines the Japanese had deployed astride the expected route of the American fleet lured into battle at Midway. By the time the Japanese had arrived on station, the ships they had hoped to ambush had, in fact, eluded them.

While the American force managed to remain undiscovered, the Japanese soon began coming into view in bits and pieces of the armada bearing down upon Midway. At 0904 on 3 June, a Midway-based PBY saw what looked like two enemy cargo ships (actually two minesweepers). While this PBY's report heralded the approach of Japanese forces, a second overshadowed it in importance. Another PBY, at 0925, told of the presence of a larger group of Japanese ships—the occupation force—bearing 261° from Midway, 700 miles away, at the limit of the PBY patrols being carried out from the atoll.

Fletcher, on the basis of these reports, made an "estimate of the situation" and decided, correctly, that the ships the PBYs had spotted were not the ones he sought. Knowing that his "great advantage lay in surprise" in this high-stakes game, he chose not to tip his hand until certain that the situation required it. He thus maintained his force north of Midway, keeping station at courses and speeds to allow him to stay in the vicinity and carry out aircraft operations that ensured the security of his own forces, TF-16 ten miles to the south of TF-17.

Yet Fletcher regarded land-based aircraft and their search capabilities warily, having experienced some frustration in that regard when operating in the Coral Sea. Unwilling to rely wholly on Midway's planes, he wisely ordered Yorktown to launch a second scouting mission on 3 June. At 1300, ten more SBDs took off to scour the same sector searched earlier that morning (240°-260°) but only to a distance of 175 miles (vice 200) from TF-17. Although Fletcher's choice of sector was excellent, the SBDs found nothing.

At the time of the sighting of the occupation force by the PBYs earlier that day, at 0925, TF-17 and TF-16 were bearing 013°, 320 miles from Midway. A little over ten hours later, at 1940, Fletcher ordered a course change which would take TF-17 to a launch point approximately 200 miles north of Midway at daybreak on 4 June. As it had done since the rendezvous on the morning of the 2d, TF-16 remained ten miles to the south of TF-17. At midnight, Yorktown and her consorts were 271 miles from Midway.

At Pearl Harbor on 3 June, ADM Nimitz and his staff waited, enjoying the advantages of "exceptionally fine" radio and cryptanalysis intelligence. No one harbored any illusions about what rode on the success, or failure, of ADM Nimitz' deployment of his three precious carriers. Nimitz' Memorial Day speech at Pearl Harbor had perhaps revealed much of his private thoughts on the battle that lay ahead. "The whole course of the war in the Pacific," wrote CINCPAC's war diarist in the "Graybook," "may hinge on the developments of the next two or three days."

That same evening, another naval man was penning quite different thoughts in a diary. On board the battleship Haruna, a Japanese junior officer ruminated: "I wonder what the people on Midway are doing now? Not knowing tomorrow they are going to Hell."

CHAPTER 9

A Godawful Lucky Coordinated Attack

BY DAYBREAK ON 4 JUNE, 1942, the searches conducted by VS-5 had not been very productive due to the poor visibility and rain squalls that hampered them considerably. *Enterprise* and *Hornet*, meanwhile, maintained their air groups in readiness. In the pre-dawn darkness that morning, Frank Jack Fletcher, through the reports from Midway and CINCPAC, only knew, in general, that the Japanese were to the westward. The enemy ships sighted by the PBY, though, were not the striking force so eagerly sought, but the occupation force.

At 0447, though, the American striking force intercepted a message from a patrolling PBY to Radio Midway: "Large enemy forces bearing 261° T, distance 500, course 080, speed 13 . . . ten ships." At dawn, *Yorktown* launched ten SBDs of VS-5 "as a security watch against surprise by enemy carriers not previously located by our forces . . ." as well as six F4Fs for a combat air patrol. The SBDs searched a northern semicircle to a distance of 100 miles, but found nothing.

At 0734, however, TF-16 and TF-17 received word which disclosed the position of enemy carriers, and, later, "many planes heading Midway . . ." heralding the approach of the Nakajima B5N2s and Aichi D3A1s making up the bulk of the attacking Japanese strike. The reports, however, did not tell of the *number* of carriers until 0808. Upon receiving this Fletcher directed RADM Spruance in TF-16 to "proceed southwesterly and attack enemy carriers when definitely located . . ." Within a half hour's time, the VS-5 SBDs were returning from the morning search, while another group of F4Fs was relieving the combat air patrol over TF-17. *Yorktown* then changed course and increased speed to 25 knots. At 0910, the first attack planes began taking off from *Enterprise* and *Hornet*.

Fletcher, though, perhaps recalling the all-out strike launched on 7 May that only ended up bagging *Shōhō*,

Yorktown near-twin sister *Enterprise* launching her attack group on 4 June (an F4F-4 is just clearing the bow ramp); *Northampton* (CA-26) is in the background. Some previous identifications of this carrier as *Yorktown* are incorrect; this ship has the forebridge peculiar to *Enterprise* as well as CXAM-1 radar at the foretop (*Yorktown* had CXAM). View taken from *Pensacola* (CA-24), the first of a series she would take this day. (80-G-32224)

LT(jg) Frank Fisler of VP-51, flying a VP-23 PBY-5B (BuNo 2389) flies near TF-17 at around 0930 on 4 June while *Yorktown* prepares to fly off the day's first CAP (VF-3), followed by the VB-3 and V"S"-5 search flights, and the TBD-1s from VT-3, which are spotted to lead the strike. (80-G-21628)

As *Yorktown* prepares to begin launching her strike with LCDR "Lem" Massey's VT-3 TBD-1s spotted aft, an SBD makes a low pass over the ship, perhaps to drop a message container to avoid breaking radio silence. (80-G-23842)

A TBD-1, Mk.XIII torpedo visible beneath its belly, heads for the Japanese fleet. Varying theories of the identity of this aircraft have been advanced over the years, but the most likely is that this is a VT-3 aircraft from *Yorktown*, since other photographs in the sequence appear to have been taken from on board heavy cruiser *Portland*, in the screen of TF-17. (80-G-21668)

LT(jg) William N. Leonard, XO of VF-3, takes off in his Grumman F4F-4 (BuNo 5244) on CAP on the morning of 4 June, as photographed by PhoM2c William G. Roy. Note .50 caliber Browning MG (R), its crew protected in rudimentary fashion by splinter mattresses lashed to the lifelines. The lack of cooling hoses to the barrel indicates that it is one of those mounts jury-rigged wherever there was room. Each .50 caliber gun required two and a half gallons of cooling water; it could be fired without it, but accuracy diminished as the barrel heated and the pattern of shots became more widely dispersed. (80-G-312016)

cautiously husbanded his air strength in TF-17. Unwilling to commit all three carrier air groups to attack only two carriers, he had ordered those in TF-16 to locate and destroy the ones he knew about; he held *Yorktown*'s air group for the others, hoping that Midway-based aircraft would soon locate them. As he saw his flagship's flight deck, though, packed with planes and spotted for launch, concern that the enemy would catch these aircraft by surprise prompted him to modify his hitherto cautious stance. He elected to launch half the bombers, all of the torpedo planes, and six fighters to cover the TBDs. He would retain the other half of his SBDs for use as a reserve strike force, in case the other Japanese carriers *were* sighted. The word proved a tonic for the restive pilots and radioman-gunners, some of the latter assigned to VT-3 bantering about future "what did you do in the war" questions. Some feared they would have to tell their children and grandchildren that all they had done at Midway was wait around.

By 1106, 17 SBDs from Bombing Three, 12 TBDs from Torpedo Three, and six F4Fs of Fighting Three had left *Yorktown*'s deck, dispensing with the lengthy rendezvous over the task force to form up en route, which saved time and gasoline. "Given complete information on the seriousness of the situation,"

ENS Richard H. "Dick" O'Brien, USNA 1942, known by his friends for his "never failing good humor, thoughtful consideration and abounding generosity," graduated with his class in December 1941 because of the wartime emergency. He had been a fine intercollegiate pugilist. Naval Academy fight fans considered O'Brien knocking out his University of Virginia opponent at the final bell of their bout as one of the highlights of the 1941 season. Here he rests beside an Oerlikon machine gun in the battery he commanded on *Yorktown*'s port side. SBDs of V"S"-5 or VB-3 are spotted on the flight deck in the background. (80-G-312008)

before they took off, every pilot . . . indeed "every man on board" knew that it was up to them to stop the Japanese carriers. So important, too, was the necessity for clear contact reports that LCDR Ray told his yeoman to round up all of the code books in use by the squadrons and put them in the safe. The lessons of the Coral Sea fresh in his mind, "Jug" Ray told the pilots that if they had anything to report, use *plain language*.

Soon after the last of the attack group had rolled down the deck and over the bow ramp, toward the same objective sought by *Enterprise* and *Hornet* groups, *Yorktown* launched six F4F-4s for a combat air patrol. She then respotted her flight deck with 12 F4F-4s and 17 SBDs from the veteran Scouting (ex-Bombing) Five, ready "for immediate takeoff." Due to this launch, which required *Yorktown* and her consorts to steam to the southeastward, TF-16 and TF-17 drew apart, "out of sight of each other." Once she had gotten her planes airborne, *Yorktown* set course 240°, 25 knots.

Upon departure from *Yorktown*, meanwhile, Bombing Three climbed to 15,000 feet, en route to the reported enemy position, staying well above the lumbering TBDs

LCDR Maxwell F. "Max" Leslie, CO of VB-3, seen here in late April 1942, while serving a tour of temporary duty in *Enterprise*. A star baseball player at the USNA, Leslie once purportedly told a classmate: "We can't all be heroes but we can all try." He evidenced plenty of an "old bull dog spirit" on 4 June 1942. (NH 95555, cropped)

and their six plane escort. The latter two elements of the air group proceeded at low level, navigating by the whitecaps on the sea and using convenient clouds to screen their passage.

"We were a bit jittery," Thach later said of the experience, when suddenly, an explosion in the water ahead of the "Wildcats" sent up a geyser of spray, adding nothing whatever to the fighter pilots' peace of mind; then another occurred, and two more. Above Thach, four Bombing Three pilots roundly cursed their luck; LCDR Leslie, along with ENSs Isaman, Lane, and Merrill, had accidentally dropped their 1,000-pound bombs, due to "faulty electrical release connections." *These* were the mysterious missiles hurtling from the heavens into the ocean!

At about noon, "Lem" Massey, at the head of Torpedo Three, sighted the Japanese Mobile Force, 35 miles to the northwest and heading east at about 20 knots, busily evading *Enterprise*'s torpedo planes. The enemy's formation appeared "scattered" as the Ameri-

cans swung to the northward. Thach, watching VT-3's movements, then noticed the enemy ships; so did Leslie, who swung northward, too. They awaited the word from Massey that Torpedo Three was ready to commence its attack.

To Thach, leading the escorting F4Fs, the Japanese ships, still engaged in evading the last gasp of the VT-6 attack, appeared not to be damaged in any way, not on fire, "not even making a light brown haze." Two bursts of anti-aircraft fire that blossomed ahead of them soon warned the Americans that the enemy had them in sight. At about that time, Leslie asked Lem Massey if Torpedo Three was ready, as the TBD-1s circled toward the north side of the Japanese force at 2,600 feet. Directed by the shell bursts, two "Zeroes" from the combat air patrol moved in, some 14 to 18 miles from their carriers. Almost as soon as Massey answered Leslie in the affirmative, LT D.W. Shumway, leading the third division of Bombing Three, heard Massey's frantic voice crackling through the static, informing Thach "that there were fighters attacking his squadron."

Almost simultaneously, a large group of enemy fighters, estimated by Thach to be anywhere from 15 to 20, tore into the covering "Wildcats" and Massey's "Devastators." One of the F4Fs—ENS Bassett's—fell out of formation, smoking on its inexorable downward flight, breaking into flames shortly before it impacted with the water. The Mitsubishis and Grummans became entangled in a fierce dogfight while the TBDs lumbered on, attracting ever-growing numbers of "Zeroes," their rear-seat men faced with an aggressive avalanche of the ash-gray fighters.

"Jimmy" Thach gave credit where credit was due—the Japanese attack on VF-3 and VT-3 seemed "perfectly timed" and coordinated beautifully. "Zeroes kept coming at us," Thach later recalled. "It was like being inside a bee hive."

MACH Tom Cheek, an ex-TBD pilot, and ENS Dan Sheedy, A-V(N), USNR, astern of Torpedo Three as close escort, endured their own separate battle for survival. Both were roughly handled, Sheedy wounded in the right ankle and shoulder; but each gave as well as

Designer Norman Bel Geddes' depiction of VB-3's attack on carrier *Sōryū* on 4 June. (80-G-701885)

he got, Cheek flaming the first Japanese pilot to attack VT-3, and downing a second "Zero" into the sea as well. Separated in the melee, both pilots ultimately got out of the battle, glad to be alive.

As Fighting Three had left the ready room on board *Yorktown*, Thach had told his men to stick together. "I don't want any lone wolves," he said. "The wolves don't last long." Having drilled his VF-3 pilots in the skies over Oahu in the necessity of staying and fighting as a team, he rallied his three pilots, himself, Dibb, and Macomber (a VF-42 veteran), to survive the onslaught, and soon, the tactic of "weaving," leading an enemy plane in front of the guns of one's wingman, began to work.

"Skipper, there's a Zero on my tail," sang out ENS Robert A.M. Dibb, A-V(N), USNR, Thach's wingman. "Get him off." As trained, Dibb led the "Zero" across Thach's gunsight, the enemy turning and coming at him head-on. Having heard about the "fanatical" Japanese tendency to never pull out of a head-on

attack, Thach murmured to himself, "*This* one's going to . . ." and triggered his .50-calibers. He knew he was hitting, but the "Zero" pressed on, growing larger in his sights. A collision loomed. Then, at the last instant, the "Zero" lifted his left wing and slid past, Thach catching a glimpse of the flames streaming out of the Mitsubishi's belly.

Although "pitifully inferior in climb, maneuverability, and speed," the F4F-4s proved rugged in the desperate air battle over the Mobile Force, as Fighting Three claimed six "certain" kills and seven "probables" in the melee. ARM3c Lloyd F. Childers, in T-3, occasionally glimpsed the desperate dogfight above him, and, after he saw a "Zero" plummet into the ocean, thought to himself, at least "the F4Fs were not losing every encounter." Unable to tell at one point if the planes falling from the sky were friend or foe, he thought, "My God, this is just like watching a movie."

Thach lost count of his victories; initially marking them down on a pad strapped to his knee, he soon de-

VB-3 pilots and radio-gunners on board *Enterprise*, 12 June 1942. Front (L-R) (all A-V(N), USNR, unless indicated): ENS Robert H. Benson, ENS Alden W. Hansen, ENS Charles S. Lane, ENS Robert K. Campbell, LT(jg) Gordon A. Sherwood, USN, LT DeWitt W. Shumway, USN (acting CO), LT Harold S. ("Sid") Bottomley, USN, ENS Roy M. Isaman, ENS Paul W. Schlegel, ENS Philip W. Cobb. Rear (L-R) (all USN unless otherwise indicated): ENS Milford A. Merrill, A-V(N), USNR, ARM3c Frederick P. Bergeron, AMM1c Horace H. Craig, ARM2c Harmon D. Bennett, ARM1c Ray E. Coons, AMM2c David F. Johnson, ARM3c Sidney K. Weaver, RM3c Leslie A. Till, ARM3c Jack A. Shropshire, ARM2c Clarence E. Zimmershead, ENS Bunyan R. ("Randy") Cooner, A-V(N), USNR. Both Cooner's and Merrill's radio-gunners (AOM2c Clifton R. Bassett and ARM3c Dallas J. Bergeron, respectively) were recovering from their wounds on the day the picture was taken. (80-G-95556)

cided that was "silly" because he had to look down, and "might get shot doing it." No one was going to see the knee pad anyway, Thach reasoned, "so let's give them hell and forget it." And give it to the enemy they did, and the "Thach Weave," as the "beam defense" maneuver became known, received its baptism of fire.

The supreme effort by Thach and his pilots, though, did not save Torpedo Three. "Lem" Massey led the TBDs toward their objective, the formation of "Devastators" maneuvering considerably, gaining or losing altitude as necessary in order to evade the multiplying number of fighters. Too low to commence an attack effectively— the TBDs could not get up enough speed from low altitude—Torpedo Three nevertheless pressed on, the last of the carrier-based torpedo squadrons to attack the Mobile Fleet. Torpedo Eight had been first; Torpedo Six had followed; no planes got away from the first attack; few from the second. But who could have reasonably expected the slow "Devastators" to go on in on their own, bereft of fighter cover and

LT(jg) Paul A. Holmberg, USNA 1939, scored the first bomb hit on Japanese carrier *Sōryū*; he was awarded a Navy Cross for his pressing home his attack on 4 June. (Holmberg)

not coordinated with the dive bombers? Torpedo Three's gallant charge would accomplish much more, though, than had those of VT-8 or VT-6.

Bullets and cannon shell from the "Zeroes'" guns slammed into the lumbering TBDs early on. One, plane no. 12, the "tail-end Charlie" of Torpedo Three, staggered from the formation aflame, and slanted toward the sea. Its pilot, ENS Wesley F. Osmus, A-V(N), USNR, a 23-year old Chicagoan, bailed out from the burning "Devastator"; his radioman, ARM3c Benjamin R. Dodson, Jr., did not. His face, hands and arms burnt, the short, stocky, dark-haired Osmus inflated his Mae West and tred water. He was an athletic young man, and a good swimmer; a "persevering" type, he watched the battle draw on without him; he watched his shipmates from Torpedo Three battle for its collective life.

To Childers, the sight of the Japanese ships was "awesome" as flak blossomed ahead. Suddenly, in his high-pitched voice, his pilot, MACH Harry Corl, yelled excitedly, "Look at the skipper!" Childers saw Massey's plane burst into flames and crash.

CAP Bill Esders, flying on the other wing on Massey, also saw the squadron leader's TBD hit the ocean, leaving Esders, a highly skilled enlisted pilot, leading the formation. Maneuvering violently to escape the tracers zipping by and into his "Devastator," Esders glimpsed another TBD splash into the ocean. From his vantage point, no more than five other TBDs had survived to that point to drop their Mk.XIIIs.

Esders dropped his torpedo, feeling the plane suddenly lighten after being relieved of the burden of the "fish." Suddenly he heard the voice of his gunner, ARM2c Robert B. Brazier, telling him that he had been hurt—badly—and "would be of no further use" in warding off the fighter attacks. Unbeknownst to Esders, "Mike" Brazier had been mortally wounded in his back and legs.

Esders cleared the formation's target, *Hiryū*, by several hundred yards; four other TBDs crossed directly over the bow of the ship; one crashed directly into the sea. Eager for the "kill" the "Zeroes" pressed home more attacks on the remaining TBDs, bent on exterminating the last of them. One of the deadly enemy fighters riddled MACH Corl's TBD, painfully wounding ARM3c Childers, whose twin guns jammed just after he had taken a 7.7mm slug just above his right ankle. Not one to admit defeat, the radioman grimly drew his .45 and squeezed off four rounds at one "Zero" and three at another. For 20 miles the chase continued, but the enemy broke off the pursuit—there were now different attacking planes to deal with.

While Thach's F4Fs had been swirling and weaving in the melee with the "Zeroes" and Torpedo Three had gone in "on the deck" to occupy the attention of the combat air patrol—which, at that point consisted of at least 40 "Zeroes"—Bombing Three had approached from the north and picked out its target. She looked big, and had a deck full of aircraft, spotted aft, gassed

"No ship commander was more beloved by his men . . ." CAPT Yanigamoto Ryusaku, commanding officer of carrier *Sōryū*, sunk by *Yorktown*'s Bombing Three on 4 June, was so revered and respected that when members of his crew saw that he was not among those who had abandoned ship, they elected CPO Abe, once a champion wrestler in the Imperial Navy, to bring off Yanigamoto forcibly if he had to. Abe, however, turned away in tears when the captain wordlessly confronted him with unyielding resolve to die with his command. As Abe left the bridge, he heard Yanigamoto softly and calmly singing the "Kimigayo," Japan's national anthem. (Author)

and armed for take off. Lookouts on board *Sōryū* must have spotted VB-3 almost the same time Leslie's SBDs began the descent, for *Sōryū* slewed northward, the sides of the carrier turning "into a veritable ring of flame" as her anti-aircraft guns opened up.

Max Leslie gave the attack signal and headed down—bomb or no bomb—the men behind him taking their attack intervals as the first plane began rolling down *Sōryū*'s deck. Satisfied that the squadron was ready to carry out its mission, Leslie veered off. "Diving from the north, all pilots had a steady dive along the fore and aft line of the target." LT(jg) Paul A. Holmberg, now in the lead, concentrated on placing his bomb where it would do the most damage. The thought paramount in his mind that he had only one chance, Holmberg pulled both electrical and manual release: his 1,000-pounded exploded "directly in the midst" of the 18 Type 99 dive bombers on the flight deck; one cartwheeled over the side as if tossed by an invisible, giant hand, with the force of the explosion. Ordnance and aviation fuel soon erupted in "sheets of flame" from the after part of the flight deck; nine fully gassed and armed Type 97 carrier attack planes on the hangar deck soon erupted in flames. Two more direct hits sealed *Sōryū*'s doom. Meanwhile, almost simultaneously but quite independently, *Enterprise*'s Scouting Six and Bombing Six loosed their lethal loads on *Akagi* and *Kaga*—both of these ships caught in the same vulnerable condition. "Jimmy" Thach caught glimpses of the destruction being wreaked upon the three enemy carriers; although not *looking* in that direction, he couldn't *help* but see it—the "best bombing" he had ever seen!

ENS Robert M. Elder, A-V(N), USNR, and ENS Bunyan R. Cooner, A-V(N), USNR, seeing that *Sōryū* was practically finished, attacked the "light cruiser plane guard"—actually the destroyer *Isokaze*—claiming a near miss and a hit on her fantail; likewise, ENS John C. Butler, A-V(N), USNR, and LT(jg) Osborne B. Wiseman shifted their dives, too, to what looked like a "battleship" nearby, claiming a direct hit on her stern, and a near miss.

As they pulled out of their dives, all Bombing Three planes withdrew to the northeast, maneuvering radically "at high speed close to the water amidst heavy anti-aircraft fire." ENS R.M. Isaman, A-V(N), USNR, reported being engaged by a "twin float biplane" but no damage resulted in the encounter. As Bombing Three cleared the area, "the carrier was an inferno of flames and undoubtedly a total loss" while the "battleship was smoking from the stern, the light cruiser . . . was stopped and had settled by the stern but was not afire." By contrast, none of the *Yorktown* SBDs had even suffered a scratch to its paint. Unmolested by enemy aircraft, Bombing Three set course for home, satisfied with a job well done. Holmberg led at the outset, clearing the area at such a good clip that LT Sid Bottomley came on the radio with a "Dammit, slow *down!*" Behind them lay three burning Japanese

ENS Wesley A. Osmus, A-V(N), USNR (seen here as an aviation cadet) was designated a naval aviator on 25 March 1941, was appointed ENS, A-V(N) on 22 April 1941, and joined VT-3 on 15 August 1941. (*The Flight Jacket, 1941*)

LT Kobayashi Michio led *Hiryū*'s carrier bombers launched to attack *Yorktown* on 4 June. Kobayashi had not taken part in the attack on the Pacific Fleet at Pearl Harbor on 7 December 1941 because of a balky engine, but did take part in bombing Wake Island a fortnight later, and flew in the devastatingly accurate onslaught against British heavy cruisers HMS *Cornwall* and HMS *Dorsetshire* in the Indian Ocean in April 1942. Kobayashi most likely survived the attack on *Yorktown*, but was splashed by VF-6 fighters (from *Enterprise*) as he attempted to return to *Hiryū*. (NH 81560)

carriers—*Akagi*, *Kaga* and *Sōryū*. What *Yorktown*'s air officer, CDR Murr Arnold, later termed a "God-awful lucky coordinated attack" had turned the tide of the war in the Pacific in just a few minutes.

Meanwhile, Bill Esders in T-2 was all by himself for a few moments after the "Ze-roes," compelled by the developing crisis over their carriers, had finally left his shot-up TBD alone. Soon, however, another "Devastator" hove into view, flown by another enlisted pilot, MACH Harry Corl. The two joined up—the only surviving planes of the twelve launched that morning—and shaped a course back toward *Yorktown*. As Corl flew alongside, he signalled to Esders that his radio was out of commission, and from where he sat, the latter could see the oil-dirtied fuselage of T-3, Corl's engine evidently pumping oil, badly. Noticing at that

Yorktown heels as she turns into the wind to launch a 12-plane combat air patrol early on the afternoon of 4 June. Soon after this launch, the carrier recovered two VB-6 SBDs that had been damaged in the morning's strike on the Japanese Mobile Force. (80-G-21626)

ENS Leif W. Larsen, A-V(N), USNR, with ARM2c John F. Gardner in the back seat, warms up his 1,000-pound bomb-armed SBD-3 on the afternoon of 4 June, shortly before "Scouting" Five was launched to look for an undamaged enemy carrier (*Hiryū*). Larsen's mount, however, may have been given a "down" shortly after this photo was taken, for it did not participate in the mission. Note very weathered upper surface paint finish, plane number (17) on the leading edge of the wing and aft of the fuselage star (indicating previous assignment to VS-5). (80-G-312000)

Enterprise orphans on *Yorktown*'s deck: ENS George H. Goldsmith, A-V(N), USNR and his gunner, ARM3c James W. Patterson, Jr., converse with plane handlers after landing on board *Yorktown* around 1340 on 4 June. Their aircraft, B-15, a badly holed SBD-3 (BuNo 4542) was damaged in the attack on *Kaga* earlier that day. LT(jg) Wilbur E. Roberts, A-V(N), USNR, flying B-5 (another VB-6 SBD-3, BuNo 4581) had just landed ahead of Goldsmith. (NH 100740, via Walters)

point that his own port fuel tank had been holed, Esders switched to his other tanks and throttled back for the return trip.

Carefully observing the sky for signs of enemy fighters, Esders started climbing. He asked his radio-man, Brazier, to "change [the] coils in the radio receiver so we could pick up the YE." Brazier, although reporting his critically wounded condition, and saying at the outset that he doubted if he could carry out Esders' instructions, labored grimly in the after cockpit. Ten minutes later, the dying Brazier gamely reported that he had changed the coil, thus improving their chance of reaching TF-17. So the two TBDs headed home; as far as they knew, they were the only survivors of Torpedo Three.

However, unbeknownst to them, another VT-3 pilot had indeed survived: ENS Osmus. Unfortunately for him, his rescuers turned out to be Japanese: *Arashi*, the destroyer returning to the Mobile Force after fruitlessly hunting for the submarine *Nautilus* (SS-168). Lookouts had spotted a swimmer in the water, prompting the ship's commanding officer, CDR Watanabe Yasumasa, to order the man picked up. *Arashi* hove-to, lowered a boat whose crew retrieved the flyer and brought him back to the ship. There, the ship's doctor treated his wounds, and Osmus was fed.

Initially, they learned who their "catch" was, and where he was from. Soon, *Arashi* rejoined the Mobile Force, only to find that three of the majestic carriers—the core of the fleet that had ravaged the Allies, from Pearl Harbor to the Indian Ocean—were floating infernos—the handiwork of the SBDs from *Yorktown* and *Enterprise*. *Arashi*, ordered to assist in firefighting and rescue operations, closed the force, and neared *Akagi*, as the destroyermen—and their captive—beheld the destruction wreaked by the American planes. Did this sight trigger greater effort to extract information from their captive—increase the "duress" to which they subjected him? At that point, somehow, the Japanese extracted from young Osmus the exact composition of TF-16 and TF-17, containing the significant fact that the Japanese were facing *three* American carriers instead of none. That night, Osmus was brutally murdered—a blow to the neck by a fire axe—and his body dumped into the sea.

How significant was the information obtained from the Torpedo Three pilot? Delays in transmission kept this intelligence from reaching ADM Nagumo for some time, but it did give the Japanese the first inkling of the forces which confronted them. By that point, however, a strike from *Hiryū*, the only carrier to escape the destruction that had befallen the other three, had already been launched. At 1258, eighteen *kanbakus* and six "Zeroes" departed *Hiryū* under the command of LT Kobayashi Michio. Soon, the heavy cruiser *Chikuma*'s search plane stalking TF-17 began sending back position and weather reports for the benefit of Kobayashi's group.

Yorktown, however, had not been idle. At 1330—shortly after *Hiryū* had launched planes to find *her*—*Yorktown* launched ten SBDs from Scouting Five under LT Short, each armed with a 1,000-pound bomb, to search for the undamaged fourth carrier, in a sector ranging from 280° to 020°, out to 200 miles from the ship.

Seven more "Dauntlesses," "fully gassed, and armed with 1,000-pound bombs" remained on the hangar deck. *Yorktown* then maintained her course into the wind and launched a 12-plane combat air patrol.

No sooner had the SBDs and F4Fs taken off on their respective missions when LT(jg) Wilbur E. Roberts, A-V(N), USNR, and ENS George H. Goldsmith, A-V(N), USNR, of VB-6, low on fuel, brought their SBDs on board, the latter's, B-15, badly shot-up. Pushed forward to clear the deck, the Bombing Six SBDs were soon struck below as ten F4Fs formed up to begin coming on board: six from the previous CAP under LT(jg) Leonard and four under LCDR Thach from the VF-3 strike escort.

The need to bring in the F4Fs to top off their tanks and get them ready for any eventuality assumed a higher priority than landing Bombing Three which had reached TF-17 at about the same time. "Max"

TACTICAL ORGANIZATION,
SCOUTING (BOMBING) FIVE SEARCH
Afternoon of 4 June 1942

Pilot/Radioman	Plane No.	Sector
LT Short/ACRM Trott	2	A
LT(jg) Horenburger/ARM3c Forshee	13	A
LT(jg) Berger/ACRM Phelps	1	B
LT(jg) Berry/ARM2c Clegg	AGC	B
LT Dickson/ARM2c Lynch	11	C
LT Adams/ARM1c Karrol	15	C
	(BuNo 4634)	
LT Nielsen/ACRM Straub	4	D
ENS Preston/ARM1c Cowden	16	D
LT(jg) Christie/ARM1c Sobel	7	E
LT(jg) McDowell/ARM2c Strickland	3	E

Credit: CAPT C.N. Conatser, USN (Ret)

Leslie's men thus orbited the task force, while far astern lumbered the two surviving "Devastators" from Torpedo Three, their fuel dwindling and wounded radio-gunners on board each crippled aircraft.

The last of Thach's men to come on board was MACH Cheek, whose plane, no. 16, crashed upon landing and flipped over, crumpling the tip of the F4F's tail and momentarily fouling the barrier. Aft, on the LSO platform, "Soupy" Campbell, the LSO, softly muttered a "damn" while his assistant, LT(jg) John P. Preston, said: "Gol-darned old Snafu-maru, up to her old tricks." From beneath the inverted "Wildcat" came Cheek's anxious voice: "Get this thing to hell off of me!" The flight deck crew soon extricated the NAP from his predicament and struck no. 16 below. Others set to work repairing the damaged barriers four and five.

Thach, meanwhile, amazed that *any* of his men had emerged alive from the lopsided aerial battle over the Mobile Force, climbed to *Yorktown*'s bridge, and recounted to CDR Arnold, the air officer, the destruction of Torpedo Three. He added, though, that "three Japanese carriers were completely out of action and that it looked like the battle was going our way." They planned to see the task force commander.

At 1320, however, RADM Fletcher signalled TF-17 that the force had apparently been sighted by the enemy, following that up moments later with a signal that told of *Yorktown*'s planes receiving credit for sinking a Japanese carrier. *Yorktown*ers found the latter message infinitely more cheering than the first, but imminent danger did not permit the Americans to savor the victory for long. "Jimmy" Thach, meanwhile, hurried down to the flight deck to see if there were any fighters that could be gotten into the air.

CHAPTER 10

Planes Were Falling in Every Direction

BOMBING THREE HAD BROKEN UP into sections and entered the landing circle, now led by Leslie, but soon found itself being directed, by voice radio, to clear the area. The reason for the wave-off, rather than a richly deserved welcome, soon became vividly apparent.

At 1352, *Yorktown*'s radar had picked up a contact, bearing 255°, 32 miles away and closing. The Japanese had learned their battle lessons well—unlike at Coral Sea, where their planes had come in high, to be detected by radar and intercepted, this group of attacking aircraft came in low, and then ascended to attain position to commence their attack. Detection of the incoming "bogies" prompted a purposeful flurry of activity on board *Yorktown*: she told VB-3 to clear the landing circle "and the general area of (our) own anti-aircraft fire," discontinued the fueling of the planes on deck, and an auxiliary gasoline tank, containing "800 gallons of clear aviation gasoline" was dropped over the side, aft. All compartments were closed down and secured; and MACH Oscar W. Myers drained the fuel lines of avgas, blanketing them with CO_2.

The fighter director circuit crackled with activity: "All Scarlet [*Yorktown*'s call sign] planes keep a sharp lookout [for] a group of planes coming in at 255 [°] unidentified," LCDR Pederson radioed his airborne "Wildcat" pilots at 1358; two minutes later he directed ENS Richard L. Wright (Scarlet 9) to take his group and look for the incoming "bogies": at bearing 255. Almost simultaneously, LT(jg) Brassfield (Scarlet 19) asked LT(jg) Woollen for his position, but only elicited the response: "Many bogies, angels 10." The fighter direc-

tor burst in, directing his airborne interceptors to the location of the enemy, urging them to "step on it." At 1355, LT Kobayashi caught sight of *Yorktown* and her screen, their wakes curving gently behind them as they maneuvered to meet the threat headed their way, and radioed: "We are attacking the enemy carrier." At about the same time, Kobayashi's incoming strike must have passed over the head of LT(jg) Brassfield, who sounded the alarm—"Bandits above me heading for ship. Appears to be 18"—and then gave chase. "This is Scarlet 19," he reported at 1402. "Formation appears to be breaking up." He continued tracking the *kanbakus*, keeping tabs on their position for the benefit of the men monitoring the action below. At 1404, the fighter direction circuit came alive again: "O.K. Break 'em up." Brassfield had needed no such urging; soon thereafter, he radioed *Yorktown* that he was "going to attack three enemy bombers about five miles" away from the ship.

LT(jg) Arthur J. Brassfield, a former Missouri schoolteacher, led VF-3's fourth division during the CAP action on 4 June, attacking a formation of three Type 99 carrier bombers. "The leader pulled up and made an excellent target," Brassfield later recounted, "the other two followed as if the leader were a magnet. The first one went down easy. And I caught the next one at a right angle from above, an ideal situation. I saw the bullets cut into his engine cowling and smash back in a straight line right into the cockpit. He flew right into those bullets. By the time they reached his cockpit his plane exploded into nothingness." The third bomber "turned tail and ran," but Brassfield gave chase and flamed him, too. The whole action consumed less than 60 seconds. (A still from John Ford's "The Battle of Midway")

139

In this Bel Geddes diorama, *Yorktown*'s CAP decimates the incoming *kanbaku*s under *Hiryū*'s LT Kobayashi early on the afternoon of 4 June. While the markings and color scheme of the F4Fs here are inaccurate for the time period, this view shows how it must have looked as VF-3's "Wildcats" pounced on the incoming Japanese strike. (80-G-701874)

A "Tally Ho" over *Yorktown*'s fighter director circuit signalled the start of Fighting Three's vigorous attack on Kobayashi's *kanbaku*s. CAPT Buckmaster, watching through binoculars, noted that the "Wildcats" slashed into the Japanese formation with deadly precision, breaking up the attack. "Planes were falling in every direction," he noted, "and many were falling in flames." Vectored to the scene, F4Fs from *Enterprise* and *Hornet* came to lend a hand.

An interested onlooker to the scene was Bill Esders, in his TBD. With Brazier, gravely wounded but gamely working the radio and homing into *Yorktown*'s "hayrake" (YE homing antenna), Esders had kept a close eye on his fuel gauge as they neared TF-17. Happily sighting the friendly forces, he maintained altitude at 5,500 feet only to sight Kobayashi's Type 99s deploying for their attack, only four to five miles away but fortunately preoccupied with getting through the combat air patrol and attacking *Yorktown*. He anxiously pushed the TBD's nose over and headed for the clouds—from where he saw at least three Aichis go down in flames—perhaps the trio methodically splashed by Art Brassfield.

The dogfight flashed and swirled closer to *Yorktown*, as she and her escorts awaited anxiously the incoming Type 99s. Her largest ensign streaming in the wind from the foremast, *Yorktown* prepared to do battle, her gunners standing to their weapons and

her engines throbbing as she cut through the ocean at a 30.5 knot clip, a bone-in-teeth curling at her forefoot and roostertail wake frothing astern. For a ship the Japanese had "sunk," *Yorktown* was very much alive. Informed by a member of his staff of the enemy's imminent attack, RADM Fletcher replied genially, "Well, I've got on my tin hat. There's nothing else *I* can do now." Elsewhere on board, LT(jg) Leonard, among the stranded VF-3 pilots, felt *he* could do something about his predicament—he drew his .45 and prepared to add to the ship's close-range anti-aircraft barrage! In the pilot house, CDR Wiltsie gulped down the last of a sardine sandwich.

At least seven Type 99s managed to run the gauntlet of F4Fs of Fighting Three. The first came under fire from all automatic weapons on the starboard side: ten 20-mm Oerlikons, the four 1.1-inch quads, a dozen .50 caliber and two .30 caliber machine guns; the torrent of metal hurled up by these weapons chopped the leading *kanbaku* into "at least three large pieces before he reached the bombing point." The bomb—a 242 kilogram "land bomb" (high explosive type)—tumbled as it fell and struck home just abaft number two elevator, at about frame 132, exploding on contact, blowing a 12-foot hole in the deck and sending jagged shards of metal in all directions—including into the two 1.1-inch mounts (III and IV) after of the island, decimating their crews.

140

Yorktown embattled!

In this magnificent sequence of photographs taken from on board heavy cruiser *Astoria*, TF-17's flagship comes under the brief but intense attack of LT Kobayashi's *kanbaku*s on 4 June. TOP LEFT: a bomb has splashed in *Yorktown*'s wake while a tail-less Type 99 plunges toward the sea.(80-G-32355) TOP RIGHT: the *kanbaku* seen in the first photo has splashed into the sea ahead of the ship; a burst of smoke above the forward part of the flight deck indicates that the forward 5"/38s have just fired; AA bursts spatter the sky; while what is most likely the *kanbaku* flown by WO Nakazawa Isao can be seen its dive. (80-G-32310) BOTTOM LEFT: fires begin to consume the inside of the funnel after the bomb hit on the uptakes, the bomb dropped by the plane in the second picture of the sequence having hit home. (80-G-32394); BOTTOM RIGHT: trailing a banner of thick black smoke, *Yorktown* shows signs of being heavily hit. (Author)

On Mount III, partly shielded by the big crane aft of the island, ENS John D. Lorenz, USNR, found himself among the few survivors—14 men had been wounded and five killed outright of the 19 men in the crew. Sea1c Harold O. Davies, the only unwounded crewman—the mount's pointer—stayed coolly at his post; 18-year-old Sea2c D.M. Smith, painfully and severely wounded in the back and in both legs, kept loading clips of shells into the gun while CGM Albert S. Nolan, also wounded in both legs, and in his right arm, "stepped in place of a dead loader, corrected the casualties to the guns and loaded" them; these three men, under Lorenz' direction, continued firing. Mount IV fared far worse—ENS Charles R. Broderick, USNR, suffering wounds in back and legs, discovered that 12 of his men were dead and four wounded.

In another view from *Portland*, *Yorktown* maintains speed after being hit three times; smoke indicates how fires have taken hold forward and in the uptakes. VF-3's F4Fs are spotted near the bow. (Author)

Unlike at Coral Sea, when *Astoria*'s photographer was inexperienced and his film of poor quality (resulting in no pictures), lensmen on board *Astoria* and *Portland* on 4 June captured very competently the full fury of combat. At left, in a view taken from *Portland*, smoke issues from the hole in *Yorktown*'s flight deck, while "The Mighty Y's" largest colors stream from the fore.

He literally stood to his guns, though, resolutely assisting in the removal of the dead and wounded until, weak from loss of blood, he could no longer stand.

The splinters also wreaked havoc in their downward flight, too, starting fires in three aircraft—the two *Enterprise* SBDs and one from Scouting Five, the latter machine fully-gassed and with a 1,000-pound bomb shackled to its belly. LT Alberto C. Emerson, the hangar deck officer, reacted with the quickness that had enabled him to stand out on gridiron and diamond at his alma mater, the University of Maine, when he promptly triggered the sprinkler system "by remote push button control," activating hangar deck water curtains and sprinklers, extinguishing the flames immediately, thereby saving the ship from a serious conflagration.

Anti-aircraft fire also accounted for the second plane, cutting it to pieces as he reached the bomb release point; his bomb also tumbled in flight and struck the water close astern, while pieces of the aircraft landed in the ship's churning wake. Splinters from the bomb, however, killed or wounded the crews of the .50 caliber machine guns on the port side of the superstructure deck, aft, and on the port quarter of the flight deck, started several fires. ENS Michael R. Pessalano, the battery officer, soon directed the survivors in extinguishing the fires. Four more Type 99s—flown by WO Nakazawa Iwao, WO Nakagawa Shizuo, PO1c Matsumoto Sadao and PO1c Seo Tetsuo—came on in rapid succession. All dropped bombs and claimed hits (Nakagawa's and Seo's actually near misses) but only Nakazawa actually scored: his 250-kilogram semi-armor piercing bomb penetrated the flight deck at frame 95, ten feet inboard of the island, and continued downward, outward and to starboard, piercing the port side of the uptakes in the hangar; hit the second deck in the vicinity of a passage at frame 95, inboard of the executive officer's office and the C&R office, and exploded in a "high order detonation" that wrecked the latter spaces and blew a 15-foot hole in the deck, as well as in the intakes and uptakes to firerooms 2, 3, 4, 5 and 6. The concussion ruptured the comparatively thin steel of the uptakes, completely disabling two of the ship's six boilers, and extinguished the fires in five. Smoke and gasses began filling the firerooms.

Again, repair parties swung into action; fire parties from Repair II and III dispatched to the fire on the second deck and laundry; those from Repairs I and VII to the photographic laboratory on the first deck. The raging fires, fed by film and the assorted processing chemicals, blazed fiercely, confronting the fire-fighters with a difficult task. CDR Kiefer led the fire-fighting efforts in the photographic lab, although he had been unable to obtain a rescue breathing apparatus from his own gutted office, conducting the first fire-fighting efforts in that area despite the infernal heat. Paint on the inside of the stack, meanwhile, caught fire and flaked off in patches, starting fires wherever it fell.

Meanwhile, below, the six men at number one boiler, under CWT Charles Kleinsmith, remained at their stations, despite the broken, red-hot boiler casing and fumes from the ruptured uptakes from their boiler. By closing the throttle, the men at boiler number one were able to maintain steam pressure at 180 pounds, enabling this boiler to carry the auxiliary load.

Topside, heavy black smoke soon obscured the after main battery director, the automatic gun batteries on the starboard side, aft, and Group III, 5-inch guns.

A sixth Type 99—flown by WO Nakagawa Shizuo—circled forward and dove from ahead, facing "considerably lessened fire" than his shipmates. Nakagawa's bomb pierced number one elevator, "at frame 36, about 17 feet to the right of the centerline," continued forward and to port, penetrating the elevator pit at about frame 32, some seven feet from the centerline, where it exploded in a high-order

A photographer on board *Portland* (his M-1 helmet on backwards) takes a picture of the damaged carrier. (Author)

detonation in A-305-A, a compartment used to stow rags and cleaning gear. The blast blew a four-foot hole in the deck and ruptured bulkheads within A-305-A; splinters, some of them an inch in diameter "travelled upward piercing the second deck in No. 1 elevator pit in several places . . . ." Other splinters pierced armored bulkheads at frame 38 in compartment A-405-A—a deck below A-305—and even pierced the overhead of compartments on the fifth deck. All lighting forward of frame 60 went out, but emergency lighting came on instantly.

Fire broke out immediately amidst the rags in A-305-A and the stores below, in A-405-A, the former emitting a heavy volume of smoke; heat from the blaze caused paint to blis-

Yorktown goes dead in the water about 1438. The heavy volume of smoke convinced Japanese observers that the ship would soon sink. (80-G-32244)

Astoria's number two motor whaleboat comes alongside the heavy cruiser to transfer RADM Frank Jack Fletcher (wearing a windbreaker beneath his lifejacket; his binocular straps, from pre-war days, are white) and the first increment of his staff. CAPT Spencer S. Lewis, Fletcher's chief of staff, is mounting the Jacob's ladder to Astoria's well deck while the ship's XO, CDR Chauncey R. Crutcher, oversees the operation at top (L). LCDR Berton A. Robbins, Jr. (like CDR Crutcher, wearing a regulation cap), flag lieutenant for RADM William Ward Smith (who commanded TF-17's cruisers and who wore his flag in Astoria) is at left. (80-G-32350)

ter and bake on the surrounding bulkheads of the two compartments. Had the fire been more intense, the blaze could have been transmitted to those areas. The blast had also ruptured a fire main riser, flooding A-405-A, A-406-A, and A-410-A through the splinter holes in the transverse bulkheads, as well as blew the forward magazine group sprinkling and flooding control panels from the bulkhead in A-306-L. A damaged circuit rendered the remote control for sprinkling the forward magazine, just aft of the fire, inoperative.

Men from two repair parties, II and VII, converged on the area, the former utilizing CO_2 and a fire hose hooked up to a plug abaft frame 80 while the latter attacked the blaze from the elevator pit using water and foam. The one group used an oxy-acetylene torch and cut through the deck beneath their feet in the elevator pit, and aimed fire nozzles on the flames below. To avert an explosion in the magazines, those spaces located directly abaft the burning storerooms were flooded.

The seventh and last kanbaku jettisoned his bomb, but did not score a hit; his ordnance missed on the starboard beam. But the damage had been done. Yorktown had taken three hits, one of which, at frame 95, had proved debilitating. The Japanese lost 13 of 18

kanbakus and three of six kansens; they claimed six direct hits, though, setting the ship afire "and causing her later to explode." To the Japanese pilots, the clouds of smoke that obscured the ship gave rise to the conclusion that they had inflicted mortal damage on her.

Yorktown, though, was not out of the fight yet. The men from Repair I and the flight deck repair crew converted on the damaged area at frame 132. Directed by LT Albert H. Wilson, Jr., these men, working without any protection while the enemy attack unfolded, "very expeditiously" effected repairs, securing wooden beams to the steel transverse ones bordering the 12-foot square hole, and then laying ½-inch steel plates over them. They then dragged "five large, square, 10-pound steel plates" into place over the gap, driving spikes into the wooden flight deck, around the edge of the steel, to hold them in place. They finished the task in about 25 minutes. Unfortunately, while Yorktown now had a flight deck capable of receiving planes, she could not enjoy her good fortune—she went dead in the water, as speed dropped to zero due to the casualties to the boilers.

The thick, choking black smoke pouring from the stack had rendered the communication office and flag

Destroyer *Benham*, her 5"/38s trained to port, hurries to join TF-17, making 30 knots around 1436 on 4 June, as seen from heavy cruiser *Pensacola*. Also steaming in company were heavy cruiser *Vincennes* and destroyer *Balch*, all four ships detached from TF-16 to help RADM Fletcher's force. (80-G-34222)

"And our flag was still there . . ." *Yorktown*'s largest ensign snaps from the fore while thick black smoke billows from the carrier's stack after the *Hiryū* Air Unit's first attack on 4 June. (Author)

While the crewmen of *Yorktown*'s after Mk.XXXIII gun director (upper left) take a breather at their battle station, the grim business of cleaning up the carnage around the aftermost 1.1"/75 mount (Mount IV) proceeds (lower right). The tarp on deck most likely covers the remains of some of the 12 men from the mount's crew who had been killed. (Author)

ENS Dan Sheedy, his shoulder wound looked after soon after his rough landing on board *Hornet*, is helped from the carrier's flight deck. (A still from John Ford's "The Battle of Midway")

ing whaleboat, and was soon on his way, with the first increment of his staff, to *Astoria*, clambering up that ship's Jacob's ladder to her welldeck, and boarding the cruiser at 1524, the boat then shoving off to make a second trip to bring off the rest of the staff.

Bombing Three, waved off from *Yorktown* as Kobayashi's Type 99s showed up, went instead to *Enterprise*, which had already recovered her air group. ENS Paul W. Schlegel, A-V(N), USNR, and LT(jg) Wiseman were the first to land on board, at 1437 and 1438. One of these pilots recounted that *Yorktown* was "in bad shape," a statement easily confirmed by gazing in the direction of TF-17. "From the heavy smoke that appeared," RADM Spruance later wrote, "I judged that she (*Yorktown*) had been hit." War correspondent Wendell Webb saw it, too, from on board *Pensacola* (CA-24), in TF-16, as did fellow journalist Robert J. Casey, on board heavy cruiser *Northampton* (CA-26). "The black puffs attenuate and lose color and mingle with the stratus clouds in the low distance," Casey wrote later, "The fires of the burning planes are quickly

plot untenable, forcing RADM Fletcher and his staff to assemble on the flight deck. With *Yorktown*'s radar out, with the difficulty in communicating with the other ships in the task force, and with *Yorktown* now immobile, Fletcher decided to shift his flag to *Astoria*. A motor whaleboat from the cruiser soon chugged over and bobbed alongside as the admiral and his staff prepared to disembark. Fletcher, about to go over the side, hesitated at the last, claiming that he was "too damned old" for that sort of thing. He was thus lowered to the wait-

LEFT: In this view, believed never before published, *Astoria* approaches *Yorktown* (visible in the distance above the Curtiss SOC on the cruiser's starboard catapult) after the carrier had been damaged by LT Kobayashi's *kanbaku*s. *Astoria*'s Mk.XXXIII director is trained to starboard, as is the 1.1 mount above the bridge. Flak burst (top right) indicates that the battle is still underway. (Author)

Fragment damage to the bulkhead of the torpedo repair workshop and sheet metal shop that resulted from the bomb hit at frame 132; note Mk.2 torpedo trucks and bomb skids in the foreground. A sailor sifts through the wreckage at right. (80-G-21601)

Hoses lie on deck in serpentine fashion as damage control parties toil on *Yorktown*'s hangar deck. Note TBD-1 (BuNo 0333) (once coded 5-T-4) triced up in the overhead: this VT-5 "Devastator" had been retained on board as a spare, and still wears the outdated markings (rudder stripes and red-centered star). MACH Cheek's inverted F4F-4 (BuNo 5143) can be seen in center background. (80-G-312023)

Panoramic view taken by PhoM2c William G. Roy showing damage control efforts underway on board *Yorktown* (R) while *Astoria* comes up to assist (L). Note dense smoke billowing from the stack; the signals two-blocked at the yards indicate flight operations had been in progress when the attack came. Also note the carrier's CXAM radar and YE homing antennas at the foremast; and 1.1" batteries (Mounts I and II) on alert. [80-G-312019 (L); 80-G-312018 (R)].

out. The carrier [*Yorktown*] has gone over the horizon again and the ocean is as it was before save for one strange and terrifying thing—a column of smoke...is rising straight into the air. . . Something is afire over there . . . We cross our fingers and hope it wasn't the carrier. . . "

Over the next several minutes, *Enterprise*'s LSO brought in seven SBDs, followed by four F4F-4s, six more SBDs, and two more F4Fs—all *Yorktown* planes were on board by 1505. Spruance, meanwhile, detached heavy cruisers *Vincennes* (CA-44) and *Pensacola*, and destroyers *Balch* (DD-363) and *Benham* (DD-397) to help screen the damaged *Yorktown*.

Hornet soon maneuvered to recover another *Yorktown* orphan: ENS Dan Sheedy, survivor of the desperate fight over the Japanese fleet to defend the lumbering TBDs of Torpedo Three, was flying with a badly wounded foot and shoulder. He managed to reach *Hornet* and bring his crippled fighter to a friendly deck, but although Sheedy had switched off his guns so that they would not cut loose in a hard landing, damage to the "Wildcat's" electrical system tragically negated his careful performance of duty. His

As *Astoria* steams close to the crippled *Yorktown*, one can see VF-3's F4Fs (that had been recovered before *Hiryū*'s carrier bombers had attacked) still spotted forward. Note SOC on *Astoria*'s starboard catapult (L), plane no. 2, its .30 caliber MG in the stowed position in the lowered turtleback. (Author)

While damage control efforts continue to put out the fires in the uptakes, flight deck crews push VF-3's F4F-4s toward the stern to prepare them for launch. Two (Thach's and Macomber's), however, are found to be unflyable. *Portland* turns to port in background. (Author)

The persistent blaze defies *Yorktown*'s damage control parties, but the flight deck crews have spotted VF-3's flyable "Wildcats" aft. With the roller curtains up, one can see at least two SBDs parked on the hangar deck. *Portland* can be seen faintly through the smoke (R), while destroyer *Balch*, newly arrived from TF-16 to reinforce *Yorktown*'s screen, can be seen at left. (80-G-32301)

LCDR Leslie and LT(jg) Holmberg, from VB-3, returning from the strike on *Sōryū*, fly over *Yorktown* in hopes of coming on board, but the carrier is not ready to recover aircraft because VF-3's "Wildcats" are spotted aft; *Astoria* is at right, with a circling PBY visible in the far distance. (Author)

Their fuel states militating against reaching TF-16, LCDR Leslie and LT(jg) Holmberg have to "ditch." Here, Holmberg makes a water landing alongside *Astoria* in his SBD-3 (BuNo 4662), side code B-2. (Author)

F4F-4 touched down and skidded to starboard; the right landing gear collapsed, and the impact of the wing hitting the deck caused a devastating two-second automatic burst from the six .50-caliber guns that tore into the after portion of *Hornet*'s island, killing four enlisted men and LT Royal R. Ingersoll, II, USNA 1934, the after 5-inch gun control officer (and son of ADM Royal E. Ingersoll, CINCLANT). Additionally, 20 men had been wounded as the .50-caliber bullets penetrated the one-inch specially hardened armor plate of the carrier's after conning station.

CAP Esders, who had ducked his "Devastator" into the clouds when he saw Kobayashi's attack force approaching TF-17, ultimately ran out of fuel. Radioing *Yorktown* that he was going to ditch on bearing 270°, ten miles away from her, he lowered his flaps and made a full stall landing. As the "Devastator" began settling, nose-down, Esders immediately tripped the flotation gear, which worked, keeping the TBD waterborne. He scrambled out of the cockpit and headed back to help "Mike" Brazier, who was calling for him, and noticed, in passing, that the second cockpit canopy had been holed "several" times. Gingerly assisting Brazier from the rear cockpit to the wing, Esders then broke out the rubber boat. He began inflating it—only to discover that it had been holed—but it had enough buoyancy to keep Brazier afloat, after Esders had helped him into it. After giving his radioman a drink of water, the pilot attempted to patch the hole. The two men conversed briefly about "the attack, the squadron, the *Yorktown* and shipmates, the Navy and of home" before Brazier breathed his last. At that moment, at the sound of airplane engines, Esders looked up and saw two SBDs flying overhead; one of which he recognized as B-1, the SBD-3 flown by Max Leslie of Bombing Three as he

LT(jg) Holmberg's "Dauntless" (BuNo 4662) lies alongside *Astoria* while a *Sims*-class destroyer steams in the background; faintly visible is LCDR "Max" Leslie's SBD-3 (B-1) as VB-3's CO prepares to make a water landing himself (L). (80-G-32328)

Two minutes after LT(jg) Holmberg ditched his SBD-3 (B-2) into the Pacific, LCDR "Max" Leslie brought in his. While *Astoria*'s number two motor whaleboat proceeds to their assistance, Leslie and his radio-gunner, RM1c W.E. Gallagher, prepare to abandon B-1 (BuNo 4518). At lower right are LT(jg) Holmberg and his radio-gunner, AMM2c George A. LaPlant, both men soaking wet from their brief swim; also visible is *Astoria*'s exec, CDR Crutcher. (80-G-32305)

around; Esders, assuming that he was about to be strafed, dived into the water and submerged beside the still-floating TBD.

Whatever the Japanese pilot's plan had been, his curiosity proved his undoing. Apparently preoccupied with the TBD, he didn't notice an F4F closing the range. LT(jg) Brassfield sighted the Aichi and got him in his sights, pressing home a vigorous attack that shot him down. It was his fourth "kill" of the day.

Shortly thereafter, *Hammann*, on a search for downed pilots, after picking up a Scouting Six crew, spotted the TBD in the water, bearing 240°, eight miles away, and altered course to close, spotting Esders and the raft containing the body of Brazier. *Hammann* stopped at 1525 and brought them on board, before she sank the badly-damaged TBD by piercing the flotation bags with rifle fire. The "Devastator" T-2 (BuNo 0286) then sank by the nose. The next day, Brazier would be buried at sea.

Two more pilots, meanwhile, were still flying around in *Yorktown*'s vicinity—LCDR Leslie and his

circled the area out of range of TF-17's guns. The other SBD flown by "Lefty" Holmberg dropped a float light to mark the TBD in the water for a rescuing ship. At about that time, after the SBDs had flown away, Esders, now alone, said a prayer for Brazier: "I prayed the Lord would take care of Mike and his family."

It looked, though, like Esders' troubles were not over. Soon after Brazier died and the two SBD shad departed, one of the surviving planes from the *Hiryū* attack group circled the area, ominously, overhead and astern. The Japanese pilot brought his plane

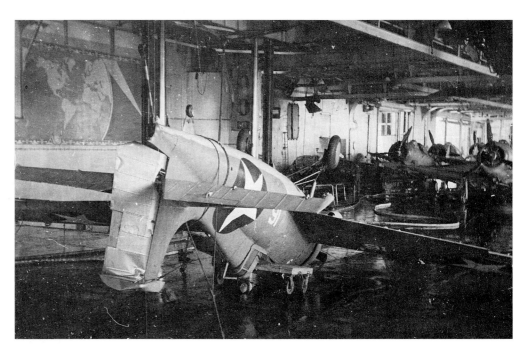

MACH Tom F. Cheek's Grumman F4F-4 (BuNo 5143) on *Yorktown*'s hangar deck, with at least four SBDs in the background. Check's aircraft had been damaged in landing, the last of the returning F4F-4s to come on board, and temporarily fouled the deck. The plane carries the standard blue gray/light gray paint finish, with the "Felix the Cat" insignia barely visible on the fuselage, just above the dolly on which the plane rests. The individual aircraft number 16 is repeated on fuselage and upper wing panels. (80-G-23979)

Sailors (L) (one wearing a M-1917A1 helmet and the other a newer M-1 model) from either Repair I or flight deck repair crews, perform preparatory work to begin laying wooden beams across the hole at frame 132. In the background are the four .50-caliber MG of battery no.9, the scene of heroism of GM3c Theodore B. Metcalf. Painfully wounded when the bomb exploded, Metcalf, with one arm useless, nevertheless went to work immediately, repairing or replacing the damaged guns, helping remove the dead and wounded and stationing and instructing new men to replace the casualties. For his meritorious service, Metcalf would be awarded the Silver Star. (80-G-312020)

wingman, LT(jg) Holmberg—both anxiously awaiting whether or not the carrier was going to get underway and be able to bring them on board. As each moment passed, though, their fuel gauges showed their more critical fuel status. Unable to wait any longer, Leslie directed Holmberg to land first; he would follow. Holmberg put his SBD-3 (B-2) within a veritable stone's throw of the side of the cruiser *Astoria* and within sight of *Yorktown* at 1546, the cruiser's number two motor whaleboat—the same one that had already made two trips to *Yorktown* to bring off RADM Fletcher and his staff—picking up the pilot and his radioman, AMM3c G.A. LaPlant. Two minutes later, Leslie, in B-1, alighted alongside, too, at 1548. As Holmberg and LaPlant, drenched from their dip in the Pacific, watched from atop *Astoria*'s plane hangar, the ship's number two motor whaleboat again chugged out to another nose-heavy SBD-3, bringing off Leslie and his radioman, ARM1c W.E. Gallagher.

MACH Corl had arrived on the scene just in time to see *Yorktown* under attack. Clearing the area, he pressed on for *Enterprise*, and ditched within sight of TF-16. Corl insisted that the boat dispatched from *Monaghan* pick up his wounded gunner first, the destroyermen dragging Childers —found floating face down—into the boat where artificial respiration brought him around.

Meanwhile, for an hour, the "Black Gang" had worked feverishly to light the fires off in

the *Yorktown*'s boilers, and their efforts paid off. At 1550, the engine room force reported that they could make 20 knots or more if required. "Look, the *Yorktown*'s moving," said a gunner next to correspondent Webb on board *Pensacola*. The breakdown flag descending from *Yorktown*'s yards, and her flag signal, "My speed five," as the ship began moving, elicited a "spontaneous cheer . . . from every ship in the screen . . ." On board the carrier, the F4Fs on deck were being fueled to ready them for the combat air

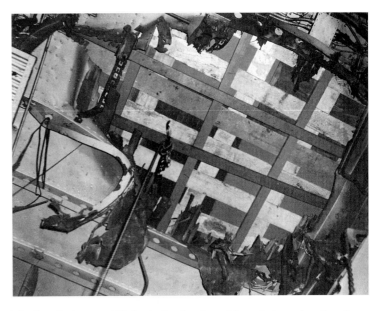

The bomb-damaged flight deck, aft, viewed from below, showing the timbers and plates fitted to patch the hole. (Author)

patrol. When asked if he could take off into a 13-knot wind (13 knots being initially the best the engineers could hope to coax out of the damaged engineering plant soon after getting underway), Thach responded that he could. A frustrated observer during *Hiryū's* dive bombing attack, Thach told a shipmate later "that he would be damned if he would ever be aboard ship again when the other fellow was attacking . . ." preferring instead to "be in the air, doing the attacking . . ." Too soon, he would have the opportunity. At 1555, radar plot reported a group of planes approaching from 340° (T), 35 miles away and closing—the 10 *kankōs* under LT Tomonaga Joichi, *Hiryū's* air group commander, who was still riding in his colorfully marked plane damaged in action with the Marine fighters near Midway that morning, and the six Type 00 *kansens* under LT Mori, as escorts, that had taken off from *Hiryū* at 1531. Like the American air groups that would take the battle to the

enemy, this Japanese group was a composite one, too—one of the torpedo planes was from *Akagi*; two of the fighters from *Kaga*. Each of the Nakajimas carried a "type 91 modification-3" torpedo, like those that had crippled the battle line at Pearl Harbor six months before.

As she had during the earlier attack, *Yorktown* shut down the fueling on her flight deck—only one of the ten planes on deck had more than 23 gallons of gasoline in its tank; two (the ones flown that morning by Thach and Macomber) had so little that they had to be left behind in the scramble. LCDR Pederson, the FDO, vectored four of the six already-airborne F4Fs into the fray, retaining two directly overhead to cover the launch of the eight "Wildcats" under Thach. Machinist Myers again purged the gasoline lines with CO_2.

The wet deck planking near the nest of rafts on the main deck, aft, bears mute testimony to *Pensacola*'s steaming at 32 knots to reinforce TF-17, while the 1.1"/75 crews at the fantail and the 20 mm. Oerlikon crew at upper right stand on the alert near their weapons. In the afternoon sunshine on 4 June, *Pensacola* heels as she turns and joins the ships in *Yorktown*'s screen, some of which (heavy cruiser *Portland* and three destroyers) are visible in the distance. Assigned duty as radar guard, *Pensacola* begins to circle *Yorktown* at 25 knots while damage control efforts continue on board the carrier. (80-G-21649)

CHAPTER 11

She Was Putting Up a Scrap
If Any Ship Ever Did

Y ORKTOWN SURGED through the Pacific swells as if straining for every knot—12 at 1620, 15 by 1622, 18 by 1628 as she and her escorts deployed in anti-aircraft formation to meet the expected onslaught. At 1635, CTF-17, now on board *Astoria*, signalled: "Prepare to repel air attack . . . ." Four minutes later, lookouts on board the cruiser spotted "about 16 enemy torpedo planes . . . 15 miles from the ship . . . ." It was a situation Frank Jack Fletcher had feared: *Yorktown* caught with planes on her deck!

While Tomonaga's formation was breaking up into four sections, to divide the combat air patrol and the

ship's gunfire, *Yorktown* commenced launch at 1640. With the jerky motion peculiar to the Grumman "Wildcat" and its hand-cranked landing gear, the F4Fs, led by a grimly determined "Jimmy" Thach in a fresh plane (the one he had flown that morning, no. 23, too damaged to risk in flight again) began wobbling skyward while all of the carrier's guns which could be brought to bear trained to port. *Yorktown*'s forward gun director had picked up five of the incoming Nakajimas approximately 19,000 yards out, and as John Adams cleared the bow ramp, the carrier's port 5-inch battery let loose at 15,000 yards. The bursts blossomed in the

As *Hiryū*'s torpedo planes approach from the port quarter, all guns that can be brought to bear are pointed that direction. In this view, taken from *Yorktown*'s compass platform, what appears to be smoke may indicate that fire has already been commenced. In the foreground can be discerned at least three .50 caliber MG's, one in its regular mounting and two apparently mounted on stanchions without cooling hoses; the 20mm battery visible beyond, on the port side, is the same one shown on p. 85. Close examination of the original print also discloses the presence of a Grumman F4F, apparently being vectored to attack the onrushing torpedo planes, visible just to the left of the stanchion to the left of the port leg of the tripod foremast, as well as .30 caliber MG's taken from grounded aircraft, mounted on stanchions on the catwalk on the port bow! (80-G-312002)

sky ahead of the charging Type 97s, but as CAPT Buckmaster could see, his guns—and those of the ships deployed around his—were not scoring hits. Tomonaga's planes, from the ship, appeared to relentlessly press onward in a loose "V" formation; from *Yorktown* it appeared that the altitudes of the attackers varied considerably, even as low as 50 feet off the "deck," the Nakajimas jinking and changing course to avoid the heavy anti-aircraft fire being strewn in their path. Wendell Webb, on board *Pensacola*, observed that *Yorktown* was "putting up a scrap if any ship ever did." Correspondent William F. Tyree, on board *Vincennes*, opined that the enemy's determination "to get the carrier seemed fanatical . . ."

But *Yorktown*ers matched the enemy's "fanatical" determination with their own brand of resolve. With ENS George A. Hopper, A-V(N), USNR, bringing up the rear, *Yorktown*'s combat air patrol took off—eight planes strong—and soon began tangling with the Japanese carrier attack planes, both sides braving the intense anti-aircraft barrage from the surrounding cruisers and destroyers. LCDR

LT Tomonaga Joichi, *Hiryū*'s Air Unit commander at the Battle of Midway. Although his Nakajima B5N2 Type 97 *kankō* had been holed by USMC fighters earlier that day, he persisted in using his damaged carrier attack plane to lead the strike on *Yorktown*. LCDR "Jimmy" Thach shot down Tomonaga's colorfully marked aircraft; killed with Tomonaga were ENS Akamatsu Saku (observer) and PO1c Murai Sadamu (radio-gunner). (NH 81559)

Thach had taken off, banked to starboard, and soon came square into the charging Japanese torpedo planes. He picked out one—Tomonaga's as it turned out—and summarily splashed him into the sea. Among the "friendlies" was ENS Dibb, who had been Thach's wingman that morning, and had been the second F4F to get off, just ahead of LT(jg) Leonard and ENS Adams. The enemy's attack now "close in and fully developed" by the time he had become airborne, Dibb ignored his own ship's barrage and, "realizing the serious predicament" of the ship he had just left, pressed home determined attacks on two planes.

ENS Milton C. Tootle, IV, A-V(N), USNR, the tall, athletic son of a St. Joseph, Missouri, bank president, had taken off behind LT(jg) Tom Barnes and Adams, banked left into "every bit of anti-aircraft fire from our whole force" and proceeded out about a mile before he spied an incoming *kankō* and gave chase. Tootle closed and opened fire at short range, seeing his tracers hitting home. Down below, CDR Jarrett, on *Morris*' bridge, noticed an enemy torpedo plane with an F4F-4 no farther than 25 yards (!) astern, and saw that his own ship's 20 millimeter Oerlikons appeared to be striking home, too. Tootle had been flying through the veritable hail of anti-aircraft fire, momentarily oblivious to it at the outset. Even as he was shooting at the Japanese plane his own plane was taking hits, too—perhaps from *Morris*. He claimed a "kill," but soon had much to worry about. Tootle knew that "all was not well" on board his own "Wildcat," from the alarming telltale signs of smoke gathering

A *Hiryū kankō* banks away, apparently having fired its torpedo, trailing a thin ribbon of smoke from its left wing, as seen from one of *Yorktown*'s 20 mm. galleries. LCDR "Jimmy" Thach chased LT Tomonaga's Nakajima into friendly fire, setting its left wing ablaze. Note the shadow of the gun shield that shows the lack of a "V"-shaped cutout that allowed the gunner to have a better chance to track his target. (80-G-312006)

Five B5N2s, most likely *Hiryū*'s second *chūtai* under LT Hashimoto Toshio, torpedoes slung beneath them, charge TF-17 in this view that is part of a series (distinguished by the aiming cross prominent near the center of each picture) taken by Photographer William Smistik, on board *Pensacola*. (80-G-32248)

Anti-aircraft fire intensifies as *Hiryū*'s *kankō*s press home their assault. (80-G-32249)

One *Hiryū* carrier attack plane can be seen at far right, with another almost out of Smistik's viewfinder above and behind it, banking to port. (80-G-32247)

Torpedoes already fired against *Yorktown*, two *Hiryū* B5N2s try to escape the tremendous storm of anti-aircraft fire being hurled at them. *Pensacola*'s CO, CAPT Frank L. Lowe, later wrote that his ship continued firing her starboard 20 mm. and 1.1" guns at the attacking *kankō*s "as they passed between the *Yorktown* and the *Pensacola*, the *Yorktown* guns doing the same; both ships accepting the danger to each other in an effort to stop the planes." (80-G-32241)

The anti-aircraft fire peppering the sky between *Yorktown* and *Pensacola* proves unavailing as a Type 91 torpedo barrels into the carrier's port side at about 1644 on 4 June. Destroyer *Morris* is at left; heavy cruiser *Astoria* (partially obscured by smoke) at far right. (80-G-414423)

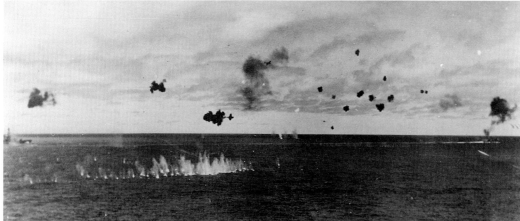

As seen from on board *Yorktown*, at least two *Hiryū kankōs* try to escape the maelstrom of anti-aircraft fire over TF-17. Heavy cruiser *Pensacola* is at left, destroyer *Benham* at right. (80-G-11644)

Two *kankōs* retire from their attack on *Yorktown* (one barely visible behind the lines at center, the other at upper right) in this view taken from the carrier's compass platform during the second *Hiryū* Air Unit attack on 4 June. At lower right a gunner, wearing an M-1917A1 helmet, levels his .50-caliber MG at another of the retiring carrier attack planes. (80-G-312003)

Crewmen negotiate the steep list following the ship's being torpedoed on 4 June. Note fire extinguisher on deck and alongside the island (right); also note knotted line hanging down in foreground, evidently used by men on the island to reach safety on the flight deck after the earlier attack damaged the ship. (80-G-21603)

Balancing themselves to keep their footing on the precariously canting flight deck, *Yorktown*ers go about their business, preparing to abandon ship after *Hiryū*'s torpedo plane attack on 4 June. Grumman F4F-4 (BuNo 5165) is visible abaft island; flown on the strike escort mission that morning by LT(jg) Brainard T. Macomber, A-V(N), USNR, of VF-3, the plane did not have enough fuel to allow its being flown off as the torpedo attack unfolded on 4 June. Its individual plane number, 6, is visible on the folded wing panel. (80-G-14384)

in his cockpit. He managed to join up with another Fighting Three plane and signalled its pilot, who radioed "when it gets bad go down and land beside the destroyer" nearby and below. At about the same time the fighter director broke in: "Scarlet 18 (the call sign for Tootle's plane), are you in the air? Scarlet 18, are you in the air?" Tootle had a lot on his mind, however, afraid to be trapped in a burning plane, too low to jump, he climbed to 1,500 feet and bailed out. ENS Hopper, the last man off *Yorktown*'s deck, was not as

fortunate—shot down by an escorting "Zero" his F4F-4 crashed into the sea, carrying the young ensign with it. He had not been airborne long.

On board *Yorktown*, CAPT Buckmaster saw one Nakajima splash off the port bow, and the tracks of "several" torpedoes. Only making 19 knots, *Yorktown* could not comb the wakes as she had done at Coral Sea: one torpedo barrelled into her port side at frame 80, 15 feet below the waterline at about 1645. A heavy explosion shook the ship, and she quickly assumed a

Destroyer *Balch*, her main battery trained to port, steams slowly past *Yorktown* as the latter abandons ship. The destroyermen gave the *Yorktown*ers three cheers as the carrier's crew purposefully went about their sad task. *Yorktown*'s men responded with three cheers of their own. (80-G-17061)

6° list. For an instant, it looked as if *Yorktown* was going to make it; she was still underway and the damage appeared to be confined to "internal flooding in the vicinity of the forward generator room." Then, however, as the column of water generated by the first hit subsided, a second torpedo hit the ship; another towering geyser shot up alongside, this one so violent that it disfigured the gallery walkway above it. All lights went out below decks; the list increased from 6° to 17° and then continued until the inclinometer read 27° in Repair III. *Yorktown* lost way, and went dead in the water, with a jammed rudder and a steep list to port. Among the dead was the indefatigable Kleinsmith.

Those at topside battle stations saw that, by and large, things weren't too bad. However, down below, their shipmates saw a different picture—darkness; silence—and felt the stomach-tightening fear of being trapped if the ship were to continue going over.

LCDR John F. Delaney, the engineering officer, soon reported that the shock of the two torpedo hits had snuffed out the fires in six boilers and that the ship had lost power. CDR Clarence C. Aldrich, the damage control officer, soon provided CAPT Buckmaster with more bad news, the dismal corollary of the loss of power: no power, no pumps. The ship could not control the flooding. Below decks, all communication had ceased with main engine control, the forward and after generator compartments, the repair parties, and pump control stations. A quick investigation of the forward generator room through the door leading to central station disclosed that that compartment was flooded—preventing the forward damage control pumps to either drain or counterflood

the affected areas. Further, the total loss of steam and electric power meant that no fuel could be pumped from the tanks on one side of the ship to those on the opposite side to correct the list. A grim possibility confronted CAPT Buckmaster as he stood on his canted bridge: *Yorktown*, his proud command of 16 months' duration, could turn turtle before the officers and men, who had fought the ship so gallantly, could get off. He ordered Aldrich and Delany to secure their respective departments and direct all of their men to lay topside to put on life jackets.

Since the list had increased steadily, CAPT Buckmaster and CDR Aldrich agreed that it looked as if the ship would capsize soon, perhaps "in a few minutes." There was no time to lose. "In order to save as many of the ship's company as possible," Buckmaster later wrote, "I ordered the ship abandoned." No captain relishes the thought of losing his ship; no captain could also relish the thought of losing men's lives if there is a chance that they can be saved. No one knew whether or not the Japanese would be back again, with *Yorktown* a sitting duck.

Lit by the glare of the battle lanterns, men toiled below, bringing wounded and injured shipmates topside. The only ladder leading "up from the vicinity of sick bay" hung crazily at an angle, loose on one side, making it precarious, at best, adding to the difficulty of getting the patients out. Slippery decks and the steep list rendered carrying stretchers impossible; some had to be dragged across the deck. Some patients had to be carried bodily.

Among those whom LT(jg) Kearney alerted was Sea2c Norman M. Pichette, USNR, who had suffered an abdominal wound while manning one of the .50-caliber MGs aft. Not in shock, Pichette had walked in to sick bay, albeit in pain, under his own power, after *Hiryū*'s warriors had struck the first time. With others more seriously wounded ahead of him, though, a shot of morphine for the pain and dressing for the wound had had to suffice for treatment until he could be operated on. Kearney told Pichette that the ship was being abandoned, and then as the doctor continued back into the maze of bunks that comprised sick bay, he saw the wounded sailor move his legs out and begin to roll out of his bunk.

Soon after leaving Pichette, Kearney found a sailor who had been left for dead; the man had suffered a compound fracture of both legs and was in shock. *Yorktown*'s junior medical officer hurried back to the entrance to sick bay and called for help, which soon materialized in the form of HA1c Vernard W. Hier.

Kearney and the corpsman, armed with their flashlights, hurried past empty bunks (including the one Pichette had been occupying) at the front of the compartment and plunged back into the dark maze. Working as quickly as they could, they got the man out of the bunk and began carrying him topside. Assisted en route by two sailors who opened the main hatches to allow Kearney and Hier to get their dying charge topside, they finally reached the canting hangar deck; they procured ropes to haul the man across the incline to the starboard (high) side to lower him from there. Sadly, the effort expended to save the wounded sailor's life, however, proved unavailing, for the wounded man died before he could be evacuated from the ship.

The *Enterprise* orphans on board *Yorktown* became separated in the abandonment. LT(jg) Roberts went to his plane, parked aft on the hangar deck, and found, while the SBD had been badly holed, the life raft, carried in the compartment in the after fuselage, was still intact. Salvaging his camera (also still intact), Roberts made his way to the high side of the ship to abandon from there, when he encountered a *Yorktown* sailor, who proposed that they abandon ship together and utilize the pilot's two-man rubber boat. It seemed like a good idea to the pilot. The sailor went down a rope first, and Roberts threw down the raft; he then started down the rope. Unfortunately, he lost his grip about 15 feet from the water and fell in; struggling to the surface, encumbered by camera, .45 pistol and holster, and leather flight jacket, Roberts could see neither sign of the sailor nor his rubber boat, so swam to a nearby life raft and hung on.

Ships nearby pitched in to help rescue the survivors, in efforts interrupted thrice by alerts of air raids that fortunately did not materialize. *Balch* lowered her motor whaleboat, under the command of ENS William G. Weber, at 1705 and it proceeded to the waters near *Yorktown*. Those men without life jackets, or wounded, took priority; Bill Weber found nearly two percent of the men swimming in the water without life jackets. Survivors who had swum the farthest from the ship, exhausted, clung tenaciously to the gunwale of *Balch*'s boat, threatening to swamp it. Weber found it "necessary to wave a gun in the faces of some of them to get them to take the lines towed astern" of the boat, two trailing in its wake with life rings attached. Weber took one load of survivors to the nearest ship and then returned for more, the operations interrupted at 1800 by an air raid alert that scattered the ships for a brief time before the "all clear."

Anxious survivors nearly swamping the boat was not the only problem confronting ENS Weber; he soon discovered that even lying alongside an abandoning ship could be hazardous. He took *Balch*'s boat close-in to take off stretcher cases; the craft bobbed alongside beside the "high" side of the ship while four men, two or three of whom looked like officers, began lowering a man overboard in a makeshift stretcher made of pieces of 4×4-inch shoring. When they had him three-fourths of the way down, a piece of timber came loose, splashing close aboard and nearly holing the comparatively fragile motor whaleboat.

Weber's crew managed to get the first man aboard, and waited for the second, who lay strapped to a bed cot as an improvised stretcher. Unable to see his progress, the men on *Yorktown* lowered away, the wounded man's foot catching on the turn of the bilge and rotating "gruesomely" through 180°. Shouting aloft from the boat below prompted the lowerers to pull the man upwards a few feet to try again. Perhaps the abrupt change in direction loosened the straps holding the man in place, for a few seconds later, unconscious, he came hurtling down toward the boat from eight to ten feet up; fortunately *Balch*'s sailors caught him before he was hurt still further, but the destroyermen found the man to be "extremely battered up . . . some of his insides hanging out . . . ." ENS Weber considered the "spirit of the job" as "commendable," but the method "crude."

An officer taken on board then ordered the *Balch* boat to lie off and wait for the captain. After another *Yorktown*er remarked that the captain was still on the bridge "and wouldn't leave," though, ENS Weber decided to pick up a raft and tow it to the destroyer nearest to him, and transfer the wounded and injured *Yorktown* survivors from his own boat before returning to *Balch*. Even transferring survivors was not without an element of danger; while Weber's boat was transferring its last man to one destroyer, the ship backed down; its motor whaleboat, rigged out, narrowly passed over the heads of the *Balch* sailors, who barely missed being smashed into its bottom by the passing swells that lifted them within inches of destruction.

Meanwhile, on board, the gregarious and energetic Kiefer, far from being one who merely gave orders, had directed the abandonment and pitched in and helped wherever possible. He lowered a wounded man over the side to a life raft but burned his hands on the rope. Then, after being informed that the last of the sick bay patients were over the side and in the rafts and boats below, and seeing no one else in sight, he reported that to the captain. Kiefer then began to lower himself down a rope. However, his hands, already seared by the painful rope burns, caused him to lose his grip and fall. While he caromed off the armored belt, suffering a painful "compound fracture of the foot and ankle," it would take a lot more than that to stop the indomitable executive officer, for he swam to a nearby destroyer, helping to push a life raft toward the rescuing ship.

Kiefer had left the side of the ship only moments before CAPT Buckmaster began a last tour. He looked her over from the catwalk along the flight deck on the starboard side, and from the 5-inch gun platforms. He then returned to the flight deck abreast number one crane, before he proceeded down through number one dressing station and forward, his steps taking him through "flag country" and his own cabin—used little in the long weeks the ship had been at sea—to the port side and then down a ladder to the hangar deck. He saw no one alive, as well as the water lapping at the port side of the hangar deck. He hurried astern, and then, hand over hand, went down a line trailing into the water at the fantail. While in the water, he heard a man calling for help, and turned to see Matt2c William Fentress, one of VS-5's cooks, floundering in the water. Buckmaster swam over to the young negro, kept him afloat, and got him to a raft. Buckmaster was soon picked up by the *Hammann*, which COMDESRON 2 had ordered to leave the screen and pick up survivors.

MACH Lewis N. Williams, who had been on board a little over two months, joined a young sailor in towing a life raft away from the carrier, when suddenly the lad began swearing a blue streak. Williams "took the trouble of asking him what was eating him so much that he cussed," and elicited the response from the youngster: "That damn recruiting officer didn't tell me about this!"

Gradually, *Yorktown* sailors, aircrew and marines—and the four *Enterprise* orphans from VB-6—reached the relative havens of nearby destroyers. *Benham* took top honors in the rescue efforts, LCDR Joseph M. Worthington's command picked up 721 men; the division flagship *Balch* picked up 544,

"The Naval Academy Peter Pan—the Little Boy who never grew up"—so said his USNA classmates of Dixie Kiefer. Executive officer of the seaplane tender *Wright* (AV-1) at the time of the Japanese attack on Pearl Harbor, the stocky, thinning-haired CDR Kiefer became *Yorktown*'s XO at noon on 12 February 1942, relieving "Jocko" Clark. Some deemed Kiefer responsible for *Yorktown*'s high morale and fighting spirit, and, in fact, he received the DSM for bringing that ship's air group, and the ship herself, "to a high state of morale, efficiency, and readiness for battle" that allowed them to achieve such good results at Coral Sea. Awarded a Navy Cross for his heroism at Midway, Kiefer later won a Silver Star for bravery after his ship, the carrier *Ticonderoga* (CV-14) was hit twice by suicide planes off Formosa on 21 January 1945. Despite severe injuries, Kiefer remained on his bridge for 12 hours directing his ship's defense and until he deemed her out of danger. Attaining flag rank (commodore) on 14 May 1945, the colorful Kiefer was ultimately killed in a plane crash in the Fishkill (N.Y.) Mountains on 11 November 1945. He is seen here on *Ticonderoga*'s bridge on 5 November 1944, as he awaits an inbound Japanese air attack. (80-G-469523, cropped)

Destroyers, ordered to close in and pick up survivors, stand by while *Yorktown* abandons ship late on 4 June: (L-R) *Benham*, *Russell, Balch* and (far right), *Anderson*. Of interest are the three different camouflage schemes seen in use on the ships: *Benham* and *Balch* in Measure 11, Sea Blue; *Russell* and *Anderson* in two different variations of Measure 12 (Mod.); and *Yorktown* in her original Measure 12, Graded System. View taken from *Pensacola*. (80-G-21694)

two of her men, F2c H.E. Prideaux and Sea1c A.E. Lewis, distinguished themselves in actively and tirelessly carrying buoyed lines to struggling survivors as far as three or four hundred yards away. Other men who dove in to help did so with the knowledge if a second attack materialized during the operation their own chances of survival were correspondingly slimmer. *Russell* rescued 499 men and *Anderson* 204 (including ENS Tootle of VF-3, who was rescued soon after his plane had crashed, just about the time the second attack ended). *Morris* pulled 193 men from the water; *Hammann* picked up 85; *Hughes* 24.

Morris enjoyed a unique honor, for among the 193 men she rescued was CDR Michael B. Laing, RN, the Royal Navy officer whom ADM Nimitz had allowed to go out in *Yorktown* to observe U.S. Navy carrier operations. After someone had observed how Laing seemed to be taking "very good care of his hat," CBM C.S. English heard the British officer respond: "By Jove, yes. In England it takes three weeks to get one of these things made."

Morris' experience was typical among the screening destroyers; *Yorktown*'s oil-covered men dragged themselves, with great difficulty, up the lines and cargo

nets to reach the deck. However, with their hands and feet so slippery with the oil from the ship's ruptured tanks, "it took a good deal of assistance to get even the strongest aboard." The two worst injured men who came to *Morris* on rafts, had to be placed in the ship's whaleboat and hoisted up to the gunwale from there, to be placed on stretchers; the remainder of the injured men came up bowlines, a task made especially difficult by oily lines, a slippery deck, and oily hands.

Several *Morris* men, unwilling to stand idly by, dove over the side and assisted swimmers in the water. All hands on board the destroyer donated clothing willingly, as well as gave up a precious commodity on a man-of-war—fresh fruit—after their visitors had bathed and been given dry clothing. Although there were no extra bunks to be had on board *Morris*, her men gave up their own for the sick and injured from *Yorktown*.

Benham, after rescuing well over 700 men, soon added one more man to her "bag." An alert lookout spotted a downed aviator in his rubber boat at 1818. Altering course, *Benham* soon came upon LT(jg) Woollen, of Fighting Three. As his ship approached, LCDR Worthington heard the pilot call out: "Take

Yorktown after being abandoned on 4 June; the sponson of the hangar deck catapult is only a few feet above the water. "The Mighty Y" clearly shows signs of battle: the twisted catwalk amidships, the patched flight deck, and the blackened stack. Two VF-3 F4F-4s seem to cling "like struggling beetles to her tilting deck." A 26-foot motor whaleboat from one of the screening destroyers stands off in the right foreground, most likely engaged in a last check of the waters around the stricken carrier. (80-G-21643)

your time, Captain—I'm in no hurry. This raft won't run out of gas!"

The opportunity to avenge *Yorktown*'s crippling damage, though, soon came—thanks to Scouting Five. The search that *Yorktown* had launched at 1330 on 4 June had proved singularly un-fruitful for over three hours, the five two-plane scouting sections finding nothing. Heading for home, however, their collective luck changed. At 1630, LT Sam Adams, a short, stocky officer once given the typically inappropriate nickname of "Goliath" by his USNA classmates, flying plane no. 15 and in company with LT Harlan R. Dickson (plane no. 11), saw something which quickened his pulse—a formation of ten ships— four destroyers, three heavy cruisers, and . . . a carrier!

Adams immediately broke radio silence and reported, in plain language, what he had found, following it up with a keyed transmission. A "Zero" soon showed up to attempt to drive off the shadowing SBDs, but Adams' gunner, ARM1c Joseph J. Karrol, and ARM2c J.M. Lynch, his wingman, put up such an effective fire with their free guns that the "Zero" pilot soon went off to pick on less feisty prey!

Elsewhere in the vicinity, LT Nielsen and ENS Ben Preston, A-V(N), USNR, met a Nakajima E8N ("Dave") from the battleship *Haruna*—one of those launched at 1500—which radioed Commander, Mobile Force, at 1630: "I am being engaged by two enemy planes. apparently there are carriers in the vicinity." Each SBD made five runs on the seaplane, causing heavy damage and killing the rearseat man, but the pilot proved exceptionally skillful—he managed to get away, avoiding Preston's head-on attack and those by Nielsen. Two more SBDs, also on the return leg of the search, sighted an unidentified formation of six to eight planes, but did not engage them.

Upon completion of the search, all ten planes returned to the vicinity of TF-16, two planes—flown by LT(jg) W.F. Christie, A-V(N), USNR, LT(jg) H.M. McDowell, A-V(N), USNR—landing on board *Hor-*

LT Samuel Adams of "Scouting" Five (seen here as an ENS at Pensacola, 31 January 1938), "the type of man and pilot who gives strength to a squadron." From previous observation of his reporting and navigation, CDR Murr Arnold, VB-5's former skipper, believed Adams to be "one of the best carrier plane pilots and navigators in the Navy attached to carrier squadrons at that time...From my own limited experience I have always believed that Adams' contact report was by far the best, clearest, most accurate, and deliberate contact report made from any carrier based aircraft in the entire war..." (80-PA-1A-32)

net; the rest including Adams, on board *Enterprise*, which had received Adams' contact report disclosing the position of the enemy carrier, at 1645.

At 1730, while rescue operations were underway around the listing *Yorktown*, *Enterprise* commenced launch of an attack group of 24 SBDs. Fifteen of these were SBD-3s of Bombing Three, now grouped in five three-plane sections. Fourteen were flown by Bombing Three pilots, one by a Bombing Six pilot temporarily transferred to the unit to round out the complement. LT Shumway, who was now the senior man in the squadron (Leslie being on board *Astoria*), led the formation. The rest of the attack group were *Enterprise* aircraft, ten from Scouting Six and four from Bombing Six. LCDR Wilmer E. Gallaher, commanding Scouting Six, would lead the attack.

On board *Hiryū*, meanwhile, flight deck crews worked mightily to put one last strike in the air, with the pitiful remnants of the once-proud 1st Air Fleet: six Zeroes, five *kanbakus*, and four *kankōs*. *Sōryū*'s Type 2 experimental carrier bomber ("Judy") which had landed on board *Hiryū* after her near sistership had been put out of action, was warming up on deck. The heavy cruiser *Tone*, nearby, began maneuvering to pick up her scout plane when her sistership, *Chikuma*, suddenly spotted planes over *Hiryū*; almost simultaneously, the carrier's anti-aircraft battery opened up.

Acting on Adams' exceptionally precise contact report, the combined *Yorktown-Enterprise* group had again caught a Japanese carrier in a vulnerable position—with planes on deck. Shumway's group pushed over at 1910 and dove from 19,000 feet, coming from out of the sun—14 planes from VB-3 and one from VB-6. Six VS-6 planes headed down through the thick anti-aircraft fire and attacked *Hiryū* as she maneuvered radically, swinging to the southeast, to avoid the SBDs heading inexorably in her direction.

All of the Scouting Six planes' bombs, however, missed. Shumway saw this and abruptly switched his target from the cruisers to the still-unhit carrier. The orphaned *Yorktown*ers led the way, the four SBDs from Bombing Six swinging in astern of Bombing Three. The remaining "Zeroes," estimated at about a dozen, swarmed over the SBDs like stinging creatures from a disturbed nest. Three of them swept in from the rear at Shumway's "Dauntless," B-13, their guns winking fire; others attacked "Randy" Cooner's B-15, "Sid" Bottomley's B-10, and ENS M.A. Merrill's B-17; two SBDs jumped by the "Zeroes" were never seen again—gone were ENS Butler and his radioman, ARM3c D.D. Berg, and LT(jg) Wiseman and his rear-seat man, ARM2c Grant Ulysses Dawn.

Shumway's SBDs dropped nine 1,000-pounders on *Hiryū*, two on a nearby ship. Shumway reported four direct hits that turned *Hiryū* into a hellish floating cauldron of exploding ammunition, gasoline, and ordnance. They had knocked out the fourth Japanese aircraft carrier of the day and avenged *Yorktown*. There was no time for self-congratulation, though, for Bombing Three still had to disengage.

One "Zero" stayed with Shumway's SBD throughout the retirement phase of the action; several 20mm shells from the enemy fighter tore into his plane's right wing, damaging the right diving and landing flap, right

ARM2c (later ARM1c) Joseph J. Karrol, LT Sam Adams' radio-gunner, turned 27 years of age only a month before the Battle of Midway. (USN)

main gas tank (resulting in the loss of all fuel in it), right elevator and stabilizer; one shell exploded in the baggage compartment and threw fragments into the rear cockpit, injuring Shumway's gunner, ARM1c R.E. Coons, as well as holing the fuselage and nose section with 7.7mm slugs.

Cooner's SBD also suffered the attention of a trio of "Zeroes," for a time; one put a 20mm shell into the rear cockpit which exploded in the radio transmitter, "seriously wounding" AOM2c Clifton R. Bassett in the right knee. Another 20mm shell hit at the base of the fin, which exploded in the baggage compartment and shredded the life raft carried there; Cooner suffered a slight leg wound. Bassett, although weak from loss of blood, extracted a small measure of revenge for their predicament by claiming one of their tormentors, and later drove off a seaplane that had attacked them after the fighters had disappeared.

ENS Merrill's SBD took several hits from small caliber fire and two 20mm shells which "struck just aft of [the] rear cockpit," which temporarily froze control cables slightly and injured ARM3c Dallas J. Bergeron in both feet. LT(jg) Sherwood was attacked in similar fashion but "sustained no damage." A "Zero" made an overhead pass on Bottomley's SBD, but Bottomley opened his diving flaps, and the en-

Hiryū, as seen from a plane from carrier *Hōshō* on 5 June, burns, her flight deck forward rendered useless by multiple bomb hits the previous day; a violent explosion has blown the number one plane elevator almost into the island structure. (NH 73065)

emy fighter zoomed by, overshooting him; his adversary then pulled up, spoiling the aim of two other "Zeroes" awaiting their turn on the SBD. Another fighter appeared during Bottomley's dive, but his rear-seat man, AMM2c Daniel F. Johnson, drove him off with fire from his free guns. ENS Merrill spotted a single-float seaplane—perhaps the same one that attacked Cooner's SBD—heading for the "protection of scattered clouds to eastward," but wisely refrained from making runs on the seaplane due to the proximity of the still-deadly "Zeroes."

Hiryū, though, lay "aflame from bow to stern." The flames and smoke had prevented an accurate counting of hits, but regardless of the number, *Hiryū* was in bad straits. In fact, *Hornet*'s dive bombers, arriving on the scene at 1920, didn't waste any ordnance on her, electing to go after the heavy cruiser *Tone*. *Hornet*'s bad fortunes, however, still held; none of the 14 bombs dropped hit their target! The composite *Yorktown-Enterprise* air group headed back toward *Enterprise*, reaching the ship at 2008; three of their number had gone down (one VB-6 plane, and Wiseman and Butler of VB-3). By 2034 all were on board, but Shumway's,

Merrill's, and Cooner's SBDs were deemed "inoperative for further combat." By 2059, *Hornet* had recovered all of her brood, and by 2120, the last plane of *Enterprise*'s tenth, and final combat air patrol of the day had been recovered.

Almost at the same time LT Shumway's SBDs were pushing over to loose their lethal loads on *Hiryū*, RADM Fletcher decided to take TF-17 clear of *Yorktown* and join TF-16. His ships formed a column and moved off. "The aircraft carrier *Yorktown*," war correspondent Wendell Webb observed from on board *Pensacola*, "is a lonely blotch against the western sun tonight and there is a lump in many a throat. The fleet is moving on." War seldom allows much time for reflection; Fletcher knew that his most powerful concentration of ships under his tactical command, formed around *Hornet* and *Enterprise*, was operating to the east of him, too far, perhaps, to provide adequate cover for TF-17—a problem that had been a contributing factor to *Yorktown*'s troubles earlier that day. Enemy "snoopers" still lurked about, prompting Fletcher's concern about a third air attack on his force, as well as fear that the Japanese might launch a night attack to destroy *Yorktown*. How to repel such an attack was problematical, given the fact that four of his destroyers were crowded to the gunwales with survivors from the carrier—hardly the best way to fight one's ship in action.

It had been a difficult decision to make, and illustrates why the burden of command rests heavily upon those who exercise it. *Yorktown* was, for all intents and purposes, irreplaceable; carriers didn't grow on trees and the U.S. Navy had few in June, 1942. After she had been abandoned, *Yorktown* rode easily in the swells; she had ceased settling and her condition, while serious, had stabilized. Yet, ships could be replaced—trained men could not. Weighing all the options, Fletcher decided to clear the area to redistribute survivors and send a salvage party back the following day to try and save *Yorktown*. In the meantime, he radioed for assistance, asking that a salvage tug be went to

ENS "Randy" Cooner (top) follows as plane handlers and corpsmen rush AOM2c Bassett, his wounded radio-gunner, below for treatment. (USN)

begin to tow *Yorktown* clear of the area. Hindsight, always clearer after the fact and after a detached view of events that have transpired before, offers what might have been a better solution: put a party on board to work on salvaging the ship at night, with a guard of two destroyers, whose radar could detect the approach of enemy forces and which could pull off the salvagers and sink the ship with torpe-does before retiring. But—that is hindsight.

At 2000, as TF-17 drew away from *York-town* in the gathering darkness, Fletcher di-rected COMDESRON 6, CAPT E.P. Sauer, to detach *Hughes* to stand by *Yorktown* with instructions to prevent anyone from boarding her, or to destroy her to prevent

capture or if serious fires should break out on board. *Hughes* departed TF-17 at 2015.

As TF-17 then continued eastward, RADM Spruance, in TF-16, radioed Fletcher at 2016, telling him of the attacks being carried out by TF-16's aircraft on *Hiryū*. Spruance asked if CTF-17 had any instructions for him, to gov-ern his future operation. "Negative," Fletcher responded. "Will conform to your move-ments." TF-17 then drew away from TF-16 around midnight, steering east.

The situation at the end of the day on 4 June found the U.S. Navy having gained "incontestible mastery of the air." TF-16, her air groups recov-ered (*Enterprise* and *Hornet* both having *York-town* planes on board) then stood eastward, southward, and back to the westward. RADM Spruance, to whom Fletcher had passed tactical command, did not feel "justified in risking a night encounter with possibly superior enemy forces." On the other hand, he did not want to be too far away from Midway the following day. "I wished to have a position from which either to follow up retreat-ing enemy forces," he later explained, "or to break up a landing attack on Midway." The question of whether or not the Japanese possessed a *fifth* carrier in the area also weighed heavily on Spruance's mind.

Benham, with 720 *Yorktown* survivors embarked, comes alongside *Portland* around 1900 on 4 June, while the carrier drifts, listing steeply to port, in the distance. Shortly after this photograph was taken, an air raid alert (which proved to be false) prompted *Benham* to cast off without having been able to transfer any *Yorktown*ers to the cruiser. The next morning, though, the destroyer would transfer some to *Astoria* and some to *Portland*. (NH 95574)

CHAPTER 12

With All Battle Flags Flying

*H*ughes HAD ARRIVED in *Yorktown*'s vicinity around 2124, and commenced patrolling around the dark, silent carrier. It was a fitful watch. At 0145 on 5 June, *Hughes*' radar, and her lookouts, spotted a "dark, low-lying object" 3,000 yards away off the destroyer's starboard bow. The ship increased speed to investigate but found nothing. Had it been a group of life rafts appearing as one object, or a submarine?

Daylight brought the ubiquitous enemy search aircraft. At 0826, *Hughes*' radar watch picked up a plane bearing 295°, 20 miles distant. Correctly believing it to be enemy, *Hughes* increased speed and went to general quarters, her gunners standing by to repel an air attack. The stranger cleared the screen, though, ten minutes later, heading west. Had they been seen? Yes. Lurking out over the Pacific was the heavy cruiser *Chikuma*'s no. 4 plane, launched at 0641 on a search mission. This aircraft soon sent off a contact report (0852) of an "enemy *Yorktown*-class carrier listing to starboard and drifting" and telling of the solitary destroyer in the vicinity.

Hughes could do nothing to hinder the progress of the enemy's aerial reconnaissance, since the plane which had made the sighting and appeared briefly on the destroyer's radar screen was far out of range. The aircraft gone, *Hughes* resumed her lonely vigil near *Yorktown*.

Unbeknownst to the destroyermen nearby, there *were* still men alive on board *Yorktown*. One was 18-year old Sea2c Pichette, whom LT(jg) Kearney had last seen preparing to get out of his bunk in the carrier's sick bay during the abandonment late the previous afternoon, who manned a .50-caliber machine gun jury-rigged in the boat pocket aft on the port side and fired it into the water at 0941.

As *Hughes* drew alongside to investigate, her men spied Pichette, waving. After lowering a boat, the destroyer got underway and resumed circling *Yorktown* as her whaleboat chugged across to the listing carrier. The boarding party soon found Pichette unconscious beside the weapon he had fired to attract their attention, and carefully embarked him in the boat for the trip over to *Hughes*, which they reached at 1035.

Those who attended the wounded man, however, heard him mumble something about someone else being alive on board. Consequently, *Hughes*' captain, LCDR D.J. Ramsey, sent his ship's motor whaleboat back to *Yorktown* on its second mercy mission. The boarding party soon returned with Sea1c George K. Weise, who claimed to have suffered a fractured skull and other injuries. Interestingly, Weise, whom LT(jg) Kearney would later remember as a "frequenter of the sick bay from way back . . . well known by me and all the corpsmen" had walked into *Yorktown*'s sick bay unaided after the first attack, and although Weise appeared to have been hit by fragments, Kearney, having many more serious wounds to treat and who had examined Weise himself and had seen the comparatively minor nature of his complaint, told the sailor to lie down in a bunk.

How Weise and Pichette came to be left behind provokes questions. LT(jg) Kearney had searched sick bay; he later asserted that no one, except the dying sailor that he and HA1c Hier had taken to the flight deck, where the mortally wounded man died before he could be removed from the ship, had been left behind—especially not Weise and Pichette, neither of whom were seen when the junior medical officer and the corpsman were carrying the last man out of sick bay. What had compelled them to remain on board? For Pichette, the act of staying in *Yorktown* proved a death sentence: peritonitis, which may have been averted had he been treated within six hours of his wounding (which treatment could have been rendered on board *Astoria*) had set in in the interim.

While *Hughes'* boat had been away recovering Weise, a PBY circled the destroyer, whose signalmen took down the message from the lumbering flying boat that there were no ships in the area to the north and west. At that, LCDR Ramsey sent *Hughes'* boarding party back for another look at the abandoned carrier.

At about the same time, lookouts reported seeing a man in a rubber boat, determinedly rowing toward *Hughes.* At 1138, she picked up ENS Harry Gibbs of Fighting Three (one of the four VF-3 pilots who had been shot down in the melee over TF-17 on 4 June during the *Hiryu* carrier attack planes' torpedo attack). He had been in the water since 1705 the previous day, and had rowed at least six miles to reach safety. With people turning up unannounced, *Hughes* searched the vicinity for others, but found none.

At 0744 on 5 June, TF-17 reversed course and reduced speed. By 0800, TF-17 was steaming some 054° (T), 240 miles from Midway. By that time, CAPT Buckmaster had been transferred to *Astoria* from *Hammann*, and had discussed with RADM Fletcher the possibility of saving *Yorktown,* whose remaining in a stable condition throughout the night had buoyed hopes for salvage. Buckmaster wanted to return to his ship with a hand-picked crew of volunteers, specialists in their respective departments. To do so, however, required the time-consuming gathering of his men on one ship.

Between 0804 and 1129, a series of high-line transfers took place as the ships drew together and passed lines between them, across which came the men necessary to attempt to save the listing *Yorktown.* *Benham, Anderson, Hammann* and *Balch* transferred all of the carrier's survivors—save the select salvage party—to *Portland,* while the salvagers gathered on board *Astoria.* At 1235, *Hammann* came alongside *Astoria* and began bringing on board Buckmaster's crew, a process that took almost one hour; she cleared the heavy cruiser's side at 1327 with 30 officers and 141 enlisted men embarked.

After the high speed steaming necessitated the day before, Fletcher deemed it provident to fuel his destroyers from *Portland,* an evolution which commenced around 1430 and ceased at 2000. Then, their tanks topped off, Fletcher ordered *Hammann, Balch* and *Benham,* all three ships as a task unit under CAPT Buckmaster, to return to try and save *Yorktown.*

While Buckmaster was gathering his salvage team, other ships were converging on the scene. One, *Vireo* (AT-144), LT James C. Legg in command, had been at

Portland brings on board *Yorktown* survivors rescued by *Benham* the day before; the evolution took place on 5 June between 1055 and 1327. Thus unencumbered, *Benham* would join the force earmarked to try and save *Yorktown.* (80-G-32387)

Pearl and Hermes Reef in the opening phases of the battle, guarding the gasoline tanker *Kaloli* (AOG-13), and was lying-to there until ordered to go to *Yorktown*'s aid. Built as a minesweeper, *Vireo* had served as such through the 1920s and 1930s, until newer and more capable minecraft began coming into the Fleet. She and her sisters were being assigned other duties, including those of tugs.

Hughes sighted *Vireo* at 1144 on the 5th, ten miles distant, shortly before the destroyer's motor whaleboat returned to the ship with three ECMs and all secret and confidential publications that were found in two safes or loose in the code room—evidence of considerable haste by the abandoning carrier crew. *Hughes'* boat officer reported that the destroyermen could find no more men alive on board the carrier, and that the ship did not appear to be sinking. He also reported that the smoke, seen forward, was apparently a waste fire and confined.

Vireo soon joined *Hughes*, and the former's skipper, LT Legg, an experienced sailor who had come up through the ranks, agreed to the feasibility of taking *Yorktown* in tow. *Hughes* contributed men to assist *Vireo*'s sailors in rigging the necessary tow line. This done, Legg ordered course set at 100° (T) and rang down for 110 revolutions.

LT James C. Legg, photographed at about the time he received his commission in May 1942. Fifty-two years old at this time, he had entered the Navy in 1919, and had been XO of *Vireo* at the time of the attack on Pearl Harbor. Assuming command in the spring of 1942, he was awarded a Navy Cross for his gallantry in the attempt to salvage *Yorktown* on 5 and 6 June 1942; among the survivors his ship picked up on the 6th was CAPT Buckmaster. (NH 100171)

The plucky little minecraft started ahead at 1636, but Legg soon discovered that two or three knots was all that he could coax out of his ship, in view of her unwieldy charge. Forced to slow down, and making very little headway, *Vireo* labored on, lacking power and possessing only a small rudder; all Legg could do was keep *Vireo* holding *Yorktown* into the wind. The heavy load imposed on the tug's engines, though, meant slow going; and the heavy sea making up compounded the problem. *Hughes*, meanwhile, monitored the fighter direction circuit for TF-16 and learned of "enemy" planes in the vicinity. Neither the destroyer's lookouts, nor her radar, however, spotted any.

While *Vireo* had been preparing to take *Yorktown*

in tow, two more ships arrived: *Monaghan* (from TF-16) and *Gwin*, one of *Yorktown*'s old Atlantic consorts. The latter had departed Pearl Harbor on the morning of 3 June with orders to join TF-16; at 1900 on the 4th, however, she had been directed to join TF-17. She had sighted *Yorktown* on the horizon, 12 miles away, at 1530 on the 5th, and arrived on the scene soon thereafter.

Gwin's commanding officer, LCDR John M. Higgins, could see that *Yorktown* was in a bad way. Not content to stand idly by, Higgins immediately ordered a salvage party on board the listing carrier "in [an] endeavor to improve list and trim . . . ." *Gwin*'s men, assisted by those from *Hughes*, then boarded *Yorktown*; they jettisoned the carrier's port anchor and the 50-foot motor launch from the skids in the after boat pocket before they knocked off work to return to their ships after nightfall.

Meanwhile, later that same afternoon, at 1740 on the 5th, as *Vireo* was towing *Yorktown* toward Pearl Harbor, and *Gwin*'s sailors were jettisoning topside weight from the carrier, elements of *Yorktown*'s orphaned air group again took to the air: ten planes from VB-3, led by LT Shumway, and seven from VS-5, led by LT Short; the remainder of the group consisted of 15 SBDs from VB-6 and VS-6. The object of their search: a "burning CV" reportedly accompanied by two battleships, three heavy cruisers, and four destroyers. All planes, each armed with a 500-pound bomb, headed toward a position estimated from the original 1000 contact report sent by a PBY. As RADM Spruance later admitted, the trail of the Japanese ships was "rather cold," but was "the best we had."

However, instead of finding a "burning CV" (*Hiryū* had sunk a long time before), part of the group, comprising nine planes of VS-6 and seven from VS-5, found only a single ship. Reported as a "destroyer leader" or a "light cruiser," the ship they saw was the destroyer *Tanikaze*, a fast, modern ship with a main battery of six 5.5-inch guns. Although she was not

The minesweeper *Vireo* (AM-52), seen here during salvage operations on *California* (BB-44) at Pearl Harbor in December 1941, was reclassified as a fleet tug, AT-144, on 2 June 1942. Pictures of the ship are very rare, and the inclusion of a view of her in this rig is because her appearance had not changed between December 1941 and June 1942. After the Battle of Midway she was extensively modernized, and went on to participate, with much glory, in the Solomons campaign. (NH 95569)

what the pilots had been sent out to attack, the pilots of VS-5 and VS-6 decided, in view of the length of the search and the amount of gas remaining, to attack anyway: sixteen planes vs. one destroyer.

Although the odds were against her, *Tanikaze* put up a worthy fight and squarely beat them. Seeing the approaching SBDs, she bent on speed and commenced maneuvering, putting up what LT Short later considered a "relatively weak and inaccurate anti-aircraft fire" at the outset. *Tanikaze* then made violent "S"-turns and put up a high volume of anti-aircraft fire, evading every bomb dropped (although she later reported at least eleven "very near misses"). Her guns also downed one plane—that of LT Adams and his

gunner, Karrol. A group of *Hornet* SBDs attacked *Tanikaze* a little later, soon after the mixed VS-5/VS-6 group departed, but they, too, could not score a hit.

The attack group returned to *Enterprise* and *Hornet* in the gathering darkness; all Scouting 5 planes (except Adams') were on board by 2200, as were all but one Scouting 6 plane—the solitary exception within that squadron was ENS Vammen, who made his first night carrier landing on board *Hornet*. (Five other Scouting 6 pilots had also made *their* first night carrier landings as well!) Despite the danger of lurking enemy submarines, RADM Spruance ordered the use of lights to guide the fliers home; success rewarded his bold consideration for his pilots—all landed safely.

At 0530 on 6 June, another ship was nearing *Yorktown*, but she was not friend but foe; her men not interested in salvage, but in destruction—the Japanese submarine *I-168*. Acting on information initially provided by *Chikuma*'s number four plane, *I-168*'s commanding officer, LCDR Tanabe Yahachi, had been directed to sink a crippled carrier. As she neared the

Japanese submarine *I-68*, seen running her trials in March 1934, was the lead ship of six Type KDa 6 Sensuikans. Laid down on 18 June 1931, launched on 26 June 1933 and commissioned on 31 July 1934, *I-68* was reclassified as *I-168* on 20 May 1942. *I-168*'s success at Midway proved to be the only noteworthy enterprise of any of the six boats in the class, none of which survived World War II. *I-168* was sunk by submarine *Scamp* (SS-277) on 20 July 1943. (NH 73054)

Hammann at Charleston (S.C.) Navy Yard, January 1942, shortly before she sailed for the Pacific, and as she looked when lost at Midway six months later. Painted in Measure 12 (mod.) and sporting new FD fire control and SC air search radars, *Hammann* has also undergone the tophamper reduction common to *Sims*-class ships. (19-N-26593)

area on the surface in the first wash of the day, the submarine was 11 miles away from the carrier when a lookout spotted the dark shape of *Yorktown* on the horizon; *I-168* dove to make her approach, unseen.

As the Japanese submarine commander was skillfully bringing his craft toward the Americans, *Hammann*, accompanied by *Balch* and *Benham*, neared the crippled carrier, too. At 0615 on 6 June, *Yorktown*'s salvage party began clambering and climbing on board, from *Hammann*, prepared to carry out their predetermined plan. The damage control party was to extinguish the tenacious fire in A-305-A and carefully inspect the lower deck spaces, determining the extent of the damage. They were also to reduce the list by jettisoning topside weight on the port side and by implementing counterflooding and pumping,

the pumps to be powered by the destroyer until the arrival of a salvage tug. The gunnery department was to prepare machine guns in case of an air attack, and assist the damage control party by cutting loose and casting overboard all five-inch guns on the port side and any other "removable weights" that could be let go. The air department was to jettison all planes left on board and all "removable weights" on the port side, while the engineering personnel were to carefully inspect the lower decks to determine the extent of the damage and assist the damage control officer in correcting the list. Other specific tasks involved having a navigation party "attempt to bring the rudder amidship," men from the communications department to "maintain visual communications with other ships in the task group," supply department hands to prepare to subsist the salvage party on board; and, lastly, the medical department to collect and identify the dead.

To MACH Williams, the experience of boarding a ship that had been abandoned was unforgettable. "*Yorktown* was dark and dead and silent," he recalled. "Darkness isn't black enough for the void that was in her. The silence was overwhelming. You

Mikuma, pounded into junk by SBDs from *Hornet* and *Enterprise* (including in the latter some from the orphaned *Yorktown* squadrons), wallows in the Pacific swells on the afternoon of 6 June, as photographed by *Enterprise*'s veteran CP J.A. Mihalovic. (80-G-414422)

Bel Geddes' diorama depicting *Hammann* lying alongside *Yorktown* during salvage operations on 6 June while another destroyer conducts anti-submarine watch nearby. (80-G-701899)

got an eerie, unearthly dream-like feeling when you walked her decks and went below. I can't quite put into words the lonesome dead feeling that was in her . . . ."

After placing the salvage party on board *Yorktown*, *Hammann* had taken a screening station until CAPT Buckmaster directed LCDR True to bring his ship off the carrier's starboard bow to provide hoses and water for the fire-fighting effort being carried out on board to contain the persistent blaze there in the rag stowage. True found it "impossible to lie clear of *Yorktown* and maintain position accurately enough to permit effective assistance," so he brought *Hammann* alongside, splinter mattresses and large fenders hanging between the two ships, the destroyer resting against the carrier's projecting bilge keel. *Hammann* then led out two foamite hoses to *Yorktown* and one water hose to the carrier's flight deck, to attach to the latter's own foamite system. She also rigged a hose aft to pump in salt-water for counterflooding, and an oil suction hose to take oil from the carrier's port tanks to correct the list. *Hammann*'s galley hands, meanwhile, turned to with a will, providing coffee and food for the salvage party.

While CAPT Buckmaster and his men strove to save their ship, *Balch*, *Benham*, *Monaghan*, *Gwin* and *Hughes* screened *Yorktown* and *Hammann*, the destroyers in an anti-submarine and anti-aircraft screen, 2,000 yards distant, steaming at 14 knots. Sound conditions, though, were poor, and maximum echo range was only 900 yards at best. "Submarine propeller noises," LCDR Higgins of *Gwin* lamented, "could not be heard at any range."

"Considerable progress" had been made, during the forenoon and afternoon watches, in reducing the list, the men working in spite of the hazardous footing imposed by the canted decks; those working below decks had to contend with "stale and foul" air. The firefighters had finally extinguished the smoldering rag stowage. CDR Aldrich directed the battle to right the ship; LCDR Davis, the gunnery officer, supervised the cutting away of guns on the port side. Meticulously taking care that no fire hazards developed in doing so, Davis and his volunteers had cut away one 5-inch gun and dropped it over the side, as well as five 20mm mount foundations. Work was progressing well on a second 5-inch mount. The aviation members of the salvage team, meanwhile, lowered aircraft from the overheads, forward, and began pushing them over the side, too.

At 1240, while salvage operations were still proceeding apace on board *Yorktown*, Bombing Three and Scouting Five were again going forth to fight. Shumway, now flying B-3, led two divisions (10 planes, five planes per division) from Bombing Three, one (of five planes) from Bombing Six. Launching at 1240, the formation took departure from *Enterprise* at 1300, in company with a mixed formation of planes from Scouting Five and Scouting Six, twelve F4F-4s of Fighting Six, and three TBDs of Torpedo Six. The whole was under LT Wally Short of VS-5.

Shumway and his group proceeded on a southwesterly heading. Climbing to 15,000 feet, they made contact with the enemy at 1400, 30 miles away. Two heavy cruisers (one erroneously identified as being from the *Atago*-class) came into view—the crippled *Mogami* (looking smaller from a distance because of her crumpled bow suffered in a collision with *Mikuma* the night before) and *Mikuma*, with two destroyers

in attendance. It was an attacking pilot's dream—perfect visibility, ceiling unlimited with scattered clouds, winds 18 knots from the southwest.

Told that a battleship was in the area, however, the pilots flew on, swinging to the south, hunting for bitter game. In due time, when they realized that a battleship was not to be found, Short gave the order to attack "the *Mogami*-class cruiser" (as both proved to be). With no fighters to hinder them, and very little anti-aircraft fire to speak of, it was a catch-as-catch-can attack, "divisions and sections" making "individual approaches from all directions . . . ." *Mikuma* shuddered under the impact of hit after hit; LT Shumway estimated that Bombing Three, alone, scored four direct hits and five near misses. "After the attacks," Shumway reported, "the topside was burning heavily;" the ship, a complete shambles, slowed to a stop. Many topside personnel had either been blown or jumped into the water. Internal explosions were seen to follow." Scouting Five then tagged *Mikuma* with what LT Short deduced were "five direct hits" and "two close misses." The accompanying F4Fs, meanwhile, strafed the accompanying destroyers; seeing the flak, though, however, weak the volume, the trio of TBDs retired, having been specifically ordered *not* to go into anti-aircraft fire. They headed back to *Enterprise* carrying their torpedoes.

Between 1527 and 1615, the elements of Bombing Three and Scouting Five returned in triumph to *Enterprise* without loss. LT Nielsen and

Bel Geddes' diorama depicting the torpedoing of *Yorktown* and *Hammann* by *I-168* on 6 June. (80-G-701900)

LT Dickson, of Scouting Five, lingered in the vicinity of the crippled *Mikuma*, watching her death throes. Dead in the water, burning, and emitting heavy black smoke, *Mikuma* was near death. While the sight of her demise moved one *Enterprise* pilot to pity, it did nothing of the kind to one of the other pilots in the air at the time; the sight provoked little pity from Dickson, a man, whose USNA classmates once said, held a "deep-seated hatred for all that was . . . unjust." Not content that the enemy ship was doomed, Dickson only wanted to go back to *Enterprise* to get another bomb to drop on the hated enemy!

While elements of her air group were returning to TF-16, elsewhere *Yorktown* was being watched carefully by LCDR Tanabe, who took sightings at inter-vals and brought his ship nearer to the unsuspecting carrier. Her approach concealed by the poor sound conditions, *I-168* pierced the screen successfully. Tanabe, however, found himself too close, and brought his boat around second time to open the range. He carefully laid his plans, determining that four torpedoes, fired with a minimal spread, would do the job— *Yorktown* was incapable of maneuvering in her crippled state, so "leading" the target was unnecessary. During the final leg of the approach Tanabe could not believe that he had escaped detection: "Either they [the escorts] were poor sailors, had poor equipment or *I-168* was a charmed vessel." When 1,200 yards away from his quarry, the Japanese I-boat commander ordered four torpedoes fired.

Hammann's stern plunges deeper while *Yorktown* sailors watch in foreground (R); knotted lines used earlier in the abandonment of the carrier dangle at right. (80-G-32320)

Hammann having disappeared beneath the waves, one sailor who had been watching the destroyer's dramatic demise has turned to look toward the camera. (80-G-32322)

Up to that point, *Yorktown*'s salvagers had had good reason to congratulate themselves, although they knew full well that much work lay ahead. Three submersible pumps on the "low" side of the ship, on the third deck, had transferred liquid from that area to the fourth deck on the starboard side, counterflooding into empty starboard fuel tanks. One submersible pump in the after engine room had suction, and was pulling water overboard. Pumps had also transferred water from *Hammann*'s bilges into empty fuel tanks on the starboard side as well. That, in conjunction with the losing of topside weight—guns and aircraft, chiefly—had reduced the water level on the third deck, aft, by three feet; no further flooding was occurring, and the list decreased two degrees. The inclinometer now read 22°.

At 1534, lookouts on board *Balch* noted a disturbance in the water, some 2,500 yards beyond *Yorktown*; at 1535, *Monaghan* opened up on the TBS: "Torpedoes headed your way. . . ." Around 1536, lookouts in *Hammann* picked up emergency signals from screening destroyers. Almost simultaneously, that ship spotted four torpedo wakes about 600 yards away on the starboard beam. *Yorktown*, too, sounded the alarm in the form of 20mm fire while on board the carrier, "Torpedo attack" spread quickly by word of mouth. On board *Hammann*, the bridge signalled the engine room: "Full speed astern on inboard engine" as LCDR True sought to pull clear; meanwhile, gunners on the starboard side Oerlikons—GM3c Willie V. Allison, forward, and Sea2c Roy T. Nelson, aft—opened fire in the hopes of detonating the onrushing torpedoes.

Hammann's sailors headed for their battle stations as the general quarters alarm sounded; most reached them before one torpedo penetrated the destroyer's hull plating abreast the number two fireroom, breaking the ship's back. In a shattering instant, the

Soon after *Hammann* disappears beneath the waves, a terrific explosion—probably the destroyer's depth charges—rumbles up from the deep with destructive and deadly force, killing and maiming many men in the water. This Bel Geddes diorama depicts this dramatic event. Ship at left is *Vireo*, doubling back to pick up survivors after cutting the two line to *Yorktown*, in an action that earns for her skipper, LT James C. Legg, a Navy Cross. (80-G-701902)

explosion of the torpedo warhead carried away the forward bulkhead of the forward engine room; large quantities of oil, water, and debris cascaded into the air as two more torpedoes barrelled into *Yorktown*, one at about frame 84, the other at frame 95. A fourth torpedo passed harmlessly astern. Onlookers on board *Balch* noted "three huge columns of water" reaching skyward alongside the carrier.

The heavy blasts rocked both ships; *Hammann*, mortally stricken, began to sag immediately. All mooring lines and hoses parted as the destroyer, blown away from the carrier's side, drifted aft and began to sink. The explosion hurled LCDR True hard against a desk in the pilot house. Temporarily unable to either speak or breathe, and having unknowingly suffered a broken rib, True paused to recover his wind. Seeing the ship was doomed and the captain incapacitated, LT Ralph W. Elden, the executive officer, passed the word: "All hands abandon ship . . . ."

LT(jg) C.C. Hartigan, *Hammann*'s gunnery officer, had been knocked from the gun director to the lookout platform; regaining his senses a few seconds later, he saw *Hammann*'s foc'sle awash. After then making sure that the director crew and lookouts had all put on life jackets and laid below, Hartigan followed, reaching the bridge to find Elden going down the ladder paralleling the mast, LCDR True the last man on

the bridge. Then, after inspecting the pilot house, chart house, and radar room, finding no one, True joined Elden and Hartigan and jumped into the water, swimming to get clear of the sinking ship. He looked around, perhaps to take a last glimpse of his command, when he suddenly spotted StM1c E.W. Raby emerging on deck without a life jacket; he pointed in the man's direction and LT(jg) Hartigan swam back.

Yorktown, too, had trembled hard as if struck in the solar plexus. Close to the side while supervising the cutting operations on the second five-inch gun to be tackled by the salvage party, LCDR Davis was thrown overboard by the shock of the torpedo explosion; he soon swam aft to grab a line dangling in the water and climb back on board. LT Wilson was below inspecting compartments to determine the extent of fire damage when he heard the alarm being passed. He started topside, but the torpedoes struck the ship before he reached the hangar deck. A heavy hatch jarred loose, and fell on his head and arm.

Just about the time *Yorktown*'s LCDR Davis reached the line dangling in the water, and *Hammann*'s LT Hartigan reached the mess attendant, a "terrific explosion" rumbled up from the deep—probably *Hammann*'s depth charges going off at a predetermined depth. *Yorktown*'s communication officer, LCDR C.C Ray, had begun to ascend a ladder when "something" compelled him to "turn and look back" to see the heads of men floating in the water in the slick where *Hammann* had been only a few short moments before. In what Ray declared was "the most remarkable and awesome sight that I think I have ever seen, those heads that had been on the water . . . suddenly disappeared, somewhat like the windshield wiper erases the droplets from your windshield when it's raining—they were all gone."

The combination of the torpedo hits and the explosion from the destroyer's depth charges jostled *Yorktown* still further, carrying away number three auxiliary generator; shaking numerous fittings loose from the overhead of the hangar and sending them crashing to the deck below; collapsing the landing gear on two planes left on board; shearing all rivets on the starboard leg of the foremast, and throwing men in every direction, causing injuries and breaking bones.

The sudden, devastating presence of the Japanese submarine changed all plans in one destructive moment. As *Gwin*, *Monaghan* and *Hughes* turned aggressively to the task of hunting *I-168*, whose captain had set course to pass directly beneath *Yorktown* at the outset, and *Balch* and *Benham* commenced rescue operations, CAPT Buckmaster decided to postpone the salvage attempt for the moment, "to remove the salvage party to destroyers and to return to *Yorktown* the following morning.' A large salvage tug was expected the next day. *Yorktown*'s captain then directed *Vireo* to come alongside.

Legg, however, had needed no such orders. Looking aft from his bridge, the tug's commander had thought that *Yorktown* was going to sink immediately, and ordered the tow line cut. An acetylene torch soon severed the wire linking the tug with the carrier, and *Vireo* turned back toward *Yorktown*. She began picking up *Hammann* survivors, as did *Benham*, the latter rescuing three officers and 163 enlisted men (as well as 16 bodies) from *Hammann* and three officers and 19 men from *Yorktown*.

On board the carrier, her salvagers prepared to abandon ship—again—closing all watertight doors below the main deck that they could reach. Those

CDR Arnold E. "Everett" True, October 1942, receiving the Navy Cross for the heroism he had shown while commanding *Hammann* at the Battle of the Coral Sea when his ship rescued *Lexington*'s survivors. True, who would receive the Distinguished Service Medal for his service at Midway, had been *Hammann*'s only CO, having put her into commission in August 1939. (80-G-40170)

making the lower deck inspection noticed "a heavy pounding of water . . . apparently through the torpedo hole on the starboard side and against the centerline bulkhead," causing those who heard the ominous sound to feel a "very pronounced shock" each time the sea surged through. All hands then lay topside and began leaving the ship for the second time, transferring to the tug that now lay close by.

Legg, in an impressive example of "seamanship of the highest order," brought *Vireo* alongside smartly, closing from astern and then shifting to the exact spot where *Hammann* had been only a few minutes before, still picking up destroyermen and carriermen alike. *Yorktown*, as if resenting the rough treatment accorded a lady of her stature, rolled considerably, giving *Vireo* a "terrific pounding" for the 40 minutes she lay alongside bringing off the salvage crew. Then, after having taken on board the last of *Yorktown*'s men—CAPT Buckmaster among them—*Vireo* gathered momentum and moved away from the carrier's side, LT Legg noting no appreciable change in the bigger ship's trim and list. CAPT Buckmaster noted the phenomenon, too, but noted that the torpedo hits had counterflooded the ship, reducing the list to 17° but causing her to settle deeper in the water.

At 1715, CAPT Buckmaster conducted a burial service for the three bodies of the *Hammann* men whom *Vireo* had received from a destroyer's boat over an hour earlier—StM1c Raby and two officers who had been killed by the concussion of the destroyer's depth charges. One of the latter could only be identified by his lieutenant's bars (making it either LT Elden, the XO, or LT M.H. Ray, Jr.); the other, identified only by a laundry mark and the initials "R.P.F.E." on his USNR midshipman's ring, was the gallant ENS Enright, whose heroic perseverance off Cape Henslow over a month before had resulted in the rescue of McCuskey and Adams of VF-42.

Balch closed *Vireo* at 1738 and transferred her medical officer and two pharmacist's mates over to the tug to help in treating the wounded before resuming the search for more survivors in the waters surrounding *Yorktown*. At 1828, *Balch* picked up LCDR

Portland (R) transfers *Yorktown* survivors two at a time to *Fulton* (L) on 6 June. Steaming at 15 knots, *Portland* commenced the evolution at 1420, but had to discontinue it upon receipt of a submarine contact at 1930. The cruiser wrapped up the transfer, using her motor launch to transport the *Yorktown*ers, between 2022 and 2145. (80-G-312028)

maximum speed; both ships opened fire on their target—*I-168*, as she fled on the surface. The two destroyers set off in hot pursuit.

Throughout the force, all hands awaited the dawn, to see whether or not there would be another chance to save the much-battered *Yorktown*. Given the "recognized inadequacy of the torpedo protection system," it was amazing that *Yorktown* was remaining afloat as long as she was. As if unwilling to yield her life to the sea, she remained stubbornly afloat during the first and mid-watches. *Balch, Benham* and *Gwin,* with *Vireo* in the vicinity, too, formed a circular screen at 2200, 4,000 yards from the carrier, moving at 14 knots. *Monaghan* and *Hughes* rejoined the vigil at 0213 on the 7th, *I-168* having eluded them. On board *Yorktown*, weakened and sprung bulkheads far below decks allowed progressive flooding while the pounding heard and felt by the salvage party had intimated ominously at what probably happened next: the surging sea ultimately broke down her centerline bulkhead; denied access be-

True, who, although "semi-conscious," was gamely supporting two men: Sea1c Robert J. Ballard and COX George W. Kapp, Jr., the latter one of the ship's Coral Sea heroes. True survived the ordeal, but Ballard and the gallant Kapp never regained consciousness after two hours of artificial respiration.

The destroyer than altered curse to close the tug. While approaching *Vireo* at 1937, to pick up *Yorktown*'s survivors that the latter had rescued, *Balch* latched onto a submarine contact and laid down a barrage of depth charges—six from her tracks and four from her "K"-guns—only 400 yards away from the venerable tug. The shock waves from the exploding charges shook *Vireo* again, straining her hull still further. *Benham* picked up a contact at 1956 and attacked, with no results. *Balch* returned at 2046 and took on board all but eight of the *Yorktown* survivors (these being deemed too badly hurt to experience yet another transfer at sea) including CAPT Buckmaster. At 2047, *Monaghan* and *Hughes* sighted smoke on the horizon, and soon worked up to

Preparing a muster list of survivors transferred on board *Fulton* from *Portland*, on 6 June, en route back to Pearl Harbor. (80-G-312030)

Yorktown rolls over to port on the morning of 7 June 1942. This view shows clearly the massive damage wreaked by the two torpedoes from *I-168* which holed the ship below the turn of the bilge at frames 85 and 94. (NH 95575)

Close examination of this photo shows the massive torpedo damage, the projecting hangar deck catapult sponson, 5-inch guns trained on the beam, and the bow LSO platform, all identification features unique to *Yorktown*. (NH 95576)

Yorktown almost completely turned turtle. CCM George D. Clare later related how the carrier "rolled over on her side and dropped sharply" on 7 June; CWT George Vavreck recounted how *Yorktown* "started listing to port when she sank. The flight deck was absolutely vertical—a fighter plane was still lashed to the deck when the ship went under." (NH 95577)

fore, the sea rushed relentlessly through the remaining spaces on the port side on the third and fourth decks, amidships, carrying all before it.

By dawn, those who watched from the warships nearby could detect an increasing list to port around 0530. By 0635, to watchers on board *Benham*, the carrier appeared to be listing heavily to port and sinking. The minutes passed, *Yorktown* slowly turning to port; with the end appearing inevitable, all hands topside on the ships in the screen, on signal, came to attention and removed their caps or helmets; all ships half-masted colors. Then, at 0658, *Yorktown* "turned over on her port side and sank in about 3,000 fathoms of water with all battle flags flying." Many *Yorktown*ers who watched from the destroyers wept unashamedly, saluting the vessel that had been their home, and which had almost survived the worst the enemy could throw at her. From on board *Balch*, "we saluted her," recalled "Jug" Ray in later years, "and I'm sure the tears which came from Captain Buckmaster's eyes were no more salty than my own . . . ." Tears even moistened the eyes of others who had not served in the ship.

After *Yorktown* disappeared beneath the waves, the rest of the ships in the screen then set course for Pearl Harbor, *Benham* carrying *Hammann*'s survivors and *Vireo* bound for Midway. Ultimately, the lion's share of *Yorktown*'s men were transferred at sea to the submarine tender *Fulton* (AS-11) on the 6th, the ship having been sent out from Pearl Harbor for that purpose. *Fulton* arrived at Pearl on the 8th and, assisted by the usual bevy of tugs, soon warped into her

ADM Chester W. Nimitz (CINCPAC) and his staff watch as *Fulton* docks at Pearl Harbor. (80-G-312025)

berth, lines of ambulances and trucks awaiting the new arrivals. ADM Nimitz stood among those gathered at dockside to see the returning *Yorktown*ers.

"The Commanding Officer cannot praise too highly the aggressive fighting spirit of the entire complement of the *Yorktown* and her Air Group," CAPT Buckmaster reported within two weeks of the battle, "not only in the Battle of Midway but in all the actions in which they have participated." He then listed the attacks on the Gilberts and Marshalls, the raid on Lae and Salamaua, the three attacks on Tulagi, the Battle of

Assisted by tugs, *Fulton* (AS-11) docks at Pearl Harbor on 8 June, with *Yorktown*'s survivors on board. Note sailors lining the rails and standing atop the ship's Mk.37 director. *Hoga* (YT-146) and *Nokomis* (YT-142) are among the craft assisting the tender to her berth. (80-G-312058)

Yorktown survivors embark in open trucks and busses at the Submarine Base, Pearl Harbor, after disembarking from *Fulton* on 8 June, en route to their temporary billets at Camp Catlin. They would not, en masse, again man another *Yorktown*, but would return to the fleet to give it the benefit of their experience that had been gained in the crucible of combat. The loss of "The Mighty Y," besides resulting in the reassignment of her men, also caused a change in orders for CAPT Arthur C. Davis. Slated to relieve Elliott Buckmaster as *Yorktown's* CO, Davis received command of sistership *Enterprise* instead. (80-G-312056)

the Coral Sea, and the engagement recently brought to a successful conclusion for American arms. Buckmaster added that "during all these actions an the many weeks at sea in preparation for them the fighting spirit of *Yorktown* was peerless." That "fighting spirit" remained vibrant and animated, although the ship herself had "perished gloriously in battle."

"The wish closest to the hearts of all of us who are privileged to serve in that gallant ship," Buckmaster concluded fervently, "is that she might be preserved not only in memory but by the crew's being kept together to man, commission, and return against the enemy a new aircraft carrier, preferably another *Yorktown*." Hopes for this eventuality, though, began to fade as the survivors, initially billeted in Camp Catlin, a Marine Corps base on Oahu, began to be shipped out to other ships—replacements on old ones, some

to new construction. One large group, 209 men strong, soon reported to *West Virginia* at the Pearl Harbor Navy Yard. Buckmaster himself soon attained flag rank.

As the result of the experience with *Yorktown's* loss, ADM Nimitz soon directed that special salvage teams—such as the one so laboriously gathered from many ships—be formed beforehand, so that in the event of an emergency they could go into action, only abandoning ship last if the need arose. Although *Yorktown* had finally succumbed to her mortal wounds, her travail had not been in vain. Future ships could be saved by lessons learned from one that was lost.

RADM Frank Jack Fletcher (second from left) received a Distinguished Service Medal for his workmanlike leadership of TF-17, in ceremonies on board *Enterprise* at Pearl on 17 June 1942; others with him are (L-R): RADM William L. Calhoun, RADM Thomas C. Kinkaid, RADM William Ward Smith, RADM Marc Mitscher and RADM Robert H. English. Of this group of flag officers, only Fletcher is not wearing any campaign ribbons—his may have been lost with *Yorktown* at Midway. (80-G-10403)

CHAPTER 13

We Had Found the *Yorktown*

To HONOR "THAT GALLANT SHIP" and perpetuate the name, Secretary of the Navy Knox renamed CV-10, then *Bon Homme Richard* (an incorrect rendition, incidentally, of the original French), to *Yorktown* on 26 September 1942, the day upon which the Navy officially announced CV-5's loss in the Battle of Midway. Knox also invited Mrs. Roosevelt to reprise her role as sponsor.

"I wonder whether I should sponsor the new U.S.S. *Yorktown*," she responded, "inasmuch as the one I sponsored met such a sad fate?" Knowing that the Navy had its superstitions, the First Lady wanted to "be very sure that it was wise for me to this" before she would accept the invitation. Only after being assured that there was an "exact parallel" in Mrs. Douglas Robinson's sponsoring *Lexington* (CV-16) (she had christened the first carrier of that name that had been lost at Coral Sea) did Mrs. Roosevelt agree to break the ceremonial bottle on the new ship's bow.

Launched on 21 January 1943 at Newport News, *Yorktown* was commissioned on 15 April 1943; her first commanding officer was Capt. "Jocko" Clark, who had been CV-5's first wartime exec. *Yorktown*'s survivors, whom CAPT Buckmaster had desired fervently to serve together in another ship of the same name, for the most part leavened the influx of green recruits as the fleet grew in response to the exigencies of global war. *Yorktown* (CV-10) earned a Presidential Unit Citation and 11 battle stars for her World War II service in the Pacific. Modernized and refitted to handle the heavier planes that entered fleet service in the 1950s and 1960s, *Yorktown* went on to earn a further five battle stars for her service off Vietnam. She is currently memorialized at Patriot's Point, South Carolina.

Subsequently, another *Yorktown*, a guided missile cruiser (CG-48), entered the fleet on 4 July 1984. Her

motto summed up the proud spirit of her predecessors, not the least of which was "that gallant ship" *Yorktown* (CV-5): "Victory is Our Tradition."

The ship that had rolled over and sunk at Midway, however, still lived in the hearts of her former crewmen; her veterans gathered year after year, their numbers diminishing. Their *Yorktown* remained in the blackness that envelopes the bottom of the Pacific, undisturbed and unseen, for over a half-century, three miles down. The lure of what lies underwater, however, proves strong, particularly when cutting-edge technology gives explorers freer reign to venture into the depths. Eventually, *Yorktown* came under serious consideration for exploration.

On 1 May 1998, *Laney Chouest*, the base ship for the National Geographic Midway Expedition, sailed from the atoll that had been a sought-after prize of war to find, plot, and photograph *Yorktown* and her adversaries *Akagi*, *Kaga*, *Soryū*, and *Hiryū*, under the direction of Dr. Robert D. Ballard, the noted underwater explorer who had led similar missions of discovery and exploration to the lost luxury passenger liner *Titanic*, the German battleship *Bismarck*, and U.S. and Japanese warships off Guadalcanal in "Iron Bottom Sound." Embarked on board the research vessel as honored guests were two Japanese veterans of the battle as well as two Americans, one of whom, William F. ("Bill") Surgi, Jr., had served in *Yorktown*'s VF-42.

The following day, *Laney Chouest* deployed the *MR-1*, the University of Hawaii's sonar vehicle, to begin the search. The U.S. Navy's ATV (advanced tethered vehicle), launched on 6 May to look for the sunken destroyer *Hammann* in hopes that a debris trail might lead the explorers to *Yorktown*, encountered the first of the troubles that would dog it; following repairs, it was deployed again on 7 May. When

Yorktown in her prime, her crew mustered in whites forward, her air group parked on the flight deck, utility planes in the hangar space, aft; photographed by *Enterprise*'s CP J.A. Mihalovic, off Gonaives, Haiti, 23 February 1939. (80-G-64784)

the ATV neared the bottom, however, its crew on board *Laney Chouest* detected trouble, and brought it to the surface. They soon discerned the problem with chilling clarity: there had been a pressure sphere implosion that had caused considerable damage.

On 8 May, meanwhile, operations began with the *MR-1* to try and locate the Japanese carriers, data having been obtained on a possible location of *Yorktown*'s resting place. Repairs proceeded apace on the ATV, enabling it to be launched on the 10th to look for what was hoped to be *Kaga*. Ultimately, the search for the Japanese ships proved fruitless, and was abandoned on the 12th. Three days later, *Laney Chouest* returned to Midway for supplies, and disembarked some of her passengers; Bill Surgi, however, the *Yorktown* veteran, remained on board. He still retained the M-1917A1 helmet he had worn when he had abandoned ship over a half-century earlier.

Subsequently, Ballard ordered the repaired ATV deployed on 17 May but two more mishaps meant further "down" time. Ultimately, however, the vehicle that had proved so vexing earned its keep. On the morning of 19 May 1998, the ATV descended and reached the ocean floor; subsequently, as those in the control van on board *Laney Chouest* watched, the vehicle "moved closer and rose slowly, lights and cameras working perfectly. I could see," Ballard recounted later, "the edge of a dark hole

with flat decking around it. An elevator opening. Then I saw the ship's superstructure—the island—and I knew where we were. We were at the stern of an aircraft carrier. We had found the *Yorktown*."

Ballard found *Yorktown* to be in remarkably well-preserved condition. Mapping, exploring, and photographing the wrecked carrier occupied two subsequent dives; a further search for *Hammann* proved unsuccessful. On 25 May, Bill Surgi, in a touching ceremony held on *Laney Chouest*'s foredeck, memorialized his lost ship and his fallen shipmates; the next day the expedition returned to port. On 4 June 1998, 56 years to the day that *Yorktown* and her crew battled the Japanese at Midway, Robert Ballard showed an awed audience breathtaking images of "The Mighty Y."

Yorktown (CV-5) thus rests on the bottom of the ocean that she had helped to assert mastery of. Seeing footage of the carrier as she reposes three miles beneath the surface of the ocean evokes images of her last battle: surging ahead with a bone-in-teeth, her stem cutting through the Pacific swells, her anti-aircraft guns firing at attacking Japanese planes and her own "Wildcats" wobbling aloft, some into the teeth of friendly fire. As CAPT Buckmaster had written, and doubtless each man who ever served on board *Yorktown* and who felt pride in her name would agree, she was, truly, "That Gallant Ship," whose memory will never die.

ABBREVIATIONS

Miscellaneous Terms & Abbreviations

(AA) Acting Appointment

A-V(G) USNR Aviation officer holding designation as naval aviator, qualified for general detail afloat or ashore

A-V(N) USNR Aviation flight officer, detailed to active duty in the aeronautic organization of the USN following the completion of their training and designation as naval aviators

AOL Absent Over Leave

BATDIV Battleship Division

BuAer Bureau of Aeronautics

BuC&R Bureau of Construction and Repair

BuNo Bureau Number

BuOrd Bureau of Ordnance

CAP Combat Air Patrol (or Chief Aviation Pilot, see *Ranks and Rates*)

CARDIV Carrier Division

ChC Chaplain Corps

CINCLANT Commander in Chief, Atlantic Fleet

CINCPAC Commander in Chief, Pacific Fleet

CINCUS Commander in Chief, U.S. Fleet (1940–1941)

CLAG Commander, *Lexington* Air Group

CNO Chief of Naval Operations

COMAIRBATFOR Commander, Aircraft, Battle Force

COMAIRLANT Commander, Aircraft, Atlantic Fleet

COMATRON Commander, Atlantic Squadron

COMBATFOR Commander, Battle Force

COMANZAC Commander, Australia and New Zealand Area

COMCARDIV Commander, Carrier Division

COMCARPAC Commander, Carriers, Pacific Fleet

COMDESDIV Commander, Destroyer Division

COMDESRON Commander, Destroyer Squadron

COMINCH Commander-in-Chief, U.S. Fleet (1942)

COMSCOFOR Commander, Scouting Force

COMSOWESPAC Commander, Southwest Pacific Area

CTF Commander, Task Force

CTG Commander, Task Group

CXAM Air Search Radar

CYAG Commander, *Yorktown* Air Group

DESDIV Destroyer Division

FDO Fighter Director Officer

FRUPAC Fleet Radio Unit, Pacific

GUN Gunner

LSO Landing Signal Officer

MC Medical Corps

MG Machine Gun

mm Millimeter

NAS Naval Air Station

NOB Naval Operating Base

OPNAV Office of the Chief of Naval Operations

PATRON Patrol Squadron

RDF Radio Direction Finder

RN Royal Navy

SC Supply Corps (when used with a rank)

SC Search Radar

SOPA Senior Officer Present Afloat

TBS A low frequency voice radio

TF Task Force

TG Task Group

T.H. Territory of Hawaii

USMC U.S. Marine Corps

USN U.S. Navy

USNA U.S. Naval Academy

USNR U.S. Naval Reserve

XO Executive Officer

YE Homing signal transmitter

ZB Homing signal receiver

Ranks and Rates

ACMM Aviation Chief Machinist's Mate

ACRM Aviation Chief Radioman

ADM Admiral

AMM3c Aviation Machinist's Mate, 3d Class

AOM1c/2c Aviation Ordnanceman, 1st Class/2d Class

ARM2c/3c Aviation Radioman, 2d Class/3d Class

AVCDT Aviation Cadet

BGEN Brigadier General

Bkr3c Baker, 3d Class

BOSN Boatswain

BM2c Boatswain's Mate, 2d Class

CAP Chief Aviation Pilot (or Combat Air Patrol, see *Miscellaneous Terms and Abbreviations*)

CAPT Captain (USN & USMC)

CARP Carpenter
CCS Chief Commissary Steward
CDR Commander
CEM Chief Electrician's Mate
CGM Chief Gunner's Mate
COX Coxswain
CP Chief Photographer
CQM Chief Quartermaster
CWT Chief Watertender
EM1c Electrician's Mate, 1st Class
ENS Ensign
F3c Fireman, 3d Class
1stMus 1st Musician
GM3c Gunner's Mate, 3d Class
HA1c Hospital Apprentice, 1st Class
LCDR Lieutenant commander
LT Lieutenant
LTCOL Lieutenant Colonel (USMC)
LT(jg) Lieutenant (Junior Grade)
MACH Machinist
MAJ Major
Matt2c Mess Attendant, 2d Class
NAP Naval Aviation Pilot
(PA) Permanent Appointment
PhoM2c Photographer's Mate, 2d Class
PO1c Petty Officer, 2st Class (Japanese rating)
Ptr3c Painter, 3d Class
PVT Private (USMC)
RADM Rear Admiral
RE Radio Electrician
RM1c/2c/3c Radioman, 1st Class/2d Class/3d Class
Sea1c/2c/3c Seaman, 1st Class/2d Class/3d Class
2dLT Second Lieutenant (USMC)
StM1c Steward's Mate, 1st Class
VADM Vice Admiral
WO Warrant Officer (Japanese rating)
WT1c Watertender, 1st Class

Ship Types

AC Collier
AD Destroyer Tender
AF Storeship
AG Miscellaneous Auxiliary
AK Cargo Ship
AO Fleet Oiler
AS Submarine Tender
AT Fleet Tug
AV Seaplane Tender
AVG Aircraft Carrier, Escort
BB Battleship
CA Heavy Cruiser
CL Light Cruiser
CV Aircraft Carrier
DD Destroyer
SS Submarine

Squadrons

VB Bombing Squadron
VF Fighting Squadron
VMF Marine Fighting Squadron
VMO Marine Observation Squadron
VMS Marine Scouting Squadron
VP Patrol Squadron
VS Scouting Squadron
VT Torpedo Squadron

Aircraft Names

JAPANESE AIRCRAFT NAMES

In November 1942, in order to provide a uniform system of code-names to designate Japanese aircraft encountered in the Pacific War, "person" names were given to enemy planes. For the wartime period covered in this book (December 1941 to June 1942) the names were not even in existence, with perhaps the exception of "Zero" to describe the Mitsubishi A6M2. Therefore, to preserve the spirit of the time, they have not been used; the Japanese terminology was used instead (the names assigned them in November 1942 are in quotes after):

Aichi D3A1 type 99 carrier bomber (*kanbaku*) ("Val")
Aichi E13A1 Type 0 reconnaissance seaplane ("Jake")
Kawanishi E7K2 type 94 reconnaissance seaplane ("Alf")
Kawanishi H6K4 Type 97 flying boat ("Mavis")
Mitsubishi A5M4 Type 95 carrier fighter (*kansen*) ("Claude")
Mitsubishi F1M2 Type 0 observation seaplane ("Pete")
Nakajima B5N2 type 97 carrier attack plane (*kankō*) ("Kate")
Nakajima E8N2 Type 95 reconnaissance seaplane ("Dave")
Yokosuka D4Y1 Type 2 experimental carrier bomber ("Judy")

USN AIRCRAFT NAMES

In October 1941, the Honorable Frank Knox, Secretary of the Navy, approved "popular nicknames" for the USN aircraft then in operation or projected. Prior to that time, the bulk of the time in which the operations described in this book took place, these names were not used. To thus adhere more closely to the spirit of the times, they have not been used until appropriate in the narrative, and even then, sparingly, since the names appear to have been used rarely in the official record. For quick reference these are:

Grumman F4F-3, -4: "Wildcat"
Douglas SBD-2, -3: "Dauntless"
Douglas TBD-1: "Devastator"
Consolidated PBY: "Catalina"
Consolidated PB2Y: "Coronado"
Grumman J2F: "Duck"
Curtiss SOC: "Seagull"
Grumman TBF-1: "Avenger"
Vought SB2U-2, -3: "Vindicator"

NOTES

THE BASIC SOURCE for Chapters I through IV is the *Yorktown* (CV-5) deck log covering the period from 30 September 1937 through 30 April 1942; the log for May and the first few days of June 1942, was lost while being lowered over the side during the abandonment on the afternoon of 4 June. The log that exists is an invaluable single source for its day-to-day recounting of events on board the ship. After the 30 April 1942 date, *Yorktown*'s activities have been drawn from her action reports for the Battle of the Coral Sea and the Battle of Midway as well as the war diaries, logs, and action reports of the ships which operated with her. Full titles of the books cited below, and citations of reports, will be found in the bibliography at the end of the work.

CHAPTER I

GENERAL BOARD HEARINGS, 1931-1934, and subject files 420-5 and 420-7 (1933–1940); *Records Relating to United States Navy Fleet Problems* describe the operations during Fleet Problem XX; material on the first two *Yorktowns* comes from their respective Ship History files; material on christening and launching CV-5 comes from the *Yorktown* (CV-5) Ship Name and Sponsor File; and Commissioning Booklet for CV-5 (courtesy of Pete Montalvo); BuC&R *Newsletter* describes the conditional acceptance of the ship; *Our Navy* Mid-December 1937 issue describes the first day's flight activities; flight schedule for that day comes from CAPT William E. Scarborough, USN, (Ret.); candid comments about Fleet Problems XX from E.J. King letters to J.B. Sykes (16 March 1939) and M.S. Tisdale (15 March 1939), in King Papers; comments about the Hawaiian Detachment come from Stark's letter to Bloch (8 September 1939) in Bloch's papers; background from contemporary press accounts of the Albanian Crisis from *New York Times* and Norfolk *Virginian-Pilot*; Halsey and Bryan, *Admiral Halsey's Story* contains material on Fleet Problem XX and the fleet movement Pacific-ward in April 1939. Additional sources: FDR's quote about the New Deal from Schlesinger, *The Coming of the New Deal*; Huntington's comments about shipbuilding at Newport News from *Virginia: A Guide to the Old Dominion* (1941); FDR's 18 April 1939 Press Conference.

CHAPTER 2

GENERAL SOURCES USED, besides the log, include *Records Relating to United States Navy Fleet Problems* (for Fleet Problem XXI operations and critiques); and Dyer, *On the Treadmill to Pearl Harbor* (for Fleet Problem XXI and the fleet's basing in Hawaiian waters). COMAIRBATFOR to CINCUS "Embarkation of VMF Squadron Two in USS *Yorktown* for Fleet Problem" (6 March 1940), COMAIRBATFOR to CO, USS *Yorktown*, "Operations with Full Strength Complement" (24 February 1940) and COMBATFOR's endorsement of COMAIRBATFOR to CINCUS' 6 March 1940 "Embarkation . . ." memorandum related to the operation of VMF-2 for Fleet Problem XXI; composition of the squadron from VMF-2 Muster Rolls; Megee letters to Woods (7 and 9 May 1940) in

Woods Papers; Radford's MSS autobiography as well as correspondence with Caldwell and Arnold were helpful on matters of *Yorktown*'s operations in Hawaiian waters during 1940. Comments on the effectiveness of *Yorktown*'s radar come from Halsey and Bryan.

CHAPTER 3

GENERAL SOURCES: CTF-2 to CNO, "Surface Patrol Tasks"; TF-2 to CINCLANT, "Neutrality Patrol Operation"; TF-2 to CINCLANT, "operations of Task Group Two Five"; Convoy CT-5 file; Translated BdU War Diary; Rohwer, *Axis Submarine Successes*; CINCPAC Graybook; Radford MSS, Clark, *Carrier Admiral*; "History of Naval Fighter Direction;" Abbazia, *Mr. Roosevelt's Navy*, Xanders, Hartlove and Morris; also: Honolulu *Star-Bulletin*, 1 January 1941; CNO Memo to FDR, "Ocean Escorts in Western Atlantic," enclosure to Stark to Kimmel, 4 April 1941, in PHA 16, 2163; CINCPAC Ser 162346 of 16 April 1941 in PHA 11, 5502; Stark to Kimmel, 19 April 1941, PHA 16,2164; Nomura Dispatch to Japanese Consul (Izawa), Panama, 2 June 1941 in *"Magic" Background to Pearl Harbor*, A-127; OPNAV-CINCPAC 13 May 1941 in PHA 17,2466; COMCRULANT to CINCUS, "Observation of Experimental Painting," 23 April 1941; CINCLANT to LANTFLT 22 March 1941 re: instructions for painting ships engaged in patrol duties in File C-519-7, Vol. I, RG-19; Turnbull and Lord, *History of United States Naval Aviation* for description of Cook; CINCLANT to COMAIRLANT msg, 29 august 1941 and COMAIRLANT to CINCLANT msg, 30 August 1941, in RG-19 BuShips General Correspondence File C-CV5, Vol. I, Box 714; Department of State *Bulletin*, Vol. V, No. 116 of 13 September 1941 for text of FDR speech of 11 September 1941; Stark to Thomas C. Hart, 22 September 1941, in PHA 16, 2209; William E.G. Taylor testimony in PHA 26,368 ff.; King to Cook, 10 October 1941, in King Papers; Hewitt "Record of Events" (20 October-7 November 1941) in Hewitt Papers; Norfolk *Virginian-Pilot*, (December 1941); and *Army-Navy Journal* (December 1941). James C. Sawruk research in BuAer records. McCormack to Fenton, 29 October 1942 ltr. provided by John B. Lundstrom; Mulligan.

CHAPTER 4

GENERAL SOURCES: CINCPAC Graybook; "Informal History of Second Marine Brigade from December 24, 1941 to March 31, 1943"; YAGC Report to CO, *Yorktown*, in CTF-17 to CINCPAC "Report of Engagement, January 31, 1942"; CTF-11 Action Report for Lae-Salamaua Raid; Willmott, *The Barrier and the Javelin*; Lundstrom, *The First Team*; Hipple articles in Honolulu *Star-Bulletin* (21-22 May 1942); Clark; Morison, *Rising Sun in the Pacific*; Japanese Monographs No. 102 and 116; Nielsen; *Kaskaskia* (AO-27) WD; Layton, "24 Sentai . . ."; McCuskey to Pete Montalvo in *"Yorktown Crier,"* July 1984 Halsey and Bryan; Biard; Dull; Action Record for *Yubari* on Reel JT-1; Kimball, *Churchill and Roosevelt*.

Chapter 5

General sources: Fletcher to Nimitz, 29 May 1942; NWC Analysis, *Battle of the Coral Sea; Yorktown* Air Group Tulagi Report; Ewoldt; Burch; Ray; Nielsen; CINCPAC Graybook; Edward Taylor *Diary,* in *Astoria* (CA-34) Ship History File; Drury, *History of the U.S. Navy Chaplain Corps;* Honolulu *Star-Bulletin;* Lundstrom, *The First Team* and *The First South Pacific Campaign;* Clark; CINCPAC/CINCPOA "Weekly Intelligence," Vol. I, No. 4 (6 August 1944), "*Mutsuki*-class Destroyer Refloated" (which confirms torpedo damage to *Kikuzuki*); Lord, *Lonely Vigil;* Layton notes, NHF; Machalinski interview in *Naval Aviation News* April 1960; Jentschura; *Hammann* Action Report for 4 May 1942; CTF-17 Report, Coral Sea; CTG-17.5 Action Report, 7-8 May 1942; McCormack to Fenton, 29 October 1942; *Bridge* (AF-1) WD; Johnston, *The Grim Reapers,* Faulkner.

Chapter 6

General sources: *Yorktown* Action Report for operations in the Louisiade Archipelago on 7 May 1942; ACA Reports for VF-42, VB-5, VS-5 and VT-5; Action Records for *Kako, Aoba, Furutaka* and *Kinugasa* on Reel JT-1; CTF-17 Report, Coral Sea; CTG-17.5 Action Report, 7-8 May 1942; *Yorktown* Air Group Report, Action of 7 May 1942; Tillman, "The Indispensable Man"; Burch; Lundstrom, *The First Team;* Johnston, *Queen of the Flat-tops, Neosho* Report, *Sims* Report; Dull, *Battle History;* Fletcher to Nimitz, 29 May 1942; Pilot reports for VF-42 c/o John B. Lundstrom.

Chapter 7

General sources: *Yorktown* Action Report for operations in the Louisiade Archipelago, 8 May 1942; *Yorktown* War Damage Report, Coral Sea; CTF-17 Coral Sea Report; CTG-17.5 Report, Coral Sea; Caldwell; Nielsen; CYAG Action Report, Air Operations on 8 May 1942; CA Reports for VF-42, VB-5, VS-5 and VT-5; Schindler, Johnston *Queen of the Flat-tops* and *The Grim Reapers;* Lundstrom, *The First Team;* Burch; Ray; Harrington and Frank, *Rendezvous at Midway; Japan Times & Advertiser;* Dull; Xanders; James C. Sawruk interviews with CAPT Arthur Schultz, USN (Ret.) (ex-VS-2) and CAPT Stanley W. Vejtasa, USN (Ret.).

Chapter 8

General sources: Layton Notes; *Japan Times & Advertiser;* CINCPAC Graybook; Pearl Harbor Navy Yard War Diary (which shows that *Yorktown* did not go *directly* into Dry Dock No. 1 as practically every secondary Midway source, except Prange, *Miracle at Midway,* states); *Morris* and *Anderson* War Diaries; Xanders; Potter, *Nimitz;* Wadleigh, "Memories of Midway . . ."; *Yorktown* War Damage Report; Tillman, "Dauntlesses at Midway"; James C. Sawruk Research into BuAer records; Lundstrom, *The First Team;* Esders; Myers; Fletcher to Nimitz, 27 May 1942; Nimitz to King, 29 May 1942; Ray; Nimitz Memorial Day speech in Honolulu *Star-Bulletin* 30 May 1942; Adams; VF-6 Log; Naval War College Analysis, Midway.

Chapter 9

Midway Action Reports: *Yorktown;* COMCRUPAC (CTF-17); CINCPAC; COMCRUTF-17; CTG-17.4; *Hammann; Enterprise* and *Hornet;* Spruance to Nimitz, 8 June 1942; COMCRUTF-16; VB-3, VS-5; Esders; VF-3 ACA Report; Lundstrom, *The First Team;* Barde, "Tarnished Victory"; *Osmus* (DE-701) Name & Sponsor Folder; Thach "Red Rain of Battle"; Holmberg; "Japanese Story of the Battle of Midway"; Tuleja, *Climax at Midway;* Lord, *Incredible Victory;* Prange, *Miracle at Midway;* Ray.

Chapter 10

Same general Midway sources as above; CTG-17.4 Report (incl. *Benham* and *Balch*); Kiefer Navy Cross Citation; Thach interview in *Topgun Journal;* Citations for Tootle, Dibb, McCuskey, Adams, Crommelin, Leonard; Tootle interview in Honolulu *Star-Bulletin,* 12 June 1942; Lundstrom, *The First Team;* "Japanese Story of the Battle of Midway," Prange, *Miracle at Midway;* Smith *Midway: Turning Point . . .;* Lewis N. Williams narrative in *Oklahoma City* (CL-91) Commissioning Booklet, in *Oklahoma City* (CL-91) Ship History File; Kiefer Citation; Action Reports for *Benham, Balch, Morris, Hammann, Hughes;* Info on composition of the "VS-5" search from Capt. Charlie N. Conatser, USN (Ret.) and CDR John W. Trott, USN (Ret.) (both former VB-5 members), via James C. Sawruk; Nielsen; Harlan R. Dickson biography in Ship Name & Sponsor File for *Harlan R. Dickson* (DD-704).

Chapter 11

Yorktown Action Report, Midway; *Yorktown* Loss Report; Reports of *Hammann, Russell, Anderson, Morris, Wing, Balch, Hughes, Enterprise, Hornet, Astoria;* ACA Report, VF-3; Lundstrom, *The First Team;* Lewis N. Williams narrative; Kiefer Citation; NWC Analysis, Midway; Spruance to Nimitz, 8 June 1942; Nielsen; VB-3 and VS-5 reports included in *Enterprise* Midway Report; "Japanese Story of the Battle of Midway"; *Hughes,* "Operations in Connection with USS *Yorktown . . . .*"; Kearney letters to Joseph D. Harrington (18 March 1964) and Peter Montalvo (1 June 1982) in *Yorktown* Command File.

Chapter 12

Hughes Report, *Yorktown* Loss report; *Yorktown* Action Report; "Japanese Story of the Battle of Midway"; Pichette citation in Ship Name & Sponsor File; *Vireo* Action Report and WD; *Gwin* Report; Spruance to Nimitz, 8 June 1942; VS-5 Report; Tanabe and Harrington; Harrington and Frank, *Rendezvous at Midway;* Williams Narrative; VB-3 Report, Nielsen; Dickson quote from 1936 *Lucky Bag; Hammann* Report; Ray; Legg Navy Cross Citation; Kearney letters.

Chapter 13

Yorktown (CV-10) (ex-*Bon Homme Richard*) Ship Name & Sponsor File; *Yorktown* (CG-48) Ship History and Ship Name and Sponsor File; *The Battle for Midway* Press Kit, National Geographic Television; Allen, "Return to the Battle of Midway."

BIBLIOGRAPHY

Primary Sources

National Archives Facility, College Park, Md.

Action Reports and Correspondence (RG 45)

CTF-2 to CINCLANT, "Neutrality Patrol Operations, 20 June–13 July 1941" (22 July 1941)

CTF-2 to CINCLANT, "Operations of Task Group Two Five during Period 1 August to 10 August 1941" (11 August 1941)

CTF-2 to CNO, "Surface Patrol Tasks Executed by Task Groups of Task Force 2 during Period 26 April to 30 August 1941" (9 September 1941)

CDD-3 to CINCLANT, "Attack on Submarine, October 30, 1941—Report of" (November 6, 1941)

CTF-17 to CINCPAC, "Report of Engagement January 31, 1942" (9 February 1942) (Includes *Yorktown* Action Report and pilot/aircrew narratives for VB-5, VS-5 and VT-5, as well as Action Reports for *Sims, Russell, Hughes, Walke, St. Louis* and *Louisville*)

CTF-11 to COMINCH, "Report of Attack on Enemy Forces in Salamaua-Lae Area, Mar. 10, 1942" (25 Mar. 1942) (Includes *Yorktown* Action Report)

CTF-17 to CINCPAC, "The Battle of the Coral Sea, May 4–8, 1942" (27 May 1942)

CTG-17.5 to CTF-17, "Action Report, Coral Sea, May 7–8, 1942"

CO, USS *Yorktown,* "Enemy Submarine, Contact with, 2 May 1942—Report of" (7 May 1942)

CO, USS *Yorktown* to CINCPAC, "Attack Made by *Yorktown* Air Group on Enemy Forces in the Tulagi and Gavutu Harbors" (11 May 1942)

CO, USS *Yorktown* to CINCPAC, "Attack Made by *Yorktown* Air Group against Japanese Forces in the vicinity of the Louisiade Archipelago on May 7, 1942" (16 May 1942)

CO, USS *Yorktown* to CINCPAC, "Report of Action of *Yorktown* and *Yorktown* Air Group against Japanese Forces in the vicinity of the Louisiade Archipelago on May 8, 1942"

CYAG to CO, USS *Yorktown,* "Air Operations of *Yorktown* Air Group against Japanese Forces in the vicinity of the Louisiade Archipelago on May 8, 1942"

CO, USS *Yorktown* to COMINCH, "U.S. Aircraft, Action with the Enemy, Report of, 2–8 May 1942" (26 May 1942)

BuShips, Navy Department, "USS *Yorktown* (CV-5) Bomb Damage, Coral Sea, 8 May 1942, War Damage Report No. 23 (28 November 1942)

CTU 17.2.2 to CINCPAC, "Action Report," (17 May 1942) (Includes Action Reports of *Astoria, Portland,* and *Chester*)

CTU 17.2.4 to COMINCH, "Engagement with Japanese Forces 7–8 May 1942" (22 May 1942) (Includes reports of *Phelps, Dewey* and *Aylwin*)

CO, USS *Hammann* to CINCPAC, "Report of Action May 4, 1942 near Tulagi, Solomon Islands," with "Enclosure A: Report of Rescue of *Yorktown* Aviators from Guadalcanal Island" (11 May 1942)

CTU 17.5.4 to COMINCH, "Action Report of May 7, 1942," "Action Report in the Coral Sea, 8 May 1942," (18 May 1942) (Includes reports of *Morris, Anderson, Hammann* and *Russell*)

CO, USS *Neosho* to CINCPAC, "Engagement of USS *Neosho* with Japanese Aircraft on May 7, 1942, Subsequent Loss of USS *Neosho,* Search for Survivors" (25 May 1942)

COMDESPAC to SECNAV, "Sinking of the USS *Sims* (DD-409) by Japanese Bombers in the Coral Sea on May 7, 1942" (8 July 1942)

COMCRUPAC to CINCPAC, "Action Report, Battle of Midway" (14 June 1942)

CO, USS *Yorktown* to CINCPAC, "Report of Action for June 4, 1942 and June 6, 1942" (18 June 1942) (Includes Executive Officer's Report, War Damage Report)

COMCRUTF-17 "Report of Action 4 June 1942" (12 June 1942) (Includes reports of *Astoria* and *Portland*)

CTF 17.4 to COMINCH, "Report of Action June 4, 1942" (1 June 1942) (Includes reports of *Anderson, Hughes, Morris,* and *Russell*)

CO, USS *Hughes* to CINCPAC, "Operations in connection with the USS *Yorktown* from time of abandonment until sinking (11 June 1942)

CO, USS *Hammann* to CINCPAC, "Action Report 4–6 June 1942" (16 June 1942)

CTF-16 to CINCPAC, "Battle of Midway" (16 June 1942)

CO, USS *Enterprise* to CINCPAC, "Battle of Midway Island, June 4–6, 1942, Report of." (8 June 1942); also "Air Battle of the Pacific, June 4–6, 1942, Report of" (13 June 1942) (Includes VB-6, VF-6 and VS-6, and VT-6; VB-3, VF-3 and VS-5)

CO, USS *Hornet* to CINCPAC, "Report of Action" (13 June 1942) (Includes "VF-3 Partial Bag")

COMCRUTF-16 to CTF-16, "Report of Action, June 4, 1942" (11 June 1942) (Includes reports of *Pensacola* and *Astoria*)

CTG 17.4 to CTF-17, "Japanese Torpedo Plane Attack on USS *Yorktown* during Battle of Midway, June 4, 1942, Report of" (12 June 1942) (Includes reports of *Benham* and *Balch*)

CO, USS *Vireo* to CINCPAC, "Damage to Ship, Grounding—Report of" (10 June 1942)

War Diaries (RG 45)

Ships: *Yorktown, Kaskaskia, Morris, Anderson, Russell, Walke, Astoria, Portland, Vireo, Bridge*
Pearl Harbor Navy Yard (May 1942)

Deck Logs (RG 24)

Yorktown, Kaskaskia, Walke, Anderson, Hughes, Russell, Morris.

Operational Archives, Naval Historical Center, Washington, DC

Personal Letters: RADM Frank Jack Fletcher to ADM Chester W. Nimitz (27 May 1942), ADM Nimitz to ADM Ernest J. King (29 May 1942), RADM Raymond A. Spruance to ADM Chester W. Nimitz (8 June 1942) (FADM Chester W. Nimitz Papers)

Interviews: LCDR William O. Burch, Jr. (3 September 1942), LCDR Leonard E. Ewoldt (10 September 1943), LCDR Clarence C. Ray (15 July 1942) and LCDR John S. Thach (26 August 1942) (Interviews and Statements File)

Tabular Record of Movements and Action Records of Japanese Battleships and Cruisers, Reel JT-1

War Plans Division, CINCPACFLT Staff, "CINCPAC Graybook," Volume I (7 December 1941–31 August 1942)

Kriegstagebuch der Befehlshaber der Unterseeboote (War Diary of Commander in Chief, Submarines)
USS *Yorktown* (CV-5) Files, World War II Command Files
ADM Arthur W. Radford Manuscript Autobiography

Ship's History Branch, Naval Historical Center, Washington, DC
Ships' Histories Files on the four ships named *Yorktown*; also *Astoria* (CA-34) and *Oklahoma City* (CL-91); Ship Name and Sponsor Files for *Yorktown* (CV-10) and *Yorktown* (CG-48)

Marine Corps Historical Center, Washington, DC
LTGEN Louis E. Woods, USMC, Papers (PC-228) (Personal Papers)
Muster Rolls (Microfilm) for USS *Yorktown* (CV-5) Marine Detachment, 1937–1942; also VMF-2 (1940), VMO-1 and VMS-1 (1941) (Reference Section)

Oral Histories, U.S. Naval Institute, Annapolis, Maryland
ADM James S. Russell; VADM Gerald F. Bogan

Library of Congress Manuscript Division, Washington, DC
FADM Ernest J. King Papers, ADM Claude C. Bloch Papers, ADM H. Kent Hewitt Papers

Participants

(All ranks are USN, Ret., unless otherwise specified)
VADM Walter G. Schindler (Staff, CTF-17)
RADM Murr E. Arnold (VB-5 and Air Officer, *Yorktown*)
RADM William N. Leonard (VF-42 and VF-3)
CAPT John N. Myers (VT-3)
CDR Wilhelm G. Esders (VT-3)
CAPT John P. Adams (VF-42, VF-3)
VADM Turner F. Caldwell (VS-5)
CAPT John L. Nielsen (VB-5, "VS-5")
COL James L. Neefus, USMC (Ret.) (VMS-1)
RADM Paul A. Holmberg (VB-3)
RADM Wilbur E. Roberts, USNR (Ret.) (VB-6)
CAPT John P. Preston (VT-5, Assistant LSO)
CAPT Forrest R. Biard (Staff, CTF-17)
CDR Norman L. Tate
CDR George H. Goldsmith (VB-6)
Peter Montalvo
William G. Roy
James S. Xanders
Harry F. Asbury (VB-5)
Joseph P. Hartlove
Salvatore P. Monteleone
Charles R. Morris

In addition, James C. Sawruk provided the author with information gleaned from correspondence and/or interviews with the following:

CDR James H. Cales (VB-5)
CAPT Charlie N. Conatser (VB-5)
CAPT Thomas B. Ellison (VT-5)
CAPT Leonard E. Ewoldt (VT-5)
CAPT Francis B. Sanborn (VT-5)
CAPT Arthur J. Schultz, Jr. (VS-2)
CAPT Lawrence G. Traynor (VS-5)
CDR John W. Trott (VB-5)
CAPT Frederick L. Faulkner (VS-5)
CAPT Stanley W. Vejtasa (VS-5)

John B. Lundstrom shared material provided him by:
RADM James H. Flatley, III (son of the late VADM J.H. Flatley, Jr.)
LTCOL Lloyd F. Childers, USMC (Ret.) (VT-3)

Published Sources

Abbazia, Patrick, *Mr. Roosevelt's Navy: The Private War of the U.S. Atlantic Fleet, 1939–1942*, Annapolis: Naval Institute Press, 1975.
Churchill, Winston, L.S., *The Grand Alliance—The Second World War*, Vol. III, London: Cassel and Co., Ltd., 1950.
Clark, Joseph J., with Clark G. Reynolds, *Carrier Admiral*, New York: David McKay Co., Inc., 1970.
Department of Defense, *The "Magic" Background of Pearl Harbor, Vol. II, Appendix* (Government Printing Office, Washington, D.C., 1982).
Dorris, Donald H., *A Log of the Vincennes*. Louisville: The Standard Printing Co., 1982).
Drury, Clifford M., *The History of the Chaplain Corps, United States Navy, Vol. 2, 1939–1949*, Washington: GPO, 1949.
Dull, Paul S., *A Battle History of the Imperial Japanese Navy (1941–1945)*, Annapolis: Naval Institute Press, 1978.
Dyer, George C., *On the Treadmill to Pearl Harbor: The Memoirs of Admiral James O. Richardson, USN (Ret.)*, Washington: GPO, 1973.
Francillon, Rene J., *Japanese Aircraft of the Pacific War*, London: Putnam and Co., Ltd., 1970.
Frank, Pat, and Joseph D. Harrington, *Rendezvous at Midway: U.S.S. Yorktown and the Japanese Carrier Fleet*, New York: The John Day Co., 1967.
Friedman, Norman, *U.S. Aircraft Carriers: An Illustrated Design History*, Annapolis: Naval Institute Press, 1983.
Fuchida, Mitsuo, and Masatake Okumiya, *Midway: The Battle that Doomed Japan*, Clarke H. Kawakami and Roger Pineau, ed., Annapolis: Naval Institute Press, 1955.
Halsey, William F. and J. Bryan, III, *Admiral Halsey's Story*, New York: McGraw-Hill Book Co., 1947.
Holmes, Wilfred J., *Double-Edged Secrets: U.S. Naval Intelligence Operations in the Pacific During World War II*, Annapolis: Naval Institute Press, 1979.
Jentschura, Hansgeorg, Dieter Jung and Peter Mickel, *Warships of the Imperial Japanese Navy, 1869–1945*, Antony Preston and J.D. Brown, trans., Annapolis: Naval Institute Press, 1977.
Johnston, Stanley. *Queen of the Flat-tops: The U.S.S. Lexington and the Coral Sea Battle*, New York: E.P. Dutton & Co., Inc., 1942.
_____, *The Grim Reapers*, Philadelphia: The Blakiston Co., 1943.
Kimball, Warren F., *Churchill & Roosevelt: The Complete Correspondence, Vol. I, Alliance Emerging, October 1933–November 1942*, New Jersey: Princeton University Press, 1984.
King, Ernest J. and Walter M. Whitchill, *Admiral King: A Naval Record*, New York: W.W. Norton and Co., Inc., 1952.
Lewin, Ronald, *The American Magic: Codes, Ciphers, and the Defeat of Japan*, New York: Farrar, Straus, Giroux, 1982.
Lord, Walter, *Incredible Victory*, New York: Harper and Row, 1967.
_____, *Lonely Vigil: Coastwatchers in the Solomons*, New York: The Viking Press, 1977.
Lundstrom, John B., *The First South Pacific Campaign: pacific Fleet Strategy, December 1941–June 1942*, Annapolis: Naval Institute Press, 1976.
_____, *The First Team: Pacific Naval Air Combat from Pearl Harbor to Midway*, Annapolis: Naval Institute Press, 1984.
Mingos, Howard, *American Heroes of the War in the Air*, Vol. I, New York: Lanciar Publishers, Inc., 1943.
Morison, Samuel E., *The Battle of the Atlantic, September 1939–May 1943, History of the United States Naval Operations in World War II*, Vol. I, Boston: Little, Brown and Co., 1950.

_____, *The Rising Sun in the Pacific, 1931–April 1942, History of United States Naval Operations in World War II*, Vol. III, Boston: Little, Brown and Co., 1948.

_____, *Coral Sea, Midway, and Submarine Actions, May 1942–August 1942, History of United States Naval Operations in World War II*, Vol. IV, Boston: Little, Brown and Co., 1949.

Prange, Gordon W., et. al., *At Dawn We Slept*, New York: McGraw-Hill Book Co., 1981.

_____, *Miracle at Midway*, New York: McGraw-Hill Book Co., 1982.

Rohwer, Jürgen, *Axis Submarine Successes, 1939–1945*, Annapolis: Naval Institute Press, 1983.

Smith, William W., *Midway: Turning Point of the Pacific*, New York: Thomas Y. Crowell, 1966.

Tillman, Barrett, *The Dauntless Dive Bomber of World War II*, Annapolis: Naval Institute Press, 1976.

_____ *The Wildcat in World War II*, Annapolis: Nautical and Aviation Publishing Company of America, 1983.

Tuleja, Thaddeus V., *Climax at Midway*, New York: W.W. Norton, Inc., 1960.

Turnbull, Archibald D., and Clifford L. Lord, *History of United States Naval Aviation*, New Haven: Yale University Press, 1949.

Willmott, H.P., *The Barrier and the Javelin: Japanese and Allied Pacific Strategies*, February to June 1942, Annapolis: Naval Institute Press, 1983.

Periodical Articles

Akimoto, Minoru, "Nakajima Type 97 Carrier Attacker," *Koku-Fan* 31:9 (September 1982), 31:10 (October 1982).

Allen, Thomas B., "Return to the Battle of Midway," *National Geographic* (April 1999), 80–103.

Barde, Robert E., "Midway: Tarnished Victory," *Military Affairs* (December 1983) 188–192.

Codman, Charles, "24 Hours on Carrier Patrol," *Saturday Evening Post*, 10 January 1942.

Green, William (Ed.), "The Zero Precursor . . . Mitsubishi's A5M," *Air Enthusiast XIX* (November, 1978).

Hailey, Foster, "Valor at Midway the Casual Brand," *New York Times*, 23 June 1942.

Hersey, John, "Friends of the Snafu-Maru," *Redbook*, January 1943.

Hipple, William, "Our Navy Strikes Again! March 10 Blitz is Revealed," Honolulu *Star-Bulletin*, 21 May 1942.

_____, "Lae and Salamaua! Fighters of U.S. Navy Teach Japan a Lesson," Honolulu *Star-Bulletin*, 22 May 1942.

_____, "At Sea on a Carrier," Parts 1 through 7, inclusive, in Honolulu *Star-Bulletin*, 22–23 May 1942, 25–29 May 1942, inclusive.

Layton, Edwin W., "24 Sentai—Japan's Commerce Raiders," U.S. Naval Institute *Proceedings*, June 1976.

"Mac," "*Yorktown* News," *Our Navy*, Mid-December 1937.

Mulligan, Timothy, "The German Navy Evaluates its cryptographic Security, October 1941," *Military Affairs* (April 1985) 75–79.

Ray, Clarence C., "Saga of the *Yorktown*, Part II, Midway," *Shipmate*, June 1982.

Tanabe, Yahachi, with Joseph D. Harrington, "I Sank the *Yorktown* at Midway," U.S. Naval Institute *Proceedings*, May 1963.

Thach, John S., "The Red Rain of Battle: The Story of Fighter Squadron Three," *Colliers* for 5 and 12 December 1942.

Tillman, Barrett, "Dauntlesses over Midway," *American Aviation Historical Society Journal*, XXI, No. 3, 1976.

_____, "The Indispensable Man," Part I, *The Hook* 10, No. 3, 1982.

Wadleigh, John R., "Memories of Midway, Thirty Years Ago," *Shipmate*, June 1972, 3–10.

Newspapers

New York *Times*
Honolulu *Star-Bulletin*
Norfolk *Virginian-Pilot*
Japan *Times and Advertiser*
Washington *Star*
St. Louis *Post-Dispatch*

Unpublished Studies

Barde, Robert E., *The Battle of Midway: A Study in Command*, Ph.D. Dissertation, University of Maryland, 1971.

U.S. Army, Headquarters Far East Command, Military History Section, Japanese Research Division, *Japanese Monographs*; specifically:
No. 96 Eastern New Guinea Operations.
No. 102 Submarine Operations, December 1941–April 1942.
No. 110 Submarine Operations in Second Phase Operations, Part 1, April–August 1942.
No. 116 The Imperial Japanese Navy in World War II: A Graphic Presentation of the Japanese Naval Organization and List of Combatant and Non-Combatant Vessels Lost or Damaged in the War.
No. 139 Operations of the South Seas Force.

U.S. Naval Administration in World War II
DCNO (Air) Essays in the History of Naval Air Operations, Carrier Warfare, "History of Naval Fighter Direction"
"Aviation in the Fleet Problems"

U.S. Naval War College, *The Battle of the Coral Sea, May 1 to May 11, Inclusive, 1942, Strategical and Tactical Analysis* (NAVPERS 91050), Newport, 1947.

_____, *Battle of Midway, including the Aleutian Phase June 3 to June 14, 1942, Strategical and Tactical Analysis*, Newport, 1948.

U.S. Navy, Office of Naval Intelligence, *Combat Narratives* (Washington, D.C.: GPO, 1943)
"Early Raids in the Pacific Ocean, February 1 to March 10, 1942"
"The Battle of the Coral Sea"
"Battle of Midway, June 3–6, 1942"

Index

195